s-AKTIEN-GESELLSCHAFT

-Schein № 0778

Aktie

Bezugsrecht 1928 ausgeübt

BEZUGSRECHT 1912 AUSGEÜBT.

BEZUGSRECHT 1905 AUSGEÜBT.

gs-Aktien-Gesellschaft

Bezugsrecht 1921 ausgeübt.

RLIN.

Maffei in München ist mit dem Betrage von

ND MARK

Solawechsel beseitigt lt. Gen.-Vers.-Beschluss v. 24. Mai 1910.

as Aktienbuch der Gesellschaft eingetragen.

dertfünfzig Mark baar eingezahlt; für die übrigen 75 Procent ist ein

Heraufgestempelt auf RM 375.— i.W. dreihundertfünfundsiebzig Reichsmark gem. Div. Abg.V. 12.6.41; Aufs. R. Beschl. 5.6.42 Resteinzahlungsverpflichtung RM 121.50 2

mit Genehmigung des Aufsichtsrathes geschehen (oder den Statuten.)

gs-Aktien-Gesellschaft.

Der Vorstand:

EINTAUSEND MARK

RLIN.

ebr. Parcus) in München.

Barbara Eggenkämper
Gerd Modert
Stefan Pretzlik

ALLIANZ

Barbara Eggenkämper
Gerd Modert
Stefan Pretzlik

ALLIANZ

The Company History
1890–2015

translated by
Jefferson Chase, David R. Greeves,
Timothy Slater, Patricia Sutcliffe,
and Patricia Szobar

Verlag C.H.Beck

Includes 150 illustrations

© Verlag C.H. Beck oHG, Munich 2015
Copy-editing: Patricia Sutcliffe
Typesetting: Fotosatz Amann, Memmingen
Printing and Binding: CPI – Ebner & Spiegel, Ulm
Cover Jacket Illustration: Europahaus in Berlin with a neon ad pictured in
an Allianz image brochure. Completed in 1931 in the style of New Objectivity,
it was the largest modern office building in the city. Allianz's neon
advertisement quickly became an established attraction.

Printed in Germany

ISBN 978 3 406 67821 9

www.beck.de

CONTENT

Foreword   9

Credits   11

1. 1890–1918 The First Years and the First World War   13
(Stefan Pretzlik)
The Founding of Allianz   13
The Early Years   24
The Insurance Official and the "Fräulein"   28
New Insurance Branches and First Mergers   39
Sales and Marketing   53
Foreign Business and the First World War   58

2. 1918–1933 Crises, Rationalization, and Growth   71
(Gerd Modert)
A New Allianz – A New Generation Takes Over   76
Mastering Crises: Moderation, Conversion, and Mergers   84
How Allianz Survived Hyperinflation   98
Roaring Twenties? – Rationalization, Growth, Crisis   105
Communication: Newspapers, Advertising, Public Relations   123
International Markets   135

3. 1933–1948 Allianz: The Nazi Years and Reconstruction   143
(Gerd Modert)
1933: Kurt Schmitt, Allianz, and National Socialism   147
"Insurance Must Make Money" – Economic Development
and Adaptation   159

Allianz, its Jewish Employees and Clients, and the
Anti-Semitic Policies of the National Socialist Regime   172
War, Peace, Reconstruction   186

4. 1948–1970 **The Economic Miracle and Unlimited Growth**   205
(Stefan Pretzlik)
A New Corporate Headquarters   206
A New Head Office   210
Allianz Pensions   212
The Clients Come with Their Cars   215
Sag' es heiter, Du kommst weiter (Say It with Cheer, and You'll
Keep on Going!)   218
Hoffentlich Allianz versichert (Hopefully Covered by Allianz)   222
The Company Undergoes Change   224
On the Way to Becoming Allianz Staff   231
Codetermination in the Company   234
Allianz Agents   237
The Little Man and Life Insurance   242
New Investment Principles   244
Dealing with New Risks: The Dawning of the Atomic Age   249
The Difficulty of Rebooting International Business   251

5. 1970–1990 **Paths of Internationalization**   257
(Barbara Eggenkämper)
Change of Command and of Generations   259
1970: Losses and Restructuring   264
Restructuring Automobile Insurance   266
Customer Service and Safety Research   268
Rationalization and Cost Management   271
Success in the Life Insurance Business   276
1977: A Corporate Identity for Allianz   281
Nuclear Energy: Insuring a Radiant Vision of the 1970s   285
The View across the Borders: First Steps Abroad   289
The Founding of Allianz International Insurance Co. Ltd., London   296
Forced Expansion of Foreign Business   298
1985: Becoming the Allianz AG Holding Company   305
1985–1990: Changes in Allianz's International Business after
Formation of the Holding Company   308
The European Single Market   318

6. 1990–2015 The International Financial Services Provider   323
(Barbara Eggenkämper)
Allianz during the 1990s   326
Change in Allianz's Corporate Culture   328
The Process of Transformation in the 1990s   334
From Reunification to Global Player Status   340
Allianz in Asia   345
Asset Management and Banking Operations   352
1999: A New Corporate Design   358
Allianz at the Start of the 21st Century   362
The Founding of the SE   365
A Strong Community with a Future   374

Appendix
Notes   377
Picture Credits   423
List of Archives   423
Index   424

FOREWORD

Allianz was founded in Berlin in 1890 by Wilhelm von Finck and Carl von Thieme. For the company's 50th anniversary, several months after the beginning of the Second World War, Allianz chronicler and member of the board of directors Rudolf Hensel wrote in his commemorative volume: "Allianz's name is its program: Allianz meaning alliance, consciously chosen in the early years of Imperial Germany." Community has been and is part of the company's identity. Today, 125 years after its founding, Allianz has passed through several decisive stages on the journey to becoming the world's strongest financial community.

Over the impressive period of 125 years, a multi-layered worldwide community has arisen, where Allianz has been and remains a stable, crisis-proof, and reliable partner to quite different groups. There are almost 150,000 employees, as well as agents and brokers in this unique worldwide sales network. The basis for their work are 83 million clients who put their trust in Allianz daily. This community also includes some 430,000 shareholders who have decided to invest in Allianz. Allianz also has regular dialogs with associations, non-governmental organizations, legislators, and regulatory authorities. And as an insurer and investor, and because it believes in corporate responsibility for the future, Allianz takes account of important global developments, such as demographic shifts or climate change, and their consequences.

In the 1990s, public expectations of the company changed. Increasing numbers of people demanded more and more information and insisted that Allianz take responsibility for its past and present actions. Spurred on by Henning Schulte-Noelle, Allianz opened itself up to political and social questions. One expression of this change was the founding of the company's historical archive, the Allianz Center for Corporate History, whose task, among other things, is to address the ambivalent and difficult periods in the company's history. It has done this by means of a series of projects and publications directed by Barbara Eggenkämper, for instance, on the history of the state insurance company in East Germany. This book, written by Eggenkämper and her fellow historians Gerd Modert and Stefan Pretzlik on the occasion of Allianz's 125th anniversary, offers an overview of the company's history since its founding. It follows Gerald D. Feldman's groundbreaking study on the history of Allianz and the German insurance business under National Socialism, published more than a decade ago, to which the three authors also contributed. Both books demonstrate the company's interest in its own past. The knowledge that as a large-scale financial company Allianz is a major player and component within both German and global economic and insurance history, obliges the company to continue to critically evaluate its own history now and in the future.

In the past 125 years, Allianz has been transformed from a German into a global enterprise. Its development reflects that of Germany, Europe, and the world as a whole. Against this backdrop, this book traces, in six chapters, the path Allianz has taken, based on a wealth of oral testimony and a variety of historical sources. On February 5, 1890, Allianz started business as the "Allianz Versicherungs-Aktien-Gesellschaft" ("Allianz Insurance Stock Corporation"). The first three chapters deal with its development during the late years of Imperial Germany and the First World War, during the political instability, inflation and economic depression of the Weimar Republic, and during the Nazi dictatorship, the "zero hour" of 1945 and the incipient economic stability in the wake of the German currency reform in 1948. The final three chapters deal with the astonishingly rapid reconstruction of economic life and entrepreneurship as part of the German "economic miracle," in which Allianz became Europe's largest insurer, with its return to the international community of insurers, and with its development into an international corporation that today serves a globalized world as both an insurer and financial services provider.

Despite all of the political, economic and entrepreneurial fractures, shocks, crises and catastrophes, Allianz's history has been one of remarkable continuity. Amid the constantly changing historical conditions of the past 125 years, Allianz has always retained its identity, expanding the original idea of a partnership between the company and its clients into the concept of a global alliance. Since it was formed in 1890, Allianz has offered people of all ages, from all walks of life, and – today – all over the world the opportunity to obtain insurance coverage for practically every risk under the sun. The foundations, as this book amply illustrates, have been laid throughout the company's 125-year history.

I am extremely pleased that this book has found a place in the C.H Beck publishing company's program and wish to express my gratitude to the editor Dr. Sebastian Ullrich for his excellent work.

Emilio Galli-Zugaro
(Head of Group Communications, Allianz SE)

Credits

The authors would like to thank a large number of people who supported us in a variety of ways: Emilio Galli-Zugaro was an outstanding mentor for the project; Flavia Genillard was our go-to person for advice on the recent history of Allianz; Dr. Wolfgang Winter served as a legal advisor; Pietro Marchetti and Gaia Furlan provided information and materials on insurance in Italy, as well as extraordinary hospitality; Elisabeth Fahlbusch completed extensive transcription tasks and supported Dr. Petra Spona who, together with Ruth Alexander, mastered the cataloguing of enormous amounts of papers from the archives; Bianca Döring performed laborious research into photographs and their rights holders; Dr. Michael Westdickenberg helped us with his advice, hospitality, and expertise in questions concerning photography, as well as with extensive research in the Berlin archives and libraries; and Dr. Barbara von Benthem and Roberta Brown copy-edited the text of the German and English versions.

We owe a debt of gratitude to all those we interviewed who, over the years, helped us to bring essential aspects of Allianz's history to life: Dr. Peter Adolff, Michael Beckord, Heidemarie Brandl, Dr. Benno Freiherr von Canstein, Heinz Dollberg, Hansjörg Dorschel, Barbara Eichberger, Horst Fickel, Peter Haas, Bernd Honsel, Christian Maenz, Ulrike Mascher, Alexander Metz, Heinrich Niemöller, Helmut Perlet, Erika Remmele, Dr. Henning Schulte-Noelle, Luise Stepken, Dr. Günter Ullrich, Alexander von Yxkull.

Finally, we extend our thanks to all the employees of C.H. Beck Publishing Company, who participated in making this book, and to our colleagues Susanne Bluhm, Stefan Fister, Christine Gandowitz, Susanne Gehring, Karl Grimm, Bernhard Härter, Dr. Rolf Herkelrath, Rosa de Simone, Karl Snethlage, and Christopher Worthley, who helped us with their spontaneous assistance, their knowledge, and their enthusiastic support.

1890-1918

THE FIRST YEARS AND
THE FIRST WORLD WAR

On February 5, 1890, the First District Royal Court of Prussia in Berlin entered a new enterprise into the corporate trade registry. The name of the company read: "Allianz" Versicherungs-Aktien-Gesellschaft (Allianz Insurance Stock Corporation). This is the official founding date of Allianz. However, in order to understand how Allianz came to be founded, one has to look back even further.[1]

The Founding of Allianz

It was the year 1880 when two young men founded the Münchener Rückversicherungs-Gesellschaft (Munich Reinsurance Corporation, hereafter Munich Re). Until this time, 35-year-old Carl Thieme (1844–1924) had been the regional director of the Thuringia Versicherungs-Gesellschaft in Bavaria and had proved to be very successful. Wilhelm Finck (1848–1924), 32, was a partner in the banking company Merck, Finck & Co., as well as an authorized signatory and "from the beginning its heart and soul." Both Thieme and Finck were later granted noble titles by the Bavarian crown for their services.[2]

By then, there were 13 German reinsurers in existence. Although their premium revenues reached an impressive 13 million marks, this paled compared to the 45.5 million marks in premium revenues collected by direct insurers. With the exception of the independent Kölnische Rückversicherungs-Gesellschaft (Cologne Reinsurance Corporation), all the reinsurers belonged to German direct insurance companies that were interested in securing their business development through the help of their subsidiaries.[3]

Munich Re, however, was not founded by the Thuringia Corp. or with its capital but instead followed the example of the Kölnische Rück and remained independent. As the rumor nevertheless grew that Munich Re was a subsidiary of the Thuringia, Carl Thieme took decisive action to counter this view in a letter to the Wallmann's Insurance News Magazine: "This [corporation] will in no way place itself in any sort of subsidiary relationship to a direct corporation but rather will be open to joining in reinsurance partnerships with any solid German business." In fact, the starting investment capital for the venture came from the banking company Merck, Finck & Co., as well as from other corporate partners outside the insurance business. Carl Thieme wanted to create a reinsurance company that would not pose a threat to any direct insurer and thus be open to all insurance companies. His success proved him right: 20 years later the insurance expert Albert Ehrenzweig wrote in the Austrian Assecuranz Yearbook, reflecting the spirit of the times, that "the German reinsurance industry has become a major power." He attributed this to reinsurers no longer patiently submitting to the dictates of insurance corporations but instead focusing on improving their own businesses. Ehrenzweig left no doubt who was responsible for this: "The Munich Re caused this revolution." The records do not indicate whether this was Thieme's original intention. In any case, he was successful in establishing Munich Re as an independent and significant factor within the insurance industry.[4]

Barely ten years later, Thieme and Finck planned to repeat the success story. On the one hand, Munich Re needed a partner for its fire reinsurance policies, which made up the vast majority of its premiums; on the other hand, Thieme and his partners had found a new branch that was earning good profits from which they hoped to reap good profits in the future: accident insurance.[5]

In 1871, the newly formed German Reich passed a "law concerning the liabilities for compensation for bodily injuries and deaths occurring within the services of the railway, mines, etc." This was desperately needed as more and more accidents leading to bodily injury and death had been occurring in the newly developing industrial companies. In 1869, for instance, 300 miners died in a mining catastrophe caused by an explosion set off in a lightning storm in the Ore Mountains in Saxony. The Reich Liability Law now stipulated that the employer had to compensate an employee in the case of an occupational accident. In order to alleviate the risks to employers, several accident insurance companies, such as the Allgemeiner Deutscher Versicherungs-Verein (General German Insurance Association) (ADVV), were

Carl Thieme (1848–1924) was a founder and first head of Allianz until 1904. Thieme also directed Munich Re from 1880 to 1922.

established in the 1870s. Many of these companies, however, discontinued operations after German chancellor Otto von Bismarck introduced a mandatory national accident insurance program in 1884. These companies believed that the new legislation no longer left enough room in the marketplace for private accident insurance companies. Carl Molt, on the other hand, director-general of the ADVV, saw this as a golden opportunity; as insurance historian Ludwig Arps impressively elaborated in his biographical sketch on Molt: "The German Accident Insurance Law did not insure all employees and did not hold for all branches of industry and commerce. Non-insured workers would therefore be more likely to expect higher amounts of compensation in light of the benefits granted and received under the new accident legislature; in the branches not covered in the accident legislation, injured employees would look into whether and how they too could demand high amounts of liability compensation. The affects would carry over into other areas such as compensation and liability of homeowners, hotel businesses, and independent professionals. Finally, the professional unions within the companies could, under certain circumstances in cases of occupational accidents, demand redress and sue the companies in court, thus creating more costs for businesses. Demanding workers' compensation, in a sense, became fashionable, and liability insurance therefore more important than ever before."[6]

The co-owner of the bank Merck, Finck & Co, Wilhelm Finck (1846–1924), chaired the Allianz supervisory board from 1890 until his death.

Indeed, by 1886 already Molt was able to report record numbers of new applications for both liability as well as accident insurance and only two years later was for the first time able to boast of over a million marks in premium revenues. Unanimously and with a standing ovation, the general assembly formally released the board of directors on May 25, 1889. This was not only a formal legal procedure but rather also expressed the members' satisfaction in the – for many completely unexpected – positive business development of the ADVV.[7]

Munich Re shared the ADVV's satisfaction with the accident insurance business, particularly as it earned profits at an average of almost one-third of the premium. Internal discussions thus arose about how revenues could be increased in the market, which it was assumed would continue to grow at profitable rates in the years ahead. Unfortunately, according to a memorandum ascribed to Thieme, the demand for reinsurance in this branch was only slight; only a direct insurer could hope to tap sufficiently into this source. Should Munich Re sacrifice its very successful business model after only ten years and instead become a direct insurer in the accident insurance business? It was decided otherwise: Thieme, along with Wilhelm Finck, lawyer Hermann Pemsel, Friedrich von Schauß (director-general of Süddeutsche Bodenkreditbank), and Hugo Ritter von Maffei (Bavarian industrialist) – who all belonged to Munich Re's supervisory board – founded a new corporation for direct accident insurance in Berlin. Their plan was supported by the Rhine industrialist Heinrich Lueg and a strong Berlin faction including Otto Oechelhäuser (representative of Deutsche Bank), Friedrich Hammacher (economic politician), and Bruno Pohl (accident insurance expert). Together with Merck, Finck & Co., this circle held the entire capital stock of Allianz, amounting to 4 million marks, although it was determined at the beginning that Deutsche Bank would pass on a portion of their shares to Bayerische Vereinsbank and that Merck, Finck & Co. would pass on a portion of their shares to Dresdner Bank, both of which soon transpired.[8]

The stock market culture at the end of the 19th century is hardly comparable to today's speculative capital market culture. Around 1900, stock corporations had proved their worth and were becoming more and more popular due to the organizational advantages they offered and the fact that they simplified the flow of capital. That being said, shares and liquid capital reserves at that time were reserved for only a small class of the wealthy. This is reflected in Allianz's case as well: for one thing, the number of stocks was only 4,000 shares, which led to a starting capital stock of four million marks with a value of 1,000 marks per share (an extremely high value from today's perspective). For another, investors only paid in 25 percent of their share – that meant that they had to be ready to pay the remaining 75 percent if the business experienced financial difficulties. Allianz therefore had an increased interest in 'liquid' shareholders and thus distributed only registered shares. These were printed out in the names of the owners whose rank, place of residency and date of purchase were compiled and entered into a shareholders' register held by the company. Transferring of the share to a different owner – and this is exactly why the shares were registered – was contingent on the approval of the supervisory board. Needless to say, the gentlemen of the board surely knew who should or should not be allowed to buy a share. Allianz did not make use of this additional payment duty, despite all the crises including the Great War and inflation, until 1926 when it raised the capital base from 25 to 26 percent. The founders paid 40 marks in addition to the share price of 250 marks per share as organizational and founders' fees. This 160,000 marks sufficed for Allianz as a liquid capital base in the initial years. The costs for personnel and office space were manageable since the number of employees was small. At first only a few offices were rented in an office and apartment building at Kochstraße 75, in what was then Berlin-Friedrichstadt (today's Berlin-Kreuzberg).[9]

Yet what drew this subsidiary-like company of Munich-based Munich Re to Berlin? To answer this question, we must now take a few steps forward and look at testimony from a later date, since so little is recorded from the founding and early years of Allianz. Therefore, we can formulate hypotheses only and assumptions rather than draw sound conclusions based on actual facts. Nevertheless, we can assume that a combination of factors led to the choice of Berlin. For one, the position of Berlin as the capital of the German Reich formed only twenty years before. The political center developed an enormous economic dynamic and soon became the financial center of Germany. Helped perhaps by new shareholding legislation, 35 banks were established in Berlin between 1870 and 1873, including Deutsche Bank. Other banks, such as Dresdner Bank, moved their top management to Berlin or opened new subsidiaries there, as, for example, Commerz- und Diskontobank of Hamburg.[10]

The development of the insurance branch was less rapid as efforts to reform the regulatory process had stalled to such an extent that it was more difficult to found an insurance company than to found a bank or an industrial concern. Nonetheless, there was a discernible increase in start-up activities in this branch, albeit over a longer period of time. In 1925, of the roughly 40 Berlin insurance groups which had already been in existence prior to 1920, 19 had been formed between 1863 and 1898, including such well-known companies as Nordstern or Deutsche Transport Versicherungsgesellschaft (German Transportation Insurance Corporation), which later became a part of Allianz. That political concerns also played a role in the choice of Berlin as Allianz's headquarters is suggested by the fact that Friedrich Hammacher was among its founders. An elected representative and member of the German parliament in the Reichstag as well as an important economic policy maker in the National Liberal Party, he had considerable influence in Berlin's political arena.[11]

The presence of banks in Berlin must also have motivated the founders to settle there; after all, the focus within the transportation insurance business, which Allianz had also engaged in from the beginning, would shift to personal property insurance for valuables like savings bonds, stock shares, precious metals, jewelry, gold, silver, diamonds, cash, and similar items – insurance policies that financial institutions, above all, made use of. Thus, it proved particularly practical that Munich Re had a staff member with some of the best contacts in the finance sector, one who had persuaded Deutsche Bank to become a founding member of Allianz: Paul von der Nahmer (1858–1921), the Munich Re representative in Paris. Before holding this position, he

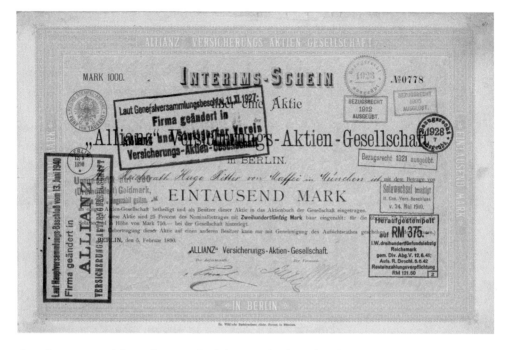

One of 4,000 original shares that were divided among the eleven founders of Allianz. The owner of the share with the serial number 778 was Hugo Ritter von Maffei.

had served in Paris as a representative for a private French bank and had also trained at a bank.[12]

Other sources on the history of Allianz point to the special political culture of Germany as a reason for the choice of Berlin for Allianz's headquarters. The German Reich was highly federalized, i.e., decentralized in its organization. It went so far, in fact, that the Reich did not initially collect taxes directly but was financed by means of the customs and duties of the German states. The stewardship over the insurance industry was within the jurisdiction of the 25 federal states. To offer insurance in the entire Reich, it was necessary to deal with 25 bureaucracies and 25 different license application processes. This held not only for Prussia, Bavaria, and Saxony, which were the most densely populated states in 1890, but also for the least densely populated states such as Schaumburg-Lippe or the District of the House of Reuß, the Elder which, along with five other federal states, had fewer than 100,000 inhabitants.[13]

The awarding of a license was at that time anything but a purely formal, procedural act and could drag on for years. Companies used all means to try to speed up the process. When the ADVV applied for a license in Prussia in 1885, it not only made reference to its past successes but also touted its status as a long-standing effective partner in the fight against the Social Democratic Party, at that time a declared public enemy of Otto von Bismarck. Von Wolff, a member of the administrative board and of the state parliament, as well as a retired lieutenant general, summarized the matter in the following terms: "By completing the social security insurance scheme in categories I and II, the above-mentioned company has declared as its purpose, in accordance with German national intentions, to act conservatively and to paralyze where possible the Social Democratic movement." Apparently, they wanted to make an impression in this rather direct manner and win over the public agencies.[14]

Allianz was supposed to be founded as quickly as possible in order to profit from the then current boom in the insurance business. The most important goal had to be to receive a license as rapidly as possible in Prussia, because Prussia represented at the time almost 60 percent of the entire German population with approximately 30 million inhabitants. Although the legal hurdles in Prussia were no higher than elsewhere, each federal state had its own idea of how a company was to prove that it was sound. If one can believe a 1930 retrospective report by Victor Bernhardt, a long-time employee and director of Munich Re, on the history of the founding of Allianz, officials at the Prussian Interior Ministry demanded that companies from outside the state, for example, Bavarian ones, prove their solidity with annual account statements from the preceding two years. That would have meant that a Bavarian Allianz would have had to wait a good two years after its founding before it could move to Berlin. In Bavaria, it would have been necessary to survive with comparatively few customers. The second largest state in the German Reich had only 5.6 million inhabitants in 1890.

Since Allianz was a Prussian company, its founding ran smoothly for the most part: on September 17, 1889, the company's founding article was notarized. The approval to operate a business in Prussia was granted on January 13, 1890. Official entry into the commercial register in Berlin followed on February 5, 1890. With that, Allianz attained legal status. This is why Allianz chose this date as its official founding date on its 50th anniversary in 1940. Bavaria would seem to have been more liberal concerning the approval of insurance companies from outside the state. Only a month later, on March 7, 1890, Allianz was granted a license to do business in Bavaria. Slowly but surely, Allianz received licenses in all of the other federal German states with the exception of the District of Schaumburg-Lippe where the Prussian model seems to have been followed and proof of several years of successful business was required. After the end of this period, Allianz apparently forgot about this missing link in its German armor and did not reapply for a license.[15]

"The company's purpose is to guarantee accident and transportation insurance policies as well as reinsurance policies for accident, transportation, fire and life insurance policies" states the official entry in the commercial register from February 5, 1890. Not every contemporary understood why a new insurance company made business sense. Wallmann's Insurance News Magazine, for example, predicted it would quickly fail: "Of course, older, more traditional companies have been able to generate satisfying dividends in the last years; however, the dominant opinion in insurance circles is that these results are undoubtedly due to the special circumstances of these businesses, above all, their good connections, the many years of experience the leading personalities in the industry have, the great caution taken in maintaining the business, etc. In short, their positive results are due to circumstances that the new enterprise more or less completely lacks." The editor was quite sure of himself: "It is not the time to found new corporations in this segment." He stated this in reference to the transportation insurance business and, we can say in hindsight, displayed little clairvoyance. The rapid boom in the transportation insurance business soon presented Allianz with dreamlike growth figures.[16]

What may initially have been even more important to Allianz's founders, however, was the simple fact that the company received permission to offer reinsurance. This corresponded to Munich Re's urgent need as many direct insurers were reluctant to pass on a large portion of their business to reinsurers. Arvid Johansson, a Munich Re agent negotiating a contract with the Swedish company Skandia, was instructed by Thieme as follows: "If, by the way, Skandia finds it difficult to give <u>one</u> reinsurer two quotes, suggest to the company that it transfer the second quote to our newly founded insurance stock corporation in Berlin, Allianz, also directed by Mr. Thieme." This procedure seems to have been a complete success. After all, almost half of Allianz's premium revenues in 1890 came from fire insurance. The citation also illustrates Munich Re's self-concept. The company saw itself as the "mother" company of Allianz – and rightfully so. This self-image can be found on display in the language of the contract agreed upon by both Allianz and Munich Re. If Allianz wished to guarantee reinsurance in the fire branch, it

*Favag insurance certificate of 1911:
the name of the company alone
fills four lines of the cover sheet.*

first had to gain the approval of Munich Re; it also had to terminate a contract at Munich Re's request. This becomes clear when one later reads in the contract that Allianz was to transfer 100 percent of its fire insurance to Munich Re. Similar arrangements were also made between the two companies for accident insurance.[17]

What did one associate with the insurance corporation "Allianz" at the end of the 19th century? It is not known how the founders came to choose the name, Allianz. At the same time, the choice was not completely original. Ludwig Arps uncovered numerous examples of insurance corporations in other countries around 1890 that carried the name Allianz, for instance, the "Alliance British and Foreign Fire and Life Insurance Company" in London (established in 1824), the "Aliança da Bahia" in Brazil, the "Alliance Maritime" in France, the "Alianza de Santander" in Spain, and even, closer to home, the reinsurer "Allianz" in Vienna (1871 to 1897). As an alternative choice, one could have followed the path of Munich Re and the tradition of many German insurers and chosen the name of the city where the headquarters were located and combined it with the service branch in question: instead of Allianz, it could have been called the Berlin Accident Insurance Corporation, for instance. At that time one could already find examples of a Berlin life, a Berlin hail and a Berlin fire insurance company in the industry. Aside from the confusion such a choice might have easily led to, it is important to note that from the start Allianz did not limit itself to doing business in one single branch. The era of the classic one-branch company was slowly coming to an end in Germany.[18]

The gentlemen of Munich Re might have considered this and studied the example of the Frankfurter Glasversicherungsgesellschaft (Frankfurt Glass Insurance Corporation – Favag) and the difficulties that could ensue concerning a corporation's name. This company served as a point of comparison repeatedly for Allianz before finally in 1929, in the wake of a large scandal, it became a part of Allianz itself. The company had been founded in 1865 and then expanded into other branches, changing its name after each expansion. When Favag added burglary insurance in 1897, the company finally decided to spare customers and employees alike the torment of another name change. In 1911, it changed its name to Frankfurter Allgemeine Versicherungs-AG (Frankfurter General Insurance Corporation), and the abbreviation Favag quickly caught on. Allianz, by comparison, only changed its name once for a relatively short period of time in 1927 when Allianz and the Stuttgarter Association (the ADVV mentioned above) became equal partners after a merger. The name 'Allianz and Stuttgarter Association' never caught on and after thirteen years was changed back to the popular and expressive name 'Allianz,' which because of its brevity, resisted all abbreviation attempts.[19]

Thieme seemed to have been very satisfied with the choice. Eight years later, in fact, when Munich Re founded a subsidiary in Italy, it imported the name of its German subsidiary: the new insurance company was named "Alleanza Società di Assicurazioni." The globalization of Allianz that soon ensued, however, revealed the weaknesses of the corporate name. While the original French word is known in many languages of the world, its pronunciation varies dramatically. This fact made Allianz wary; for example, in the 1970s when the company started to offer insurance in the United States, it launched a huge public relations campaign to popularize the German pronunciation of the name in the United States (with mixed results).[20]

In Allianz's early years, the name was sometimes translated into the other languages and a corporate image used for easy identification purposes. This was common practice with many insurers and was especially effective in early forms of advertising for fire insurance that included highly defined and artistically designed fire insurance shields. When customers signed a contract, they received a shield that was then proudly mounted on the fence or on the side of their house. Close to the name of the corporation a small emblem or the figure of a saint was placed on the shield. The Landschaftliche Brandkasse Hannover, for instance, used a Saxon horse; the Deutscher Phönix (German Phoenix) used the image of this mystical bird; and the fire insurance society for small farmers chose the emblem of the city of Rostock, the griffin. As in the last case, insurers often used figures with a strong connection to the region or the city from whence they came. Horses, Bavarian or Hessian lions, as well as eagles, were the most popular motifs. The Badische Feuerversicherungs-Bank went a step further and used the state coat of arms of the imperial Earl of Baden, as did the Magdeburger Feuer Versicherungsgesellschaft, which used the coat of arms of the city of Magdeburg. Allianz first used fire insurance shields when it began offering direct fire insurance in 1906. However, even before this it did not want to miss out on the use of a symbol in its own logo. After all, one could decorate the insurance documents nicely with a logo, thereby increasing policies' value by improving their appearance. Allianz's first emblems and logo design were thoroughly deliberated. Although the company followed the tradition of other insurers, it did not just leave it at that. Rather, it set higher goals and chose the emblem of the German Reich, the imperial eagle. Just as it had avoided merely using a city or region in choosing its corporate name, it also avoided reference to a city or region in its choice of logo. Instead it wanted to signal its national status. Allianz's logo is unique, for one thing, because of its calligraphic display of the word Allianz in the center, and, for another, because of the two coats of arms – the coat of arms of Munich and that of Berlin – held in the eagle's talons. Furthermore, heraldry experts could recognize the message behind the logo immediately: the Munich coat of arms, the 'Munich Kindl', is placed on the right hand side thus signaling its higher rank. Allianz's logo symbolizes an accord between three partners: the alliance between Munich and Berlin, the alliance between reinsurers and direct insurers, and the alliance between the insurer and the customers.

The Early Years

It is worthwhile to take a closer look at the relationship between Allianz and Munich Re, especially from the early years up to 1895. The companies were perhaps most accurately characterized as two sides of the same coin. This thesis is impressively corroborated by the very

Allianz's first premium revenues came from its founder Wilhelm Finck, who paid an annual premium of 155 marks for an accident insurance policy.

first contract between them (mentioned previously). It was signed by director-general Thieme for Allianz and by two deputy directors, Paul Szelinski and Marcus Mauel, for Munich Re. Why these three signed the contract is unknown. What we do know is that Thieme, of course, could have just as well signed for Munich Re and Paul Szelinski and Marcus Mauel for Allianz, since all three held their respective positions in both of the organizations. This configuration is reflected in early correspondence. Letters were diligently sent from the directors of the Allianz headquarters in Munich located at Maffeistraße 1 to Munich Re, also located at Maffeistraße 1. Whoever happened to be present signed these letters and documents. Berlin seemed to have played a minor role at this time. Although there was also a director located there, namely Bruno Pohl, who was recruited from the Transport- und Unfallversicherungsgesellschaft Zürich (Zurich Transportation and Accident Insurance Company), he was concerned primarily with the accident insurance business. Thieme in Munich, however, clearly had the final say. This explains why the office space remained so sparse in Berlin at the time.[21]

In the first year of business, there were 121 claims against accident insurance policies at Allianz, as recorded in its first annual report, a slim four-pager. Despite a fatality case and two cases of invalidity, a profit of 22,000 marks was made on the premium revenues of 174,000 marks in the accident insurance branch. Almost half of Allianz's revenues were generated by the fire insurance branch, which resulted in profits of 18,000 marks. Overall, revenues reached over half a million marks, with a profit of 55,000 marks. A dividend of 4 percent could be paid out to the shareholders, in proportion to their capital investment. In the following years, premium revenues, interest yields, and profit continuously increased: it was soon the transportation insurance branch that was responsible for the largest portion of premium revenue growth.[22]

With success came increased envy. In 1893, Deutsche Bank considered going public and listing on the stock market; it announced that it would like to sell a portion of its Allianz holdings. Wilhelm Finck took some of the wind out of the sails of this idea, explaining that "the development of the company had been a good one" and confessed to his colleagues from Deutsche Bank that he was unable to persuade himself to "decide to introduce a new security with fluctuating yields" to the Munich stock market. Nonetheless, he did declare himself ready to at least search for buyers for Deutsche Bank's shares. Deutsche Bank accepted this proposal and sold its last Allianz shares at the end of 1894 to Carl Thieme, among others. Perhaps Hermann Wallich, who together with Georg Siemens directed Deutsche Bank for many years, also had Allianz's engagement in mind as he said, reflecting on Siemens: "The businesses that my brilliant colleague originated, stood, one could say, on a cemented foundation and absorbed our liquid assets, often crippling our freedom of movement in another direction." If Deutsche Bank truly needed "liquid assets," then a sell-off could not be postponed; if, on the other hand, the sale of the shares was motivated by lack of faith that Allianz would continue to grow, then Deutsche Bank lacked good business sense. When Allianz debuted on the Berlin stock market a year later on December 12, 1895, the share price was 750 marks. The Deutsche Bank had sold its shares a year before for 327 marks. Paul von der Nahmer barely refrained from gloating in commenting on Allianz's success (which was already apparent before the stock went public) in a letter to Deutsche Bank director Max Steinthal: "Mr. Finck told me that the sale of the Allianz shares on the part of Deutsche Bank – premature and against our advice – was all the

Paul von der Nahmer joined the board of directors in 1894 and headed Allianz from 1905 to his death in 1921.

more regrettable in that he would have been very happy, in light of the friendly support Deutsche Bank had constantly shown to us, if [the bank] had also earned a few hundred thousand marks on us." As a gesture to make amends, Thieme proposed to Steinthal that Deutsche Bank could support Allianz's listing for 10,000 marks, although Dresdner Bank had offered to introduce the stocks for free. Deutsche Bank did not refuse the offer.[23]

If one believes the reports about Carl Thieme that his contemporaries left behind, it appears that he recruited a corps of co-workers at Munich Re who were completely loyal to him. This and Thieme's tendency to make decisions without consulting the supervisory board made Wilhelm Finck and the members of this board uneasy. The situation at Allianz was probably not much different, nor did it change significantly in 1894 when Paul von der Nahmer was appointed as an additional director in Berlin. Since he was the nephew of Thieme's first wife, this almost turned Allianz into a family business. Paul von der Nahmer was born on May 25, 1858, in Rheydt in the Rhineland and had worked since 1886 for Munich Re. He sat on Allianz's board of directors from 1894 until his death on April 15, 1921.[24]

With the addition of von der Nahmer, the distribution of power within Allianz shifted toward Berlin. Operations had developed so satisfactorily that one could now begin solidifying the organization. For the impressive sum of 345,000 marks (which made up about 10 percent of the premium revenues in 1895), Allianz bought a piece of real estate on which the head-quarters was to be built. This new home was still to be in the Friedrichstadt district; Allianz moved a few blocks to the north and thus landed close to the center of political power in Germany. Various ministries of the German Reich were here, as well as Berlin's banking quarter, with all of the illustrious and reputable banks. Also, at the same time as Allianz's new head office was being built, the largest consumer temple in the world, the Wertheim depart-ment store at Leipziger Platz, was going up. At the start of Taubenstraße, some 100 meters away from the Brandenburg Gate, architect Helmuth Schus-ter created an imposing Neo-Renaissance building in the style of an Italian palazzo. Because the spatial capacity of the building (whose total costs came to over 1.7 million marks) more than met the demand, the corporation de-cided to rent out some of the rooms when it was completed in 1900. And who could have been a better taker for such a proposition than the Berlin branch of Munich Re, led, naturally, by Paul von der Nahmer? Slowly but surely the public also became aware of Allianz's successful business. In 1895, the Aus-trian Insurance News gave Allianz only satisfactory grades; four years later Allianz had already climbed the ranks to become the favorite subsidiary of Munich Re in the eyes of the same newspaper editors, benefiting from good fortune and expanding handsomely in its development.[25]

The Insurance Official and the "Fräulein"

Industrialization in the 19th century not only created new places of employment and jobs in manufacturing, but also led to an expansion of administrative and bureaucratic activities. Economic development also increased the per capita income and awoke new consumer needs. Levels of consumption rose and new jobs were created everywhere, which were filled by a new group of dependent employees: white-collar workers. While in 1892 there had been a total of only 307,000 white-collar workers in Germany, their numbers nearly quadrupled to 1.3 million in the next 25 years. Although dependent on their employer, white-collar workers enjoyed a clearly different social status from the working class: they received a stable and constant monthly salary instead of blue-collar workers' performance-related weekly wages, their working hours were shorter, they had more self-control over their working con-ditions, were more independent, had more responsibilities, and, therefore, more chances to climb up the social ladder.[26]

If, however, one believes the reports of retired Allianz employees, life in Berlin as an Allianz staff member at the turn of the century was no piece of cake. Director Paul von der Nahmer lorded over the company, untouchable, unapproachable, and often not even visibly recognized by the workforce. It was important to hold the proper distance and von der Nahmer let it be known that he did not wish to be greeted by his employees in public on the street. In the office, he appeared in a bowler hat; the other top managers, those who regarded themselves as important, appeared in fur capes and a top hat. Once in the office, they slipped into house shoes and even changed their pants. The normal employees were probably rather simply clothed, most likely as a result of their modest wages. The monthly salary was reported to be 60 marks, below the average per capita income in industry and trade in 1900.

This figure becomes meaningful when we compare it to the prices of the day. In 1900, according to official sources, a kilogram of pork cost 1.34 marks in Berlin, a kilogram of butter 1.33 marks, 100 kilogram of potatoes around 4 marks and a kilogram of wheat flour 35 pfennigs.[27]

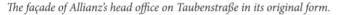

The façade of Allianz's head office on Taubenstraße in its original form.

Employees could bring in a few more coins by taking and delivering Allianz business mail to their own neighborhood. That was enough to pay for a ride or two with the horse-drawn trolley on Taubenstraße. Yet employees' privation was still great; they often worked on the side as a waiter, a musician, or as an usher. There were even Allianz employees who worked evenings for a competitor, the Viktoria, collecting premiums. And having received the paltry paycheck from the director's treasury, the tailors and shoemakers with whom they had outstanding debts for mending clothes and shoes were waiting right outside the door ready to receive their fair share. Despite these hardships, being an Allianz employee was a privilege. Of course, the prestige of being an insurance official did not approach that of a bank employee, who was seen as leading a dream life; yet insurance officials did enjoy a higher social standing than salespeople or the simple blue-collar workers. The grand aim was to be equal to a civil servant, a "Beamter" in German, hence the title 'insurance official' (Versicherungsbeamter) for employees in the insurance industry.[28]

This held also for Rudolf Reich. After completing his vocational training in sales with the asbestos and rubber factory Alfred Calmon, followed by a one-year internship with the Preußische National-Versicherungs-Gesellschaft (Prussian National Insurance Corporation) and then another three years as office errand boy at the Gothaer Feuerversicherungsbank (Gotha Fire Insurance Bank), he applied to Allianz's general agency in Munich. Allianz hired him on April 1, 1906, granting him a monthly salary of 110 marks and placing him in the fire and burglary department. Besides his expertise in fire insurance, which Allianz had just begun to offer as first insurers at that time, Reich also possessed an encyclopedic knowledge of office operations which much impressed Alwin Kleinschmidt, the general office agent for Allianz in Munich: "This employee shows much knowledge and diligence in handling his required duties such as the preparation of document copies, the design of policy and clausal concepts, entries into the maximum control accounts, completion of bordereaux and other small correspondences; what's more, he always exemplifies the best behavior." With this monthly salary, Reich was not forced to find part-time work. In addition, his salary increased considerably in the following years and grew to around 2,000 marks a year in 1914. At about the same time, Gustaf Körner applied in Berlin to become an employee in the accident and liability department of Allianz. He was motivated by an advertisement Allianz had placed in the Vossische Zeitung seeking a young man with good penmanship. Körner completed his training in the department store Hermann Tietz and then worked for a short time in various jobs, including for the Edison Company. Allianz reacted quickly to the application and invited Körner to a personal interview. Allianz was not prepared to meet his salary demands of 90 marks per month, but it was ready to offer him a handsome starting salary of 75 marks, and his salary was raised to 1,740 marks per year by 1914.[29]

The limited potential workforce is probably the primary reason that ADVV had a second group of employees that Allianz fully lacked until the beginning of the First World War – women. After the apprentices, who even at the end of the 19th century were expected to somehow survive completely without compensation for their services, women earned the lowest wages. Twenty-year-old Miss Sautter, in her second year at the ADVV, for instance, earned no more than 480 marks a year in 1889. Miss Grüneisen, on the other hand, outdid this after twelve years of service, earning 840 marks per year. She was the only female employee to earn a higher wage than some male employees. The so-called daily writer received 2.50 marks per day – in the case of excellent penmanship perhaps even 2.75 marks– and thus could reach an annual salary of 750 to 825 marks. The vast majority of insurance officials already earned over 900 marks a year in 1889; many, including department heads, crossed the 2,000-mark line, and deputy director Barrenscheen received 3,700 marks. The total cost of wages came to 82,580 marks and made up less than 7 percent of premium revenues.[30]

Like Allianz, the ADVV also had a paternalistic structure. Molt had founded the company in 1875 and was its director-general for 35 years until his death in 1910. Germany had only slowly transformed itself from an agrarian society into a modern industrial one. Some traditions from the feudal age still held sway and influenced the relationships between supervisors and their workers. Just as the feudal lord had earlier controlled every aspect of his serfs' and vassals' lives, the patriarch at the top of the company took care of the employees in good times as well as bad. The official regulations for ADVV office employees give a good indication of the spirit of these times: "The administration of the [ADVV] considers it […] one of its most important duties to care for and uphold the well-being of [its] officials and employees to the greatest extent possible; the administration expects at the same time that it will be supported by these same people and that they will make every effort to maintain the peace and harmony between the supervisors and their subordinates, as well as to maintain harmonious relationships among themselves."[31]

With the well-being of the employees in mind, the employer took responsibility for seeing that the premiums for workers' health insurance were paid and when necessary paid the insurance premiums for those who were not required to pay them. Additionally, a relief fund was created to support insurance officials in emergency situations, as was a pension fund. All officials were automatically members of the officials' circle, a union of staff members that served to promote social interactions among staff but also to better channel workers' interests to the company management. In return, the company demanded that the employees "behave impeccably outside of work." An "immoral lifestyle," for instance, could lead to an employee's immediate dismissal. When reading the official regulations, one can imagine Molt sitting at his mahogany desk with quill in hand thinking up clauses for his subordinates for the well-being of the ADVV. On the occasion of one of his regular inspections of the officials' quarters, he must have noticed that the gaslights were lit and the curtains drawn. To prevent this from ever happening again, Molt added the appropriate paragraphs to the official regulations: "Mornings when the gaslights are being used, the curtains should not be drawn on the windows so that one can immediately put out the gaslights when sufficient sunlight allows." Employees' desks were regularly inspected as well. The officials had to use formal forms of address during working hours, and conversations on private matters were subject to penalty and fined; tardiness could lead to a reduction in pay or even to dismissal. The officials' entrance was occupied by two assistant workers whose task was to note who entered and left the building and when they did so. Each employee had his place in a detailed and highly structured hierarchy determined in the end by his wage level. Whoever earned more had a right to take longer vacations, received more sick leave, and enjoyed a greater notice of termination. This created a culture of loyalty even among the lower-wage employees because they knew that they could only climb the wage ladder and hope for a better future by means of loyal behavior.

Allianz had very similar rules with similarly structured social benefits (such as an internal retirement fund). The Munich employees profited in addition from Munich Re's "breakfast," a free lunch that was served in Munich Re's rooms. In Berlin, on the other hand, the apprentices were sent out to fetch lunch until Paul von der Nahmer prohibited this practice after catching an apprentice delivering food on the steps; from then on, von der Nahmer had the custodian's wife prepare milk, cocoa, and soup for the employees instead.[32]

Allianz's head office was at first free of any office technology. Writing and arithmetic were a must if one wanted to climb the career ladder. These fundamental skills were quite widespread at the turn of the century. Allianz

View of an office of the ADVV at the beginning of the 20ᵗʰ century: insurance officials filled out the policies by hand.

had a large reservoir of workers at its disposal. Thus, the insurance branch developed a diverse workforce comprised of, among others, craftsmen, retired or dismissed military officers, and persons supposedly of "ruined existences." One day, for instance a young man applied for a position as a window cleaner in the Berlin branch of the North British and Mercantile. Since he was elegantly dressed, he was given a temporary position as an assistant waiter in the company cafeteria. There, his fine penmanship was noticed and he was given a position filling out policies. Ultimately, he reached the rank of executive secretary. At the ADVV, workers were also judged by their penmanship abilities as one can clearly read in the passages quoted above and from the payroll lists. Next to the column in which comments on individual workers like 'hard-working' or 'thorough' were made (as well as such comments as 'could be more diligent' and 'slow'), there was also a column for grading the penmanship of almost all employees (up to the deputy director himself) on a scale of one to three.[33]

The "instructions concerning the department and direction of the insurance business" describes the office tasks very vividly. At first the four agents directly subordinate to the directors, the "department managers," had to personally check the incoming correspondences twice a day. So that this should not lead to a prolonged reading hour, it was made abundantly clear that "hereby the individual reader restrains himself from a lengthy reading of those documents and pieces of correspondence that do not pertain to his business duties." All insurance forms and compensation papers had to be "thoroughly and immediately" examined and then the more important documents sorted from the less important. The normal operational routine went as follows: an official of the respective department drafted a response by hand. The department managers then took these in turn (at least at the ADVV) and presented them to the director and subsequently discussed them. Then the draft was modified as desired, revised, and written out. A subordinate official then wrote it up in careful penmanship, the so-called fair copy. Two officials subsequently collated the fair copy and the draft to check whether the fair copy corresponded to the draft or contained any errors. Everything at every step was noted with check marks and a subordinate daily writer wrote up a copy for the copy book in order to satisfy legal requirements, and finally, a letter of response was given to the director to sign. At Allianz, workers also delivered the letters personally. If the letters went to the directors of associated companies, Thieme drew up the letter himself or wrote out at least the draft (or outline). This had the effect of speeding up the process and making the letter more personal. What is amazing in this rather complex process was the speed with which the responses reached the addressees. One can find many examples of completed letter exchanges taking only a few days. Obviously, the work took a lot of personnel, but it was organized very tightly. What's more, the mail was delivered daily. In especially urgent cases, it was thus possible to get the mail delivered even on Sunday.

Filling out and managing the insurance policies proceeded in a very similar manner. For this, dozens of writers were kept busy doing nothing but writing out premium receipts. Others, who had distinguished themselves with their arithmetic skills alongside their fine penmanship, were in charge of bookkeeping and maintaining the registry. At the general agency for Bavaria, for example, it was necessary to add several hundred pages of copies to the so-called extension registry every month. There were also revision and cancellation registries – as well as monthly and premium transfer registries – that had to be maintained "most punctually."[34]

Around the turn of the century, insurance offices began to be technologized. In Munich on Maffeistraße, there was already a telephone line and Carl Thieme could also be reached privately by telephone. From 1892, if not before, Berlin's Telephone Exchange No. VI allowed callers to reach Allianz at its Berlin headquarters on the telephone number 1971. Other machines, however, would have a greater influence on officials' daily routine. These, of course, did not generate as much astonishment as the telephone booth, but two devices would evoke a considerable amount of anxiety among the workforce – the typewriter and the calculator. The first typed letter from Allianz that survived is from 1895. Handwritten letters continued to be made at the same time. In the beginning, typewriters did not really catch on at Allianz. For one thing, this was because they were impractical, awkward, and taxing to operate. If one wanted to see what one had written, one had to lift up the ribbon. Officials with fine penmanship were only partly qualified to work with the typewriter. Although the younger officials, for instance, at the Wilhelma in Magdeburg, at first fought for the chance to write with the new American product, it soon became clear that they were quicker without such technical progress. After that, a retired teacher operated the typewriter. Since he had been a pianist and had nimble fingers, it was thought that he would be quicker. The lesson was learned that new technologies at first only cause higher expenses. After all, a typewriter cost as much as the annual wages of a female employee at the ADVV. To use the new technology effectively, qualified personnel were needed. For that reason, Allianz apprentices were invited to attend evening courses for typing and stenography with part of the costs paid.[35]

The industrial revolution drove masses of people to places where work could be found or could, at least, expected to be found. They migrated from rural areas that could no longer feed them into the cities with newly developing industries. And after the old credo from the feudal Middle Ages – city air is freeing (which of course is a characteristically 19th-century version of the motto) – these rural masses-turned-workers experienced completely unknown freedoms in the city (but also completely new rules and regulations). When a worker was disgorged from the factory gates at the end of his shift, he could, if he still had enough energy and money, enjoy himself at the ever-growing number of pleasure and amusement parks in and around the cities. Social control was considerably more lax than in the rural towns. To be sure, wages were miserable, rents high, and life amounted to not much more than mere survival. At the same time, however, employees at least had more opportunities here to get together with fellow working-class brethren. Working-class political groups and unions arose and fought for higher

A "Fräulein" room at the ADVV in Stuttgart before 1914.

wages and more rights. Not only men from rural regions migrated to the cities, but young women or daughters from the small farm milieu who were used to working the farms moved to the cities as well. The women were hired primarily as service girls; over time, however, they began to find employment as industrial workers. In this context, these women had the same experiences as their male colleagues under tyrannical business management, money-grabbing landlords, and an invariably inhospitable and unsupportive bureaucracy. In addition, they had to fend for themselves against the discrimination that they were subjected to in a society dominated by men.[36]

By taking on jobs, working-class women also took on a pioneering role. The conventional 19th-century picture of a woman's role in the world saw her in the kitchen at the stove cooking or taking care of children. Especially in higher-ranking circles, it was normal for girls and young women of the family, after completing their schooling, to prepare for their roles as wives and mothers by enrolling in home economics courses. Driven by their social need and invigorated by the first successes in the women's movement in the 19th century, young women from higher social ranks, too, now began to work. For the most part, they found jobs as salespersons, but increasingly, also as office assistants in industrial companies and in commerce. In 1907, there were already almost 640,000 female employees, including domestic workers who made up over half of the total. 11,000 females were employed as office assistants; approximately 3,500 were employed in the insurance business. With the total insurance workforce at about 50,000, female employees thus accounted for around 7 percent.[37]

Elisabeth Branthin was one of the "Fräulein." She described her professional development up until the time when she joined the Wilhelma in Magdeburg in 1899 in the following terms: "We were trained in stenography, typewriting, etc., and had to be able to show proof of our strong moral fiber and good character to various experts, and then we were ceremoniously released into the hands of the company." Writing out dictations and completing written correspondence on the typewriter constituted the daily routine for many young women. Together with Ms. Branthin, another 16 or 17 young women began working for Wilhelma on October 1, 1899. In her words, this represented "the first time that such women were introduced in a larger company as office employees, and this generated quite some resistance." It was, in truth, not the first time because there were other insurance companies that were further along in this respect; by contrast, her description of the resistance the new arrivals aroused is credible. Their entrance into Wilhelma was made possible by Wilhelma's director at that time, Ferdinand Hahn, who himself had six daughters and was said to be "ahead of his time." Elisabeth Branthin transferred out of the writing room after a year and a half and moved into an area that had already become a women's domain by that time: as a "switchboard girl," she operated the brand new telephone system at Wilhelma.[38]

The ADVV also owned a telephone system, and theirs was operated by women as well – at least, that is, in fair weather. The official regulations specified that use of the telephone was not allowed in foul weather – such as in a storm – since this could damage the nerves of the person telephoning and of the "telephone operator". Whether this concern was based on experience or simply the result of human fear of the new technology is unknown. Yet it is this preventive measure we have to thank for the knowledge that at the ADVV at this time, around 1900 the same occupational title, "telephone operator" in this case, could be applied for men and women. At ADVV, there was clearly a distinctively progressive thinker because, normally, women were identified either as office assistants (Bürogehilfinnen) or as "Fräulein." At ADVV *Fräulein*" had been in the workforce since 1878; Molt seems to have recognized many years earlier than all the others that the employment of women could increase the company's profitability. When in 1892 the board of directors was discussing the acquisition of a fourth typewriter, Molt explained that "the association's board of directors recommends the purchase of another (and in fact the fourth) typewriter of the Yost system at the wholesale price of 427 marks. The same body also mentions that although the price of the machine is high, the efficiency of the device is, however, equally so; with such a machine two to three copies can be made along with the original and more quickly than with the quill. The practice by which the officials normally first draft their correspondence and then have an original fair copy written out by the office girls has proven itself successful; time is saved, the need for corrections reduced and the fair copy looks more prestigious. For the latter reason the typewriter is mainly used." The new technology was worth it because the work could be taken care of more rapidly and less expensively. Only the argument that a typewritten letter was more "prestigious" than a handwritten one might have generated little understanding then, as today. Consequently, the ADVV continuously hired more women. While in 1889 it had employed only nine women, already ten years later there were over 200 women employed at the ADVV and around 500 men.[39]

At this time, women worked in so-called writing rooms. Insurance officials were prohibited from entering these rooms. The overseers of these rooms were selected female employees under the direction of manageress Miss Mohr. She was thereby one of the first female top managers in the history of an insurance company. Her tasks included hiring and firing women employees. It was also important to segregate female employees from their male counterparts, not only during working hours, but after hours as well. The working hours of female employees began for that reason ten minutes earlier and also ended ten minutes earlier than the working hours of male officials. In addition, there were separate entrances and exits for male and female employees. When a retirement fund was created in 1903, by contrast, the company's progressive spirit showed itself again: explicit reference was made to the right of the female employees to receive retirement benefits along with the officials. The female employees, however, in return demanded to be freed from the retirement fund fees with the argument that "the vast majority [of female workers] does not attempt to achieve a lifelong position in the company; at a certain age they leave the company and thus the retirement fund benefits – such as providing for survivors (widows and orphans) – plays no role for them." The management agreed and complied with their demands; Miss Mohr was initially the sole female employee participating in the retirement fund. In the following years, it became apparent, however, that more and more women were searching for a lifelong position. Looking at the collection of photographs of the offices of the ADVV from the period before 1914, it becomes clear that not only young women are sitting at the typewriters but also more mature women. Furthermore, some female employees had by this time left the segregated writing rooms and can be seen seated side by side with their male co-workers in several administrative departments including the main payment center, the advertising department, or the bookkeeping and accounting department. Reading reports from women from the 1960s about their time in the insurance company, the gratifying retirement payments that arrived monthly from Allianz are frequently mentioned. The female workers had long since recognized how beneficial the establishment of a retirement fund proved to be, especially for employed women.[40]

New Insurance Branches and First Mergers

In 1894, the Prussian government granted Allianz the right to offer "insurance protection against financial loss due to fraudulent behavior on the part of officials or employees." The so-called fidelity bond insurance (Kautionsversicherung), which replaced cash bonds for employees in positions of trust with annual insurance premiums, represents Allianz's first step, albeit a somewhat indirect one, toward becoming a company that would cover every conceivable risk and insurance need of its customers. Two years later, it took over the fidelity bond insurance and accident insurance business of Fides Insurance Company, which, after it had introduced fidelity bond insurance to Germany, had now decided to go in a different direction.[41]

With fundamental support from Munich Re, Fides had tried since 1895 to establish burglary insurance in Germany. Carl Thieme negotiated a reinsurance contract with Fides and, along with Munich Re, invested in Fides' capital stock in 1896. Thieme seems to have been convinced that this type of insurance would be successful because he exported the idea to his European neighbors. The French company Réunion Française and the Erste Oesterreichische Versicherungs-Gesellschaft gegen Einbruch (First Austrian Insurance Society against Burglary), both of which Munich Re had invested in, introduced burglary insurance in France and Austria, as did Swiss National after Munich Re had bought shares in it.[42]

As the standard of living rose, burglaries increased: burglary insurance became established as a new insurance sector at the start of the 20th century.

Allianz approached the new branch in a roundabout way. In 1897, it took over the assets of the Germania, which specialized in bicycle theft insurance; such companies were springing up everywhere at that time. The business prospects for the branch were promising considering that the bicycle had progressed from a purely hobby or leisure article into a serious means of transportation for the gainfully employed. Doctors especially seemed to enjoy visiting their patients by bicycle. Perhaps not unexpectedly, thieves quickly developed a taste for their bicycles. Doctors in the large cities paid hefty premiums for their insurance policies. Simple, straight-up bicycle theft insurance continued to be a difficult business, although new, sophisticated types of locks and chains were constantly being devised. One design, for instance, transformed the saddle into a type of bed of nails for the thief. If the potential thief wanted to avoid a painful injury to a sensitive area, he had to push the stolen bike instead of pedaling quickly away on it and was thus easier to pursue.[43]

Allianz offered theft insurance in combination with liability insurance and thus packaged several risks together in a policy – a procedure that would soon prove to be effective in the automobile insurance branch as well. In 1899, Allianz referred to burglary and theft insurance as an independent branch in its overall business summary for the first time. In February 1899, the company received the official approval in Prussia for bicycle theft insurance as well as for burglary and theft insurance. Thieme seems to have shown his strong business acumen in this case, too. In 1900, there were already eleven insurance companies that published figures solely concerning burglary and theft insurance, and Allianz topped the list with premium revenues totaling 117,000 marks (although these figures also included the fidelity bond insurance premiums).[44]

Allianz was regarded, as mentioned previously, as Munich Re's favorite subsidiary. Yet Munich Re, as before, did not own Allianz stock. This was soon to change. Until that time, Munich Re's investments were almost exclusively in life insurance companies. Fides also had a life insurance branch when Munich Re climbed aboard. A few years later, the company was restructured and Fides concentrated on liability and burglary and theft insurance. Perhaps the reason Munich Re was reluctant to play a more active role as a participating shareholder in German insurance companies was that, in Thieme's eyes, Allianz had already covered this corner of the market. Supporting this theory is the obvious fact that Munich Re soon lost interest in Fides and that then (and only then) did Fides merge with Allianz. On this occasion and because the business had experienced strong growth in the previous fifteen years, Allianz raised its capital stock from 4 to 8 million marks through the sale of 4,000 new shares and exchanged these for Fides shares. As a shareholder in Fides and because it took over the shares not needed for the exchange, Munich Re advanced to a major stockholder of Allianz through these transactions. This new official role for Munich Re as major stockholder was also expressed by the fact that Thieme, even before the plan was implemented, left Allianz's board of directors and was elected during the second annual general meeting in 1905 to Munich Re's supervisory board (to which he belonged until his death on October 10, 1924). He was the head of Munich Re then until 1922. After Thieme's departure, the board of directors of Allianz was comprised of the two directors Paul von der Nahmer and Otto Andrée, as well as the deputy directors Franz Enß in Berlin, and Marcus Mauel, and Paul Szelinski, both in Munich.[45]

In the meantime, it became clear to Allianz that it could not simply maintain its leading position in the burglary and theft insurance branch. In the previous years, the very close race between Allianz, Aachen-Münchener, and Favag intensified; in 1905, for example Favag was leading. It relied on a system of cooperating with fire insurance companies that acquired theft and burglary insurance policies for Favag, and it also expanded resolutely in foreign countries. In exchange, Favag voluntarily withdrew from the fire insurance business so as not to compete with its own allied business associates. Only when the same companies over time took on the burglary and theft insurance themselves did Favag decide in 1914 to offer fire insurance policies, too. Burglary and theft insurance gradually became an offshoot of fire insurance. The Imperial Private Insurance Supervisory Office, established in 1901, also regarded it this way; it finally bundled together the supervision of the insurance system across the Reich and collated the theft and burglary figures under those of fire insurance in its official publication of insurance statistics. Already in April 1904, some on the supervisory board of Allianz had begun to doubt whether burglary and theft insurance could subsist profitably without fire insurance.[46]

It was probably not an easy decision for Thieme to make. After all, Allianz (upon its founding) had consciously chosen not to offer fire insurance in order not to affront the business partners of Munich Re. This time, however, Allianz's potential market growth outweighed the dangers of causing Munich Re to lose a few customers. In November 1905, Allianz received the license from the Imperial Supervisory Office for the entire German realm as well as for many parts of other countries and cities abroad. The German fire insurance companies, as a result, did indeed reduce the number of policies they passed on to Munich Re. Thus, for example, the fire policies that Aachen-Münchener handed over dropped from 1 million marks in 1905 to 42,000 marks in 1909; other companies terminated their relationships with Munich Re completely.

Thieme had probably reckoned with such an outcome. On the other hand, he also certainly expected an increase in Allianz's premium revenues, which would then benefit Munich Re through the reinsurance policies. The premium revenues from burglary and theft insurance continued to increase tremendously until 1913, rising to 2.7 million marks. With this, Allianz was at least able to distance itself considerably from Aachen-Münchener. Favag's strategy was less successful than Allianz's. Of course, in the fire insurance newly established in 1913, Allianz did not quite reach the level of the older, established fire insurance companies. Including the reinsurance policies that Allianz still took on, the premium revenues reached over 9 million marks, so that profits naturally spilled over to Munich Re as well.[47]

The damage from the 1906 San Francisco earthquake is carefully assessed.

In 1905, one of the cities that the German Supervisory Office gave Allianz approval to sell fire insurance in was "Saint Francisco," as it was named in the official certificate of approval. Only six months later, not even the extremely self-confident German ministerial bureaucracy would have had the gumption to write the name of the city in this form. By then, San Francisco was known worldwide as a symbol of the sheer uncontrollable violence of nature. A catastrophe of biblical proportions had occurred that modern communications technology had transmitted to practically all corners of the world. Early in the morning of April 18, 1906, an earthquake – with a magnitude of 7.8 on the Richter Scale – shook the city. An eyewitness vividly reported what he had observed and experienced in the Münchener Neueste Nachrichten (Munich Latest News): "The catastrophe came suddenly and unexpectedly like a bolt of lightning from nowhere. Tuesday was a beautiful California day with a colorful sunset. The night was quiet, hundreds of wagons and automobiles transported their guests to the opera to hear Caruso perform in *Carmen*. The hotels were booked with patrons of gay and lively parties who were still celebrating together as the noise of falling buildings and ruins and terrified screams were heard instead of raucous, joyous cheers. I was standing before the Colombian building when the ground began to rock. At first, one thought that it was a normal quake; then the roof beam supports on the buildings across the street began to collapse, then the crunch of falling rocks mixed with the terror-stricken cries of the wounded and maimed filled the air. On top of that, there was a horrible sinking and rising, and one had the feeling that one was a helpless atom in a vast maelstrom that meant the end of the world." After about three minutes, the earthquake subsided. The fires – which in part were caused by the earthquake and in part by the emergency rescue squads – raged for days throughout the city and left in their wake a completely destroyed city district that had housed approximately 25,000 homes. Over 3,000 people lost their lives in the catastrophe; hundreds of thousands of inhabitants lost their homes. It took some time before San Francisco recovered somewhat from the shock of the events. San Francisco's position as the leading city on the West Coast was passed on to Los Angeles, whose position was considered less susceptible to earthquakes.[48]

The earthquake set off shockwaves not only in the Bay Area but also in the insurance business, which was already astonishingly globalized. 78 American and 31 foreign insurers, 19 of which were British and 6 German, were approved to sell fire insurance in California. Especially hard hit was the American fire insurer Fireman's Fund, founded in 1863 (which became an Allianz subsidiary in 1991). With its headquarters in San Francisco, this company's business was focused in the region that had experienced the catastrophe. This meant that not only did its customers suffer more than the average amount of damage, but also that its own invested assets and real estate lost much of their value. In addition, many of its own employees were personally affected.[49]

Jacob Bertha Levison, who later became president of Fireman's Fund, woke on this morning to "a crunching of timbers – a roaring, apparently from above and below – and to the house rocking back and forth. It was most terrifying and frightful. I did not realize what was happening; it seemed like a nightmare [...] My only thought was to get the family together so that when the house went down we should all go together." Levinson and also his family survived unscathed, as far as we know. When he tried to reach the site of the company's headquarters located in the heart of the hardest hit area, he had to give up and turn back home to his family. The building on California Street burned completely to the ground; only a few documents were saved. The company's official documents were completely devoured in the flames of the fire. Despite the severity of these losses – or perhaps because of them – the company was somehow able to find a way to cover the liability claims of the insured (the sum amounted to $11 million). The claimants received half of the payments in cash, the other half in shares of Fireman's Fund. The insured thus became co-owners of the company, simultaneously helping it overcome an existential crisis. The press and the San Francisco Chamber of Commerce praised this approach highly.[50]

Others, including the six German insurers directly active in the affected region, invoked a clause stating that damage occurring in the aftermath of an earthquake was not insured and offered only partial payments or refused to pay anything. Not only was the Californian press outraged by this behavior, so too was Imperial German Consul Franz Bopp. In fact, he feared that there would be political repercussions if the German companies continued to regulate the damage claims so restrictively. Rhein & Mosel was the most consistent in its actions. Its policies explicitly excluded any damage directly or indirectly related to or caused by earthquakes. It paid half of small claims up to $500 and denied all the other claims or sent them to court. An agreement with the majority of claimants was not settled until December 1909; Rhein & Mosel agreed to pay 25 percent of the damage claimed. Allianz and Munich Re also paid: they were involved via Rhein & Mosel reinsurer, Helvetia, in the San Francisco business of that company. One can assume that Thieme had an important voice in these companies' discussions about how Rhein & Mosel and the other direct insurers should treat their clients. His position had already been articulated along with that of other European reinsurers in an open letter to the direct insurers involved, which was the result of a meeting of the reinsurers on April 30, 1906, in Frankfurt am Main. Among other things discussed it was stated that: "Whatever the sitation, it remains the case that a fundamental principle of fire insurance companies should be that the insurer is not liable for damage directly or indirectly caused by an earthquake. It is according to this principle, and to this principle alone, and not according to any forced interpretation of the policy documents, that any claim for damage compensation is to be treated."[51]

As we have seen, the reinsurers were not even able to maintain this position with Rhein & Mosel, let alone with the American and British companies, most of which had paid the total sum of claims of the insured and thereby gained a good argument for selling future insurance policies. In all, about 80 percent of all total insured sums were paid out, although at the same time the payments often marked the end of many businesses. By the beginning of 1907, 19 insurers had already declared bankruptcy. The Transatlantische Feuer-Versicherungs-AG of Hamburg was liquidated, as was the Norddeutsche Feuerversicherungs-Gesellschaft, since it had bought reinsurance from two American companies, both of which went bankrupt themselves, as well as from two subsidiaries. Here it becomes abundantly clear that the system of in-house reinsurance did not function. The model of independent reinsurers co-developed by Thieme, on the other hand, was exceptionally successful. In contrast to the other great catastrophes in the past, the vast majority of the 243 businesses involved survived the calamity fairly well.[52]

Munich Re, which had initially opposed paying the claims, in the end covered approximately 11 million marks. In December 1906, Thieme revealed how it had come to such a reversal. At Munich Re's annual general meeting on December 28, 1906, he was asked whether Munich Re wanted to continue its business in the U.S.; Thieme's response, according to Wallmann's Insurance News Magazine, was that: "In America, one can earn from the hundred as much as can be earned in Germany from the thousand; and while in Germany profits of 5 percent are considered normal, one can earn five times as much in the US." The newspaper went on to quote Thieme word for word: "I will not do without America." The U.S. was and continued to be an extremely attractive market in Thieme's eyes; the earthquake presented Allianz with the chance to make a name for itself as a reliable partner to U.S. and British direct insurers. Varying the well-known saying, "time is money," the phrase "Thieme is money" was supposedly coined in American insurance circles. This, at least, was recorded in internal documents and can be corroborated by the impressive business growth in the following years. By 1913, the premium revenues of all German reinsurers had doubled.[53]

How much of this increase was directly attributable to business in America is difficult to say; Munich Re in any case left a lasting impression. Five years after the earthquake, the German government assessor, Dr. Ernst Avellis, while visiting the U.S., was able to report positive results to Berlin: "The events of San Francisco are beginning to recede into the past. That this crisis situation did not cause lasting damage to the name of German fire insurers should be credited, above all, to the past and present efforts of the largest active German insurance company in the US – the Munich Re company. The directors of a number of top companies in the North American market, including Home Fire, United States Casualty in New York City, and Travelers in Hartford, with whom Munich Re maintains good business relations, praised the work and the reliability of Munich Re." The total damage caused by the catastrophic earthquake – which not only affected San Francisco – amounted to around $524 million (according to Munich Re's current calculations); about $180 million worth was insured. In today's figures that would be equivalent to around $4 billion. It took almost 90 years before the insurance business had to deal with greater damage caused by a single earthquake; again this occurred in California when on January 17, 1984, an earthquake caused $44 billion in damage; around $15 billion of this was insured. Allowing for inflation, this would amount to about $24 billion in today's dollars.[54]

Allianz had not begun offering direct fire insurance in San Francisco at the time of the earthquake. For this reason there was little need to comment on the insurance calamity of the century in its 1905 annual report, which was published in May 1906: "For our involvement in the 1906 earthquake in San Francisco we have already allowed for sufficient reserves in the above-mentioned balance sheet as well as the above-mentioned profit forecasts." From the total surplus revenues in 1905 of over 1 million marks, Allianz set 300,000 marks aside as an emergency reserve fund for the fire insurance branch. It reported to the supervisory office in June 1906 that, due to a reinsurance contract with Munich Re, it was involved to the sum of $161,000. It calculated that an insurance liability rate of 50 percent was to be expected. The rate was probably much higher. Assuming a rate of 80 percent, which had previously been quoted, it would amount to a sum of around 540,000 marks. The annual report for the following year only states that the damage was completely covered in the previous year's figures. Also in that year, profits continued to increase and the paid-out dividend remained at the level of the previous year at 24 percent of the initial paid-in capital investment; that is to say, around 60 marks.[55]

Along with the Norddeutsche Feuer and the Transatlantische Feuer companies, some other German insurance companies ran into liquidity problems due to the catastrophe in San Francisco. Süddeutsche Feuerversicherungs-Bank in Munich, founded in 1883, "had become involved in business in California that was offered to them by a friendly company," its director, Heinrich Bothe, reported to the annual general meeting on November 17, 1906, according to Wallmann's Insurance News Magazine. No name was mentioned, but this probably referred to Munich Re as the friendly company, as Thieme also attended the annual general meeting. With astonishing honesty, Heinrich Bothe related that he had hoped for large profits as had been typical over the previous 50 years. Now he had to announce something completely different: "The catastrophe is, unfortunately, for us so hard to bear that we are now forced to give up our independence." Fortunately, Allianz stood ready in the wings as a merger partner, since Munich Re was already a shareholder in Süddeutsche Feuerversicherungs-Bank. An agreement was quickly reached: for the second time in its short history, Allianz raised its capital stock, this time by 1 million marks, and thus helped the shareholders of Süddeutsche Feuerversicherungs-Bank. In return, Allianz gained all of Süddeutsche Feuerversicherungs-Bank's assets, business and, above all, its workers and agents, including Gustav Henning from the Baltic Sea resort town, Warnemünde. Upon his death in 1923, he was the chair of the supervisory board for the Warnemünde Bank and through his contacts provided valuable support to the company.[56]

Heinrich Bothe was also able to recover from the catastrophe. Beginning in 1907 with the start of the merger, he joined Allianz's board of directors as a deputy member and from his office on Salvatorstraße 18 (the former headquarters of Süddeutsche Feuerversicherungs-Bank) he directed the Munich branch of Allianz. Barely in office and without the official contract documents from Allianz, which were still at the old branch office in the Domhof, he caused a stir by stepping on the toes, unwittingly, of the major player on the Bavarian turf, Bayerische Versicherungsbank (Bavarian Insurance Bank, BVB). Bothe had given the insurance accounts of the Maffeische Lokomotivfabrik in part to the insurance company Globus, although this decision was supposed to have been made by BVB, which was leading the operation. BVB's director, Ernst Drumm, assumed it was done on purpose, although it must be said that he thought the director of the fire insurance branch at Allianz's general agency in Munich was responsible. Drumm did not trust him at all; only after a thorough investigation and detailed explanation of the transaction did the defamatory attacks stop. Drumm's complaints may also have been motivated by the fact that the merger now allowed a powerful Bavarian competitor to become established in the fire insurance branch. This time, they reached a settlement in goodwill; 17 years later, however, shortly after Ernst Drumm became director-general of BVB, another conflict situation with Allianz arose that would not end so harmoniously for Drumm.[57]

Within a year Allianz had thus gone from newcomer to serious contender in the fire insurance business. Yet, the business from Süddeutsche Feuerversicherungs-Bank – Paul von der Nahmer spoke of 160,000 insured – generated many worries for Allianz for years to come. Whether it was due to the many wood-working factories, sawmills and spinning mills insured by the agencies in Sonneberg, Magdeburg, and Hanover, whose

Total loss in the case of a turbo generator at the Königsberger Werke in the early 1920s.

number von der Nahmer had incidentally wanted to reduce as early as 1906, is not known. But in 1910, he was still complaining about the heavy risks that Süddeutsche Feuerversicherungs-Bank had left behind, which led to large damage claims and to an unfavorable end result. A sense of deep satisfaction can be read in the words of von der Nahmer two years later when he told Thieme about considerable damage at a roof-tiling factory in Sömmerda. Allianz had inherited a portion of an insurance policy amounting to almost 300,000 marks from Süddeutsche Feuerversicherungs-Bank; the risks, however, were great because of a flammable drying system, and Allianz was thus able to get out of the contract at the right time, thereby also saving Munich Re from having to pay a large claim.[58]

Finally, in 1909 the Bayerische Lloyd, a transportation insurer from Munich Re's circle of associates, merged with Allianz. Whether this was due to the difficult situation in the transportation insurance industry – circumstances that Allianz also noted in its annual reports for the years 1908 and 1909 and that had a negative impact on its annual figures – or whether Munich Re no longer needed the Bayerische Lloyd in the same capacity as before and therefore wanted to simplify its organizational structure – is not known. The pattern of the merger nevertheless remained the same: Allianz raised the capital stock by 1 million marks in order to finance the merger and took on the top managers of the Bayerische Lloyd. Alfred Leube, director of the Bayrische Lloyd, joined Allianz's board of directors, which Heinrich Bothe had already left in early 1908. The new major player in fire insurance was now the deputy director in Berlin, Hermann Siefart, who had been recruited from the Preußische National in 1905 to strengthen the fire insurance department. One last capital infusion, this time in 1912, served to increase the amount of money in the reserve fund.[59]

By this time at the latest, Allianz had, once and for all, become one of the largest German insurance companies. Only a few other insurance companies had more capital stock, including Magdeburger Feuer, Norddeutsche, or Favag. Favag was the only competitor that managed to keep pace with Allianz's rapid growth to any degree. Nonetheless, the growth of Favag was built upon extremely shaky ground, as would become clear over the next fifteen years. "While the premium revenues in the German insurance business doubled between 1900 and 1913, Allianz's grew by nearly five times as much, namely, from 10.24 million marks to 50.31 million marks. On the eve of the Great War, Allianz was the direct insurer with the highest premium revenues in the German insurance industry – when life insurance is taken out of the comparison. At that time Allianz was still not involved in this branch of insurance." This picture is relativized, however, when one relates Allianz's revenues to the total premiums in the German private insurance industry. Allianz recorded just over 2 percent in its books.[60]

A small portion of this two percent came from machine insurance, which Allianz had introduced in Bavaria in 1900. The idea originated in England, which was then the leading country in levels of industrialization and actuarial calculations. It became necessary to find insurance protection for increasingly expensive machinery in industrial companies that would cover damage beyond that due to fires. The demand was there, as the numerous machine claims in the printing industry in Munich at the turn of the century show. Was it possible to offer an attractive enough insurance package to these companies? The efforts in Bavaria to offer such policies appear to have proceeded in a promising way. With the assistance of Munich Re, Thieme expanded the project to include the entire German Reich and even moved into other European countries. In Germany, Allianz formed a cooperative venture with Stuttgarter Mit- und Rückversicherung (Stuttgart Co- and Re-Insurance Company) and Kölnische Unfall (Cologne Accident Insurance Company); they all offered machine insurance at the same prices and under the same conditions. Along with Germany, the group wanted to offer insurance protection in Switzerland, the Netherlands, Belgium, and Luxembourg. With Alleanza in Italy and Providentia in Austria, Munich Re gained two further subsidiaries to take up machine insurance in their respective countries. Somewhat later, perhaps because the German companies remained unsuccessful in these countries, other companies from Switzerland and the Netherlands joined the circle of companies offering this type of insurance.[61]

In the commemorative publication celebrating the 50th anniversary of Allianz in 1940, Wilhelm Kisch proudly reported, in the spirit of those times, that in 1913 Allianz had "marched to the front of the machine and fidelity bond insurance branches." This is misleading in that both of the other companies in the co-operative were slowly reducing their activities in the machine insurance branch. On the eve of the First World War and with total premiums below half a million marks, "marching" was hardly the appropriate term. Allianz restricted its machine insurance sales almost exclusively to Germany, even though it had been granted permission to operate in Switzerland in 1909. Perhaps it was Munich Re's strategy to help the new branch achieve a breakthrough in several countries simultaneously while at the same time protecting direct insurers – who each tried in their respective countries to promote the new insurance – from competition from within. However, it was not until some years later that the branch became profitable for Allianz, when it had set up a materials testing laboratory in 1932 and began applying scientific methods to research the causes of damage and how to prevent it.[62]

Allianz had become the largest property insurer in Germany and certainly had Munich Re to thank for this. Since Thieme's departure from Allianz's board of directors, though, the relationship between the two companies had changed markedly. The areas of responsibility apparently became more clearly structured. Thieme was now the director of Munich Re; Paul von der Nahmer, on the other hand, was responsible for Allianz. The uncle and nephew liked to handle complicated and contentious items of business congenially in personal correspondence between them. Of course, not everything was resolved in the manner the father figure in Munich wished. Especially in the newly developing fire insurance branch, Allianz proceeded with extreme caution and occasionally against the advice of Munich Re. Such was the case, for instance, with Wiedes Papierfabrik Rosenthal in Blankenstein. (Today this is located in Thuringia; at that time it belonged to the principality of the House of Reuß, the Younger.) Munich Re wrote to Allianz, proposing fire insurance for the company and announced that Thieme would travel to Berlin for talks. The discussions resulted in a classic compromise: it was agreed that more information was first of all to be gathered and that a Munich Re employee would be sent out to investigate the premises since Allianz was not keen on the presumed design of the building nor on the location. Six month later, a contract had apparently still not been agreed upon, and Munich Re made another attempt to persuade Allianz; Allianz, however, remained skeptical and complained about the factory's handling of rags and straw materials. In fact, Paul von der Nahmer confessed that "whenever possible we prefer to avoid insuring paper factories, because the risks have proven to lead to losses." Munich Re sarcastically dismissed these fears with the passing remark that Leipziger Feuer and Berlinische Feuer would be taking on 30 percent and 15 percent of this "bad risk," respectively. Whether a last attempt by Thieme in the form of a face-to-face meeting succeeded in convincing Allianz is unknown. One factor in these discussions was certainly that the paper factory had already concluded policies with Allianz for liability and burglary and theft insurance and that exactly on the day that Munich Re received Allianz's refusal, it had raised its insured sum from 103,000 to 253,000 marks.[63]

Almost a year and a half later, Allianz asked Munich Re to "send a list of those companies with which you have concluded reinsurance policies." Now it was Munich Re's turn to get upset. Fritz Thieme, Carl's son and at the time an authorized signatory for both Munich Re and Allianz, recorded in a note that von der Nahmer would not receive the list without explaining his rationale for this decision. One can assume that Munich Re wanted to protect its own clients and did not want to reveal any business secrets. This seems to be corroborated by von der Nahmer's response, in which he expressed that Allianz naturally would "only make discreet use" of the information.[64]

A third spotlight on the relationship between the two insurers can be found in the way they interacted with a company that repeatedly played an especially important role in the history of Allianz – Österreichischer Phönix (Austrian Phoenix). Founded in 1860, the property insurance segment of this company later became a part of Allianz as Wiener Allianz (Viennese Allianz); today, following the merger with Anglo Elementar in which it became Allianz Elementar, it belongs to the core of the Allianz group in Austria. Around the turn of the century, Munich Re and Phoenix had close reinsurance ties. One day in early 1906, Carl Thieme appeared before a group of Allianz employees and made them a startling proposal. In exchange for a salary raise of 25 percent, these employees were to switch to Phoenix. Paul

Bezzenberger, an official in Allianz's claims department, was named the chief authorized agent of the German Reich and took over, together with Freiherr von Sternbach, the directorship of the Munich Phoenix branch. Max Schertel, a young independent agent who himself had switched to Phoenix after only a few months at Allianz, observed how "Österreichischer Phönix established itself as Allianz's strongest competitor." With the aid of special contracts with farming cooperatives in the rural areas of Bavaria, Allianz became the dominant liability insurer. Phoenix followed Allianz's model, since, of course, its independent agents knew Allianz's conditions only too well. Spectacular results were the consequence, as Schertel self-confidently reported: "I was very successful, for example, in the area of Glött-Offingen in Swabia in 1906; within one week I closed 180 farming contracts; in other words, I was able to almost completely, to 100 percent, steal them from Allianz on Allianz's own conditions, but all in the interest of Munich Re." The latter was involved as a reinsurer with Allianz as well as with Phoenix.[65]

In 1909, Providentia took over the German assets of Phoenix and began offering machine insurance. This act may have relaxed the competitive antagonism considerably because Providentia's administrative board was comprised, along with Hermann Pemsel, of Wilhelm Finck, Carl Thieme and Paul von der Nahmer. Providentia was headed by Manfred Knote, von der Nahmer's cousin and the brother of the director of the Munich branch of Allianz, Gustav Knote. But this home-grown competition was to continue in Germany until, finally, on the occasion of a new partnership agreement between Munich Re and Allianz in 1940, Providentia was integrated into the Allianz concern as a part of its Berlin branch.[66]

Sales and Marketing   How painful the loss of several independent agents to Phönix was for Allianz is not documented. On the other hand, there is much documentation on how quickly Allianz built up a comprehensive sales network. Already in the first annual reports, it proudly stated that there were 41 general agencies and 789 agents working for Allianz; ten years later, the number of agents had increased to over 3,000. This growth is understandable when one considers the circumstances of the time. Insurance companies that only handled one or two branches were still common in those days. A representative agent could only offer his client broad and comprehensive insurance protection when he worked for many diverse insurers.

The two sales agents Ernst Reischert (right) and Franz Ebert helped to shape sales at Allianz for many decades.

Since accident and liability insurance at the end of the 19th century were not yet widespread, Allianz does not seem to have had difficulty finding experienced agents who wanted to work for it in this branch. But in the end, which agents brought in all the clients? Which ones were responsible for increasing Allianz's premium revenues every year? We know only a few names and even less about their backgrounds. It would not have been much different at Allianz than it was for instance at the Magdeburger Feuer, which as a consequence of the merger with Vereinte Gruppe (United Group) became a part of Allianz in 1995. In 1892, this time-honored enterprise employed almost 5,000 agents. Farmers, bookkeepers, jewelers, goldsmiths, retired security guards, soap manufacturers, and night managers were represented in its pool of employees. But also civil servants, silo owners, elected city officials, and private secretaries earned extra income as agents. Among these – almost all men – there were also five women. All five were widows of businessmen who had probably taken over their husbands' agencies after their deaths. Especially in the bourgeoisie milieu where insurance companies advertised for clients, the employment of women was considered in poor taste. The special value of women for selling insurance products, however, had already been recognized. Stuttgarter Lebensversicherungsbank, for example, in a letter to its members in 1905, quoted the following from an article in the Sonntags-Zeitung für Deutschlands Frauen (Sunday Newspaper for Germany's Women): "If a woman possesses enough talent, discretion, drive and prudence, she could earn a handsome additional salary as an agent for life insurance policies. Of course, to direct an agency alone would be asking too much and is not recommendable as it demands a great deal of business knowledge that cannot be gained at the bat of an eye and requires much time to acquire." This time would then possibly be missing elsewhere, particularly in caring for her husband or household.[67]

Ernst Reischert, a former actor at the Royal Court Theater in Hanover, was undeniably not your typical example of an agent. In order to receive approval from the father of the woman he wished to marry, Reischert began in 1894 to build up a bourgeoisie life with a second job. It took only a few months before deputy director Otto Andrée from Berlin arrived in Hanover with a new employment contract for Reischert in his briefcase: he should get the Silesian general agency in Breslau running up to speed. His task consisted of, for one, recruiting new agents. Traders in colonial goods and hardware were especially desired, since they had enjoyed good relationships with the rural farmers in the region. Secondly, Reischert was to organize meetings with the estate lords where he would then hold lectures explaining liability risks and the virtues of insurance protection. In hordes he was able to convince the listeners to sign up with Allianz. His success reached into the highest social circles of Silesia. After two and a half years of service in Breslau, he returned to Berlin and was subsequently promoted to a top management position; he was praised by the directors as having signed up more nobility in Silesia than Allianz had previously signed up in all of the German Reich. Sometimes his earlier acting career helped him out. In 1897, for instance, when he wanted to steal the liability insurance of the chemical company Silesia in Breslau from Kölnische Unfall, the negotiator for Silesia greeted him saying, "now, Mr. Reischert, it is not too long ago that you looked down at me from the theater stage and entertained us for many pleasant hours." Reischert was not only a convincing actor, but he was soon to greet the chemical company as a new customer of Allianz.[68]

In Berlin, his responsibilities included hiring and training new general agents in all of Germany and regulating accident and liability claims. Parallel to these tasks, he also held his Breslau lectures before various Berlin associations and clubs and concluded, as he did in Breslau, special contracts with, for instance, the association of pharmacists, the association of soap dealers, or the association of German leather manufacturers. The wedding with his beloved had of course long since taken place by this time. His father-in-law could no longer come up with any objections after these successes.

Allianz used Reischert's model for many years to come throughout the German Reich. In Bavaria, it was Julius Schmidt who directed the general agency, which was initially housed, like Munich Re, in the so-called market bazaar on Maffeistraße but later moved to the Domhof on Kaufingerstraße 23. Schmidt was primarily responsible for concluding special contracts with the leading associations in Bavarian agriculture and for sending his staff of inspectors, which included former military officers, business administrators, teachers and businessmen, to presentations at gatherings of farmers. Success soon followed: "In fact, contracts came by the barrowload," Albert Köhler, a former co-worker of Schmidt's, happily reported years later in a letter to Allianz describing that time. Naturally, there were unexpected difficulties as well. Max Schertel had just begun a presentation in Kissing, outside of Augsburg, when an outraged farmer stood up and told the story about how an insurance company had refused to pay a damage claim. Tumult and chaos ensued, and Schertel had to break off the presentation with no results. Only after he had explained the mistake to the rebellious farmer during two subsequent visits – not every kind of damage falls under liability – was he able to successfully insure almost all the businesses in the region.[69]

In this case the effort was moderate, since Kissing was located on the train route between Munich and Augsburg. In the more remote regions of Bavaria like the Bavarian Forest, one could wait a lifetime for a bus. Most inspectors and agents covered the distances on foot. It must have seemed like a gift from heaven when an agent could hitch a ride in the small carriage of the local county commissioner to a meeting that the latter had organized. One can imagine the impression the gentlemanly arrival of the agent with the commissioner must have made on the local farmers. At the turn of the century, the annual premium for an agricultural business with horses (and without an additional business operation) amounted to about 6 marks. For this very early form of mass business, there was no adequate form of advertising. The brochures that did exist were nothing like today's advertising materials. There was absolutely no illustration; the text was usually regarded as incomprehensible. The one exception, surprisingly, could be found in the advertisements for machine insurance. In this insurance branch, in which specially trained engineers supervised each contract individually, Allianz supported sales by designing brochures with spectacular photographs of machine damage. Allianz's classified ads, by contrast, were quite conser-

An Allianz agency in Bonn (1908).

vative. Since 1896, for example, Allianz had advertised in the catalog of the Munich art exhibition in the Glass Palace by placing a complete page announcement and referring "specifically to the favorable conditions for the transportation of oil paintings, copper plate etchings and other works of art." The art exhibition patrons and the buyers of the art catalogs were certainly the clientele Allianz targeted. Whether Allianz at that time also insured the exhibited works of art is not known. Thirty years later, in 1931, in the great fire at the Glass Palace that destroyed almost the entire collection of art works on exhibit, only a portion of the exhibited works were insured; not only were the works of art lost forever, but their owners suffered an irrecoverable financial loss, too.[70]

Personal contacts and networking seem to have been more important for sales than advertising. Everyone was called upon to help establish and expand Allianz. For instance, in this spirit, Allianz wrote in 1906, to its shareholders and to those of Munich Re, informing them that it had now also begun to offer direct fire insurance: "As a shareholder in our company we turn to you and request that you support our efforts to establish and operate profitably in our newest insurance branch by recommending our company to your circles, as well as by showing your friendly support by transferring your fire insurance policies to us once the current terms have expired." Knowing well that people preferred to think of other things rather than about their insurance policies, Allianz also offered a special reminder service. There was a form enclosed that the shareholders could fill out giving the date of the fire insurance contract's termination, and send it to Allianz, so that Allianz could remind the sender in due time of the impending necessity to terminate contracts with other companies. The employees of Munich Re addressed as "Herren Beamten" (Officials), were similarly informed. Allianz tried to make the transfer of policies more attractive to them by pointing out the higher commissions they would then possibly receive. For signing a 10-year furniture fire insurance policy, for example, one would receive 90 percent of the initial year's premium as commission and for a 10-year burglary and theft insurance policy, 60 percent.[71]

Personal connections and networks were vital to the insurance business in industrial branches. This was recognized by the general agency in Magdeburg, which badly wished to insure the soap factory C. H. Oehmig-Weidlich in Zeitz; the soap factory's owner, however, was known not to be receptive to insurance matters. Fortunately, the general agency learned that the owner was none other than councilor of commerce Hermann Thieme, Carl Thieme's brother. Soon thereafter, Carl wrote to his brother to remind him that as a large shareholder of Allianz he should please reserve a share of the fire insurance of the business for Allianz. An answer came from Hermann's son only four days after the Allianz general agency had written the letter with the news that, alas, only a few weeks before a new contract had been concluded resulting from the addition of new buildings raising the insured amount by 75,000 marks and that the insurance policy would first terminate in July 1909; Allianz could participate then. In October 1908, Allianz announced that it had completed the deal: as a result of restructuring, Allianz was to take over an insurance policy amounting to 158,860 marks.[72]

Foreign Business and the First World War

When it came to new acquisitions, Allianz relied on the assistance of friendly foreign firms when necessary. Prompted by general agent Felix Amende from Breslau, who wanted to do business with the coal mine Charlotte in Czernitz in Upper Silesia, Thieme asked the director-general of the Wiener Versicherungs-Gesellschaft, Sigmund Nyitrai, whether he could arrange a meet-

1. 1890–1918 The First Years and the First World War

ing. The president of the mining company, Alexander von Schreiber, promised in discussions with Nyitrai to intervene on behalf of Allianz; in a letter to the general agency, however, he wrote quite coldly that "there seemed to be no reason at the moment to undertake a change in the indemnity insurance at the Charlotte mine." Once again Allianz had run up against a wall on account of special Austrian business relations. Wilhelm Kißkalt, Thieme's successor as director of Munich Re, recalled in retrospect the mixed emotions of fascination and of aversion associated with Thieme's many trips to Vienna: "Vienna always meant trouble: the subsidiary Providentia was poorly managed; worst of all, however, were the relationships with the Austrian Phoenix companies. These were under the direction of Dr. James Klang, who Pemsel once described as Thieme's evil spirit [...] Klang's priority above all was to serve his personal vanity, and only secondly running the business. It was a soft, slippery terrain in Vienna, which took up much time and brought little profit; the most objective relationships were with the two companies located in what was then Austrian Triest, Generali and Riunione."[73] Nonetheless, Austria was still an especially important foreign market for Allianz – so important, in fact, that it opened

Receipt of claims payment of $ 162 for fire damage in Tianjin on December 24, 1914.

a branch office there in 1913, the only one besides the branch office in Munich at that time.[74]

In 1913, Allianz earned over 10 million marks in premium revenues from foreign business. Unfortunately, it is not possible to say much more about how these revenues were distributed across the different insurance types or the different countries. There are only a few figures and some hints and references that could shed light on Allianz's activities abroad before the First World War. The amazingly high portion of 20 percent of premium revenues from abroad can be explained partially by Allianz's reinsurance business. In 1913, Allianz received almost two and a half times more reinsurance premiums from fire insurance than it did from direct insurance. To be sure, this was partly due to the fact that Allianz had only begun to offer direct fire insurance in 1906. In burglary and theft insurance, where over 50 percent of Allianz's premium income came from abroad, the pendulum swung strongly in the direction of reinsurance. With over 1.2 million marks, the reinsurance premiums were six times as high as the direct insurance premiums.[75]

From the beginning, Allianz offered transportation insurance along with accident and liability insurance. With good reason, Allianz's founders expected considerable growth in the transportation of goods and saw numerous opportunities for transportation insurance. Because the transportation of goods did not cease at national borders, international contacts could only be advantageous in insuring these goods. Munich Re enjoyed such contacts with general agencies in Vienna, St. Petersburg, Copenhagen, Stockholm, and with the agency in Paris managed by Paul von der Nahmer until 1894. In its founding year, Allianz also established a branch in London that Carl Schreiner managed and whence he built up Munich Re's transatlantic business. In Copenhagen, Allianz worked together with Peter Christian Olsen; in Paris with Charles Weisweiler; in Vienna with Wiener Rück; and in Zurich with Zürich Versicherung, whose former deputy director, Bruno Pohl, helped build up Allianz in Berlin. These parties are recorded in the books as partners as early as the 1890s. In 1902, Allianz took over the Pomerania in Stettin and "inherited" the transportation insurance of the ferry company Bräunlich in Stettin. "The ferry company operated extensive freight and passenger services throughout the Baltic states of Sweden, Finland, Russia, Lithuania, Estonia, and Latvia, which automatically resulted in strong ties to seaports such as Riga, Petersburg, Stockholm, and Vyborg." For Louis Dreyfus and Co., Allianz insured the transportation of wheat from South America and from the Black Sea. Since the Danube delta was

Advertising brochure of the Austrian Phoenix for a war bond insurance policy on the basis of a life insurance policy.

considered a very dangerous region where plundering was frequent, Allianz, together with its partners, stationed its own steamship, the Adagena, in Kerch on the Crimean Peninsula, from where it could quickly reach the site of an insured loss in order to assess the claim.[76]

It was not only transportation insurance or the transfer of Munich Re's fire reinsurance policies that turned Allianz into an international enterprise. The agents in Copenhagen were also negotiating accident insurance as early as 1891 (at the latest); in London, Allianz opened a branch for personal accident insurance in 1893; in Switzerland, it was granted permission to sell not only transportation insurance, but also accident, liability and fidelity bond insurance in 1897. Although the premium revenues in the first full business year in 1898 only amounted to the rather modest sum of 25,000 Swiss francs, it had already recruited its own agents in 18 of the 25 Swiss cantons with authorized agent Paul König at the helm in Bern. These efforts paid off: in 1913, a large part of the premiums from direct insurance for burglary and theft came from Switzerland. In this, as well as in accident and liability insurance, the revenues reached around 200,000 Swiss francs, which made the Swiss market one of the most important foreign markets for Allianz at this time.[77]

By 1909, Allianz had significantly expanded its radius of operations. With diverse branches, it was active in Belgium, Denmark, France, the Netherlands, Luxembourg, Austria, Sweden, and Switzerland. In Romania, it took on burglary and theft insurance, and it was precisely the fire insurance business that Allianz had taken up so belatedly that propelled Allianz's internationalization: in this branch, Allianz was active in 1909 also in Greece, Russia, Spain, and Hungary, as well as in "Egypt, America, Australia, China, in the Chinese treaty ports, the German-African colonies, England, India, Mexico and Transvaal." This seemingly strange ordering of countries where Allianz was active – first Europe, then all countries outside of Europe, with England in the middle – would have corresponded to the British self-perception then as now; yet there were also internal organizational reasons for this ordering, and it reflected the special role Carl Schreiner played for Allianz. He was one of the first staff members of – and certainly one of the closest to – Carl Thieme. In 1886, he left Munich Re and directed Badische Rück for some years before he returned to Munich Re in 1890 and established and managed its English and transatlantic business in London. Allianz adopted the same pattern when it began to expand its international business. Europe was directed from Berlin and Munich, the rest of the world from London. For instance, when Richard Dietterle approached Allianz about the possibility of taking over its agency in Egypt, Thieme passed the matter on to Carl Schreiner and not to Allianz director Paul von der Nahmer. Schreiner informed Thieme a month and a half later that the agency had been transferred to Dietterle without there being any record of Berlin having been involved. The partnership, however, does not appear to have been especially successful; merely one and a half years later, Allianz parted ways with Dietterle.[78]

Much more successful was the partnership with Siemssen and Co., one of the first German trading companies in China. How far the cooperation went back is not ascertainable. At first, the focus was probably on transportation insurance. Then, at some point between 1906 and 1909, Allianz branched out into the fire insurance business in China. What drove Allianz so far away from home, though? In the end, it wasn't just a matter of concluding insurance deals, but rather of handling claims as inexpensively as possible. Take, for example, the case of the Paukstat family, whose Christmas decorations went up in flames on Christmas Eve 1914. Fortunately, the family members present were able to extinguish the fire relatively quickly, so damage remained limited. Already on January 12, 1915, an employee from Siemssen and Co. in Tientsin (now called Tianjin) paid $ 162 to the Paukstats for a damaged silk evening gown, women's silk underwear, a corsage, a rug and a tablecloth.[79]

Allianz certainly concentrated at first on German exporters when it took up operations in foreign countries. Employees of these trading companies and industrial enterprises, for instance, in the Chinese coastal towns, were the first foreigners to have settled there since the mid-nineteenth century. They were followed by diplomats, missionaries, doctors, soldiers, engineers, and administrative officials for the colony of Tsingtao.[80] These kinds of people – who were also to be found, for example, in British South Africa or in India – had to be won over as clients. This was also the strategy of Stuttgarter Lebensversicherungsbank (Stuttgart Life Insurance Bank, Old Stuttgarter), which for this reason wrote to various Imperial German consulates general: "Our German citizens living abroad to make a living tend to put more and more of their savings into solid German insurance companies for retirement funds and survivors' life insurance. This is a fortunate situation for many reasons, but especially, because it is in the best interest of the insured, the beneficiaries and their families. Therefore, we would like, in accordance with the appeal of our welfare organization based upon pure reciprocity, to support such good intentions insofar as it is possible to take into account the interests of all our bank members." As a sign of consideration and in order to better gauge the dangers, Stuttgart asked the consulates to provide thorough information about the local situation. The reply from the general consulate in India could not have evoked an all too enthusiastic response from the directors at Old Stuttgarter. The climate was too unhealthy, a large number of infectious diseases put life in jeopardy, the hygienic conditions left much to be desired, and the Europeans drank too much alcohol. The consulate general himself, on the other hand, was all for it. He was located in a more moderate climate, in Shimla in northern India, which he warmly recommended to Europeans living in India as a spa destination.[81]

Six years later in Chinese Canton, the Chinese themselves discovered life insurance. Germans were for the most part insured by German companies; the Chinese, on the other hand, who themselves slowly began to invest in life insurance, bought insurance from US American or Canadian companies. The German consulate stationed there was sorry to see such potential go unused and was disappointed that the German insurers had undertaken no strategies up to then to tap such a great developmental opportunity. In fire insurance, on the other hand, the largest portion of the business for German insurers was insuring Chinese property. This is confirmed by Allianz records: the majority of the policies in Tientsin were concluded with Chinese customers and, in fact, in both European and Chinese districts of the city. The regulation of claims was also exemplary: in a fire on February 16, 1915, in the Chinese part of the city, the rice dealer shop Shing Chong Yuan Tung Chi burned to the ground. Employees from Siemssen and Co. inspected the damage and attempted to save what could be saved. An "enterprising Chinese" made an offer to buy the rest of the damaged goods (rice, flour, and grains were ruined by heat and water) for 100 Mexican dollars. Since the rice dealer had kept "accurate and impeccable" records, the amount of the damage was quickly assessed and merely a few days after the fire, Allianz paid the client 1,500 Hongping taels. Allianz in Munich would first receive news of the fire on February 20 and a full report on February 22. Of course, not every claim could be resolved quickly and easily. This can be seen in the case of Mr. Yu Tang Li. During the same night damage occurred in his house, too, which the insured estimated at 500 taels; Siemssen and Co. thought this a gross exaggeration (bordering on the "offensive"): "We will for the moment not comment on the claim until the insured reports serious estimates. If the customer fails to do so, we will take measures ourselves to have the building restored." Unfortunately, there is no documentation as to how the case was ultimately resolved.[82]

At this time, Siemssen and Co. corresponded directly with Berlin and no longer through Carl Schreiner in London. This was not, however, due to Paul von der Nahmer energetically taking control of the overseas operations but rather to world political events: "As a consequence of the war any and all traffic between our overseas agencies and our business locations in London, on the one hand, and between us and our site in London, on the other, is prohibited; we are now working directly with our Chinese agencies […]." The First World War was about to make far more than only the correspondence between business partners more difficult.[83]

"Now a flaming sword will appear in the heavens above." According to his children, this was Thomas Mann's comment upon hearing that the German Reich had declared war on Russia on August 14, 1914. Within a few short days, a regional conflict between Austria and Serbia had grown into a war of unprecedented proportions. All the great powers of the day entered sooner or later into the war. In England, it was therefore soon dubbed the "Great War," in France, "La Grande Guerre" and in Germany, "Weltkrieg" (World War). At the start of the war, most people believed battle veterans who said that the war would be over quickly and that Germany would be victorious. For the German insurance industry, as for all areas not directly tied to war, the war initially meant that they had to do without a great num-

From the beginning of the First World War, more and more women work at ADVV, also in specialist departments.

ber of employees. Of the 792 officials employed by Allianz, 326 enlisted for military service in the first year of the war; the ADVV, in fact, lost 757 of 1,377 employees. This was not a problem for the companies at first as the ADVV's annual report indicated: "With business slacking off, the amount of work to be completed was so reduced that it was completed in the mornings by those who had not been called up, leaving time available in the afternoons for patriotic activities." Very quickly, however, there was no time left over for patriotic activities: "Soon, as a result of the war, requests pertaining to insurance contracts grew, for suspensions or reductions of premiums, for cancellations, loans and buyouts; not to mention the work related to new war measures […] all this with increasingly smaller numbers of personnel. Conducting of business was only possible by employing ever increasing numbers of women and using them in all parts of the company." Did the war give rise to equal rights for women? At the very least, the war emancipated the female employee from the clearly outdated "girls' room." The fact that at this time the young men were missing from the standing desks at ADVV may have made the decision easier for the management to make. Even greater, however, was the revolution at Allianz. Rudolf Hansel, a veteran insurance director, described the changes fifteen years later in these terms: "It was not possible to find male replacements for all who withdrew to the field. And the first women moved in with us. Because until then women's work, which at the time maybe still carried the stigma of 'cheap labor,' was unknown at Allianz."[84]

Viewing the profit reports for 1914, one would not have guessed that a new era had begun; unimpressed by the outbreak of war, profits climbed upward to 2.47 million marks as the number of claims declined considerably. Hensel had a catchy explanation for this: "Distractedness, negligence, malice, egocentricism, and covetousness, these roots of the soul out of which so much damage occurs were in the better parts of the population repressed for a considerable period of time (only to return later so uninhibitedly)." The premium revenues, however, were also considerably reduced; above all because of losses in the transportation insurance branch, in which premiums fell from 30 million to 25 million marks. By declaring war, Great Britain had nullified all insurance connections with enemy states. This hit the German transportation insurers especially hard – they had covered about one-third of their business risks on the London market. All the other war parties behaved in a similar manner. The German insurance industry reacted to the loss of markets in the enemy states by expanding business ties with their allies (Turkey and Bulgaria) and in neutral states. Especially in the neutral states, German trading companies, their employees and German citizens were considered potential customers since they no longer could or wanted

This is how artist Norman Wilkinson imagined the sinking of the Lusitania on May 7, 1915.

to be insured by British companies. For this reason, the German government supported and even spurred on the insurers in their efforts. Allianz intensified its own efforts, for instance, in Sweden, the Netherlands, and Switzerland and began new relationships in Argentina and Chile, among other places, where German agents could no longer work for British companies and the German population was happy to get insurance coverage from German companies. Furthermore, Allianz hoped for new business prospects in Poland and the Baltic states, areas that the German Reich had taken over from conquered Russia.[85]

It soon proved more difficult than initially thought to divide the tangled network of global insurance associations into friends and enemies. On May 7, 1916, a German submarine sank the British passenger steamer, the Lusitania, an act that caused 1,198 deaths. Among the fatalities were 128 Americans, which led to strong protests on the part of the U.S. government. After a second submarine attack that killed more Americans, Germans at first stopped the unrestricted submarine warfare. Some of the American passengers were very wealthy and had been insured by American accident and life insurance companies that, in turn – the U.S. had, at this time, not yet entered the war – had bought reinsurance from German reinsurers. The payments for life insurance claims alone were estimated at over 6 million marks. Munich Re, for instance, had around 680,000 marks in net expenditures for a catastrophe caused by the German military command. When insurance to protect against damage caused by air attacks grew dramatically during the course of the war, French newspapers repeatedly reported on the complicated insurance situation. French companies that had offered insurance protection against air strikes had bought reinsurance from Spanish and Swiss reinsurers, who in turn bought reinsurance from German reinsurers. In the end, German insurers paid for a portion of the damage caused by German shells and bombs in France.[86]

In 1915, Allianz's profits sank for the first time in its history. Premium revenues also decreased slightly. However, already one year later both figures were increasing once again. What made this possible for Allianz was what insurance historian Ludwig Arps claimed for all of the German insurance industry: "Although no insurer thought the war would last four years, the length of the war did not shake the German insurance industry." On November 11, 1918, the First World War came to an end after four longs years with the defeat of the German Reich. The flaming sword had appeared, but not as Thomas Mann might have envisioned in his wildest dreams. Millions of soldiers and civilians were dead; even more came home wounded and

Allianz advertisement for auto insurance in an illustrated magazine, around 1920.

traumatized by the war experience. Of the 667 Allianz employees who had gone to war, 94 never returned. In many countries, the suffering did not end with the armistice. Hunger, famine, the Spanish flu and other diseases, inflation and massive unemployment turned the life of many war survivors into a living hell. In Germany, normalcy did not return for a long time. In the late 1920s, the year 1913 was still often referred to as the last year of peace – and at Allianz as well.[87]

Life nevertheless went on and with it the need for people to seek insurance coverage. As the war was still in progress, Allianz made a decision that would strongly shape its future development. Until then, it had not been able to establish a position in the automobile insurance business. Instead, the ADVV was the first in 1899 to offer accident, liability and collision insurance to automobile drivers. Later, Allianz brokered automobile insurance for In-terunfall, which, to emphasize the exclusivity of this branch, printed the pol-icies on cork. During the war, most private automobiles were confiscated by the military. Nevertheless, in the Kaiserlicher Automobil-Club (Imperial Automobile Club, KAC) – Kaiser Wilhelm had been an honorary member since 1904 – there was apparently still a demand for automobile insurance. In order to offer the club members (many of whom came from the highest social circles in Germany) something extraordinary, the KAC founded the "Kraft" Versicherungs-AG along with Allianz and Munich Re. The newspa-per, Annals of the Insurance Industry, expressed its skepticism of the pro-ject: "Whether now, when automobile traffic is as good as dead and it is not foreseeable when and at what level it will return, is the right time for such a new founding is naturally very questionable." In this rare case, the efforts at exactly the wrong time and in exactly the wrong place proved successful. When the first insurance policies were finally sold, though, the auto club had lost its imperial attribute just as Allianz had done away with its imperial crown in the company logo. The German Kaiser had abdicated the throne and gone into exile. Yet this did not stop the development of the new com-pany. Soon "Kraft" and Allianz would become the largest car insurers in Germany. Allianz had found a market that promised healthy growth for many years to come.[88]

1918-1933

CRISES, RATIONALIZATION, AND GROWTH

On November 11, 1918, at eleven in the morning, the guns fell silent. The day before, the German Kaiser Wilhelm II had decamped to the Netherlands. An age was ending, but people's perceptions of this varied widely. The English economist John Maynard Keynes – attached to the British delegation at the Versailles peace conference – in 1919 described in his polemical essay, *The Economic Consequences of the Peace*, the opposing views of reality on the two sides of the English Channel:

"In England the outward aspect of life does not yet teach us to feel or realize in the least that an age is over. [...] In continental Europe, the earth heaves and no one but is aware of the rumblings. There it is not just a matter of extravagance or 'labor troubles'; but of life and death, of starvation and existence, and of the fearful convulsions of a dying civilization."[1] Keynes feared the worst for Europe's future if the peace treaty were to be unbearably hard on the defeated powers. But in view of the catastrophic destruction of the First World War, and the hate that had built up, a negotiated peace could hardly be hoped for. Only a few months before, Germany had imposed the unbridled peace terms of the Treaty of Brest-Litovsk on Russia. And indeed, the German public felt the Treaty of Versailles, which put the legal seal on Germany's defeat in June 1919, to be a "peace of humiliation," which should be overcome as soon as possible.[2]

Under the immediate impression of the revolutionary events, Ernst Grumbt, a member of the board of directors of Allianz, penned a newspaper article that was published on November 23, 1918, as a call for "unity and unanimity." Vacillating between pathos, self-pity, and fear of the future, he invoked the will to struggle for a new beginning and democracy:

"The die is cast. Germany's fate is sealed; doomed to impotence, left helpless to the mercy of our enemies, we see before us a most dismal scene. As stormy as politics may be in the next few years, so lifeless and impoverished will economic life in our dear fatherland be [...] Let us admit it openly and bluntly: despite all the denials of our incorrigible optimists, we are a ruined people, who will be barely permitted to survive if the terms of the peace are of the kind that the terms of the armistice suggest, with their outrageous severity, their harshness that makes a mockery of all humane feelings [...] The plain fact is that they have no intention of granting Germany the position in the councils of nations which it formerly held, that they do not want it to become powerful and strong again. [...] The domestic struggle is still raging, and all our thoughts and feelings must be devoted for the time being to this point, so that the despotism of a few does not become a permanent structure of government, those who believe that they should consider the free development of intelligence their most dangerous opponent. Only when we know that the domestic enemy has been stopped, and, if luck is with us, democracy triumphs for good, should we devote all our self to the service of combating external obstacles [...] Let us not wait, crestfallen and downcast, for miracles that save the German people from the collapse of the realm – we might lose valuable time doing so. No – get to work, as soon as domestic conditions have consolidated. Commerce, industry, and transportation must [...] march hand in hand towards the great goal: the reconstruction of our devastated fatherland."[3]

The period of the Weimar Republic, whose dramatic beginnings Ernst Grumbt commented on here shortly before leaving Allianz, became one of the most exciting, most dynamic, and most successful eras in the history of the company. But at first, uncertainty prevailed. Allianz faced enormous economic problems and political risks. The board of directors' report to the stockholders on the situation of the company in the summer of 1919 was correspondingly bleak: "Due to the unfortunate course of the World War, the area in which we do business has been restricted, while operating costs are increasing continuously, the full weight of which will only be felt in the future. It is not possible at present to assess whether and to what extent it will be possible to compensate for this. The experiment of nationalizing the fire insurance business, currently under discussion again, would destroy tried-and-tested arrangements and threaten the livelihoods of many people; and links to other countries, which are so desirable, would be made more difficult, and German insurance companies would be

ALLIANZ-ZEITUNG
MAI   SONDER-AUSGABE   1921

One generation departs:
title page of a special edition
of the Allianz Zeitung upon
the death of director-general
Paul von der Nahmer, who
died on April 15, 1921.

deprived of the possibility of providing the desired insurance coverage for the property of German merchants abroad. The financial advantages hoped for are unlikely to be achieved to the extent expected, while they could be ensured in other ways, without destroying a flourishing business. It is to be hoped that people in authority will not close their eyes to this insight."[4]

In his address, Paul von der Nahmer, the director-general of Allianz, who was 61 by now, only touched on a few of the most urgent challenges to his company. For example, as a consequence of the territorial losses of the German Reich to Poland, Belgium, France, Czechoslovakia, and Denmark imposed by the peace treaty, Allianz lost almost 15 percent of its annual premium revenues. The future of its activities abroad, which had amounted to 20 percent of its volume of business on the eve of the war, was entirely uncertain, and access to its international assets – bank accounts, securities, real estate – had been blocked by the governments of the wartime enemies, and of some of the neutral countries, for the time being. In addition, a fundamental debate, which had already been conducted repeatedly in the 1880s and during the war, was revived. The topic was whether society and the treasury would be better served if the insurance system, and in particular fire insurance, were monopolized in the hands of the state, or left to free-market competition.[5]

As if this were not enough, numerous other questions were already on the horizon, to which the management and staff of Allianz had to respond during the few and stormy years of democracy: it was apparent that there would be a new generation of top executives in the company. Under the paralyzing influence of the war, and because von der Nahmer showed little interest in internal business processes, a backlog of necessary reforms had built up, which increased administrative costs and slowed work processes.[6] Economic pressures, but also the spirit of the time, demanded more efficient working methods and more modern management structures. Furthermore, the leading men of Munich Re and Allianz in 1917 had already begun to put the business relationship between the two insurance companies, which was mainly based on informal agreements, arrangements for individual cases, and personal agreements, on a clear legal and sustainable footing. An initial binding agreement in principle had already been concluded before. Finally, Allianz had to cut its umbilical cord to its founders and emancipate itself as an increasingly independent enterprise.

By 1917 at the latest, Allianz's bookkeepers noted the increasing premium revenues with some concern, strengthened by the fact that they personally were only able to buy less and less with their nominally growing salaries.[7] It was apparent that the mark was losing value. In the first years of the Weimar Republic, this became the fundamental challenge for Allianz, the insurance business, and the banking sector, but also for the German economy as a whole, and, in the end, a question of survival for democratic society. The war, its consequences, and the welfare policy of the post-war period were financed to a considerable extent by printing money, so that inflation finally went completely out of control. It destroyed the people's financial assets. In addition, the government administrations of the Weimar Republic only succeeded briefly in restricting the growth of unemployment, until after 1929, German society finally "descended into the abyss" of the Great Depression.[8] At first, the U.S. banking system was destabilized, and then, as a result, the German financial sector as well: the insurance company Nordstern got into trouble in 1931, and in that same year, the Danat Bank, one of Germany's largest financial institutions, went bankrupt. At the end of a rescue operation without parallel, in 1932, the largest banks in Germany were state owned, some via majority, some via minority holdings.[9] In Germany, the collapse of the financial markets initiated an economic depression of hitherto unknown magnitude, which weakened the unstable political system still further, and steered society, which was already sharply divided economically and ideologically, into conditions approaching civil war. Thus, its enemies were finally able to destroy democracy.

In view of all these events and developments, it is all the more astonishing that Allianz, which was integrated in the global, European, and national structures of the economy, society, and politics in a wide variety of ways, succeeded during this period in surviving, modernizing itself, growing, and increasing its earnings. On the eve of the First World War, after a series of mergers, Allianz had become one of Germany's major insurance companies, with 792 office staff. By 1932, the last year of the Weimar Republic, after another 80 originally independent insurance companies had been merged into the Allianz group, this number had increased to almost 9,000 employees. In addition, there were tens of thousands of full-time and part-time sales agents. The gross premium income of the company grew from 57.3 million marks in 1918, the last year of the war, to 300 million Reichsmarks (RM) in the crisis year 1932. And while Allianz's business in 1918 had been limited to insurance policies in six product lines for customers in twelve countries, in the early 1930s, it held about 4.6 million policies from almost all classes of property, accident, and life insurance, except private health insurance, of customers from more than 25 countries.[10]

When Kurt Schmitt, the head of Allianz, presented the 1932 annual report to the public, the Nazis were already extending the powers that had been granted to them on January 30, 1933, with full brutality. They smashed the labor unions, had the books of authors they disliked burned, harassed the Jewish population, and opened the first concentration camps. The newspaper Vossische Zeitung – published by Ullstein, which at the time was one of Europe's largest press groups – praised Allianz in May 1933 comprehensively for its current annual financial statement. Under the headline "Strong Foundation for Allianz," it commented: "For one thing, this shows the loyalty of its clientele, and for another, its good service to its customers, and finally the necessity of compensating for risks on a very broad basis, which has always been Allianz's supreme principle. [...] Thus, one gets the impression of an extremely cautious and forward-looking business policy. [...] The result is that the company has remained financially unweakened in every respect."[11] In the years to come, Allianz experienced economically rosy days. Board of directors' chairman Kurt Schmitt was appointed Economics Minister in Hitler's cabinet on June 30, 1933, by President Hindenburg. However, the liberal Vossische Zeitung was not able to comment on news about Allianz much longer, since it had to stop publishing as of March 31, 1934. Only weeks later, the Ullstein brothers were forced to sell their publishing house for a pittance. The Central Publishing House of the National Socialist German Workers' Party (NSDAP) was the one to profit from this Aryanization.[12]

A New Allianz –	In the midst of the First World War, Carl von Thieme on behalf of Munich Re and
A New Generation	Paul von der Nahmer on behalf of Alli-
Takes Over	anz signed a contract which was intended

to set the framework for the business relationship between the two companies for 25 years. What was covered by a bare four lines in the minutes of the meeting of the supervisory board of September 6, 1917, under the heading "Agreement" soon proved to be an important step in cutting Allianz's umbilical cord to its founders: on the one hand, the two companies strengthened their links, while on the other, they made an agreement between equals (although one that was particularly lucrative for Munich Re) that formalized and spelled out their relations – there were to be no more implied agreements. Seen purely as a business transaction, the parties had negotiated a reinsurance contract, as had been done repeatedly under comparable terms since Allianz was founded. Allianz ceded a 50-percent share of its business and the total surplus (Exzedent) to Munich Re, which for its part assigned 10 percent of its share in the profit to Allianz.[13]

The next contract followed in 1921, barely four years later. But this time, the authors drafted considerably more extensive provisions, as suggested by the designation as a 'general contract,' although the term 'association agreement' later became established. In order to emphasize the significance of the document, which was agreed upon for a term of 50 years, the contract commenced with a preamble that stated, in the style of a constitution: "Since its founding, Allianz has been in close union with the Münchener Rückversicherungs-Gesellschaft; both companies have obtained strength and benefit from their association. Directed by the desire to ensure this friendly relationship for the future, the companies had already set the term of this association for 25 years on May 10/29, 1917. Since that time, as a result

Head office of Munich Re (occupied in 1913). The reinsurer and Allianz formalized their relations in an association agreement in 1921.

of changing economic conditions, the need for […] cooperation has intensified still further. […] For this reason, the two companies have proceeded to a revision of the agreement and a new specification of the term of 50 years, in the confident expectation that future generations, which will then be responsible for its renewal, will regard the association as a lasting inheritance."

In contrast to 1917, the signatories coordinated the guidelines of their entire future business and expansion policies, delimiting their central fields of activity and specific interests. Specifically, they provided that Munich Re would increase its holding in Allianz stocks to 25 percent, and would not establish any companies that might compete with Allianz in the latter's business sectors in the future. The heads of the two companies were each to be represented on the supervisory board of the other company, and at least three people were always to be members of both advisory boards. Allianz was to concentrate on direct insurance, and Munich Re on reinsurance. In addition, the two parties extended the provision that Allianz was to cede half of its business and the total surplus (Exzedent) to its reinsurance associate for transactions resulting from future takeovers and holdings. And finally, Munich Re was granted the right to take a 50 percent share in all companies newly founded and holdings of Allianz from then on. In return, Allianz received a 10 to 20 percent share of the earnings and business of Munich Re from fire and hail insurance, and lump sums from its contracts with selected assignors. This included international business and revenue in foreign currency, which became particularly important for Allianz during the period of German hyperinflation.[14] In the last article of the agreement, its provisional term was specified as until December 31, 1970, to be extended until December 31, 2020, unless one of the parties gave notice by 1965. This was indeed long-term planning.

A few weeks before the heads of the two companies were to sign the association agreement on April 29, 1921, director-general Paul von der Nahmer died of cancer at the age of 62. His counterpart at Munich Re, Carl von Thieme, had been chairman of the board of directors for 41 years at that time and celebrated his 77th birthday the next day. A new generation had long been ready to assume leadership responsibilities. Wilhelm Kißkalt, who had been deputy chairman of the board of directors of Munich Re since 1918, had been urging for years that the relationship with Allianz be formalized, and finally drafted the association agreement himself.[15] When von Thieme retired on January 1, 1922, Kißkalt, a lawyer born in 1873 in Würzburg, succeeded him as chairman of the board of directors.

By then, a former protégé of his had already overtaken him on the career ladder: the new head of Allianz, Kurt Schmitt, had been hired in 1913 by Kißkalt at Munich Re as a 26-year-old graduate of the University of Munich. "A nice young man, whom I would like to take an interest in."[16] This was Carl von Thieme's assessment after an initial personal conversation, which Schmitt had requested in a letter, referring to his father-in-law, who had been working for Munich Re for many years. In early April 1913, Schmitt reported that he had passed his examination with honors. He wrote to von Thieme that he wanted to become a "specialist in administrative law working in business," although he knew "how difficult it is to achieve this goal, both in getting 'in' and 'on.'"[17] His wish became reality within a few weeks. But the position assigned to Schmitt in the accident department of Munich Re bored him so much that after a few days, his

The new generation takes over: Hans Heß, Kurt Schmitt, Eduard Hilgard, and Rudolf Schloeßmann on an outing on the river Elbe on the occasion of the final meeting of 1930.

superior felt sorry for him, and went to Kißkalt and told the latter that Schmitt "feels the urge to be in real work." The next day, they let him go to the Munich branch office of Allianz, where a lawyer was needed for the liability department.[18]

Kurt Schmitt had been born on October 7, 1886, as the son of a country physician in Wachenheim in the Palatinate.[19] When his father's ability to work was restricted by a stroke, the family moved to Munich in 1904, so that he could practice in town. Here, Kurt Schmitt graduated from a Gymnasium in 1905, began to study law at the university, joined the dueling fraternity Corps Franconia Munich, did his one year of military service, and passed his first state qualification examination in 1909, the year of his marriage to Marguerite Wengler. He did part of his practical training at the Munich Local Court, passed his second state qualification examination in 1912, and after placement at a credit agency, did a doctorate with a thesis on the nature of credit-agency agreements. For financial reasons, Schmitt did not enter government service but worked for a few months in a law office. He earned his first monthly salary as an insurance official in June 1913. It amounted to 200 marks.

Three months later, Schmitt was put in charge of the department for liability claims at Allianz because he managed, just a few weeks after starting his career, to simplify bureaucratic processes, and reduce the costs and numbers of legal suits against dissatisfied policyholders drastically. He promoted contacts with the agents in the field, and settled major domestic and international claims together with them. This attracted the attention of the top management in Berlin. Von der Nahmer promised him a position as an authorized signatory in the Berlin headquarters as of January 1, 1915, but the start of the First World War prevented this promotion at first. Schmitt was called up, was wounded in Lorraine, and recovered, but because of the protracted festering of a gunshot wound, his health remained affected, so that Allianz, which had lost many of its staff, succeeded in getting him exempted from a return to active military service. In May 1917, the supervisory board appointed him a deputy member of the board of directors, and in December of the next year, a full member. When von der Nahmer died in March 1921, Schmitt, who was just 35 years old, succeeded him in the position of director-general.[20] He obviously enjoyed the special patronage of von Thieme and von Finck, the two dominant representatives of Munich Re on the Allianz supervisory board, because a majority of the representatives of the larger banks had favored von der Nahmer's son-in-law, Heinrich von Tyska.[21]

Together with Schmitt, the Allianz supervisory board in 1918 also appointed Hans Heß to the board of directors. Gravely injured, he had been discharged from the military, and Schmitt got him to join Allianz. Heß was soon his most important colleague, especially as an organizer of the impending restructuring and subsequent expansion of the company. Hans Heß had been born in 1881 in Wengelsdorf in Thuringia. He grew up in modest circumstances as the son of an insurance agent in Leipzig, where he was able to attend the Nicolai Gymnasium thanks to a scholarship. Here, he made friends with Alfred Wiedemann (1883–1963), who in the 1930s rose to become head of the affiliated Frankfurt companies in the Allianz group, and one of the most influential personalities in the company. They both studied law at the University of Leipzig, played soccer with VfB Leipzig, joined different fraternities, and did their doctorates. Then they went separate ways, at first. Wiedemann, after an initial job in Stuttgart, chose to join Frankfurter Allgemeine Versicherungs-AG (Favag) – one of Germany's largest insurance groups at that time – while Heß worked for the Unfall- und Haftpflichtverband Magdeburg before becoming district director of the Winterthur insurance company for Saxony and Thuringia. The friendship between the two proved its worth in 1917, when Kurt Schmitt's attempt to hire Wiedemann for Allianz failed due to the resistance of the powerful Favag patriarch, Paul Dumcke (1859–1929). Instead, Wiedemann suggested to Schmitt that he get in touch with his old friend from school, Heß, which smoothed the latter's way to Allianz. In 1921, Wiedemann then also joined Allianz. After he had come in conflict with Dumcke, Heß hired him for the newly created position of head of the Dresden branch office.[22]

Next to Hans Heß, Eduard Hilgard (1884–1982) was the most important aid of Kurt Schmitt's successful leadership of the company until 1933. Hilgard was two years younger than Schmitt and, like the latter, came from the family of a doctor in the Palatinate. After graduating from a Gymnasium in Speyer, he studied law in Würzburg and Berlin. Since Hilgard's parents were acquainted with the Schmitt family, the children had known one another since their early days. But their contact only became closer later, when Hilgard was doing part of his practical training in Munich. From 1910 to 1919, he worked in various positions in Bavarian government service – interrupted by four years military service during the war – and shifted to the Reich Finance Ministry in Berlin in 1919. As a consultant to the Undersecretary of State for Finance, he took part in the meetings of the Allied commission on reparations in Paris, and in the conferences in Spa and London. Hilgard found fulfillment in high politics, acting on the diplomatic stage, the associated refined manners, and last not least the social prestige associated with this office, and raved about his work. However, his enthusiasm was clouded by money worries, which concerned Mr. and Mrs. Hilgard more and more. As for Schmitt and Heß, financial motives played an important role in Hilgard's decision to join Allianz.

On New Year's Eve in 1920, the telephone rang in Hilgard's apartment in the Grunewald district in Berlin. He had just, as so often, had to "do serious calculations" with his wife "in order to ensure that the domestic budget was balanced," and "the outlook this revealed was not particularly rosy." On the phone was Kurt Schmitt, who asked Hilgard without much ado whether he "was married to government service." Two days later, the two met at the Allianz offices. A discussion with Hans Heß followed, and soon after an appointment with board chairman Paul von der Nahmer. They came to an immediate agreement. Hilgard left the ministry and was appointed a deputy member of the Allianz board of directors in June of that year, with a monthly salary, already bloated by inflation, of 3,000 marks plus a profit-sharing bonus. Within a few months, Schmitt made him his closest associate, placed him in the adjacent office, and assigned major

ALLIANZ
VERSICHERUNGS-AKTIEN-GESELLSCHAFT
SEKRETARIAT

TELEGRAMM-ADRESSE: ALLIANZ-BERLIN
CODE 5th EDITION A. B. C.
Seedienst-Schlüssel im Gebrauch

FERNSPRECHER: ZENTRUM 11920-26

POSTSCHECK-KONTO NR. 4501
REICHSBANK-GIRO-KONTO

BERLIN W 8, *Datum des Poststempels.*
TAUBENSTRASSE 1-2.

Die Gesellschaft wird rechtsverbindlich gezeichnet durch zwei Direktoren oder durch einen Direktor in Verbindung mit einem Prokuristen oder durch zwei Prokuristen gemeinsam.

Die Handlungs-Bevollmächtigten zeichnen in Angelegenheiten ihrer Abteilung in der Weise, daß sie unter die Firma der Gesellschaft neben die Unterschrift eines stellvertretenden Vorstandsmitgliedes, eines Abteilungs-Direktors oder eines Prokuristen unter Beifügung der Bezeichnung „i. V." ihren Namen setzen.

Herr Generaldirektor Dr. Kurt Schmitt - - - - - -

Herr Direktor Dr. Hans Heß - - - - - - - - - -

Stellvertretende Vorstandsmitglieder:

Herr Direktor H. Siefart - - - - - - - - - -

Herr Direktor H. von Tyszka - - - - - - - -

Herr Direktor Oscar Helb - - - - - - - - - -

Herr Direktor Georg Paul - - - - - - - - - -

Herr Direktor Gustav Kaufmann - - - - - -

Herr Direktor Dr. Clemens Maiholzer - - - -

Herr Direktor Eduard Hilgard - - - - - - -

Herr Direktor Franz Köhler - - - - - - - -

Herr Direktor Paul Szelinski in München - - - - -

Herr Direktor Fritz Thieme in München - - - - -

Herr Direktor Gustav Ziegler in Hamburg - - - - -

Excerpt from the list of Allianz's authorized representatives with the power of attorney. The list includes the signatures of Schmitt, Heß, von Tyszka, Maiholzer, and Hilgard.

projects to him from the start, without Hilgard having any opportunity to familiarize himself with the technical aspects of the insurance business, and also made him his personal confidant.[23] Very rapidly, personnel management and the representation of Allianz in the associations and interest groups of the private insurance industry, as well as collaboration with government institutions, became Hilgard's domain. On the one hand, this suited his diplomatic experience and abilities, and his own interest in public appearances, and, on the other, Schmitt had always found such duties particularly annoying.

In the period up until 1933, Schmitt, Heß and Hilgard formed the inner circle of the management at Allianz, joined over the course of time by a few others with decisive influence, such as Clemens Maiholzer (1920–1946) as an expert on liability insurance and in charge of internal administration and real estate, and Rudolf Schloeßmann (1923–1945), for many years the head of Allianz Life Insurance.

The first concern of the new generation of decision-makers was to deal with the commercial consequences of the war while also seizing the opportunities presented by the years of upheaval. It would be years before they could think of working in orderly conditions. It was not until 1925 that Kurt Schmitt could tell his shareholders with obvious relief, as the conclusion from his annual financial statement for the previous year: "After an interruption of ten years, 1924 once again gave us the prerequisites for normal business operations."[24]

A new type of insurance was first created as a true child of the times: tumult insurance.[25] At first camouflaged as transportation insurance in November 1918 to protect it from possible objections of the supervisory board, it developed into a booming sector. Within a few months, 25 insurance companies were competing for customers who feared for their property in view of the unrest. Allianz was as actively involved in this as in business for automobiles, for which purpose it had specifically founded the Kraft-Versiche-rungs-AG, together with the Imperial Automobile Club and Munich Re. By 1920, tumult insurance was already producing Allianz's second-largest turnover, and in contrast to the automobile insurance business, which was also booming, it was highly profitable.[26]

In the 1920s, the insurance sector experienced a unique wave of new companies being founded. During those years, the Reich Supervisory Office for Insurance, granted new operating concessions to no less than 250 companies.[27] All the actors in this sector were affected to varying degrees by the major trends in the insurance business, which were influenced by the social, political and economic factors typical of that time. The most important trends included:

- a process of concentration in the industry, which resulted in corporate groups being formed,
- the continuous formalization of the relations between employers and employees, which strengthened the rights of the staff and improved their protection,
- the institutionalization and professionalization of the interest groups representing the industry,
- rationalization measures and the expansion of sales and marketing,
- the expansion of specialized insurance companies into insurers for all fields of business,
- the professionalization of occupational and advanced training,
- the growing competition between private and public insurers, and
- the expansion and professionalization of communication with customers, employees, and the general public.

Mastering Crises: Moderation, Conversion, and Mergers

Symptoms of a crisis were to be seen at Allianz as early as 1918. Profits had increased for 27 years, since the company was founded, with one exception in the wartime year of 1915. Now, they began to decrease. And it became apparent that the area in which it did business would be restricted in future. In 1919, Allianz's problems became more and more obvious. While the financial volume of business soared because of inflation, the amount of work involved, and thus the operating costs, increased considerably, and profits collapsed. Only a year later, the figures threatened to go completely out of control. As a first step, Allianz increased its capital stock from 12.5 to 30 million marks to keep up with inflation. In the two years since the end of the war, the bookkeepers posted a fivefold increase in premium revenues, as well as a fivefold increase in salary payments for the 1,515 employees. Foreign business, which for a long time had guaranteed substantial foreign-currency earnings – now more important than ever before – had collapsed, but was showing initial signs of recovery.[28] Assets abroad had been confiscated, or were at least, as in the case of the U.S., unavailable for the time being.[29] Furthermore, caution was called for in the core business of Allianz, the transportation insurance business, which was particularly dependent on the state of the world economy. Individual players, such as the banking expert von der Nahmer, were only gradually beginning to understand how destructive the effects of inflation of the mark could be – it was already losing value at frightening speed.[30] On the Berlin stock exchange, the dollar had traded for 8.20 marks in January 1919; in December 1920, the rate of exchange was already 73 marks.[31] The security guarantees of Allianz that were tied up in the U.S. alone, amounting to $450,000, corresponded to a sum of about 33 million marks at that rate of exchange, ten times its annual net profit or 13 percent of its annual premium revenues. Even in this tense social and economic situation, in which the number of criminal offenses related in some way to insurance and cases of attempted fraud grew, and more and more customers had difficulty in affording their insurance premiums, almost all the heads of Allianz sectors were able to post surpluses.

The Allianz management had an entirely new experience at the beginning of 1920: the Central Association of Employees, a union of office workers, called its members out on strike because they had not been able to agree with the employers on a follow-up contract to the national collective-bargaining agreement for the private insurance industry negotiated in 1919. And indeed, as everywhere in Germany, staff of Allianz – except the Munich branch office – and Munich Re went on strike on January 8.[32] It was the first, and to this day the only real strike in the industry, which even acquired an international dimension when insurance employees in Austria, Poland, Hungary, and Czechoslovakia also stopped work.[33] More important than the outcome – an agreement was reached in February, and formalized in the second Reich collective wage agreement – was the fact that the representatives of the two sides gained practice in the new forms of dealing with one another: works councils, labor unions, conciliation councils, employers' associations, and business owners had to learn how to negotiate working conditions by means of collective agreements, and follow the new rules of the game. The employers had to accept the unions as appointed representatives of the white-collar workers, and thus as negotiating partners of equal status, and grant their employees opportunities for codetermination in the company, such as were specified in the Works Councils Act of February 1920.

This did not always happen without misunderstandings and overreactions: in the Munich headquarters of the Bayerische Versicherungs-Bank (BVB), whose stocks had been taken over by Allianz in 1923 as part of a series of mergers, all the typewriters stood silent for a day because the

Wachstum der Allianz

Prämieneinnahme in den letzten fünf Jahren
(in Millionen Mark)

1917	1918	1919	1920	1921
49,9	57,2	97,4	251,6	422,5

The chart on the cover page of the Allianz Zeitung of July 1922 depicted Allianz premium revenues that were already ballooning due to inflation.

management had suspended an employee it had accused of insubordination and agitation. He had protested at work and at a meeting that the salaried staff were expected to work overtime and deal with additional work at home. The management felt challenged, and these events were discussed soon after at a conference of the directors called especially for that purpose: "Hofrat Drumm opened the meeting, and reported that on the morning of February 19, immediately after the announcement of Mr. L.'s dismissal without notice, a delegation of the works council called on him and informed him that there was turmoil in the company; some of the employees wanted to stop work. The works council wished to mediate, they informed him. [...] They had obtained legal advice and acted on that basis. The works council had not foreseen the consequences of its letter [to the staff and management], rather it had believed that the Works Council Act with its mandatory provisions could provide a way out of the situation [...]. The works council was willing to withdraw its letter, and requested the management to then also withdraw the letter of dismissal. [...] During the discussion [...] it had been reported that people were leaving their offices in order to hold a company assembly. [...] Mr. Geyer, as speaker of the works council, had thereupon rushed to the dining room immediately and had returned after a very short time with the news that he had caused the meeting to break up immediately, and pointed out in doing so that he alone had the right to call a meeting [...]. He said he would advocate order in the company at all times."[34]

The court dispute about the dismissal for cause without notice dragged on for more than a year and repeatedly occupied the board of directors. It also led, along with other conflicts with the works council about provisions for breaks, access to the rooms of the management, the handling of private matters during working hours, the posting of notices on the bulletin board, and the like, to the introduction of a code of conduct at work with mandatory rules of behavior. In the end, the dismissal remained in effect, the dismissed employee was banned from entering the premises, and was not allowed to act as an agent any more.

What became the totally predominant topic for staff, management, and customers was the effects of inflation, which increased ever more rapidly from 1920 to 1923. Concerned messages from the Austrian affiliate reached the board of directors of the BVB in Munich: "They report that things are becoming terribly expensive in Vienna. And accordingly, insane wages are being paid, in the insurance business as well. Despite this, people are not satisfied, they say, and had threatened to strike on March 20, unless a monthly raise of 200 kronen for all, regardless of position, was granted. There is no doubt that the companies will not be able to afford this."[35]

Allianz reacted by adopting a new charter, restructuring its administration and sales fundamentally, opening new and promising fields of business, thus establishing a counterweight to the property-insurance policies, which were generating losses because of the business climate.[36] A large part of the existing policies took a long time to mature – often ten years – and under terms that could no longer be met in view of inflation. Within months, premiums and insurance sums that had been agreed upon previously had only absurdly low residual values, so that all the customers were underinsured, the company was receiving hardly any substantial revenues, and thus the purpose of the business was put into question. And at the same time, the company's capital threatened to melt away.

In 1922, the newly appointed chairman of the board of directors, Kurt Schmitt, gave an accounting for the past business year, and formulated the maxim by which, he said, Allianz would have to direct its corporate strategy in the future. It would be a "good mix" that would decide its future. Risks and opportunities needed to be balanced by directing the volumes of insurance of all sectors so that a balanced and profitable mix was created. The goal was formulated boldly: while the insurance market was shrinking and the mark was reeling, Allianz would count on growth. It was not just a matter of preserving the existing business; the internal administration and the sales force were to be reformed in such a way that the volumes of insurance could grow "at bearable costs in all fields as strongly as possible."[37]

Up through 1924, Allianz used all possibilities for growth that arose, and was so successful in this that it was able to enter the phase of political and economic recovery generally known in Germany as the Golden Twenties as the strongest universal insurance company. The expansion of the business was fed mainly by three sources:

(1) As specified in the association agreement with Munich Re, Allianz assumed full responsibility for the latter's direct insurance business. It acquired the Badische Feuerversicherungsbank in Karlsruhe and Securitas Feuerversicherung in Berlin, thus doubling the volume of its direct fire-insurance business. Allianz took over Globus Versicherungs-AG in Hamburg, configured it as a specialized company for the maritime business again, where its origins had lain in the 19th century, and transferred the business of the other Globus branches to its own sector departments. By way of Globus, Allianz also came to own the Hermes Kreditversicherungsbank-AG. Its core business comprised fidelity insurance and commercial credit insurance, guaranteeing loans and mortgages. With the political support of Gustav Stresemann, Wilhelm Kißkalt of Munich Re and Erich Herzfelder as the chairman of Globus had founded the specialized insurer Hermes in 1917 since they suspected that the German economy would need to borrow a great deal of money after the end of the war while the risk for the lenders would be very much higher than in the prewar period due to the results of the war.[38] Hermes was able to make use of the Allianz sales network, being guaranteed a share of the reinsurance in return. Munich Re also demanded, despite the doubts of Hans Heß, that Allianz transferred its direct business in Switzerland to Swiss National, bought the latter's business in Germany, and received in compensation a share of National's reinsurance. The background to this exchange, which was disadvantageous for Allianz, was the fact that, at the beginning of the war, National as a subsidiary of Munich Re had first been placed on the black list of enemy companies in the U.S., and then, after the U.S. entered the war, lost its concession. In addition, there was an anti-German mood in Switzerland.[39]

(2) The second source that fed the growth of Allianz was the critical situation into which numerous specialist and general insurance companies were plunged by inflation. Such companies often failed because they could

not compensate for the losses of vulnerable lines of insurance with revenues from fields of business less affected by general economic conditions, and now their capital stock was also shrinking. Allianz absorbed a number of such failed companies, such as the Brandenburger Spiegelglas Versicherungs-AG (plate-glass insurance), Union Hagel in Weimar (hail), Badische Pferdeversicherungsanstalt in Karlsruhe (equine insurance), Deutsche Phönix Versicherungs-AG in Frankfurt (German Phoenix), and Providentia Frankfurter Versicherungs-AG – the latter two only after a prolonged struggle with Paul Dumcke, who wanted to incorporate them into the Favag Group.[40] In a number of other cases Allianz also had to woo the companies intensively and negotiate at length before it succeeded in the takeovers.

In the case of Wilhelma in Magdeburg, Allgemeine Versicherungs-AG, the deal was initiated at the Berlin race track. It was there that the banker Walter Stiehl tried to do a deal with the horse-racing fan Hans Heß in the spring of 1923. But Heß, who had little interest in mergers and financial transactions, referred him to Kurt Schmitt. Only a few days later, Stiehl and a broker contacted Allianz, and offered Kurt Schmitt a block of Wilhelma stock. After they had rapidly come to an agreement, the broker appeared

Headquarters of the Bayerische Versicherungsbank (BVB) on Ludwigstraße in Munich, built in 1911.

again the very next day, handed over the stock certificates, and received from Eduard Hilgard the agreed upon purchase price of $18,000 in cash. In parallel with this successful transaction, Schmitt negotiated with the chairman of the supervisory board of Colonia, Hans Leiden, about a merger, which only failed on the day it was to be carried out due to the objections of a sales associate of the Cologne property and accident insurance company.[41]

Banker Jacob Kahn helped Allianz to a real coup. He belonged to the supervisory board of the Bayerische Hypotheken- und Wechsel-Bank (Hypo-Bank), which wanted to dispose of the stock of the Bayerische Versicherungsbank (BVB), a wholly-owned subsidiary. In confidential negotiations, Hypo-Bank agreed with Kurt Schmitt and Wilhelm Kißkalt on the terms of the transfer, without being able to provide exact figures on the true situation of the company, since the board of directors of BVB was not initiated into the plans. After the sale, the chairman of the BVB board, Ernst Drumm, accordingly resigned his position under protest at Christmas 1923. He was afraid that the company would lose its "Bavarian character," be "swallowed up" by Allianz, and merged with it. But in fact, BVB remained independent within the Allianz group until the year 2006. Before this, Drumm had failed in an attempt to convince Magdeburger Feuer Versicherungsgesellschaft to take a fifty-percent share as a counterbalance to Allianz.[42] Hypo-Bank justified the sale by pointing to its altered investment strategy: "After we had hived off the fire, life, and accident insurance business, which we had engaged in until then, into an independent corporation in 1906, whose stock we managed in our portfolio at first, the complete or partial mobilization of the stocks of the company, whose interests were now only loosely related to our field of business, was only a question of time and opportunity."[43]

The willingness of the bank selling the stock and the buyers to take a risk was rewarded by an excellent deal, as Kißkalt reported to his fellow member of the board of directors, Carl Schreiner, in a letter: "The negotiations were difficult. We had to buy a pig in a poke, as it were. But in fact, the purchase was brilliant, since the company possesses excess foreign currency not only to the amount of 400,000 to 500,000 Swiss francs, as we assumed, but of over a million. In addition, there are assets to be considered of the company's substantial real-estate holdings, with a peacetime gold value of four to five million marks. The purchase price amounts to 5,000 Allianz shares, 2,000 shares of Munich Re, and 3,500,000 Swiss francs, payable as two million on January 2, and 750,000 each on July 1, 1924, and

January 2, 1925. So the purchase price is well covered by the existing assets, allowing for the goodwill, and then there is also the growth of the business and the strengthening of our position. The bank, on the other hand, can do such profitable deals at present with the foreign currency it is to receive from us that it can multiply the purchase price in a few years, while it would only have had a modest dividend for years from the stock. So the deal was a good one for both parties."[44] The press judged the takeover positively, and emphasized that a further step in the accelerating concentration within the German insurance business was thus being taken.[45]

(3) And the third method by which Allianz was creating potential for growth for itself consisted in establishing new companies. A very special opportunity seemed to present itself in 1921. What Allianz had been lacking until then, in order to actually become a strong company entrenched in all branches of the insurance business, was the life insurance business. A first attempt to get involved in that branch had failed in 1909. But now the situation was favorable in several respects, since it was becoming clearer by the month that Germany was headed for monetary reform. Many established

Founder's share (April 1922): after only three months of preparation, Allianz Leben was entered into the commercial register. With the establishment of this life insurance company, Allianz could offer its clients nearly all classical types of insurance except for health insurance.

and traditional life insurance companies that did business outside Germany, as well, came under pressure because their international financial obligations were not covered in the corresponding foreign currencies, but, as German law required, in German marks. In Switzerland alone, these companies had life insurance policies worth a hundred million Swiss francs, for which only coverage in German paper marks existed. Among them was the second-largest German provider at that time, Friedrich Wilhelm Lebens-Versicherungs-AG of Berlin, with which an Allianz subsidiary, the Deutsche Versicherungsbank, had been cooperating since 1920. As part of a new collaboration, the Friedrich Wilhelm was now to be able to use Allianz's sales network. The parties argued for months about the share that Allianz was to receive of this. The editor of the Allianz Zeitung promised great things to come as the result of intensified cooperation: "Two powerful organizations are linking up in order to support one another," and predicted: "Our community and all its agents are bound to experience huge successes. We cannot give further details about the implementation in this context. There will be an opportunity for this at the convention of insurance agents."[46]

For in secret, Kurt Schmitt was negotiating with Max Loebinger, the director of Friedrich Wilhelm, about a much more far-reaching project. In an internal memorandum, Schmitt developed his vision of the future. As long as two companies were only collaborating, he wrote, expensive duplication of administrative and sales structures would continue. So what was needed was to place a united and reorganized sales force at the service of all fields of business and specialized companies, under a joint organizational umbrella. Despite some doubts of his own, and even at the risk of provoking the unwilling Munich Re, Schmitt styled this as a crucial matter, claiming "the concern that grasps this task the earliest and solves it the most completely will be the number one in the future."[47]

This project matched the spirit of the times: everywhere, companies were being merged and corporate groups forged. While at first this concentration seemed only to be affecting major manufacturing industries, with Walther Rathenau – the AEG manager and foreign minister who was assassinated in the summer of 1922 – surmising "that in a decade, all Germany will be divided up into a few industrial duchies," a similar trend had in fact already established itself in the banking and insurance sectors.[48] As the main players in Germany, besides Munich Re and Schweizerische Rückversicherungs-Gesellschaft (hereafter Swiss Re), which alone set up 14 holdings by 1933, there were the Favag Group, headed by Paul Dumcke, the insurance group belonging to the Mutzenbecher family of Hamburg (Albingia, Hamburg-Mannheimer), and the rapidly expanding Gerling Group, as well as Allianz, to name only some of the most important ones.[49]

The character of Schmitt's project was supposed to find expression even in the new name of the group, "The Alliance of United Insurance Companies." The most important Allianz companies and the Friedrich Wilhelm were to be amalgamated into this group. The stability of the construction was to be ensured by an exchange of stock, and by having an equal number of representatives of the other company on the supervisory boards. But then negotiations stalled. On January 2, 1922, Kurt Schmitt wired to Munich: "Loebinger backed off again today [...]." The project had failed. Three days later, Schmitt played his alternative plan, which was favored by Munich Re. He enticed a manager of Friedrich Wilhelm away, added Allianz's actuary, and formed, together with Hans Heß and Eduard Hilgard, under his direction the board of directors of the new company Allianz Lebensversicherungsbank-AG. The Reich Supervisory Office checked their application promptly, and on March 23, 1922, the company was entered in the commercial register.[50]

Allianz Leben was not encumbered by hazardous foreign-currency obligations, nor by feeble old business, but in view of the general situation of the economy, it seemed illusory to hope that the newcomer could acquire enough new business to become a significant factor in the market entirely on its own. Here too, inflation favored Allianz's ambitions. In 1922, two life insurers, Deutsche Lebensversicherungsbank Arminia AG and Freia, Bremen-Hannoversche Lebensversicherungsbank-AG, of Berlin got into trouble because of exploding administrative costs, the fall in value of their premium revenue, and a lack of alternative sources of revenue. These were both medium-sized firms, whose combined balance-sheet value came to about two-thirds of that of Friedrich Wilhelm.[51]

Arminia was based in Munich, where it possessed a generously sized office building designed by German Bestelmeyer in a top location; together with its other real estate, this comprised the most valuable part of its balance-sheet assets. Since its foundation in 1889, it had taken over the holdings of more than thirty firms, but had never combined them, leaving them instead in thirty-six accounting units, all of which were to be balanced separately. Rudolf Hensel, a director at Allianz headquarters in Berlin, commented sarcastically in his company chronicles: "Perhaps the company would not have been able to survive, and would have calculated itself to death, even if the inflation had not happened."[52] The lawyers of the two firms organized the takeover of Arminia as a reverse merger; as the Frankfurter Zeitung remarked smugly: "The amalgamation is not initiated by youthful Allianz-Leben, of course," since the latter was unable to submit the two annual financial statements required by the authorities.[53] So Arminia played the role of the acquiring company, subsequently changed its name to Allianz Leben, and moved its head office to Berlin.

Freia had played a pioneering role when, in the years around 1890, it introduced the industrial life insurance policy on the British pattern for the large number of potential customers with a small income. It was at first administered as an independent unit within the Allianz, as was the company Die Pfalz (The Palatinate), which was founded in 1923 for the property insurance business in the French-occupied areas of Bavaria west of the Rhine.

Most of these companies newly founded, merged, or taken over from Munich Re were integrated by Allianz from April 1922 into the structures of a newly created corporate group, which was christened the Allianz Konzern in the spirit of the times. Together with the new name, the management announced the most important components of a drastic restructuring conception to the staff in the Allianz Zeitung. For this, they defined three maxims that were supposed to govern all impending or already initiated reforms. These were simple and timelessly relevant points, which, slightly revised, Allianz continues to consider basic to its activities to this day. The goal of all activity, they said, was "maximum production, first-class technical handling of the business, as cheaply as possible."[54]

The most important measures of this modernization program were intended to standardize as much as was necessary in order to do business efficiently and be perceived externally as a strong group, while at the same time not challenging the independence of the individual companies of the group, each with their specific skills and traditions. The management focused on the sales and marketing side, which as a general sales organization was to become a service provider for all sectors of all companies of the group. The group was also to represent the joint interests of its members towards politicians, business associations, and all private and public organizations, and to direct advertising and public relations work uniformly; for this purpose, a new logotype for the group was commissioned. The Allianz Zeitung, founded in 1919, was assigned the task of being the organ of communication of all the members of the group.

In its first issue of June 1919, the Allianz Zeitung printed the following report as a minor item in the section "Other News:" "On March 24 and 25,

2. 1918–1933 Crises, Rationalization, and Growth

Nr. 10 · Jahrgang 1919

Sonntag, 16. März

Der Welt Spiegel

Illustr. Halb-Wochenschrift

des Berliner Tageblatts

Wirkung einer 2½-Zentner-Mine:
Zerschossenes Haus in der Alten Schützenstraße.

Bilder von den Straßen-
kämpfen in Berlin.

Aus der Gegend des Alexanderplatzes:
Vostreffer auf einem von Spartakisten besetzten Dach.
Phototek.

Nach den Artilleriekämpfen im Zentrum.
Erschütterter Glaspavast der Rebellen.
Phototek.

During the first conference of Allianz general agents in March 1919, conditions close to civil war prevail in Berlin.

the first meeting of our general agents was held in the company building in Berlin, which a number of our general agents attended. Unfortunately, not all the gentlemen were able to attend, due to the troublesome traffic conditions and geographical difficulties, but we hope to be able to welcome all our general agents here at the next gathering. The purpose of this meeting is to establish and intensify the necessary contact between the directors on the one hand and the general agents on the other, and between the latter, to exchange experience by personal discussion, and to clarify future goals and tasks in oral presentations." The "troublesome traffic conditions" mentioned in the text were the result of the Berlin March Battles during the second phase of the November Revolution in the spring of 1919. The national government deployed the police and military to combat political and social unrest, which vented itself repeatedly in general strikes. They could rely on the order to shoot issued by Minister of Defense Gustav Noske, which was also misused to murder unarmed persons and politically hated opponents, such as the newly appointed head of the Communist Party of Germany (KPD), Leo Jogiches. In March 1919, a total of well over a thousand people died in the streets and detention rooms of Berlin.[55]

What was reported in prosaic terms in the Allianz Zeitung text represented a cultural revolution for the "old" Allianz. Until then, office workers ('officials') and sales agents had worked in strict isolation for their own agency or department. Contact and interchange were not desired, and sometimes even punished; many agents did business alone way out in the country without ever coming in contact with the all-powerful general management in Berlin. Rudolf Hensel had experienced these good old days for almost twenty years as an employee, and was then a witness of how the traditional ways of work and the associated corporate spirit was swept away in the 1920s. Looking back, he caricatured his experience: "They were really two companies. People watched jealously that no official should dare to enter the hostile zone of the other wing; otherwise, he could expect really rude remarks – and woe betide any official of the one department who wanted to do a deal for the other department! Once, when an accident insurance assessor mentioned placing a theft-and-burglary-insurance policy in his report, his expense allowance for that day was canceled. There was the same division in the field. When the new men did their first field trips throughout the country, still under the old regime, some general agents, 'typical fire insurance aristocrats' of the time, refused to have anything to do with the 'young people' coming from the accident and liability fields."[56]

One of these young people who seemed not of an acceptable social status was the energetic Hans Heß, who as the first head of sales at Allianz was to become the father figure of the sales agents. Kurt Schmitt, Hans Heß, and their colleagues broke with traditions: by 1922, they had taken over all the agencies which had previously worked only on a commission basis for Allianz, but also for other insurance companies, often against determined resistance, or terminated the old contracts where a takeover of the agency was not possible. Until then, these agencies had also done some of the administrative work for Allianz that was now assumed by the office staff. And before 1920, there were no general sales agents: instead, the sales force consisted of an army of specialized agents who only sold insurance policies of their particular field, as fire insurance, liability insurance or transport insurance agents. After the reform, in what were now company branch offices, or the independent agencies, more than 2,000 agents collaborated across fields, within the boundaries of their respective districts, and only sold Allianz policies, in accordance with the principle of exclusiveness.

In parallel with this, and at the same time as the mergers and new company establishments mentioned, the office staff was reformed. Until 1919, there had been only two administrative offices at Allianz: the Berlin headquarters and the Munich branch. In practice, all business activities outside Bavaria were directed from Berlin. All policy applications and notices of claims were sent to headquarters by mail or courier; there, the staff, divided by insurance class, processed the cases and directed claims settlement. The larger Allianz became, the more this centralization overtaxed and crippled the company. Therefore, the branch offices now took over those tasks related directly to the technical business. Following the principle of decentralization, they managed and supported the sales force of a district. Hans Heß had chosen Saxony as the test case for the reorganization of the sales force, since he was familiar with conditions there from his former employment at Winterthur. The sites for the branch offices were subsequently determined by internal competition between the existing field offices. The top management stimulated this by publishing regular reports in the Allianz Zeitung on the competition for the limited number of offices still to be assigned, and the reasons for establishing them. In the summer issue of 1923 of the company magazine, the question "Which affiliate office will be next?" ended the following article: "In accordance with the long-entertained organizational plans of our central management, in time all affiliate offices, once they have achieved the necessary size and maturity, will be raised to the status of branch offices, and as such will be able, under precise consideration of the special circumstances of their district, to conduct their business in all fields of insurance with the maximum degree of independence, like a separate company. [...] The branch offices in Frankfurt am Main and Stuttgart owe their raised status mainly to their rapid and pleasing development; in the case of Cologne, it was especially the idea of establishing a company bulwark, intended to withstand all future storms, at an exposed position in the threatened Western part of our fatherland."[57]

In 1921, there were four branch offices, and two years later, there were eight. But their number was constantly being adjusted, because the company needed to see which districts were sufficiently large and productive. Ideally, they were supposed to be balanced so that a grid of similarly productive branch offices equivalent to medium-sized insurance companies covering the entire service area would be created. By the late 1920s, the number of these units (also known as *Landesdirektionen*, or state offices) had grown to thirteen, but shrank to ten again by 1940. The heads of these branch offices were appointed by the Berlin head office. They were the most prominent part of management, next to the members of the board of directors, and offered some managers the opportunity of joining the board. Several times a year, the heads of the branch offices and of the independent subsidiaries took part in meetings of the extended board of directors that lasted several days. The board used these forums to discuss business developments, explain targets and important strategic measures, and stimulate competition between the branch offices. This sometimes reached the point that Schmitt or Heß threatened individual heads of branch offices with the closing of their branch office if they did not succeed in lowering costs, increasing sales volume, and improving customer service.[58]

There was a clear division of responsibilities between Berlin and the branch offices. The general management, which dealt with strategy, planning, and monitoring, comprised the board of directors and subordinated councils for the individual sectors, sales and marketing, foreign business, bookkeeping, and the administration of personnel, real estate, investments, and legal and tax matters. Below this, the branch offices acted largely independently. They were only obliged to report their premium revenues, information on claims settlement, and their costs to the head office every month. The heads of the branch offices were responsible for all operations and sales and marketing. For this purpose, they had specialized departments at the branch office for all classes of insurance, for administration, bookkeeping, and the sales force, to whom the affiliate offices and general agencies reported. In addition, there were inspectors for training the agents, and special officials who assessed major risks before policies were signed and dealt with industrial claims. As a result of this drastic decentralization, the number of employees in the head office dropped from 970 in the year 1921 to 811 in 1924, while the staff in the branch offices increased from 1,540 to 3,140 over the same period.[59] At that time, the basic reform of the sales force and the decentralization of the corporate structure were largely completed.

How Allianz Survived Hyperinflation	In November 1923, Kurt Schmitt and Hans Heß addressed a message to all Allianz staff, which they had entitled "The Troubles of the Times." They wrote:

"The terrible collapse of the German mark has made most of our stock of insurance worthless. It will need to be restored slowly with stable value under most difficult currency conditions. The impoverishment of large groups, the difficulties in commerce and industry, will in any case leave painful gaps among the parties we insure.

Our own growth has been strong. A large number of established and traditional companies have merged with us. Despite this, today and for

2. 1918–1933 Crises, Rationalization, and Growth

1923 became the year of the hyperinflation in Germany. The paper mark – in this case bills of over 100 million marks each – epitomizes the currency's loss of value.

the foreseeable future, the total business of our group will be considerably smaller than that of Allianz in 1914.

False hopes for speedy improvement in the general situation kept some companies from taking necessary measures in time. Allianz must not jeopardize its financial strength. That is for us what its machinery is for a factory. Its reduction or its loss would mean reduction or loss of our productivity, and thus the loss of the jobs of more or all employees, and of the financial security of our retirees.

Thus, we had to make the bitter decision to dismiss or pension off a considerable number of employees, in the interest of the commercial viability of our enterprises. Those affected may be assured that we found this measure extraordinarily difficult. Whatever can be done to alleviate it, must be done. They will not be forgotten in case of extensions of operations!

But all those who have the good fortune to keep their positions should feel especially obliged to do their utmost in the interests of the company! The more they bestir themselves, whether as office or sales staff, the sooner and better we will have overcome the general German economic and currency crisis, and the sooner and the more we will then be able to call those colleagues whom we had to part with back to work!"[60]

When Allianz published this letter, a dramatic year was ending. Conditions approaching civil war prevailed in Germany.[61] In the Ruhr, in Thuringia and Saxony, Hamburg, and Bavaria, communist and right-wing populist ('völkisch') groups revolted; everywhere, tensions were vented in anti-

Semitic outbreaks – in Berlin, an angry mob plundered Jewish businesses and attacked the Jewish residents of the Scheunen quarter. On November 5, 1923, three days before the attempted Hitler putsch in Munich, Allianz shares were valued at the absurd figure of fifty trillion (50×10^{12}) paper marks on the Berlin stock exchange.

This galloping inflation also threatened to make banks and insurance companies lose control of their costs. At Allianz, premium revenues increased by well over 800 percent in 1922. But in the same period, expenditures on out-of-control administrative work grew by more than 1,300 percent. The staff were drowning in work, since in a race with inflation, they had to increase policy amounts, recalculate the resulting premium payments, calculate price-increase surcharges, and correspond with the impatient customers. Thus, in parallel with the currency, the amount of work involved inflated to absurd levels, for the value of the premiums received soon melted in Allianz's hands, just as the claims payments did in its customers' hands. Furthermore, in the crisis many firms decided not to insure their risks any longer. Mark-based business became a minor item for Allianz. In 1922, it was already earning 90 percent of its premium revenues from business abroad, and from foreign-currency-based domestic insurance policies.[62]

But how was the insurance business supposed to function at all under these conditions? The customers demanded policies in safe – in other words, foreign – currency. But this was prohibited by law for most of the business, an exception being transport insurance for foreign goods. Therefore, Allianz made do with offers in a fictitious currency, tied to strong international currencies such as the U.S. dollar, the pound sterling, or the Swiss franc, until hyperinflation set in during 1923. These policies, known as foreign-currency-based gold-mark policies, were based on a fixed rate of exchange, such as 4.20 gold marks to the dollar. The premium and claim payments were then calculated and paid in paper marks according to the official rate of exchange of the previous day. This laborious procedure required more and more staff, so that Allianz in the end had doubled the number of employees. On October 1, the company gave up the struggle with the paper mark's twelve zeros and stopped issuing invoices. The paper-mark-based business was at an end.

A few days before, the German government had finally abandoned its objections to insurance policies in foreign currency. Customers who had foreign currency were now allowed to pay their premiums in dollars or Swiss francs. At first, the insurance companies had to deposit these amounts with the Reichsbank, but this rule was also revoked only weeks later: the government abandoned its now worthless currency, and its place was taken by a variety of makeshifts based on material assets, such as railway bonds, bonds covered by potash, gold, or rye, or on foreign currencies.[63]

At this point, the government, the Reichsbank, and the Deutsche Rentenbank founded in October 1923, had in principle already carried out the monetary reform. The Reichsbank stopped financing government expenditures and debts by printing money, and the Rentenbank issued the rentenmark, whose value was based on that of the old gold-covered prewar mark (the gold mark). The government printing office dismissed more than half of its then 7,500 employees, whose efforts had ensured that in November 1923, 192 quintillion marks (192×10^{18}) were in circulation in Germany.

For one trillion paper marks, the hyperinflation-afflicted Germans received one rentenmark, and the rate of exchange with the U.S. dollar was set at 4.2 rentenmarks. The Social Democrat Rudolf Hilferding, who served briefly as Reich Finance Minister, developed an idea for giving sufficient backing to the rentenmark, which was only acting as a transitional currency: the Rentenbank's nominal capital of 3.2 billion rentenmarks was covered by a compulsory loan from the assets of agricultural estates, industrial and commercial enterprises, and banks.[64] In return, the Rentenbank issued fixed-interest debenture bonds to cover the new currency. This proved to be stable because the Rentenbank controlled the amount in circulation strictly. It only provided loans to the state and firms very restrictively, and government expenditures were reduced massively. This austerity policy had its costs. More and more people fell on hard times, since wages and salaries were lowered drastically, as were expenditures on education, the health system, and welfare. An enabling act allowed the German government to dismiss or retire compulsorily about a quarter of all civil servants and other government employees.

There followed what Kurt Schmitt and Hans Heß had announced in their message "The Troubles of the Times." Allianz rehabilitated its insurance business, liquidating existing holdings, converting existing contracts, and building up new business. In order to become profitable again, and because the work involved in the paper-mark business was no longer needed, it stopped hiring temporary personnel, and dismissed permanent staff. In this way, the number of employees sank from 6,650 to about 4,000 by January 1, 1924. Some disappointed or desperate employees struggled with great determination against the loss of their jobs. They wrote threatening letters to Eduard Hilgard, the head of the personnel department who was responsible, or harassed him with anonymous telephone calls. The memory of this haunted him into his old age, as he admitted in his memoirs: "This meant above all a vast reduction of the staff apparatus. [...] Reading this today, I think people will hardly be able to imagine the profusion and severity of the human tragedies that accompanied these measures. I was already head of the personnel department at that time [...]. Thus, all the human distress that was an unavoidable consequence of the cuts surged directly up against my desk."[65]

In contrast to many other insurance companies, Allianz weathered the crisis, in which a large part of its business went under, because it possessed enough secure assets. These included foreign-currency revenue from its direct foreign business, and its quota shares in reinsurance, as well as long-term investments in more than 30 international currencies and extensive real-estate holdings, consisting of almost 50 office buildings in addition to the Berlin headquarters. An audit report by the Reich Supervisory Office for Private Insurance of May 1922 on the financial condition of Allianz showed freely available bank balances of 8 million Swiss francs, 1 million in other high-value foreign currency, securities worth 4 million Swiss francs, and annual foreign-currency premium revenues of about 5.4 million Swiss francs.[66] The Allianz group was also crisis-resistant because, as an all-lines insurer, it was better able to cope with a falling-off in individual fields of business and counterbalance this with revenues in fields not sensitive to economic fluctuations. Many smaller firms, or specialist insurance companies, such as those that had concentrated on the glass business, collapsed during the hyperinflation because many contracts – as was customary in that field – were drawn up on the principle of compensation for damage in kind. They had to supply the claimants with "panes of the same size and quality," as it was phrased in the terms of insurance, and were no longer able to pay the skyrocketing bills from domestic glass-works, much less pay for imported plate glass in foreign currency.[67] Much greater damage was suffered by internationally active life insurance companies and their foreign customers because the law governing private insurance companies compelled the German companies to build up their premium reserves to cover their contracts in gilt-edged securities from domestic issuers, denominated in marks. In this way, the German government hoped to obtain foreign currency and sell public-sector bonds to the insurance companies, and only loosened these rules when it was already too late. In the inflation, the reserves denominated in German currency lost their value, so that the insurance companies were ruined because they had to pay their customers' claims in foreign currency.

An Allianz image brochure from 1924: Allianz presents the names of the group's companies and advertises on the basis of its now "normal" financial figures after the end of the hyperinflation.

In Switzerland alone, 60,000 insured persons lost part of their assets, although the Swiss fiscal authorities stepped in. In addition, the reputation of German life insurance companies was severely damaged for a long time.[68] Although Allianz was hardly affected by this directly, the damaged reputation of the German insurance industry did hurt its chances of success as a life insurance company outside the borders of the domestic market.

In June 1924, two months before the Reichsmark (RM) was introduced as the new currency by the Coinage Act, Allianz published the gold-mark opening financial statement required by a statutory ordinance. At first glance, all the figures presented there seem disappointingly modest. The days of large numbers were gone for the time being. Like all other German insurance companies, Allianz had dropped below the level of earnings and reserves of the prewar period. The conversion to a gold standard showed that the premium income of the entire German insurance industry had been halved compared to 1913, to about 1 billion marks. Allianz showed its net worth extremely conservatively in its financial statement, so that even substantial assets such as real estate and holdings were assessed at very low values. Uncertain items, whose future value was still to be decided by the legislature, such as mortgages or loans to municipalities, were either not estimated at all, or liabilities of the same value were posted. In addition, Allianz formed conspicuously large reserves for outstanding premium payments and as a provision for pension payments to employees who had been dismissed or acquired through mergers. The share capital had previously amounted to 100 million marks; in the new balance sheet, it was converted to 30 million gold marks. In the long term, this more than cautious assessment of the group's financial status paid off, as was to be seen by comparison with their major competitor Favag in 1929, the fateful year for the latter company.

Now Allianz began to re-establish its lost non-life insurance business, while at the same time laying the foundations of its soon to become dominant role in life insurance. 1924 became the year of reconstruction, although in a market characterized by price-cutting, so that no profits were made in property insurance. Despite this, the restrained optimism proved to be justified. Kurt Schmitt voiced this optimism in a newspaper article of April 1924 on the mood and outlook of the insurance business: "Now that all the unfortunate concomitants of the period of constant decline of the mark for both insurance companies and policyholders have been eliminated, an especially pleasing consequence of the reorganization of the monetary system is to be seen in the revival of insurance-mindedness, demonstrated by the fact that the production figures are currently reaching peacetime levels, and often exceeding them. In particular the broad-based and medium-sized business, which vanished from insurers' books completely, has experienced an unexpected revival. It is just this 'simple' and medium-sized business that has always been the most sought-after support of the companies, because of its generally favorable course, and because of the large potential for compensating for risks due to its broad base."[69] In that year, the companies combined into the Allianz group reported a premium income of 108 million marks, and thus more than ten percent of the total German insurance business.

Roaring Twenties? – Rationalization, Growth, Crisis

Inflation was hardly over when the German economy plunged into another crisis in the winter of 1923. There was a downturn because the economy first had to adjust to the radically reduced amount of money in circulation. The following February, there was an economic upturn again in a few leading sectors, and firms hired new staff, until the Reichsbank revised its policy that spring. In order to protect the mark, it made fewer loans and controlled the money supply with rigid restrictions. Money became tighter, people consumed even less, and firms and public authorities could barely invest. As a consequence, Germany slipped into the next crisis in 1925. The alarm bells rang at Allianz because a sharply increasing number of customers in arrears caused the outstanding debts to rise to record levels. It was only in the autumn of 1925 that the crisis gradually began to ease but then remained for another year in a state of a mild depression, with persistently high unemployment figures of over 2 million. None of this sounds like the Golden Twenties (as the period is known in Germany). However, the period from 1925 to 1929 was indeed experienced as such, because the arts, the mass media, the sciences, intellectual life, high culture and subculture blossomed in a spirit of liberation, at least in the big cities, and above all in Berlin, which for a short time became a cosmopolitan metropolis of culture. And in 1927, an economic upturn finally began, as well. Financial institutions, other companies, state and local governments evaded the bottleneck on the domestic money market by obtaining money on international markets, in the U.S. in particular. At a relatively high interest level, short-term investments in Germany were lucrative for foreign investors. The German banks, which had been dangerously undercapitalized since the inflation period, then lent this third-party capital to their customers for long terms, thus laying the foundation for the collapse of the banking system during the Great Depression of the early 1930s. While industrial production flourished in Japan and the U.S., but also in Italy and Czechoslovakia, goods production and people's incomes grew only moderately in Germany, although private consumption grew noticeably, and investments and exports increased. For a few years, economic conditions stabilized, giving breathing room to the war-afflicted and crisis-afflicted society. The major economic trends of these years, which also shaped Allianz's corporate history, were the rationalization and technicalization of work processes, the modernization of industrial relations, the expansion of social benefits, a specific company culture, and a tendency towards concentration into larger and larger corporate groups, which involved many industrial, mass media, and finance sectors.[70]

Despite all the continuing economic vicissitudes, the Allianz staff was able in 1924 to return for the first time from crisis management and constantly working under exceptional conditions to normal and predictable business operations. The management sought to prepare the directors of the branch offices and subsidiaries for the opportunities and risks of this new situation at a meeting in Berlin in June 1924. They said that the new currency and the sound gold-mark-based financial statement formed the foundation for their future work, that the effective sales force covering the entire nation provided Allianz with the implements for successful canvassing, and that the Allianz spirit, which had to be instilled in all parts of the company, was what must distinguish the company from all its competitors. The board of directors also provided a definition of this spirit: "By this is to be understood not merely a healthy optimism, but also, from the technical point of view, seeking the best training and constant advancement of our knowledge and skill in theory and practice, by open discussion and exchange of mutual experience. The goal must be a maximum perfection of our enterprises, which must be second-to-none in a few years. From the personal point of view, we mean by Allianz spirit loyal friendship and camaraderie, which remain unshaken even if personal ill feelings threaten to arise temporarily."[71] This expressed, in unctuous phrases typical of the times, on the one hand Kurt Schmitt's ambition to make Allianz the largest and most efficient insurer, and on the other, Hans Heß's passion for professionalization of sales and marketing, stimulating competition, and at the same time strengthening the solidarity among the employees and their identification with the company.

What did the return to normal operations mean for the company and its employees? What was called for in the new normalcy, they claimed, was to integrate the companies that had been acquired hastily in such a way that, while operating profitably as part of Allianz, they made the group's profile more attractive with their specific capabilities and connections. Popular and respected company names such as Phönix, Wilhelma and Providentia were something that the agents should turn to good account in advertising and canvassing, they said. At the same time, all merged companies would from now on be underwriting the insurance of those sectors that they were operating in simultaneously in joint liability, and would standardize the forms they used for this purpose. So they moved closer together in organizational and business aspects.[72]

In the final analysis, Allianz resumed implementing those measures of the reform program for operations and sales that had been interrupted or slowed in the disastrous year of 1923. Among the office operations, antiquated traditions that still existed were eliminated. The labor-intensive and costly individual copying by hand of policies was replaced by a "matter-of-fact printed form, without superfluous ornamentation." The modern contract consisted of the printed general terms of insurance, to which the processor added the customer's address and a copy of the application. This saved 80 percent of the working time of the previous procedure.[73] Not only the processing of applications, but also simple correspondence, the writing of the premium receipts, statistics, and bookkeeping were simplified, rationalized, and shifted to the regional branches as part of the decentralization. Since the mid-1920s, rationalization meant increasingly that the already simplified processes were now mechanized. Since, at Allianz, such questions enjoyed the attention of top management, it is hardly surprising that a special body was created in 1926 to discuss and direct ideas and measures for technization, simplification, and adaptation of work processes, equipment, and working conditions. In October 1926, the Allianz Standardization Commission began work; the board of directors appointed directors from the head office and influential heads of branch offices, such as Maximilian Eichbaum and Hans Heß's boyhood friend from Dresden, Alfred Wiedemann, to it.[74]

The minutes of this working group, which was later renamed the Simplification Commission, and in 1931, the Technical Commission, document in

Modern data processing: hand-operated keypunch for punched cards, which were used for statistical operations in the Hollerith machines.

Monumental sculpture of the javelin thrower by Karl Möbius in the Allianz sports stadium in Mariendorf. A traveling miniature replica has been awarded annually to the most successful branch since 1924.

detail how Allianz was modernized. After a successful test phase in 1926, all the branch offices introduced addressing machines successively. These ADREMA systems prepared the monthly premium invoices, and replaced typists who had prepared the payment vouchers on typewriters until then.[75] In the early 1920s, individual departments of Allianz were already experimenting with the punched-card technology introduced from the U.S. for doing statistics. But it was not until 1926 that the administration systematized the use of this technology. The accounting department purchased Hollerith machines from the German IBM subsidiary Dehomag, as did Allianz Leben, in order to process inexpensively the relatively simply and uniformly structured industrial life insurance policies of the newly founded Allianz Spar- und Sterbeversicherung (ASS).[76] However, in order to reduce costs with this technology, they first had to invest, as the board of directors reported a bit impatiently in its report to the 1927 annual general meeting. After Allianz had been cutting costs in operations and the sales force for years, achieved synergy effects in the integration of merged companies, and repeatedly eliminated jobs, the expenditures on novel office equipment ate up several million marks in saving again. But the hoped-for cost reductions had yet to be seen.[77]

With its rationalization policies, Allianz was following the international spirit of the times. The basic ideas were not new, but had already been discussed before 1914, and quickly gained a foothold in the U.S. economy, which was less affected by the First World War. The journalist and sociologist Siegfried Kracauer analyzed the changes and their consequences for the social status of the employees in his trailblazing social study of 1930, *Die Angestellten. Aus dem neuesten Deutschland*: "Since capitalism has existed, within the limits set for it there has always been rationalization, but the period of rationalization 1925–28 marks an especially important stage. It brought about the penetration of machinery and the methods of the assembly line into the precincts of the office workers of big companies. This conversion according to the American pattern – it is far from complete – gives large parts of the new masses of office workers a diminished function in the work process."[78]

The mechanized working world offered women, in particular, new, although not always enticing, career opportunities. Allianz hired women increasingly as card punchers in the Hollerith department, as operating staff for the ADREMA technology, and as office clerks for statistical work. One reason for this was that it was able to pay women 5 percent less than their male colleagues under the Reich collective wage agreement for insurance-industry staff.[79] In practice, the income differences between male and female employees were probably considerably larger, but no clear statistics on this have survived in the company.

At the same time as Allianz began to record, simplify, standardize, and mechanize work processes and hours systematically, Hans Heß developed ideas for anchoring the principle of competition more strongly than before in the management, everyday working practices, and the corporate culture. His objective was to increase performance and earnings while intensifying the employees' emotional ties to the company, and increase their pride in their performance and in the success of Allianz. Hans Heß was without a doubt the most popular personality in the history of Allianz. More stories and anecdotes are told about him than about anybody else; he is credited with countless ideas and initiatives, and because of his affability, his energy, combined with his portly fatherly physique, and his special familiarity with the circumstances and needs of the sales force, he enjoyed not only exceptional esteem, but in many cases even heartfelt admiration.

The story about Hans Heß and the javelin thrower, for example, is legendary. The popular image of Heß included his enthusiasm for athletics in general and gymnastics in particular, which he kept even after losing his athletic figure. One day, the Allianz Zeitung reported in 1924, Heß saw in the studio of the Berlin sculptor Karl Möbius (1876–1953) the "artistically perfect reproduction of the ideal figure of a German gymnast and athlete."[80] It was a statue of a javelin thrower, which Heß first bought for his apartment, and a monumental version of which was erected in a Berlin park. Various castings of it soon decorated the apartments of other Allianz top managers. Finally, Heß declared it the symbol of the "Allianz spirit," embodying strength and the will to achieve, and thus ideally suitable as a model for Allianz employees to emulate. In 1924, this was made into a challenge trophy awarded annually to the most successful branch office by a selection commission. The competition proved so successful that Allianz retained this tradition until 2005, when the business in Germany was restructured.

"In reality, we have – thank God, I say – long since been in the midst of 'Americanization', or what is called that." Rudolf Hensel wrote this in 1927 in his account of his travels in America, which for him, as for many visitors to that country in his day, seemed the prototype of a modern, dynamic society, imbued with the principle of self-responsibility, but also unfathomable. Hensel, who was a member of the board of directors of Allianz, took the money he had saved up since the inflation period and traveled throughout the country for months. When he returned, he felt the urge to report to his colleagues and other Allianz employees how "under the impression of what I saw and experienced over there, my views of America (and not only of America, but also of much in our own country) changed fundamentally, and turned away from the predominant opinion among us." He was enthusiastic

Women's hockey team of Allianz.

about the expanse of the country, the variety of its people, and above all the size of the (life) insurance market, the confidence in technology, and the technicalization of the insurance business. This enthusiasm was only surpassed by his dismay over the power of the American regulatory agencies, and over the freedom, irresponsible in his eyes, which American insurance companies granted their agents in acquiring even the riskiest.

Despite many reservations, America also seemed to him a model for Allianz, which was reflected in his work as a chronicler – for its fortieth anniversary in 1930, he wrote an unpublished company history. His judgement on the period even before the two major mergers that assured Allianz a special position in the German insurance industry was this: "At the end of this period, around 1925, Allianz had grown to an American size. But it was not only the volume of business and its working methods that were American. Someone who has seen […] the business world over there will have been surprised by the exceptional welfare institutions that every larger firm there has created for its employees. Allianz measures up to the Americans […] in its care for its staff, as well."[81]

This applied in particular to the most valuable of the employee benefits, the company pension system. However, this was only one year old when Rudolf Hensel praised its performance, since the original pension fund had become insolvent during the hyperinflation period, and had lost its assets. Allianz thereupon assumed the obligations of the fund towards the members. The company established the "Allianz-Versorgungskasse" (company pension fund), organized according to the principle of staff self-manage-

Hans Heß (center) with soccer players at a tournament in the Allianz stadium in Magdeburg.

ment, for all permanent office and sales employees. The salaried staff paid 6 percent of their pensionable annual income into the fund, and the company contributed about twice that amount; the annual income of the person covered could not exceed ten thousand Reichsmarks, and the pension pay was set off against entitlements from the state old age pension agency, the Reich Insurance Institution. The company's benefits tied its salaried staff to the company and strengthened their identification with Allianz, on the one hand, and on the other constituted the management's reaction to the altered political conditions in the Weimar Republic, and the strengthened position of the labor unions and works councils. Managers hoped, ideally, that the benefits would enable them to influence opinion positively to the benefit of both sides. This purpose was also served by the lunchrooms that were now established at the larger sites, such as Berlin, Hamburg, Frankfurt, Munich, and Stuttgart, thus saving employer and employees the loss of time in going home for lunch. A total of five health-insurance funds offered insurance coverage to the employees and their families, until Allianz decided in 1928 to thin out this thicket and combine them under the name Company Health-Insurance Funds of the Allianz group in Berlin.[82]

At company excursions, Christmas celebrations, and sports festivals, the employees encountered the executives outside the workaday routine. In the sports clubs sponsored by Allianz and in the company's own sports facilities, Allianz staff swam, rowed, fenced, boxed, and did gymnastics and target-shooting, played handball, ice hockey, soccer, fistball, and tennis; male and female employees practiced track-and-field athletics, ice-skating, and weight-lifting. All this came about in accord with the development of a new mass culture: millions of mainly young men and women joined sports clubs at that time. Mass sporting and athletic activity boomed, as did attendance at public sports events. Companies subsidized sporting activities in order to give their employees recreation and physical exercise as compensation for sedentary work, to maintain their health and fitness, and – as Hans Heß constantly emphasized – to encourage their competitive spirit. How such considerations could rapidly become ideologically charged was shown in 1925 by some of the thoughts of the editor of the Allianz Zeitung, Jurtschat, expressed in a language that is difficult to stomach today: "The sports-hardened and supple body of the working sportsman increases the operating capital of any commercial business so significantly that any economist really ought to ask himself why physical exercise has only played a minor role in commercial and industrial businesses until now. In American factories, sports are a major factor for the high-voltage productivity of the entire

Allianz vacation home for employees in the Baltic sea resort Baabe on the island of Rügen.

labor force. [...] What about our workers? The employee who spends his spare time not in bars and cinemas, but in sunlight, fresh air, and on grass playing fields, not only eases the burden on all social-welfare institutions with his healthy body [...], but also helps to increase the national wealth by staying healthy in body and soul due to a life full of moderation, and thus does not so easily fall a burden on the public, the state. [...] True sportsmanship, fitting in voluntarily, and the sense of duty with willingness to make sacrifices have a great influence on the moral consolidation of the individual, so that it seems plausible that true sportspeople hardly commit any crimes, or only to a very limited extent."

Last but not least, the vacation homes of the Allianz companies created during the 1920s in Bad Harzburg and in Aidenbach in Lower Bavaria offered employees and their dependents novel freedoms. At a time when holiday entitlements under collective wage agreements were scarce – an annual vacation of one week was customary – they could go on vacation and recuperate at little expense. This also was in accord with the spirit of the times. In the new republic, vacations and participation in leisure-time activities were no longer considered a privilege of the well-to-do and the bourgeoisie but represented a democratic achievement.[83] In the following years, the number of these vacation establishments grew, some being newly founded, others joining Allianz through mergers. As a rule, they were located in popular tourist regions, such as in Baabe on the island of Rügen, in Oberschreiberhau in the Krkonoše Mountains in Lower Silesia, in Dornholzhausen in the Taunus hills, in Kreßbronn on Lake Constance, and in Bad Godesberg near Bonn.

In the spring of 1927, Rudolf Schloeßmann, who had been head of Allianz Leben since 1923, went to London for the eighth international congress of actuaries. The host of the 700 scholars and businessmen from the entire Western world was Sir Joseph Burns, the director-general of Prudential, which at the time was the largest life insurance company in Europe. On the floor of the congress, Schloeßmann in a good mood struck up a conversation with Adolf Kimmel, a member of the board of directors of Stuttgarter Verein Versicherungs-AG, and sensed a basic interest by this Stuttgart Group in collaborating with Allianz. Bearing this news, Schloeßmann traveled to Berlin, where he found Kurt Schmitt very willing to listen. For in 1921–22, Schmitt and Kißkalt had already discussed at length a merger of their life and property business with Max Georgii, the legendary long-term general manager of what was then the Allgemeiner Deutscher Versicherungs-Verein (ADVV), which had since been transformed into the Stuttgarter Verein.[84] But at that time, the Stuttgarters had decided in the end to remain independent, although their financial position threatened to become precarious due to inflation. But now, five years later, the Stuttgarter board of directors changed its views; the overall economic situation had brightened considerably, more and more industrial firms were forming cartels, and banks and insurance companies were merging. Kurt Schmitt consulted immediately with Munich Re, and set out for Stuttgart. Difficult and controversial negotiations ensued, lasting several months, in which conflicts between Allianz and Munich Re over their underwriting shares in the future business broke out, reservations among the various committees of the Stuttgarter companies had to be dispelled, and the determined resistance of the City of Stuttgart had to be overcome.[85] All the parties involved were doing business successfully, were well aware of their value, and accordingly contended vigorously, being willing to accept the risk of failure. After the financial and personnel questions had been resolved, Allianz in the end made extensive concessions to Stuttgart, especially in the matter of the locations of the future administrative centers. The deal was closed.

On October 8, 1927, the headlines were devoted to Allianz and Stuttgarter Verein. The Deutsche Versicherungs-Presse reported: "A huge merger project is underway," and continued under the headline "The first German insurance trust:" "On October 5–7 of this year, an act of world economic significance was undertaken: the German insurance business acquired its first trust. Without any discernible pressure, a number of leading companies have joined together and created two new firms for property and life insurance, respectively, whose business volumes and financial strengths are paramount in Germany, and which will also play an important role on the world insurance market." The resonance in the media was large and international; the focus of the reports was on the size, financial strength, and market power, but some comments also voiced skepticism. For example, the correspondent of the Frankfurter Zeitung, who remarked, "An insurance complex is being created here whose homogeneity still has to be established […]. It will not be easy to obtain a clear view of a giant complex such as the Allianz-Stuttgarter Group now represents, and manage it with the requisite organization."[86]

Allianz made the most obvious concession in agreeing to introduce new names for the two firms arising from the merger. Thus, the property insurance companies Allianz, Stuttgarter Verein and Stuttgart Berliner became the "Allianz und Stuttgarter Verein Versicherungs-AG," and the life insurance companies Allianz Leben and Stuttgart-Lübecker and Stuttgarter Leben became the new "Allianz und Stuttgarter Lebensversicherungsbank

1929 advertising calendar for the company renamed the Allianz und Stuttgarter Verein Versicherungs-AG in 1927.

AG," with head offices in Stuttgart. These names bore witness to the differing histories and character of the new firms; they were recognizably the result of a compromise and were clearly intended to placate the skeptics within the management and staff. Due to their unwieldiness, they presumably gave the experts in communication, advertising, and marketing in Stuttgart and Berlin a few sleepless nights.

With the merger, the new companies became the market leaders in the fire, accident, and liability insurance business, and in the life insurance sector. In property insurance business, the premium income increased by more than 50 percent, to roughly RM 165 million. In the life insurance sector, the premium revenues, which in 1926 had amounted for Allianz to RM 27 million for a total insured sum of RM 540 million, grew to almost RM 81 million for a total insured sum of around RM 1.6 billion in the consolidated financial statement after the merger. This represented a market share of about 16 percent of the total German life insurance business. The most important competitors were the totality of the publicly chartered insurance companies, with a market share of 9 percent, followed by Victoria with about 8 percent.[87] In 1928, the customers of the merged Allianz company were paying for almost 340,000 policies – ordinary life insurance, pension and annuity insurance, and the ASS contracts for minor insurance sums introduced in 1926.

In the following years, there was often good news from Stuttgart. Life insurance became the growth sector for Allianz. By 1931, the number of policies had already more than doubled, to almost 700,000, as had the total insured sum, which by now amounted to around RM 3.2 billion. New prospects had developed, particularly in the ASS business, which had finally become more dynamic in 1932, after difficult initial years. The ASS-Versicherung (Allianz Spar- und Sterbekasse, Savings and Death Fund) was largely independent within the group, issued all its insurance policies from Berlin, and possessed a nationwide sales and marketing network.[88] With a mean insurance amount of RM 1,150, this offer was directed towards a group of customers who were described as "middle-class" at Allianz: craftsmen, civil servants, white-collar workers, and tradespeople with small to medium incomes. At first, the agents had to struggle against a negative image of the Allianz Savings and Death Fund among customers. The latter had unhappy memories of the former People's Insurance (Volksversicherung), in which millions of such contracts had lost their principal during the inflation. The insurers were forced to discontinue them because it became pointless to collect premiums and the reserves were gone. This idea of a life insurance for everyman had ended in total loss for all concerned. Furthermore, the new ASS insurance offer from Allianz was tied to thoughts of dying and death since the insurance was intended primarily to cover burial costs and provide surviving dependents with a small sum of money. So the new, positively connoted idea of provision for daughters' trousseaus was intended as a "morning gift" for the agents' difficult task of canvassing – in the words of Wilhelm Busekow, who had been assigned the task of giving the ASS project a last chance in 1929. He took advantage of this in two ways. Life insurance for smaller amounts, marketed with new ideas, and with very strict cost control, became a complete success. For Busekow, who had just escaped from the Favag Group (Frankfurter Allgemeine Versicherungs-AG), which collapsed in an unprecedented financial scandal, this was the start of a new career at Allianz Leben.[89] Even in the year it was introduced, the agents were able to sell a third of all new ASS policies as trousseau insurance. In sales talks, they were even able to rely on the German Civil Code. They could appeal to the duty of the father of the bride, stated explicitly in Section 1620: "A father is obliged to grant a daughter, in case of her marriage, an adequate trousseau for establishing her household."[90]

The surprising figures for Allianz Leben are partially explained by the fact that Frankfurter Leben, part of Favag, of which Busekow had been a deputy member of the board of directors, merged with Allianz in the fall of 1929, causing the latter's portfolio of life insurance policies to grow by 120,000. This was preceded by one of the major scandals of the European financial industry in the twentieth century at Favag, the second-largest German insurance group. There had been rumors and some "uneasy feelings" in banking circles and on the stock exchange for years.[91] Other things seemed utter folly: for example, in 1928, promissory notes appeared that the 68-year-old chairman of the Favag board of directors Paul Dumcke had signed personally in order to obtain money on short notice. There seemed to be serious difficulties. The rumors about financial problems at Favag aroused the suspicions of the journalist Artur Lauinger. He wrote for the Frankfurter Zeitung, had acquired over the years a profound knowledge of the insurance business and the art of drawing up company financial statements and had a large circle of knowledgeable informants. Since neither the Reich Supervisory Office nor the company's own supervisory bodies took action, Lauinger began to play the role of investigator. First, he called Dumcke himself to account, who took shelter from the persistent journalist by referring him to the finance director, Philipp Becker. When Dumcke died on February 14, 1929, after 33 years at the head of the Frankfurt companies (Favag), he was

Clients in front of an Allianz agency in Munich, which is advertising an industrial life insurance policy with the image of a money box intended for ASS (originally Allianz Spar- und Sterbekasse) in 1931.

buried with all public honors, accompanied by numerous eulogies for his life's work. A month after his death, Lauinger confronted Becker with questions about the financial condition of the group: "The discussion with the slippery Mr. Becker, who tried to evade every question that seemed embarrassing, ended with me telling him, to his forceful protests, that I would have to repeat the questions I had put to Mr. Dumcke and himself in the Frankfurter Zeitung, unless I received within two weeks a written and binding explanation of the management of the companies, and a current financial statement that reflected the actual situation."[92]

When Favag continued to stonewall and published a doctored financial statement, Lauinger had already taken the offensive. He published a series of articles on Favag's credit transactions and on the thicket of sixty interlocked companies in the group, which had become impenetrable for the outside world. And he also warned the Reich Supervisory Office and the supervisory board. The latter grew hectic: an internal investigative commission discovered hidden financial obligations and manipulations, although finance director Becker and his colleague A. Kirschbaum had used all the tricks of the trade to hinder their investigations. In their predicament, the members of the supervisory board even invited Artur Lauinger as an expert witness to an extraordinary board meeting. At the same time, officials of the Reich Supervisory Office in Berlin appeared to check the files and financial statements. What they found was outrageous. Hardly any documents of the board of directors existed, and it had been working largely unmonitored by the supervisory board.

The group's financial situation was disastrous: instead of the net earnings of RM 3 million reported in the annual report, Favag had actually incurred losses of RM 29 million, with premium revenues of about RM 80 million. It owed over RM 65 million to German banks, and almost RM 40 million to foreign lenders. The losses had not been incurred in the property or life insurance business but in mortgage and credit insurance, which is especially dependent on economic conditions and had seemed particularly attractive due to the high premium revenues. For this reason, the management had even been willing to cover not only the risks of goods transactions but also of purely financial transactions, where in case of a claim, there were not even goods that could be sold off. In addition, there were enormous liabilities and losses in the group's various banking subsidiaries from consumer and commercial credits. The bookkeeping, actuarial practices, and administration did not even meet the minimum standards of the industry. And given a total of 60 subsidiaries, some newly founded and some taken over, the management had simply lost the oversight of the chaotic ramifications of the group over the years. The boundaries between this and explicitly criminal activity were fluid, so that it was no longer a great surprise when, after lengthy investigations, the police and public prosecutor's office discovered that Becker and Kirschbaum had misused company funds for private real-estate transactions and for their personal profit.

In the end, it was clear that the Favag scandal was the result of mismanagement and criminal machinations by top management, a failure of the supervisory board, and inactivity of the regulatory agencies. A great deal of time passed until everything was cleared up, during which the public's mistrust of the insurance business and of the abilities of the government agencies in charge grew. The report of the internal audit was delivered on September 30, 1929, four weeks before the crash of the New York Stock Exchange on Black Friday, which proved to be the starting signal for the world economic crisis, the so-called Great Depression. The trial of six Favag directors responsible ended in February 1932 with fines and prison sentences. On May 26, 1939, the end of Favag had come, and it was wound up with a final financial statement. Its creditors retrieved about 23 percent of their funds, while

In August 1929, one of the largest financial scandals in the history of the German insurance industry erupted. Allianz's largest competitor, the Frankfurter Allgemeine Versicherungs-AG (Favag), collapsed. In a spontaneous rescue operation, Allianz took over the portfolios of the tottering company.

the stockholders had to make do with a rate of 15 percent of their original investment.[93]

If the people insured by Favag had lost their investments and their insurance coverage upon its collapse, the downfall of one group would have become a debacle for the entire industry. This rapidly became clear to the main players in August 1929. In his memoirs, Eduard Hilgard later remembered how dramatic events became, and how Allianz decided within a few hours to intervene: "On the afternoon of August 16, 1929, the Frankfurt banker Ladenburg, a member of the supervisory board of Frankfurter Versicherungs-AG, whom I knew well, appeared unannounced in my office. He told me that the "Frankfurter Allgemeine," Favag, as it was generally known, had collapsed, and that the public would be informed of this fact the next day. His question was whether Allianz would decide on a rescue operation. […] I called Dr. Heß into my office at once, of course, where we continued the conversation with Ladenburg. We telephoned Dr. Schmitt in Munich, and arranged […] to meet him for a conference the next day at the opening of business. And this memorable and momentous conference did indeed take place on August 17 at nine o' clock in the morning in the office of our chairman. The participants were Dr. Schmitt, Dr. Heß, Dr. Schloeßmann, and I. In the course of an hour, we were clear about the measures we were to take." [94]

Schmitt, who had sounded out Favag about a possible merger even after Dumcke's death – in other words, only a few months before – now telephoned the Reich Supervisory Office.[95] The agency had still hesitated until then, and now heard with surprise the head of Allianz outlining his plan "according to which the position of the Frankfurter Allgemeine, shaken by illiquidity, should be regulated by an intervention of Allianz to the benefit of the policyholders. He explicitly requested that the regulatory agency should refrain from taking steps for a short time in order not to endanger this supporting action."[96] The office did exactly that and showed itself very conciliatory towards Allianz over the course of the following five decisive days.

Kurt Schmitt proposed transferring most of the policies, and thus the resulting liabilities, to Allianz. The plan was quite daring because Allianz hardly had time to assess the risks that it would assume with this deal. And first Wilhelm Kißkalt's reservations had to be overcome; he had been taken by surprise by these events while on vacation. In his opinion, Allianz was reacting too hastily and taking too great a risk. But as soon as he arrived in Frankfurt, he grasped what was at stake. And besides, this offered the unique opportunity to acquire Favag's valuable holdings in Karlsruher Leben, Vereinigte Berlinische, and Preußische Leben. Swiss Re, the largest competitor of Munich Re on the world reinsurance market, was also ready to make an offer.

And thus Munich Re and Allianz on August 21 founded the Neue Frankfurter-Versicherungs-AG, after the supervisory board of Favag and the Reich Supervisory Office had approved all the plans the day before with a sigh of relief. An official had scribbled on the agency's memorandum "We support merger." But in reality, a merger did not occur. Allianz acquired neither the entire Favag Group nor its debts, nor the holdings of credit and transport reinsurance, which had a bad reputation in the industry. Neue Frankfurter took over the bulk of the non life insurance holdings of the collapsed group and was now faced with the task of gradually integrating this business into the corporate structures of Allianz. In contrast, the life insurer Frankfurter Leben merged directly with Allianz's life insurance company.[97]

And in contrast to the banking crisis, which caused an uproar among the depositors in 1931, a panic was avoided among the policyholders in August 1929 largely because Allianz intervened so rapidly.[98] Thus at the same time, it gained prestige and even more influence on the German market, which its competitors criticized accordingly. In order not to increase their suspicions even more, only Munich Re appeared as the new owner of the

Favag shareholdings in the Karlsruher and two Berlin life insurance companies mentioned. In secret, Allianz was involved to the same extent but did not make this public.[99] The new shareholders promised the firms that they could do business independently for years. During the years of crises to come, Allianz had all it could manage at first in digesting and consolidating the mergers and takeovers of previous years, anyway.

In 1932, Germany reached the nadir of the Great Depression affecting large parts of Europe and North America. The gross national product had sunk by more than a third from 1928, industrial production had fallen by more than 40 percent, and more than 30 percent of all those able to work were unemployed.[100] Now Allianz also felt the economic distress clearly for the first time. Its premium income sank in almost all fields, especially in automobile and transport insurance, which were particularly sensitive to the general economic situation. At the same time, more employees than had ever worked in the company before made the largest profit of its history to that date. After the many mergers of the previous decade, employees had been dismissed again and again, but management refrained from this almost entirely in the takeover of Favag's holdings and the merger of their life insurance company. Allianz was now employing 8,835 office staff overall, and about 1,500 sales staff. A third of these employees were women, as can be estimated on the basis of the statistics prepared for 1933 by the Allianz company health-insurance funds.[101]

Among these was the young actuary Anna von Pritzbuer (1900–1971), who after studying at university and working for a time at Hamburg-Mannheimer switched to Allianz in 1925 and was granted power of attorney for the company in June 1933, the second female employee discovered to date to have this authority. The first such woman at Allianz, Dr. Gertrud Scharf, who worked in the Magdeburg branch office, had been invested with the authority to sign for the company in 1923.[102] Anna von Pritzbuer worked as a department head at Allianz Leben and was responsible for group insurance policies until 1945. Then she broke radically with her previous life: she learned Russian, joined the Communist Party of Germany, worked at first for the [East] Berlin city government, and became administrative director of what would later become Humboldt University in East Berlin. In 1950, she joined the Deutsche Investitionsbank of the GDR, and later switched to the Council of Ministers of the GDR, where she worked last in the State Planning Commission.[103]

As the end of the Weimar Republic approached, some Allianz staff members were faced with making a choice of political orientation. The most prominent of them was Kurt Schmitt. In late 1931, Reich Chancellor Heinrich Brüning had the banker Hans Arnhold inquire whether Schmitt would be willing to enter his cabinet as Minister of Finance. At that time, this would have been a truly great responsibility, but Schmitt refused since he viewed the parties of the Weimar Republic with skepticism. "It is too early," he said to Hans Arnhold.[104] His time was to come in the summer of 1933, when he apparently was no longer skeptical, as far as the party of the dictatorship was concerned.

Communication: Newspapers, Advertising, Public Relations

Communication can be difficult. Disappointments cannot always be avoided. The editors of the Allianz Zeitung had to learn this after distributing the first issue of the new company journal to the staff and agents in June 1919. In the editorial of the first issue, they explained their program to the readership: the tasks and goals that the publication was intended to accomplish, and their hopes related to this. The newspaper was to replace the previous circulars and make everything that had been done individually to date by means of "oral and written instruction," available to all. The readership was to be informed in simple language about economic, technical, and scientific aspects of insurance, as well as about the current decisions and communications from management. And one of its core functions was to stimulate and enable the ongoing exchange of information among the employees and between them and the directors of Allianz, they wrote. For this, the editors were relying entirely on the collaboration of the staff and the agents. Three months later, the editor expressed with more emphasis what he expected: "We are counting [...] particularly on the active support of our agent gentlemen, and especially on the mutual exchange of the professional opinions and experience of our office and sales groups in order to make the experience gathered from practice by individuals the common property of all our institutions. We welcome every contribution, even the smallest one, every critique, every item of experience." But since not a single employee had written even one line to the editors in the three months since the first issue had appeared, he concluded his article with an urgent appeal: "Let no one claim a lack of time, for vital tasks – and the fruitful collaboration of the agents with management is one of these [...] – the necessary time must and can always be spared."[105]

Front page of the Allianz Zeitung with a color ad for Allianz. It appeared in 1929 in the Indian newspaper "The Daily Tej" on the occasion of Allianz starting up business in Delhi.

But the journalists did not become discouraged; they reported and commented on important news, business results, and decisions, explained new insurance offerings and current problems, gave hints for acquiring new customers, presented newly introduced advertising material, reported personnel news, printed feuilleton texts to entertain the readers, and even established a column for jokes and riddles. Over the years, the range of subjects of the reports broadened: Allianz grew, absorbed the staff of the companies it took over, and expanded its employee benefits. All this was reflected in the paper: staff sports became a topic, new locations and buildings were presented, and increasingly, articles on international firms, news from the judiciary and the German and international insurance business appeared. On special occasions, such as spectacular mergers, or when Allianz presented its annual financial statement, the editors prepared a press review. So the Allianz Zeitung appeared at varying intervals, sometimes as a monthly, sometimes as a bimonthly, and occasionally as a quarterly, without

Branch offices published their own magazines for their employees. Here, a special color edition from 1932 advertises automobile insurance.

interruption until 1939, when under wartime rationing, Allianz was no longer allotted paper for this purpose.

As early as the second year of publication, the editors began to relieve the solid blocks of text at least occasionally with drawings, and sometimes full-page diagrams. Over the years, they also varied the typography, added frames, and used graphic emphases and pictograms. The first special issue printed on glossy paper appeared in May 1921, in memory of the deceased board chairman Paul von der Nahmer. It also presented on the title page the first black-and-white photograph of the man being honored. Exactly a year later, the magazine announced the creation of a new corporate structure, the Allianz group, and noted in passing that the management was having a new logo designed: "A joint symbol of the group is being created, which will be borne not only by the managements of the individual companies, but also by all the regional offices and local branches, and will appear on all the printed material of the individual companies, and on all sorts of public advertising."

The editor added: "The mouthpiece of the group is the Allianz-Zeitung, which in this way will gain in importance, and in future must be utilized in the interests of all the group companies."[106] Since February 1923, the Allianz Zeitung appeared with the new corporate logo in its title. The front page now and then contained a photograph but usually full-page artwork, which was placed under a table of contents, and explained in an article in the issue. This showed the results of one of the many modernization and professionalization measures of those years. For in April 1922, an advertising and public relations section, called at that time the propaganda office, was established for the first time in the organization department of the Allianz headquarters in Berlin. Its staff was given three tasks: they took over the editing of the Allianz Zeitung, with lawyer Wilhelm Haeselich installed as the new head at the same time; they were supposed to design all advertising materials according to uniform criteria for the first time and refine them according to the wishes and needs of the sales force, and direct all the advertising and press work of Allianz.[107]

By 1929, Allianz renovated, professionalized, and intensified all of its communications. In addition to the reworked company magazine, the new branch offices also regularly published bulletins for their employees and agents. In 1929, Allianz Leben ventured to embark on the major project of a "magazine that is to cultivate and strengthen the feeling of personal and friendly ties between our policyholders and us."[108] For this purpose, the management commissioned the journalist Eilert Pastor to edit a customer magazine entitled Lebensblätter, which was published with an initial print run of 300,000. By 1939, the number of printed copies rose to almost half a million. The A5-sized illustrated quarterly was distributed for free to all life insurance customers. Staff writers and freelance authors published articles on health matters and on life insurance. The articles of each issue usually focused on a particular topic, which was very often oriented to the history of civilization, but from the summer issue of 1933 on, they were increasingly devoted to ideological commentary also on eugenics, war, blood-and-soil topics, and aspects of Nazi social policy.

Since 1923, the Allianz eagle had served as the trademark for marketing all of the Allianz group's insurance offerings and for all communication. Karl Schulpig (1884–1948), a Berlin painter and commercial artist, had experimented for a year until Kurt Schmitt accepted his design and presented it at a meeting of the board of directors. The main problem for the designer was that the work of an insurance company is difficult to visualize, illustrate, and symbolize. Schulpig experimented first with the initials AK

Painter and advertising graphic artist Karl Schulpig drafted Allianz's new logo in 1922. The eagle was officially introduced in 1923. The fireplace tiles depict other trademark ideas from the designer's workshop.

for the Allianz Konzern, then with different versions of the letter A for Allianz, and added two hands grasping one another to illustrate how the insurer and the insured form a community to avert risks. Finally, he returned to the letter A, placed it in a grid, and developed a simplified eagle figure sitting in its nest and spreading its wings around three fledglings from this pattern.[109] On October 5, 1931, the Reich Patent Office accepted the new logo as a registered trademark, number 438015.[110] Allianz used this company symbol for more than fifty years, until 1977. For all that time, the advertising department watched with varying success to ensure that the eagle was only printed and shown in its original, trademark-registered form. Despite this, an editor of the Allianz Zeitung complained as early as 1931 that almost a dozen variants of the logo were in use and implored people to use only the "original Allianz eagle 'made in Germany.'"[111]

In the decades before the start of the First World War, advertising had become well established in North America and in many European countries.[112] The most obvious evidence of this were the advertising pillars in the streets, but by far the most important advertising medium was newspapers and periodicals, whose number had boomed in a few decades up to the turn

With the slogan "Every minute …" Allianz boasts of its productivity and performance (around 1931).

of the century: around 1890, there were already 12,500 being published in the U.S., 5,600 in Germany, about 3,000 in Britain, 2,800 in France, 1,400 in Italy, and about 800 in Russia.[113] Many of these were financed in large part by the income from advertisements. The first Allianz advertisements preserved in archives seem to be job announcements from the time of the First World War. In addition, Allianz and the companies in its group, some of which had been founded much earlier, e. g. the BVB, the Magdeburger Feuer, the Favag, and the Berlinische in Germany, the Fireman's Fund in the U.S., and Riunione Adriatica di Sicurtà (RAS) in Italy, made use of fire marks, as described above. In his company history of 1990, Peter Borscheid already noted that the beginnings of Allianz advertising are obscure: "We do not know precisely how Allianz advertised in the first decades of its existence. No doubt the emphasis was on newspaper advertisements, with which, like the Stuttgarter Verein at the same time, it addressed different target groups and indicated agencies and agents. Besides this, the sales agents had brochures, some of which were illustrated."[114]

Allianz advertising brochure for liability insurance (1932).

In contrast to the United States, advertising here in the years after the end of the war had to struggle for its freedom against the spirit of the times, before becoming the icon of modernity from the mid-1920s on. For most people, the war and the years of crisis following it meant mainly shortages; they had to economize even on the barest necessities. Under these conditions, advertising was easily seen as an immoral call for wastefulness. This attitude was reflected, for example, in the German ban, under a wartime statutory ordinance, on luminous advertising until 1923, because they were considered a waste of natural resources. But all this now changed, which stimulated the advertising people at Allianz. There was a new mood, which an author of that day invoked in the trade journal Die Reklame, in an essay with the meaningful title "Not only does the modern world need advertising, but it is advertising that creates the modern world!"[115]

Allianz agents also felt this. More and more articles in the company periodical gave tips on how to advertise effectively and successfully and have a lasting effect. The advertising department developed more new campaigns and provided brochures and posters, advertisements for the compartments of railway cars, and pictures and objects for shop-window advertising, which became more professional, attractive, and fashionable – sometimes dynamic, sometimes placid and cozy, but generally more emotional, and also more colorful. The motifs bore titles such as "Quick, quick!," "Every minute," "Wonderful person," "Escaping everyday life," or "So carefree," and appealed to potential consumers' dreams, yearnings, fears, and hopes. Overall, Allianz presented a more modern, open, bright, and earnest but friendly image. The neon sign on the Europahaus in Berlin (as presented on the cover of this book), completed in 1931, is a successful example: the city and the press talked about the neon-light tower with the Allianz lettering on what was then Berlin's largest office building, built in the style of New Objectivity.[116] The new form of advertising also became the subject of a special offering in glass insurance, which insured complex neon signs against breakage.

At the same time, in Cologne the architects Heinrich Rosskotten and Karl Wach built a new administration building for the branch office. Here, Allianz broke with its historicist architectural tradition and presented itself as up-to-the-minute architecturally. But when the building was opened in 1933, the wind had already turned. The same architects designed an extension for Allianz Leben in central Berlin in 1936 that was already an obvious product of the Nazi period.

In the late 1920s, however, Allianz, which for a long time had tended to shun publicity, did not hesitate to make use of even the most novel media: the advertising bureau commissioned four films that were screened first before the feature film in ninety selected motion-picture theaters. They also had their eyes on radio: from November 1927 on, a radio station broadcast a series of talks by the authorized representative of the Breslau branch office on "Insurance Questions of Everyday Life." Whether such formats were effective, that is, whether they reached the intended target group, and how exactly they should be designed, was still a matter of dispute at Allianz.[117] In 1929, advertising specialists from America and Europe met at the World Advertising Congress in Berlin, which attracted great interest, as did the associated advertising exhibition. The Allianz experts were aware of the findings of the booming field of advertising psychology. The Allianz correspondent at the congress commented quite critically, "The power of suggestion of advertising can be so intense that the courted consumer feels it is impossible to live without the thing being recommended: he must buy, and he buys! But the supreme principle must always remain truth in advertising."[118]

New building for Allianz's branch office in Cologne, completed in 1933.

In the end, Allianz's attitude stayed ambivalent: some leaflets seemed avant-gardistic, with elements of the styles of Futurism and Expressionism, but most of the advertising material was plain and a bit old-fashioned, in subdued or somber colors, and relied on didactic slogans in Sütterlin script. However, overall the design options were much broader, and changes and experiments were obviously welcome. The Allianz Zeitung increasingly printed photographs – on very special occasions even making use of color – and ventured to experiment with comic strips to tell stories with pictures.[119]

All these initiatives, experiments and measures, whose purpose was to communicate more intensively with employees and customers, were closely linked to a desire of Kurt Schmitt's and Eduard Hilgard's. The old Allianz had not even received its visitors in the Berlin headquarters with a doorkeeper but had left them to find a contact person in the dark corridors of the building on their own. Its venerable director-general, Paul von der Nahmer, had shunned overly direct contact with the staff or the company of other managers in the general business community, not to mention any presence in public. Schmitt and Hilgard, by contrast, wished to create a new Allianz that would not only be perceived by the public but would also purposefully steer its image and strengthen its influence in society and politics. Over the years, the two had come to divide up the responsibilities concerned with safeguarding the company's interests between them: Schmitt, for example, sat on the advisory council of the Reich Supervisory Office, was deputy chairman of the Reich Association for Private Insurance, and from 1931 on, as member of the Reich Economic Council; Hilgard belonged, among other things, to the board of directors of the insurance industry employers' association.[120]

At first, there was no public relations work at Allianz that even began to be "strategic." But with each new merger, the press began to show more interest in the company and its management. And since its acquisition of BVB at the latest, its competitors were alarmed. So there was a need. Public relations specialist had already become an established career in the early 1920s in the United States, and to some extent in Germany, as well, but the labor market was as small as the number of qualified specialists, creating opportunities for people coming from other fields. The PR history of Allianz began on an unspecified date when banker Herbert Gutmann, son of the founder of the Dresdner Bank, Eugen Gutmann, and member of the supervisory board of Allianz, asked Eduard Hilgard whether he might have a job for an acquaintance whom Gutmann wanted to help. This led to a memorable conversation, in which the candidate did his best to alienate Hilgard. When the latter asked what skills he had, the applicant replied with a clear "none," and when Hilgard then asked whether he could imagine selling insurance, he answered with a decisive "I don't know." Despite this, the job seeker was hired for the sales force.

Gutmann's protégé was Edgar Freiherr von Uexküll (1884–1952), who called himself Baron Edgar (von) Uxkull. He came from a family of Baltic-German nobility, was born in Reval (Tallinn) as the heir of the family estate, had studied in Germany and Switzerland, and as a diplomat, represented the Russian Empire in the United States, Japan, and in Rome, Berlin, and Paris.[121] He left Petrograd before the October Revolution and moved to Berlin. The newly established state of Estonia expropriated his family properties in 1919. In Germany, he is said to have worked for a bank first before entering the services of Allianz in 1924. After first giving an ambivalent impression to

Edgar Freiherr von Uexküll (1884–1952), diplomat, successful agent, and first chief press officer of Allianz.

Hilgard, Uexküll's sales abilities gradually impressed his superiors. The board of directors also heard about them. In the course of the 1920s, Edgar von Uexküll developed into one of the most successful agents in the history of Allianz. He was soon regularly acquiring insurance sums of several million marks per year, with an astonishingly small number of policies, until the beginning of the Second World War. The reasons for Uexküll's success lay in his personality: he was open, humorous, eloquent, sociable, urbane, at ease in the best society, and had excellent contacts in Berlin, in Germany, and in the world. Together with his wife, Nadine von Radowitz, he made his house a meeting point for high society in the city. The couple maintained contacts with outstanding figures in cultural, diplomatic, military, and business circles, such as Max Reinhardt, Bruno Walter, the Papal nuncio Eugenio Pacelli (later Pope Pius XII), Thomas Mann, Max and Martha Liebermann, as well as Hans Adolf and Freya and Helmuth James von Moltke, who was godfather to Uexküll's son Alexander.

Around 1929, Allianz assigned Edgar von Uexküll to direct its newly founded press department, which – as Hans Heß noted – survived its baptism of fire when the Favag scandal became public, bringing Allianz into the focus of the media and the public because of its involvement. Uexküll knew the leading figures of the most important liberal and liberal-conservative media companies, such as Ullstein and Mosse, but also had good contacts in the nationalistic Hugenberg group. He was a personal friend of Theodor

Wolff, the editor-in-chief of the Berliner Tagblatt and a person of great renown in the Weimar Republic, and Rudolf Kircher, the correspondent of the Frankfurter Zeitung in London and Berlin. He advised the Allianz board of directors on questions of communication and suggested that they cooperate more closely with the mass media, which was in fact done. The heads of the branch offices were instructed to "get in closer touch with the press, especially with the provincial press," and were also encouraged to establish press service points at their locations, working on a volunteer basis for the Reich Association for Private Insurance in order "to serve the press in all questions concerning insurance."[122] Allianz Leben and the central departments for the various sectors were subsequently urged to reinforce their press relations and make them ongoing, "making use of the relations of our press office with the press, particularly in such cases where it seems desirable to enlighten the public about questions of general significance, or promote a certain tendency among broad circles of policyholders."[123] From then on, it was part of the new Allianz style to cultivate contacts deliberately with selected media representatives. Edgar von Uexküll convinced Kurt Schmitt how important it was to establish personal relationships with journalists and created a suitable framework for this. In the case of Hilgard, no special persuasion was needed in such matters.

Only a stone's throw away from the Allianz headquarters was the Hotel Kaiserhof. Here, Uexküll arranged a loose series of gatherings at which Schmitt, Hilgard, and he himself were present, and breakfasted and talked with a small group of journalists influential in shaping public opinion. These breakfast circles were soon well known, and in Hilgard's retrospective assessment, probably contributed substantially to strengthening Allianz's reputation in the media.[124]

Uexküll himself possessed the diplomatic gift of not displaying his own political views. This safeguarded his social and professional position even during the following period of the Nazi dictatorship. Inwardly, but later also in his actions, he followed a different path than his chief superior, Kurt Schmitt. His role in the finally unsuccessful attempt to save the life of 85-year-old Martha Liebermann, the widow of Impressionist painter Max Liebermann, in 1942 by ransoming her from the hands of her Nazi persecutors shows that he was a daring humanitarian who had grasped the true nature of the regime.[125] Uexküll retained his position with Allianz until 1944.[126] The Gestapo arrested him in unclear circumstances after the attempt on Hitler's life of July 20, 1944, and kept him in detention awaiting trial for two months in the Berlin-Moabit jail. His friendly relations with Helmuth James von Moltke, and Peter Graf Yorck von Wartenburg, who were both important figures in the Kreisau Circle resistance group, may have played a role in this.[127] With the help of his wife Nadine, and due to intervention by friends, Edgar von Uexküll was released and escaped death. Afterward, he lived in various places in Germany, appeared at the home of friends in Silesia, and lived at times in Konstanz, in Upper Bavaria, and in Sweden. In 1947, he testified, as part of the proceedings against Kurt Schmitt, before the U.S. military government about his assessment of the role of the leading men of Allianz in the Nazi years. His testimony remained very general and did not present any significantly new findings. He died in Bad Nauheim in 1952.

International Markets   Like the trust between nations, the trust that had supported globalized relationships between industry, commerce, and finances in the "world of yesterday" was also destroyed on the battlefields of the First World War. The warring countries of Europe had accumulated a vast burden of debt, the demands for reparations put the brakes on economic reconstruction in Germany and burdened relations between former business associates; the question of who was guilty of initiating the war, and the hatred between the wartime enemies hindered their willingness to do transnational business. Protectionist tendencies, political instability, and turbulence on international capital markets added to this. Many governments and companies wanted to revive international exchange, but they encountered enormous difficulties.[128] Allianz experienced this wherever it ventured to return to the international stage. The account by its director stationed in Riga, Walter Helms, of how Allianz wanted to gain a foothold in Estonia and Latvia begins at a time when Germany still believed it was on the victorious side. By March 1918, the German armed forces had advanced so far in the war against Russia that they had occupied almost all Estonia and the former Livonia:

> "Then Allianz opened a branch in Riga, with general agencies and sub-agencies in many other towns of the Baltic provinces, from Liepaja to Tallinn. Business, mainly fire and burglary insurance policies, grew until, in January 1919, the German military government withdrew from the Baltic provinces, and they were largely occupied by the Red Army. This put an end to Allianz's activities in this area for a time. All the files of the Allianz insurance policies [...] were transferred to the restructured office of the commissioner of insurance. In May-June, the Red Army withdrew again;

the states of Latvia and Estonia had been founded in the meantime, and Allianz was able with difficulties to get back almost all of its seized insurance files and resume activity, but now on the territory of the autonomous new republics of Latvia and Estonia. But in 1921, the operation of 'foreign insurance companies' was prohibited in these two states, and Allianz had to cease operations. In order not to abandon its business in the East, Allianz transformed the 'Vorstädtische Rigaer' [...] into a Latvian public limited company by the name of 'Rigaer Versicherungs-Gesellschaft founded in 1804', and provided it with its capital stock of 500,000 marks. The overwhelming majority of shares and all the reinsurance business were retained by Allianz."[129]

The company's business was restricted to Latvia. In neighboring Lithuania, Allianz took a holding in Lithuanian Lloyd.[130] But the total turnover and earnings remained limited and insignificant compared to the German domestic market, as well as to the important adjacent Swiss market. Unpredictability and uncertainty remained symptomatic of Allianz's international business during the Weimar Republic.

The reputation of the German insurance industry had suffered greatly among the former wartime enemies of the German Reich, anyway. And now, the hyperinflation ruined the trust of the traditionally important Swiss customers, as well. In a milder form, this applied to business in Scandinavia, too. As mentioned previously, the Swiss treasury and the Swiss life insurance companies as a whole had to come to the rescue of the Swiss policyholders of German insurance companies in 1924.

The Allianz assets in the U.S. from its prewar business there, blocked due to the war, remained inaccessible for more than a decade but were then paid out starting in 1930.[131] And although Kurt Schmitt reported to the shareholders at the 1923 annual general meeting that 90 percent of all revenues came from foreign business and from foreign-currency-denominated policies, such figures only resulted from the complete collapse in value of the premiums paid in marks. International business remained a headache for Allianz for a long time.

In the late 1920s, the management made increasing efforts to obtain concessions for the property-insurance business, and above all the life insurance business, in Europe and the rest of the world. For although Allianz had by now become the dominant player on the domestic market and was one of the three largest insurance companies in continental Europe, along with its Italian competitors, Generali and RAS, which had traditionally been very active internationally, the British and North American insurance companies played in another league.[132] With regard to the volume of life insurance, for example, in 1931, Germany, with a market volume totaling RM 19 billion, shared fourth place in the world with Japan (Australia 10 billion, France and Sweden 6 billion each, the Netherlands and Italy 5 billion each, and South Africa and Switzerland 3 billion each), of which Allianz had 3.2 billion, and thus a market share of about 17 percent. The third-largest life insurance market was Canada, with a volume worth RM 31 billion, behind Britain with a volume worth RM 51 billion. The United States, where life insurance played an important role in the retirement arrangements of large parts of the population, possessed an insurance volume worth RM 453 billion, about 24 times the German volume.[133]

While Allianz Leben in 1931 collected premiums amounting to about RM 150 million, the corresponding amount for the Prudential Assurance Co., Ltd., of London came to RM 620 million, and for Metropolitan Life of New York City, the market leader in the United States, to over RM 2.5 billion by 1928.[134]

The international ambitions of Allianz were also reflected in its administration: the board of directors established a foreign department again in 1928, headed by Ernst-Justus Ruperti, who reported directly to the chairman of the board and later became a member of the board of directors.[135] For the first few years, Allianz's attempts to become involved in international business persistently led to losses. The turnaround seems to have been achieved in 1931, when the author of the annual report noted, "thus it can be said that the foreign business has paid for itself for the first time."[136] The previous year, it had still been necessary to post a loss of RM 1 million. But in comparison with the domestic business, the revenues earned remained very modest: Allianz's foreign business revenues of RM 15 million for the fiscal year 1929–1930 formed only a small fraction of this business year's total premium revenues of RM 340 million, amounting to a share of less than 5 percent.[137]

Allianz made use of its close relationship with Munich Re to form international contacts with brokers and independent agents. It negotiated with the Reich Supervisory Office, and at the same time, via the Foreign Ministry, which was very sympathetic to Allianz, with a number of licensing authorities, to obtain concessions in Europe (Switzerland, Hungary, Cyprus, Greece, Free City of Danzig [Gdańsk], Africa (Egypt), Latin America (Mexico, Chile) and Asia (China, British India, Siam).[138] The Hungarian authorities, and especially the Austrian Federal Chancellery, proved to be particularly intractable. The negotiations with Vienna had already been going on for a year and a half, and Allianz believed it had an advantage vis-à-vis the licensing authority after its rescue operation for Favag in August 1929, because Favag had already held an operating concession for Austria. But then the German ambassador in Vienna, Count Lerchenfeld, reported to the Foreign Ministry in November of that year, "In this connection, I mentioned the Allianz application, and stated very clearly that we attached particular importance to the licensing of this company. The deferment of its application, which practically amounted to a rejection, would be inconsistent with the November agreements in the opinion of Germany, as already remarked; furthermore, there is the special situation of Allianz, which has taken over the entire share capital of Frankfurter Leben while respecting in full the rights of the policyholders, and to which the entire insurance holdings of Frankfurter Leben are about to be transferred by a merger. By assuming the obligations of Frankfurter Leben, which was to the benefit of the Austrian policyholders, as well, Allianz had made great sacrifices, I said, and it was only fair to allow it the working opportunities of Frankfurter Leben as well." The ambassador's report then ended as follows: "I said I could therefore not be satisfied with their position concerning Allianz, [...]. The effort to pre-

vent Allianz operating in Austria is all too obvious. The driving forces seem to me to be located more in the Advisory Council on Insurance than in the Federal Chancellery. To put it bluntly, they are 'afraid' of Allianz there, and Mr. Ochsner [the Austrian head of the Supervisory Department in the Chancellery] has the not particularly pleasant task of finding suitable cover names for this concept."[139] It is hardly surprising that the negotiations, which continued for years, failed. Only under completely altered political conditions was Allianz Leben given a chance, after Nazi Germany had annexed Austria.

In the early 1930s, Allianz had established a global network of branch offices and marketing associates. The project was obviously close to the heart of Kurt Schmitt, who had the news reported proudly in the Allianz Zeitung whenever a new location was established or revived. In April 1928, he welcomed Carl Ludwig Dierring and Claude Hamilton Wedderburn as the new heads of the branch office for South Africa in Johannesburg in an article entitled "In Africa" and paid tribute to the merits of Dierring's father, who, until 1914, for many years had represented Allianz at the Cape. The new branch office would serve "the South African Union, German Southwest

Far left: advertising poster for the Allianz agency in Meshed near Tehran (Persia). The other pictures portray Allianz employees in Jaffna (Sri Lanka) and the chief inspector Mr. Nanavati (1932).

and Portuguese East Africa, an area that is about seven times as large as Germany."[140]

A mere year later, the establishment of the India branch office in Delhi was celebrated with a colorfully illustrated cover story. In 1932, the foreign department head Ruperti opened another branch in Bombay before leaving for a tour of Ceylon [Sri Lanka], where he visited the staff of the Allianz agency in Jaffna, and met chief inspector Nanavati, whom he termed a "pillar of Allianz," who had made Allianz the insurer with the largest turnover in his district.[141] The potential seemed huge, and the statistical indicators were intoxicating. With its new concession for "British India, Ceylon, and Balochistan," he said, Allianz Leben had "extended our area of operations significantly again. The population of British India amounts to over 330 million itself, and the area is ten times the size of the German Reich. Yet the volume of life insurance of all the companies operating there does not come to a tenth of the German volume, weakened as it is by war and inflation. For each Indian, there is not even three RM in life insurance." The Berlin management sent mathematician Robert Reuter there as Allianz's local authorized representative; he ran the business together with Dhirendra Rath Mazumdar. Their task was "to put Allianz und Stuttgarter in the position it merits in India, as well."[142]

But this proved to be very difficult on most international markets, although Allianz began operations with local specialists and relied on offerings such as small-sum life insurance policies, which seemed appropriate for these markets. For example, in India Allianz Leben developed a Childrens' Endowment Scheme and sold education and dowry insurance with the slogan: "Here is the way to shelter your child."[143] In 1931, Allianz was operating with branches and holdings in Spain (Plus Ultra), Italy (La Pace), France, Switzerland, Sweden (Försäkringsbolaget Bore), Latvia, and Lithuania. It later transferred the business of the Johannesburg branch to South African Liberal Insurance, in which it had a holding. In addition, Allianz operated subsidiaries and cooperated with representatives in Copenhagen, Athens, Amsterdam and Rotterdam, Dublin, Luxembourg, Basel, Vienna, Istanbul, Larnaca, Beirut, Jaffa in Palestine, Persia, Iraq (from 1934), Alexandria, Colombo, Shanghai, Manila, Bangkok, Valparaiso, and Mexico City.[144] And Bayerische Versicherungsbank (BVB) was active in Poland, as well.

But by 1933, the zenith of Allianz's international business had already passed. The effects of the Great Depression hindered growth, and finally, the Nazi seizure of power harmed the interests of Allianz greatly. The governments and many customers in the states and colonies that regarded Nazi

Germany with growing dislike understandably viewed Allianz as a representative of a hostile power. They had barely arrived on the market when the Allianz companies thus withdrew from Iraq and China again in 1936.[145] In India and many other countries, Allianz companies lost the remaining business completely with the start of the Second World War, when their portfolio was classified as enemy property, and put under trusteeship.[146] However, this business which had to be written off was far outweighed by the opportunities resulting for Allianz in Nazi-dominated Europe in the early years of the Second World War. When Munich Re complained about the share of costs which it was expected to contribute to maintaining the foreign department of Allianz, the two members of the Berlin board of directors Hans Goudefroy and Paul Lux pointed out the lucrative rates Allianz was securing for Munich Re on the international market, since "our direct foreign premium has more than tripled from 1940 to 1941."[147]

EINST
ein stiller Winkel in
der beschaulichen
Residenz

HEUTE
ein ragender Eckpfeiler
im Aufbau des Reiches
im Gebäude der Wirtschaft
in der Gemeinschaft
des Volkes

ALLIANZ UND STUTTGARTER VEREIN

Versicherungs-Aktien-Gesellschaft

1933-1948

ALLIANZ: THE NAZI YEARS
AND RECONSTRUCTION

Martin Lachmann came very close to embodying the ideal type of employee that Allianz envisioned.[1] He was dynamic, successful, self-confident, and loyal to the very end. He was born on September 16, 1881, in Glogau on the Oder in Lower Silesia. He had three sisters: Lucie, Frieda, and Judith. Little is known about his childhood, adolescence, and upbringing. The family moved to Berlin around the turn of the century; in 1907 Lachmann became an Allianz agent. He was married to Aenne Alsberg (1885–1942), who came from a wealthy family in the department store business in the Rhineland region. The couple had a daughter in 1911, who was named Ruth Ernestine. At Allianz, Lachmann climbed the career ladder as a general agent and managed a successful agency in Berlin-Charlottenburg called "Lachmann's Subagency." From its inception in 1929 until 1937, Lachmann was a member of the so-called Million Club of successful agents that Allianz celebrated annually with a huge party (which Hans Heß also participated in).

The Lachmanns separated in the 1930s; though Aenne Lachmann moved to Munich, she still maintained regular contact to her husband and daughter with frequent trips to Berlin. In 1932, their daughter, Ruth Lachmann, married Leopold Haas, who came from a farming family from the Rhön region. Their son Peter was born two years later. When Haas's employer, the Ferro-Metall und Pyrit AG, had to relocate its German business due to anti-Semitic legislation in 1938, they offered Leopold Haas a position in Stockholm, and he and his family emigrated to Sweden. In stark contrast to the majority of the Jewish population in Germany, Martin Lachmann was able to maintain his position and income for some time after 1933. But over time

Martin Lachmann (back row, far left) at a meeting of the Big Life Club in Baden-Baden, October 3–4, 1933.

even his world began to crumble and his isolation grew greater. During the course of 1938, while the Nazi regime stoked the anti-Semitic fires by means of radical measures and left no doubt that the Jewish-German members of the German population were considered outcasts in their own country, Lachmann finally began to consider the possibility of also leaving the country and emigrating. He set his trust in Allianz. Hans Heß was contacted to find ways to secure Lachmann a position at Swiss National in Basel. Lachmann sensed growing skepticism within himself. Close to three weeks before the Night of Broken Glass, on October 20, 1938, he wrote to his daughter Ruth and to her husband in Stockholm that "my future is now completely unclear. I don't believe of course that Allianz will let me down, since that would be the worst possible thing that could happen to me."[2]

One week later, the passionate Allianz agent had to withstand two powerful blows: in a personal interview, Hans Heß and his boss Georg König explained to Lachmann that Allianz felt forced to terminate its contract with him at the end of the year (1938). Surprisingly, Lachmann reacted calmly and even expressed understanding concerning this bad news: "The gentlemen of the company wish me well and acknowledge my outstanding service and the successes that I have achieved. However, the circumstances of the times are perhaps stronger than the desires of my bosses."[3] Lachmann's reaction can be explained perhaps by his serious hope of landing a position in Zurich, where both Swiss National and the directors of Allianz's Swiss branch had approached Swiss officials requesting permission to allow Lachmann to enter the country. In addition, he was expecting to receive a generous pension from Allianz from an earlier guaranteed contract. But the

*Martin Lachmann on a beach
vacation in Istria in 1925.*

next blow pertained exactly to this point: Heß and Allianz's legal expert
Hans Goudefroy (who later became director-general) explained that instead of the agreed upon 36,000 Reichsmarks (RM) per year, he was to receive only RM 1,000 per month as a pension. The political circumstances
had changed so dramatically that it would be impossible for them to pay a
Jewish retiree such a high pension. Lachmann was outraged but deliberated
further about his financial possibilities: "I wouldn't be able to receive benefits from this fund, because this fund had, for the most part, to be named an
Aryan fund and a non-Aryan is not allowed to receive money from it. That
doesn't make any sense at all to me, because at the time these contracts were
signed such laws did not exist and besides, as the contract explicitly states,
these benefits are a part of my hard-earned commission. […] I ask you as a
businessman and as a son-in-law, what should I do? Do I dare take it to
court, costing much time and the possibility of an unfavorable outcome?
What's more, as of 1.1.1939, I will receive no more income at all and will have
to starve since I also have no liquid assets – or should I, since there were no
discussions about this, accept the offer and be satisfied with what they are
freely offering me?"[4]

Martin Lachmann did not sue Allianz. A legal proceeding would probably have led to more damage, especially after the Night of Broken Glass and
the anti-Semitic laws that went into effect afterwards, which systematically

stripped the remaining Jewish population of their rights and liberties in Germany. He was forced to give up his apartment, to budget his expenses, and then to sublet a new apartment on Wilmersdorferstraße while hoping for a new life in Switzerland.[5] The Swiss officials, however, were uncooperative, so he was forced in the following years, supported by his family in Sweden and some other relatives and acquaintances, to pursue other avenues of emigration. He stood on the waiting list for emigration documents into the U.S., hoped for permission to enter Sweden, considered emigrating to Chile, via Vladivostok, Shanghai, or Tokyo; to Mexico; and to the Dominican Republic. However, over the years each of these possibilities proved to be an empty dream. Martin Lachmann's correspondence is filled with the longing to be with his family – above all to be with his beloved, yet unreachable, distant grandchild. At the same time, he made an effort to dispel their worries about his increasingly dire situation. On October 22, 1941, Martin Lachmann wrote to his family for the last time: "It is a horribly difficult age that we are living through, but hopefully it will pass harmlessly by." Four days before, more than 1,000 Berlin Jews had been deported with the first Berlin deportation train to Łódź in occupied Poland. On November 14, the deportation train pulled out of the Berlin-Grunewald train station with Martin Lachmann and 1,000 other deportees on board bound for Minsk. If the official records are correct, Martin Lachmann did not experience the train's arrival in the Minsk ghetto. He is said to have died on November 16.[6] In September 1942, his sister Frieda and her husband Professor Maximilian Fuchs "preferred to take their own lives instead of suffering the deportation to Theresienstadt" according to a newspaper announcement published later by Judith Lachmann, who lived in New York.[7] A day after receiving her official deportation notice, Martin's third sister Lucie took her life in her Berlin apartment on January 19, 1943.[8] Early in 1939, Aenne Lachmann moved into a sublet apartment in a house owned by the doctor Magdalena Schwarz in Munich-Schwabing. The Nazi regime had rescinded her doctor's license. She now worked as a medic in a Jewish hospital and rented several of her rooms to elderly German Jews who were evicted from their own apartments.[9] There, at Mandlstraße 9, not more than 100 meters from the current site of Allianz's headquarters, Aenne Lachmann was murdered in broad daylight on the street on January 13, 1943.[10]

1933: Kurt Schmitt, Allianz, and National Socialism

On July 4, 1933, Martin Lachmann wrote a letter on handmade paper to Kurt Schmitt congratulating him on his new position: "May good fortune preserve your widely acclaimed diligence and your health so that they may continue to exert such force to the weal of our passionately loved German fatherland as has been achieved in your position as boss and director-general of Allianz corporation."[11] Lachmann was one of those hundreds from Germany and around the world who congratulated Schmitt in the highest tones of praise for his work at Allianz and wished him future success in his new assignment. On June 29, 1933, the president of the German Reich, Paul von Hindenburg, had appointed Schmitt Reich Economics Minister in Hitler's cabinet after Alfred Hugenberg had failed in this position. The Basler Nachrichten newspaper announced: "The most interesting figure of all the new ministers is undoubtedly Dr. Kurt Schmitt from Allianz" and speculated further that, unlike the other newly appointed cabinet members, he was not a member of the National Socialist German Workers' Party (NSDAP, hereafter Nazi Party) and would therefore perhaps "not be in this sense bound to the party line." The Times (London) saw his appoint-

Reich President Paul von Hindenburg receives Kurt Schmitt (3rd from right) at Gut Neudeck on the occasion of Schmitt's swearing in ceremony as Reich Economics Minister, July 7, 1933.

Reich Economics Minister Kurt Schmitt at a speech before representatives of industry and politics in the large meeting room of the Reich Economics Council (March 13, 1934), next to Schmitt (left to right) the State Secretaries Hans Posse and Gottfried Feder.

ment as a "clear signal for the desire on the part of the government to find a firm ground again in matters of commerce and trade."[12] For the American consulate general George Strausser Messersmith, Schmitt embodied the type of competent, conservative and rational politician who could act as a counterweight to the radical socialistic tendencies of the Nazi Party. He was, in Messersmith's almost euphoric appraisal: "the strongest and most constructively efficient personality in the entire country."[13]

Immediately after power was transferred to Hitler, Schmitt had moved to position Allianz in relation to the Nazi Party by attending a reception for representatives of 30 top corporations in German business at the office of Reichstag President Hermann Göring, along with the chairman of the supervisory board August von Finck, on February 20, 1933. The meeting was supposedly called so that the Nazi government could present its economic principles and goals and to clear up any concerns that large privately owned corporations might have had. It was announced that Hitler would be present as a possible speaker. In fact, however, the meeting's goal was to raise funds for the Nazi Party, which was desperate for money before the upcoming German parliamentary elections.[14] According to Schmitt's testimony to American military officials in 1947, he pledged a total of RM 10,000 to the Nazi Party the next day in the name of Allianz and Munich Re. Allianz also announced its like-mindedness with and support for the Nazi Party and government to its employees over the next few weeks. On Hitler's birthday – April 20, 1933 – a celebration replete with a marching band and a speech by the representative of the Nazi factory cell took place in Allianz's head office in Berlin. Before the German national anthem could be sung by the gathered guests (employees who had been given the day off for the celebration), Schmitt revealed how he viewed the situation: he was convinced "that now our folk is headed toward a better and happier future."[15]

The forced conformity program that the Nazi regime was systematically promoting had not, by any means, always been voluntarily followed. The elections for works councils did not go well for the candidates on the National Socialist list (the Nationalsozialistische Betriebszellenorganisation, NSBO). At Allianz, where elections were already held on March 16, 1933, under the conditions of dictatorship, they had won four of ten mandates. At Allianz Leben (Allianz Life) they won only two out of ten members, but these results were from an election held in November 1932, before Hitler and the Nazi Party assumed power. At that point, though, the new regime took radical action.

This is corroborated by the events of the last days of March 1933, when the newly elected council members of Allianz and Allianz Leben came together for their constituent assembly meeting: "Shortly before the start of the meeting, around 15 men fully dressed in SA and SS uniforms appeared uninvited at the entrance to the office buildings on Mauerstraße 18, who were then greeted by members of the Nazi Party factory cells. They barricaded the entrances and exits to the building, cut off the telephone lines and entered into the foyer of the conference rooms where all the members of the works council had already assembled. […] When the meeting was opened shortly thereafter, the works council member from the NSBO, Mr. Hans Lange, read a written declaration that stated that a provisional works council would be created that would regulate Allianz's operations until a finalized legal regulation had been passed by the German government and implemented and that therefore the elected members of the Marxist-oriented central association of employees must immediately declare their resignation in writing. […] Discussions are not permitted, the unconditional compliance with this declaration must be held." Such was the complaint of the director of the Allgemeiner Verband der Versicherungsangestellten (General Association of Insurance Employees), Gustav von Tein, in a letter of the same day to the German Minister of Labor, Franz

Walter Eggerss, fire insurance expert at Allianz, arranged Kurt Schmitt's first contact with the Nazi Party. Eggerss and Schmitt first met with Hermann Göring in late fall 1930.

Seldte. Meanwhile, at almost the exact same time, a few houses down the road, SA men together with some members of the NSBO had entered into the office of Max Scholber, the Social Democratic chairman of the works council of Allianz Leben, and forced him and the other council members to declare their resignation under threat of immediate arrest. Minister Seldte announced ten days later that the matter did not fall under his purview and passed the letter on to the Prussian Ministry of the Interior. Here the entire affair was laid to rest under the pretense that "such incidents [create] an actual condition, not however a legal condition" and therefore it was not deemed necessary for the government to undertake any special measures.[16]

These actions at Allianz were part of a nationwide attack, planned and coordinated by the SA and the NSBO, on the representatives of works councils and those active in independent unions. Within a few months, the government was able to expand its totalitarian hegemony into the world of trade and commerce: other works councils' elections were annulled per Nazi decree, the property and possessions of the unions confiscated, leading union personalities harassed, arrested or forced to flee, resulting in the destruction of their organizations. Even the NSBO lost some of its influence, since it promoted traditional instruments of union work like worker representation and the right to strike. The German Labor Front (Deutsche Arbeitsfront, hereafter DAF), formed in 1933 as an affiliated National Socialist organization that employers and employees alike were required to join, replaced the unions.[17] Within one year, the National Socialists succeeded in

3. 1933–1948 Allianz: The Nazi Years and Reconstruction

penetrating all layers of German society with their worldview and garnering broad support. Already in 1934, a representative of the exiled Social Democratic Party in Prague had to admit that "large parts of the workforce had fallen for the uncritical glorification of Hitler."[18]

Kurt Schmitt's first contacts to the Nazi Party dated back to the year 1930. Walter Eggerss, a fire insurance specialist who, after a short intermezzo with the Reich Chamber of Commerce in 1934 became a deputy member of the Allianz board of directors, had had dinner at the home of Emil Georg von Stauß, a member of Deutsche Bank's board of directors, and had spoken with Hermann Göring. He reported this to Kurt Schmitt the next day. Eggerss was certain that the National Socialists would sooner or later gain political power and told Schmitt that, under such conditions, it "would be more tactical to sooner rather than later make and maintain contact with the leading National Socialist functionaries in order to be able to influence the development of the economic policies of the party."[19]

Schmitt was of the same opinion, and so it was arranged that the three – Schmitt, Eggerss and Göring – would meet in the fall of 1930 for lunch in a Berlin restaurant; this was the first of what would eventually amount to eight to ten such lunch meetings. Göring sparked Schmitt's admiration from the start with his views, so much so that Schmitt told Eggerss that he could imagine himself supporting the National Socialists. Solely his position as the head of Allianz held him back from such an open endorsement. After 1945, Schmitt could not or did not wish to remember these meetings any more than he wished to recall his first meeting with Adolf Hitler, which probably took place in early February 1931. The journalist Walther Funk had brought Hitler, Schmitt and the chair of the supervisory board of both Allianz and Munich Re, August von Finck, together. Hitler spoke of the perils of social unrest in light of the uncontrollable mass unemployment and of the risks to trade and commerce if the leftist parties were to exploit the dissatisfaction of the poor population. In consequence, Schmitt supposedly pledged the unheard of sum of RM 5 million to Hitler to arm the SA in case an attempted putsch should come about. Secretly, however, Hitler feared a putsch from right-wing conservative military circles, which could have destroyed the political ambitions of the Nazi Party, and sought to secure monetary sources to better equip the SA.[20] In the end, Schmitt did not have to meet his pledge, since there was never an uprising. The episode, however, reveals his liking for National Socialists, even though he never seriously grappled with their political program or plans. Schmitt was a man who impulsively sided with a seemingly modern and dynamic National Socialist movement out of his dislike for the

Left and an equal dislike for authoritative, corporate-state projects driven by conservative forces as well as out of a deep discontentment in light of the lack of transparency of the democratically elected regime. Gerald Feldman therefore comes to a clear conclusion concerning Schmitt's qualities: "His political sense and understanding were pathetically underdeveloped, which was truly remarkable in an otherwise so talented businessman and negotiator."[21]

Schmitt was not put off by the Nazi's notorious hatred of Jews either, which from the beginning formed a central part of their government policies and which made use of widespread anti-Jewish stereotypes as well as of the brutally violent anti-Semitism of the party's original clientele.[22] "I was no anti-Semite." Kurt Schmitt begins a passage with this often-expressed assertion in his unfinished memoirs written after the end of the Nazi dictatorship. The passages that then follow can be associated with the numerous anti-Semitic sentiments, clichés, prejudices, myths and rumors concerning Jews that many Germans of this era were filled with: "I had a number of personal friends who were Jews. In some cases I didn't know they were Jews, and it hardly interested me if I liked them. On the other hand, there was a certain type of Jew in Berlin that not only we, but also respectable Jews found thoroughly dislikable. They were lazy, frivolous, and presumptuous beyond measure [...] especially in the lawyer profession you could find this type of Jew frequently [...] when I think back on the Favag trial and recall the unacceptable manner in which I was interrogated like a common criminal by individual Jewish attorneys, I am still grateful today that the presiding judge and district attorney who spared me from having to defend myself. There were also Jews of this type in the world of commerce who engendered a characterization like 'really Jewish.' These types of people rode roughshod over the interests of other people with cold-bloodedness and cynicism; they did not concern themselves with things they regarded as unimportant, but gripped them with the greatest inconsideration in the next moment. But it is wrong to generalize these types of occurrences. There are Christians who act in exactly the same manner, and there are Jews whose fine taste and selflessness in their thinking, combined with great skill and sense of responsibility, I have always admired. Concerning the practical political situation in the year 33, before I took over the Economics Ministry, I spoke with Göring about their Jewish policies [...] I will be frank here, I didn't have any problems with this line of thinking. That the Jews were too powerful, too loud and too unhealthy especially in our public and spiritual life, starting with the Reichstag, and also in the media, in many scholarly departments, among lawyers, and above all in Berlin banking circles, cannot objectively be refuted."[23]

Nazi organizations like the NSBO and the German Labor Front (DAF) shape the workday from 1933. Kurt Schmitt, Robert Ley (head of DAF), and Eduard Hilgard as well as Hans Lange (standing), DAF company manager of Allianz in Berlin, at the general assembly to celebrate that all of the employees of the Berlin Allianz companies were members of DAF (February 3, 1936).

When exactly Kurt Schmitt joined the Nazi Party is unclear, since his party membership book, his party file and his membership card all name different dates in the period ranging from April 1 and August 25, 1933. Thus, it is unclear whether he already belonged to the party when he resigned from his post as chairman of the board of directors of Allianz and was subsequently sworn in as minister on July 7 by Hindenburg at the latter's estate Neudeck. Effective as of September 12, 1933, he joined the SS, and Heinrich Himmler immediately appointed him Oberführer (Commanding Officer).[24] From around 1935, Schmitt also belonged to the Freundeskreis Reichsführer-SS (Circle of Friends of the Reichsführer-SS [Heinrich Himmler]), a club where leading SS functionaries came together with important representatives from trade and commerce and which Himmler used to raise funds to accelerate the expansion of the SS.[25] Schmitt's political career came to an end on June 28, 1934, when he collapsed after giving a speech and was then diagnosed as suffering from an acute heart weakness and a psychological breakdown. He was discharged from his ministerial post, which he never returned to, in January 1935.

In the spring of 1933, a number of other leading Allianz figures made efforts to become members in the suddenly very popular Nazi Party. Among others, two members of the supervisory board, August von Finck and Wilhelm Kißkalt; two members of the board of directors, Georg König and Ludwig Neumüller; the heads of two subsidiaries, Wilhelm Arendts and Alfred Wiedemann; and several gentlemen who later became members of the board of directors, Hans Goudefroy, Walter Eggerss, Hans Schmidt-Polex, Gerd Müller and Martin Herzog, all joined the party on May 1, 1933. Eduard Hilgard joined them in 1934, because by then it was necessary to be a party member in order to take on the director's post of the newly created Reichsgruppe Versicherungen (Reich Group for Insurance).[26] When so many top managers – either out of conviction, inclination or opportunism – took such an open political stance, Schmitt's companion Hans Heß distinguished himself from those around him all the more strikingly. He took over Schmitt's position as director-general of Allianz. They were not simply colleagues but trusted companions who discussed political, private and personal matters together during long walks. From that perspective Heß had warned his friend not to take on the post of Economics Minister, since he, according to his letter to Schmitt from November 1945, "judged the men who had made it to the top of National Socialism differently than you, and because I instinctively felt that you would fit with these people like fire and water."[27] Heß never became a member of the party and never hid his dislike and rejection of National Socialism. Furthermore, despite his leading position, he never acted the part of the big businessman nor participated in the numerous social rallies and insisted, as he later proudly remarked, that his three children not join either the Hitler Jugend (Hitler Youth) nor the Bund Deutscher Mädel (League of German Girls). However, this did not hold him back from becoming good friends with the infamously decadent and radically anti-Semitic Wolf von Helldorf, who was the SA ringleader during the Berlin street-fighting and was named the chief of the Berlin police force by Goebbels.[28] Heß concentrated on the workings of the internal management of Allianz, while his deputy Eduard Hilgard was responsible for all external contacts to the party and government agencies.[29]

In May 1933, the members of Allianz's extended board of directors were also discussing the new political developments. They prescribed a new direction for the organization and implored the employees to actively support and help to mold the emerging National Socialist government. They noted in their discussions that traditionally, Allianz had always prudently refrained from getting involved in politics, since the two spheres of business and politics were to be separated from each other. That didn't mean that the directors had refused until then to lobby for the interests of the insurance industry in pending discussions of economic policy, and to follow economic policy decisions, as well as to make use of their influence. Now that the struggle between the political parties had been settled, they reasoned, it was time to "represent common German interests," as this could only benefit Allianz's interests as well. Thus, the board of directors in Berlin, six weeks before Schmitt took up his ministerial post in Hitler's government, came to the following conclusion: "It would be wrong to withhold our cooperation in building up our fatherland, and it can only be wished that especially leading gentlemen of our corporation make their strengths and skill available everywhere in the Reich for constructive cooperation so that the inexperienced elements in our community do not tip the scales when decisions are made." They strengthened this appeal to work for the common cause by referring to a classic concern of the private insurance business, at the same time revealing an important motive for their standpoint: "When the insurance industry completes its assigned tasks as it has until now, then there is no danger of socialization since the government has committed itself to a free-market economy."[30]

The main point was to secure the favor of the party, rendered omnipresent by its many offices and organizations, as well as by a few ambitious actors both inside and outside of the company. For instance, functionaries from the party office in Breslau had publicly questioned Allianz's stance to the Nazi government and its ideology. Schmitt's state secretary Gottfried Feder used this as an occasion to attest explicitly and in writing that Allianz was "a purely German enterprise" whose "pure German stance" Hitler himself personally did not doubt, as evident in his appointing the former director-general of Allianz minister.[31]

Likewise, some agents in sales also felt called upon to participate in the plan to bring all the representatives in line with the now one politically correct path. Alfred Zaubitzer, branch director of Allianz in Brandenburg, was elected to the chair of the Reichsbund der Deutschen Versicherungs-Vertreter (Reich League of German Insurance Agents) and was now involved in bringing the sales force in line with the party; previously, the representation of the sales force had had a pluralistic structure. From now on, the league claimed to be the first and only voice for the sales agents and published an avowal of the Nazi government, of Hitler the person as well as his function as the national leader and, for good measure, of National Socialist economic policies. It also changed its leadership since, in Zaubitzer's words, the new

Allianz takes up the projects of National Socialist economic policy. In August 1933, Allianz Leben presents the brochure "Das Erbhofrecht" (Law on Hereditary Entailment) to advertise life insurance.

direction "means that one has the duty to raise old National Socialists up to the board of directors." Along with Zaubitzer, SS man Karl Straube from Gothaer Versicherung – who took over the post of deputy chairman – and Allianz general agent and SA member Josef Jöhl – who took over the post of new business manager – took advantage of this career-enhancing opportunity. Zaubitzer announced soon thereafter in August 1933 in the in-house newsletter that it was time also at Allianz for the agents to fall in line and that they had to let themselves be persuaded "by the grand ideas of National Socialism" in order to join "freely and fully in the great German Volksgemeinschaft (people's community)." By the end of 1933, all members of agents' clubs of the different agencies were to be automatically enrolled in the Reichsbund: "There will be no more standing passively on the sidelines on the part of a full-time agent, nor will it be tolerated in the future."[32]

Apart from that, the management observed how the new German

government's plans and measures for restructuring the economy developed, and how the struggles in economic and labor policy and the ambitions of the party organizations evolved. With suspicion, Hilgard followed the demands of the rapidly growing DAF and its ability to monopolize union, industrial wage contract and workers rights' matters. At the same time, he attempted to placate himself and his colleagues by pointing out that DAF director Robert Ley had personally promised him that his association would respect the autonomy of the individual companies and, in particular, that it would not become involved in their personnel policies.[33] In matters of interest to the entire insurance industry, the associations, and with them Eduard Hilgard, chairman of the Reichsverband der Privatversicherer (Reich Association for Private Insurance) and one of the chairmen of the Arbeitgeberverband (Employers' Association), acquired an increasingly important role.

Some of the National Socialist government's founding principles could not be relativized by any amount of intensive negotiation or cooperation. This held true especially for two elements of its labor market policy: for one, the party and government officials applied ever more pressure on businesses either to hire more people than necessary or to refrain from laying people off; secondly, it portrayed dual earners as the enemy and launched a hyped-up propaganda campaign against them. Ultimately, this was a fight against the unemployment statistics that was directed above all against dual earners like working married women and people with several jobs. These individuals were stigmatized as anti-social egoists who were taking jobs and money away from honest unemployed fathers and were thus sabotaging Hitler's proclaimed attack on unemployment. This was an especially delicate situation for Allianz and the entire insurance branch, because many agents had more than one income from selling policies in their hometowns to friends, family, and colleagues, making them 'dual earners' in the eyes of many National Socialist functionaries.

Hans Heß was willing, for a time and despite growing expenses and decreasing premiums, to refrain from laying off employees out of political considerations. He, nevertheless, articulated the argumentation that could be used against the party or government officials who demanded that they hire more employees. After all, he argued, it had to be acknowledged that Allianz had done more than its share in the fight against unemployment by increasing the number of office workers by almost five percent from the summer of 1932 to the middle of 1933 and external sales staff, in fact, by 10 percent.[34] Actually, the number of employees in the entire concern increased by almost 10 percent to close to 9,700 persons in 1933; during the same period, pre-

Allianz board of directors member Eduard Hilgard speaks as the head of the Reich Group for Insurance at the 125ᵗʰ anniversary celebration of Berlinische Feuer (December 11, 1937).

mium revenues sank for the third year in a row to levels below those of 1927. The currency reserves and pure profits, however, climbed slightly. The annual report mirrored the changed political times in that it explicitly highlighted the personnel policy as Allianz's sociopolitical contribution, and it recorded for the first time money given to charities for "national and social purposes" in the amount of RM 1.7 million, for instance, to the Winter Care Fund (Winterhilfswerk), and the Adolf Hitler Donation of the German Business Community. Furthermore, the report now characterized the money paid for social benefits to employees (which it had paid in previous years as well) as especially patriotic services on Allianz's part. Allianz summarized its own investment and credit portfolio in a similar manner by underlining the fact that it had invested whenever possible in government securities and other public bonds as the government had requested help in invigorating the capital market. Indeed, almost 60 percent of Allianz's assets in securities and bonds in 1933 were placed in titles held by the state whereas it had, by comparison, invested less than 50 percent in public securities and bonds in the previous year.[35]

Looking back, France's ambassador in Berlin during the 1930s, André François-Poncet, noted that in less than a year of National Socialist rule under Hitler, "National Socialist Germany stood readymade," complete "with its customs, its institutions, its vocabulary, its salutes, its slogans, its fashion, its art, its laws, and its celebrations." He was especially irritated by the speed of the transformation, which he described as a revolution: "the effortlessness with which it was completed everywhere, the minimal resistance it met with." And he added: "There is something inhumane, unnatural in this rapidity." A few months earlier, he had already noted anxiously that Germany would have "given itself over to bondage without a single complaint or expressing any protest."[36] At Allianz, many actors were still occupied at the end of 1933 with bringing themselves and the company in line with the totalitarian state. The Nazi state was supposed to keep the basic founding principles of commerce unrestricted. All the same, it made its presence felt through more regulations than any of the Weimar governments had had and subordinated economic activity energetically to its social and foreign policy plans and especially to its war preparations. Nevertheless, the regime also cultivated and maintained an arbitrariness in economic questions from the first moment on until 1945 that, as Klaus-Dietmar Henke cites in his summary of the history of Dresdner Bank, promoted the "submission" of businesses to its will. What Henke described as the characteristic framework for business behavior in the Nazi state held equally for the leaders of Allianz: as independently responsible leaders they saw themselves forced "to perpetually adjust the balance of economic rationality, proximity to the government, and complicity."[37]

"Insurance Must Make Money" – Economic Development and Adaptation

"Insurance Must Make Money" – was the title an editor of the Frankfurter Zeitung gave his article concerning a lecture held by Eduard Hilgard before a group of real estate brokers and insurance agents on October 28, 1938, in Hamburg. Since 1934, Hilgard had been director of the Reich Group for Insurance, one of the new organizations installed by the National Socialist regime, which was supposed to coordinate and eventually replace the activities of the top associations in commerce and trade and their lobbying groups. It was to make sure that companies were informed about the government's economic policy guidelines, and that they put them into effect, which the Reich Group would also watch over. In late 1938 and early 1939, Hilgard fought intensively – and also, ultimately, successfully – against Nazi proponents of public control of private enterprises gathered around Gauleiter Franz Schwede-Coburg; Hilgard also successfully defended the autonomy of private insurers as well as his own post.[38] Proponents of a state monopoly complained about the lack of ideological and party loyalty displayed by the suspicious-eyed experts in the top management positions in the private insurance business, about their international connections and the lacking presence of old Nazis in their internal organizations. Furthermore, their self-centered interest in profit and profitable investments from the capital they had accumulated, as well as their exaggerated sense of competition, stood "like fire and water" against all thoughts of a "peaceful National Socialist reform," which wished to organize the insurance business into a central charitable trust company.[39] Schwede-Coburg used all the tricks in the book in this conflict and did not refrain from attacks on Hilgard's personal integrity. He had proven his ruthlessness in numerous other political fights and from 1939 on, distinguished himself as a pioneer in the state-organized mass murder of disabled persons and the Jewish population of Pomerania. On the front line of the insurance business, as president of the Reichsverband der öffentlich-rechtlichen Versicherung (Reich League of Publicly Chartered Insurance), he was concerned with establishing the power of the party – and also his own – within the financial world and also, more concretely, with gaining control of the assets put aside for life insurance, as Gottfried Matthes, the Deputy Minister and insurance expert in the Reich Economics Ministry, said.[40]

In this ideologically loaded power struggle, it became a problem for Hilgard in his double role as director of the Reich Group and as a member of the board of directors of a private insurance company, that Allianz was turning large profits. The regime-conforming media, on the other hand, praised the business success of the company unanimously. The Völkische Beobachter, the party newspaper, assessed its balance sheet: "Increased premium revenues at the Allianz concern [...] lowered premiums in almost every insurance branch – positive returns on investments [...] Allianz can be satisfied [...] the effectiveness of the measures undertaken to cure the economy is exemplified in the gradual increase of the average sum in all types of life insurance [...] every investment serves the tasks of the four-year plan."[41] The last sentence referred to the value of Allianz's assets and reserve funds. Already in 1935, the German law for lending was changed so that up to 50 percent of insurers' liquid assets could take the form of stocks or bonds, especially including government securities. From 1938 on, the Reich government required insurers to invest a minimum of 30 percent of their annual premium revenues in government securities. It was the task of Hilgard's Reich Group to inform companies about the required investment sums, to check up on

Life insurance becomes ever more important for Allianz in the 1930s. Advertisement for Allianz Leben from 1933.

their investment behavior, and to remind them of their duties when necessary. Via secret decree the Reich Economics Ministry also instructed insurers to invest any available funds in government stocks. Additionally, the government systematically decreased insurers' freedom to control their own capital: insurers were no longer allowed to guarantee mortgages or make loans for residential construction; even the sale of real estate was subject in each individual case to government approval.[42] During the course of the war, the government took hold of more and more of life insurers' capital assets. Finally, by 1942, insurance companies in general had to invest 75 percent of all of their available funds in Reich securities.[43]

Allianz was able to consolidate its business operations, and from 1936 to the start of the war in 1939 especially, it showed strong growth. Premium revenues grew tremendously from a low point in 1933 of RM 146 million to RM 218 million in 1939; the actuarial and claims reserves grew from RM 105 million to RM 197 million in the same period, while earning roughly the same annual net profit of around RM 6.5 million. The number of policies

In 1937, Allianz opened a newly constructed building in Marien-dorf for the materials testing laboratory founded in 1932 that dealt with researching damage for machine insurance. Pictured here are visitors to the training exhibition on the occasion of the managers' conference in 1937.

rose in the period from 4.2 to 5.6 million. The total number of full-time employees both in the office and in sales grew from 9,700 in 1933 by almost 40 percent to 13,500. The growth sectors in the 1930s proved to be automobile, transportation, and machine insurance.[44]

Parallel to these developments, the structure of business operations and the capital base changed within the Allianz companies, because Allianz Leben developed with such rapidity that, in 1939, it already accounted for one-sixth of all the life insurance business in all of Germany. From premium revenues of about RM 130 million in 1933, Allianz Leben grew to RM 230 million in 1939 while at the same time the premium reserves grew from RM 500 million to over RM 1 billion. The entire insurance sum of ordinary and industrial life insurance policies and group insurance policies ran to the amount of RM 5.1 billion in 1939. For the Nazi regime, the capital strength of Allianz Leben was interesting above all because the company had invested almost RM 500 million in stocks and bonds by the end of the 1930s. In addition, the asset managers had around RM 370 million in mortgages, RM 75 million in real estate assets (net street value), around RM 160 million in loans to public organizations, and around RM 13 million in liquid bank assets in their portfolio. These yielded around RM 55 million in 1939. In other words, Allianz Leben had become the largest life insurer on the European continent, followed closely by the rapidly growing – too rapidly according to head of Allianz Leben Rudolf Schloeßmann – Volksfürsorge (People's Welfare Group), an enterprise stemming from the business conglomerate formed by

Allianz company orchestra concert at the BVB in Munich on September 28, 1938. The members of the company brigade line up along the middle aisle.

DAF, as well as the Schweizerische Renten-Anstalt (today called Swiss Life), and the Assicurazioni Generali of Trieste in third and fourth place.[45]

Allianz had modest success, despite its great ambitions, during the early 1930s in rebuilding its international business, which the in-house Allianz Zeitung repeatedly and enthusiastically reported upon. The world economic crisis, restrictive currency policies, but above all the establishment of the Nazi dictatorship and the international critique of the ideology and policies of the new regime undermined these efforts abroad. At a board of directors meeting in May 1934, those present expressed sentiments along such lines: "Business is difficult because of the anti-German propaganda one finds abroad."[46] Whereas premium revenues generated abroad had risen to just under 5 percent of all the premium revenues in 1930, the most successful year in the attempt to rebuild international business operations, they sank to under 2.5 percent in 1934 and only slowly stabilized after that. By the out-break of the war, premium revenues from abroad amounted to around 7 million marks. If, as the Allianz Zeitung in an article entitled "The International Standing of German Private Insurance" in 1935 wrote, "every policy sold abroad" assumes "that the buyer believes in the continued existence of the German insurers and implicitly also in the economic future of Germany," then the miserable figures reveal quite clearly that this trust was not to be found abroad. The article reported above all on the international dealings of German reinsurers, which, with a world market share of around 40 percent, generated the lion's share of the total of around RM 200 million in international premium revenues for all German insurers. A large portion of these, in turn, came from Munich Re.[47]

While Allianz was economically on the rise, it slowly but surely adapted to the daily routine of National Socialism.[48] It changed its language when it seemed opportune and adopted patterns of behavior that were typical of National Socialist rituals, like the heavy use of pathos-ridden and archaic words and a dynamic and martial appearance. Whereas Allianz had been reserved in its political statements and actions up to 1933, it now fully embraced the spirit of the age. In January 1934, for instance, the board of directors gave the employees the following news as a welcome into the new year: "Under the leadership of our German Chancellor Adolf Hitler, the old has brought us the greatest revolution that our fatherland has ever seen. The desire that all German hearts felt for so many centuries has been fulfilled. We have a leader (Führer), we have a people (Volk), we have our own Reich [...] the number of unemployed has been reduced by almost 2.5 million. Everywhere, business is beginning to grow again. Great projects have been started. Above all, the lost trust has returned. We have confidence that things will continue to go forward in the new year as well."[49]

National Socialism soon saturated all aspects of the daily work routine, in business operations and in top management. The company constitution was authoritatively restructured in accordance with the "Act for the Order of National Employment," which was written by a civil servant who had previously worked for a lobbyist association serving the interests of large private corporations. In the end, it transferred the essential rights and authorities back into the hands of business owners. New neo-feudal concepts gave testimony to how the workers were to act as the "followers" of their "company leaders" in the "harmonically organized" working world of the National Socialist Volksgemeinschaft (people's community) now that the antagonisms and conflicts of the old working order had allegedly been overcome.[50] For the Berlin branches of Allianz, this post was taken on by the young Paul Lux and his patron Eduard Hilgard. At the Bayerische Versicherungsbank (BVB) in Munich, Wilhelm Arendts held the position as well as that of chairman of the board of directors; in Cologne it was branch director Otto Würz; and at the Neue Frankfurter, their director-general since 1934, Alfred Wiedemann. They were all Nazi Party members, since this was a prerequisite for heading a company. After all, the democratically elected works council members had been removed, the members that replaced them were consultative councilors who now only had an advisory function. Instead of these, now party functionaries in the form of representatives from the NSBO and the DAF spread their influence, simultaneously perceiving themselves as the voice of the workers as National Socialist agitators, and vigilant watchdogs and acted accordingly.

Allianz now highlighted paid employee social benefits (which began long before 1933), its generous pay above agreed upon rates, as well as its new hiring, which far exceeded what the business needed, as examples of its especially patriotic and socially responsible business management. Of course, it was still criticized by DAF for not publicizing this effectively enough. Therefore, it demanded that Allianz publish an annual report of their social activities that, starting in 1937, was to be added to the annual report. Internally, the board of directors observed the financial expenses for administration and social benefits with increasing skepticism; in 1935, for instance, the board had refused to raise the children's bonus for higher paid employees and to pay extra money for employee excursions as requested by the organization called Kraft durch Freude (Strength through Joy), a subdivision of the DAF that organized leisure and travel packages.

The directors accommodated other demands that had no direct financial effect but seemed politically opportune, although it often took some time for the board's decision to come to fruition. For example, not all employees were ready from the start to join DAF. It wasn't necessarily a political decision, but the employees were wary of DAF, which was known as a money-grubbing and corrupt association; many employees simply did not want to pay the membership dues. Hilgard explained to the board of directors at the end of October 1935 that it was desirable for the employees to all be members; top managers, especially, should not refrain from joining any longer.[51] At the beginning of February 1936, the Völkische Beobachter reported that the last black sheep who had stood on the sidelines had now finally joined the rest of 'the followers' at Allianz in Berlin and become members of DAF. To celebrate, Allianz organized an employees' assembly meeting complete with lectures, music, and dance at the Kroll opera house in Berlin on February 3, 1936. In the presence of Kurt Schmitt, Hilgard held a talk before 3,000 employees from the Berlin offices; this was followed by a lecture by DAF-boss Robert Ley about his deeds and the work of the Kraft durch Freude organization.[52] Before the assembled leading DAF dignitaries, Hilgard highlighted the social benefits achieved by Allianz and made the purpose of the gala abundantly clear by saying: "We see in this a manifestation of the company's cohesive will to commit itself to our Führer and his work and believe that there is no better way for a corporate community to celebrate the anniversary of the transfer of power to National Socialism than by avowing this will."[53]

Workaday life at BVB: clients in the cashiers' hall (top); employees addressing correspondence with ADREMA machines (center); employee training (bottom) (mid-1930s).

Such celebrations were common throughout the Reich from 1933 and fit into the annual liturgical program of memorials and high celebrations that the National Socialist regime used to project itself in public.[54] Allianz also invested time and human resources into repeated employee rallies and flag ceremonies, paramilitary games, demonstrations for the various National Socialist Party celebrations, broadcasting Hitler's speeches on the radio before the assembled employees, gathering employees for morning calisthenics and various other activities in the competition to receive the distinction of National Socialist Model Corporation.

A business like the Cologne branch of Allianz had good chances of getting this. The employees worked in the most modern administration building of the whole concern, enjoyed social privileges such as a cafeteria, a lending library, quiet rooms for rest and relaxation, a healthcare station, special courses for further training, but also programs for pregnant women along with the usual Allianz packages offering sports, vacations and other leisure-time activities. In the eyes of the party there was surely little doubt as to the loyalty of the Cologne "agents." In 1941, of the 440 male and 200 female employees or "followers" working for branch director and "business leader" Otto Würz, 115 were members of the Nazi Party. Forty-two minors belonged to the Hitlerjugend (Hitler Youth) or the Bund Deutscher Mädel (League of German Girls), respectively.[55] All of this information was gathered, documented and evaluated for the competition including the level of social engagement displayed by the employees. After the beginning of the war, those that stayed at home took special care of their drafted colleagues and their families. Monthly care packages, newspapers and other "love tokens" were sent, morning concerts in the hospital for the wounded soldiers were held by the company orchestra, visiting services, evenings at the theater and afternoon coffee and cake were organized for the wives and children of Allianz employees in battle.[56]

As is well known, everyday events like greetings became ideologically loaded and regulated accordingly. After the Prussian Ministry of the Interior decreed in 1935 that the greeting "Heil Hitler" (Hail Hitler) should become the "greeting pledge of Germans to each other," the organization called Wirtschaftsgruppe Privatversicherung (Business Group Private Insurance) took notice and passed this along to its member companies. At Allianz in Frankfurt, in the end, it was decided that management should be instructed as follows: "The official form of greeting is: 'with German greeting'. On special occasions, the usage of a different form of greeting is a matter at the discretion of the department director."[57]

In these ways, the party and its ideology were constantly present in language, rituals, and symbols. Hundreds of surviving photos taken at these festivities, most of them published in the DAF magazine, Der Allianz Adler, show the party functionaries and Allianz employees in uniform standing before buildings decorated with flags, in the conference rooms, and at the podium – with swastikas, Hitler portraits and armbands being salient features. They show a picture of a company that came very close to matching Ley's ideal of a specifically National Socialist working world. All of these activities and symbols ultimately served "to 'educate' the people to an acceptance of the new worldview and value system" and further to mobilize them for the National Socialist system.[58] An even more military character was stamped onto everyday work routines starting in 1936, when Allianz working troops were established in Berlin, Stuttgart, Munich, Cologne, and other cities. Hundreds of male employees trained for formation maneuvers, much like in boot camp, preparing for war. They marched, paraded and sang and absorbed the attitudes and principles of orders and obedience. They formed one element of Ley's grand vision of creating one magnificent and forceful militia out of the working troops of thousands of businesses within his DAF empire.

Since 1937, the Allianz Adler magazine acted as the voice of DAF and the party within the company; the magazine propagated the ideological viewpoints of the National Socialists on essential questions about social policy, the health-care system, and labor markets and described the organized activities related to employees – the work troops, the company sports clubs, the orchestras, choirs, theater groups, youth and women's clubs. In established columns like "Talk from the NSBO-DAF," "The Woman at Work" or "Report from the Regional Strength-through-Joy [Organization]," the functionaries of the various party organizations had a forum in which to report about current meetings or other programs and to animate employees to join the groups and take part in the activities. The editors of Allianz Adler, all loyal party members, worked independently and had no attachments to the internal newsletter, the Allianz Zeitung, which at least until 1938 featured significantly more reserved reporting on political matters, concentrated more on questions about insurance, and was presented in a more modern fashion than the monthly paper of the party's factory cell.

Beyond all political support, Allianz maintained strong contacts to the Nazi Party and to government institutions for tangible business reasons as well.[59] Already in the summer of 1933, directors Georg König and Hans Futtig explicitly indicated in an open letter to the sales department that relations to the party could be advantageous for acquisitions: "For advertising in national

Allianz ad for hunting liability insurance from 1935. This insurance became mandatory for all hunters in 1937.

Die Jagd im Schutze der Haftpflicht Versicherung

circles, it will doubtlessly be useful [to spread] the knowledge of Allianz reaching large contractual agreements with organizations largely standing on the basis of today's government." König and Futtig pointed out that Allianz Leben had already concluded a contract for group life insurance policies for one hundred thousand members of the National Socialist Reich Association of German War Victims, and that similarly, a contract had been concluded for group life and accident insurance policies with the Fraternal League of German Police Officials, which covered 150,000 members and their wives.[60] Such collective contracts, in which the organizations negotiated for their members with several insurance companies and then determined which portions should go to which insurance companies, proved to be lucrative and resulted in rapidly increasing the number of persons insured in this way – they were categorized as "risks" in insurance statistics – from around 300,000 in 1932 to more than 2.7 million in 1939. Allianz was not only significantly more successful than the publicly chartered insurers in this particular segment, but also in fact more successful than the DAF's own insurance companies. Allianz agents sold group contracts for ordinary life, accident, and liability insurance policies to associations with large memberships like the NS-Lehrerbund (National Socialist Teachers' League), the NS-Rechtswahrerbund (National Socialist Lawyers' League) – in which more than 100,000 judges, district attorneys, notaries, paralegal clerks and lawyers were members – the NS-Frauenschaft (Nazi Women's Association), which at times generated annual premiums of as much as RM 3 million for Allianz. Other extremely attractive business deals were individual contracts with the Nazi Party, for instance, for the party congresses and for the furnishings in their administration buildings.

Personal contacts of many individual agents, but also the reputation of Kurt Schmitt in party circles as well as his direct contact to Nazi bigwigs like Hermann Göring, gave Allianz advantages over the competition. One of Göring's many passions was hunting. After 1934, as he began to restructure and expand his domain of power, he gave himself many titles and ranks, among others the title of Reich Huntsman (Reichsjägermeister) and developed many projects in the areas of environmental preservation and animal protection. Beginning in 1937, all hunters had to sign a hunting liability insurance policy. A conflict arose between the various interests of private insurers and publicly chartered insurers, Göring's National Hunting Office (Reichsjagdamt), and the ministerial bureaucracy. The Reich Economics Ministry then asked Kurt Schmitt to step in as an arbitrator and to negotiate with Göring. The former Allianz boss was successful; he was able to make an offer that met Göring's expectations of a simple and inexpensive insurance policy for everyone and at the same time to secure exclusive rights to offer such policies for the private insurance industry. In the end, through Schmitt's persistent arguing and minor concessions, he had turned around the competitor's opposition and the Obligatory Hunting Liability Insurance Bureau for German Hunters was established. It should come as no surprise that this was housed at Allianz. From April 1, anyone who had a hunting license was obligatorily insured with Allianz through its contract with the Reichsbund Deutsche Jägerschaft (Reich League of German Hunters). The monopoly in this niche secured Allianz annual revenues of about 500,000 marks.[61]

Finally, it is important to look at how Allianz handled its charitable contributions, since such contributions were an instrument used to influence the company's relationship to state and party. Here, the most spectacular event is the controversial pledge described above that Schmitt supposedly gave in 1931. There are no known receipts that could be checked to prove that monies were actually paid in any sizable amount. As soon as the National Socialists had come to power, their desire for money was almost impossible to channel. A phase of open exploitation ensued in which businesses were confronted with money demands from multiple National Socialist organizations and actors who seldom asked for donations, but rather more often demanded money as protection from harassment, or simply blackmailed the money outright. And so business representatives hoped for some assistance and arguments against "the numerous and exploitative demands for charitable contributions from regional directors, SA gangs and district group leaders and town group leaders of the National Socialist Party," when Gustav Krupp took over the leadership of the Industrial Committee (Industrieausschuss) in June 1933. Krupp set up the Adolf Hitler Donation of the German Business Community, an obligatory donation from German businesses.[62] The donation could be traced back to an initiative of Krupp's, when he was the chairman of the Reich Association of German Industry, to collect money from members of the association to support the Nazi Party and other conservative, right-wing parties for the German parliamentary elections in March 1933. The Adolf Hitler Donation of the German Business Community now became an institution: members of the industry association and the employers' associations had to make annual contributions that flowed exclusively to the Nazi Party and sometimes directly to Hitler for his personal expenses. The administration of the Hitler Donation (which already brought in RM 20 million in 1935) documented the payments by issuing donation certificates. During the meeting of the Präsidialausschuss des Reichsverbands der Privatversicherung (Presidential Committee of the Reich Association for Private Insurance) in September 1933, Eduard Hilgard explained that Allianz should use this certificate to refuse to make other contributions to the SS; Hilgard recommended that the other members do the same as an example.[63] At about the same time, starting in the autumn of 1933, the government began to force companies to contribute to the Winterhilfswerk (Winter Help Charity Fund, WHV). Money was collected in part by means of door-to-door or streetcorner sites, and in part by means of set contributions from companies and employees, who had it deducted from their pay and transferred to the WHV. In the collection campaign of 1933/34, RM 350 million was collected in Germany.[64] The sources do not provide any details about Allianz's charity contributions because individual contributions were only certified in cumulative sums. According to these figures, the concern paid a total of RM 600,000 for "national donations" in 1937. In the following year, Allianz paid the Adolf Hitler Donation, the WHV, the Nationalsozialistische Volkswohlfahrt (National Socialist People's Welfare Organization), the Reichsluftschutzbund (State Air Protection Corps) and various party organizations a total of RM 620,000. The amounts increased until 1943 when the last figures were compiled and had reached RM 914,000.[65]

Allianz ad for occupational liability insurance for members of special occupational groups and for private individuals to whom courts had transferred official duties.

Allianz, its Jewish Employees and Clients, and the Anti-Semitic Policies of the National Socialist Regime

James Freudenburg and Maximilian Eichbaum are two of the few figures from the circle of Jewish employees at Allianz whose lives and careers can be reconstructed in some detail.[66] This is because both of them made it to the levels of top management in the course of their careers and were thus well known. Their fates, however, differed radically.

Freudenburg was a jurist who came from Braunschweig and began working at the Wilhelma in Magdeburg. He came to Allianz in 1919 and in 1925, at age 50, he was appointed director of the Frankfurt branch. After the collapse of Favag in 1929, he also joined the board of directors of Neufag (Neue Frankfurter), which Allianz had recently founded. The National Socialists had hardly been in power for three months, when suddenly everything changed for him. Overnight he had become a burden to his longtime coworkers. On April 21, 1933, Robert Röse complained in a letter to Paul Gehrke (both of whom were also members of the board of directors of Neufag): "As a result of the political upheaval, we have had to repeatedly defend ourselves against the objection that we side with the Jews. The loss of the youth care

contract (Jugendpflege-Vertrag) is […] likely also due to the fact that someone claimed that our company was influenced by Jews. Unfortunately, since
I was not informed of these objections earlier, I was not able to take a stand
against this in time." For this same reason, Röse continued, another large insurance contract with the public schools in the state of Hesse was almost
lost. He added meaningfully, "It will interest you to know in this context that
Dr. Freudenburg has formally resigned from the board of directors of our
company."[67] At the end of 1934, Freudenburg then asked Hans Heß, the
chairman of the board of directors of Allianz, to be released from his contract as head of the Frankfurt branch of Allianz. Heß and Georg König
thanked him in a personal letter for his services and expressed their deep
appreciation for his accomplishments. His salary was paid until the end of
the regular contract and open retirement questions were generously resolved. On December 11, 1934, Freudenburg, known for his objective and rational style, seemed deeply moved in words addressed to Hans Heß: "With
your proposals in your correspondence of December 3, I herewith agree
[…] At the same time I would like to thank you for your appreciative words
and the trust that you have shown in me for so many years. With a heavy
heart I depart from your employment. I have been an Allianz-Man with all
my soul and will remain one until the day I die."[68]

However, Freudenburg was only temporarily out of the line of fire of anti-Semitic attacks. The National Socialist factory cell at Allianz did not forget
him. The party functionaries wanted to ruin him financially. The party's regional chairman (Gauobmann), Willy Becker, intervened in 1939, informed
Paul Lux, who had quickly climbed the career ladder to become a member of
Allianz's board of directors and who would soon be considered as a candidate for the post of future chairman of the board, and requested that the retirement payments to Freudenburg and all Jewish retirees be stopped. Becker
referred to the verdict of the Reich Court on retirement income promises to
non-Aryans made in July 1939. Lux and Alfred Wiedemann, the director-general of Neufag, refused to give in. Following discussions Becker was persuaded to let the matter lie.[69] Allianz continued to make payments to
Freudenburg, who, however, sensing worse to come, had his retirement
claims transferred to his non-Jewish wife Erika. The married couple continued to live in Frankfurt, where their living conditions slowly deteriorated.
In 1943, authorities ordered the 67-year-old Freudenburg to be at the disposal
of the city street cleaning company as a forced laborer. Freudenburg's bank
accounts had already been frozen by the authorities and his wife only had
limited access. On June 11, she appeared before Favag administrators where

James Freudenburg and his wife Erika in Marienbad (1927 or 1929).

she regularly submitted health care bills; on this occasion, she explained what had happened to the official, who made the following note: "At this visit, I asked her how Dr. Freudenburg had been doing and learned that he had been summoned to appear before the Gestapo the previous week and had not returned. Mrs. Freudenburg did not know more of her husband's whereabouts nor could she find out more when she talked with the Gestapo." Erika Freudenburg never saw her husband again. On January 22, 1944, she received a form letter of three lines from the Reichsvereinigung der Juden in Deutschland (Reich League of Jews in Germany) stating that James Freudenburg had died on January 10, 1944, in Auschwitz of "debilitas corporis et senilis enteritis acuta." The document exemplifies the criminal strategy with which the Nazi mass murderers covered up the murdering of their victims in the death camps by arbitrarily choosing a cause of death from a medical dictionary and filling it in in the death certificates. Erika Freudenburg then left Frankfurt, had to leave her parents' bombed-out house in Dresden in February 1945 as well, moved temporarily to Leitmeritz and returned finally in 1946 to Frankfurt, where she died at the end of the 1950s.[70]

Like Freudenburg, Maximilian Eichbaum (1881–1958) was closely knit with Allianz as well as with his fatherland.[71] Eichbaum, his wife Erna, and their three children Eva, Heinrich Alexander, and Ursula escaped the Nazis, because they were able to leave Germany at the right time thanks to receiving much assistance. Eichbaum, who came from Mainz and was a jurist like

3. 1933–1948 Allianz: The Nazi Years and Reconstruction

Freudenburg, joined the board of directors of the Wilhelma insurance company in Magdeburg in 1923, which was still independent then; after the takeover by Allianz, he became the director of the branch in Magdeburg and then joined Allianz's board of directors in 1930, where he was able to remain until autumn 1935. He wrote down his recollections of this period in 1947 in a moving letter to his old friend Hans Heß, whom he felt provided the decisive support in making his emigration successful. Eichbaum wrote to him on June 28 from Johannesburg: "It has now been almost 38 years since I came to Magdeburg as an assessor and we first encountered each other, and next year it will have been a quarter of a century of growing closer and closer professionally – at Allianz – and in our personal friendship. When the Third Reich came some of my earlier friends turned against me and the majority of them withdrew from me – I don't blame them: they would have been the next ones themselves, and it had become impractical, reckless and even dangerous to go around with non-Aryans, to associate with them or even to openly defend them. Only a few have passed this acid test of friendship and character, and no one had stood up for me more openly, strongly, or sacrificed more for me than Hans Hess. On April 3, 1936, you wrote to my wife, 'It is for me absolutely natural that I will maintain my friendship with your entire family until death,' and you have kept your word to this very day. You know how I suffered, spiritually, in Germany from 1933 until 1937 because you were the one I could pour out my heart to, and whose support, presence and actions helped and healed [me]. I was proud that I could keep my position on the board at Allianz until autumn – without you it would not have been possible. My wife and I will never forget how you and your lovely wife came to us in Magdeburg in August 1935, in order to settle my unavoidable resignation and to help me as a human being and professionally. Then you more or less plowed the way for us to come here – what would have become of us otherwise! Even over here the wave of hate and persecution sprayed us; without fail and without fear of repercussions or disadvantage you shielded me again and again. Even during the war, I now and again felt you secretly gripping my hand in friendship. What you have done for us we cannot repay and words are too poor to express our feelings of gratitude."[72] When Eichbaum in 1935 had to give up his board position, he switched temporarily to the head office in Berlin. The board also discussed the idea of sending him to Vienna, where Allianz and Munich Re were planning to get involved in the Allgemeine Versicherungsgesellschaft Phönix (General Insurance Company Phoenix), which, however, had not yet materialized. The last life-saving possibility presented itself in 1937 when Eichbaum was able to transfer to Johannesburg and become Allianz's representative for the South African Liberal Insurance Company, a subsidiary that Allianz had taken on a few years earlier. He and his family were able to acquire British citizenship in South Africa. Eichbaum kept his post in Johannesburg even as Nazi smear-sheets like Der Stürmer and Das Schwarze Korps launched an anti-Semitic campaign against Eichbaum as a person and also publicly attacked Allianz for continuing to employ him. He was finally laid off in 1943 after he had been declared an "enemy alien" due to the war.

There are no reliable figures for the number of Allianz employees who were persecuted for political or anti-Semitic reasons.[73] Information on some individual employees, however, is available. For example, the above-mentioned SS paper, Das Schwarze Korps, published an article on November 19, 1936, entitled "Residences for elderly fat cats," which pilloried five persons who had found a safe harbor at Allianz in Frankfurt, although there ought not to have been a place for them in the National Socialist people's community anymore. The author denounced Gerhard Heiland, who in 1933 was forced out of his post as the chief of the Leipzig criminal investigation department and who was later appointed a justice on postwar Germany's highest court, the Federal Constitutional Court; in 1934 he had found employment with Allianz where he could "hibernate" during the Nazi period. It was similar with jurist Rudolph de Guehery, who was dismissed in 1933 from his post as ministerial counselor in the Saxon Economics Ministry on account of his many years of involvement in a liberal party. Neufag had hired him in 1933 and named him the director of its industrial department in Leipzig. Paul Macher was hired by Neufag as an agent after his release from a concentration camp where the Nazis had taken him in 1934 for his activities in the Social Democratic Party (SPD) and in the Reichsbanner organization, which was formed in the Weimar era to defend parliamentary democracy from extremism. Finally, the article hounded two Jewish sales agents who still worked for Allianz in some capacity: Martin Bruck, who was the branch director for Neufag in Breslau, and Joseph Rittberg, who was an assessor for Neufag in Dresden. There is at least a chronological relation between the public pressure generated by this publication and the 1936 dismissal at Neufag of several employees, of whom only the names are known. The list of dismissed employees includes Hedwig Merkel, Ilse Friedländer, and Willi Baer with "Jewess" or "Jew" next to their names. Internally, the head of Neufag, Alfred Wiedemann, announced in summer 1937 that Allianz would not dismiss Jewish sales agents for economic reasons "so long as all the operating corporations in Germany have not fully realized the Aryan principle."[74] Barely a year had passed, before these words had lost their effect: Hans Grünebaum, owner of an Allianz

Hugo Kettner, director of the Frankfurt branch, had to leave the company around New Year 1936 because his wife was Jewish. In 1945, the military government appointed him head of Frankfurter Versicherungs-AG.

agency in Frankfurt experienced this first hand. First, anti-Semitic newspaper articles appeared in which he was named, and then the regional directorate (Gauleitung) of the Nazi Party intervened at Allianz. In 1938, Allianz gave up the fight and terminated the contract with their former business partner. Hans Heß personally negotiated with Hans Grünebaum over the finances of his release. He received a payment of RM 35,000 and emigrated to the U.S.

Shortly after the Nazi government had announced the Nuremberg Laws at the Nazi Party Congress in 1935, which demoted all Jewish Germans to second-class citizens, the long-standing director of Allianz in Frankfurt, Hugo Kettner, at the age of 58, was forced to retire because he was married to a Jewish woman. Three years later, the Allianz Leben director in Frankfurt, Hans Zankl, was likewise forced into early retirement on the same grounds.

It was again a member of the company's Nazi Party organization, in this case Gottfried Bünger, the head man at the Cologne branch, who shortly after the start of World War II asked Clemens Maiholzer how many Jewish members of the retirement fund received retirement benefits. Maiholzer, the director of the fund, made the following comment in response: "At present, we have neither in the company nor at the retirement fund a list containing information about one's religious confession. Names alone are not always clear."[75] But that quickly changed. The list of Jewish retirees that was then compiled identified a total of eleven persons by name. Anton Roßmann, a radical anti-Semite and Nazi Party-head of the company in Munich, had already written a letter to his boss, the director-general of the Bayerische Versicherungsbank

(BVB), Wilhelm Arendts, requesting that he please finally strike "the retirement payments of the named Jews," which he then listed. He referred to the above-mentioned judgment of the Reich Court (Reichsgericht) on retirement claims from Jewish members of the retirement fund that he had read about in the Nazi Party paper Der Angriff and now reasoned: "In these times especially, it is hard to understand how exactly those elements that are morally part of the cause of this war forced on Germany can receive benefits from our people's assets. The doubtlessly Jewish-willed assassination attempt on our leader (meaning Georg Elser's attempted bomb attack on Hitler on November 8 in [Munich's] Bürgerbräukeller) should remind us that it is necessary to eliminate all courtesy and any remaining hesitancy."[76] This argumentation seemed too crude for the company director in Berlin, Paul Lux. Roßmann's conclusions lacked any grounds, he declared in a letter to his colleague Arendts in Munich. The members had paid their dues to the fund in the correct manner and now had a right to receive the benefits as agreed upon. Moreover, Arendts would be interested to know that the board of the retirement fund had declared on October 31, 1939, the following: "The board of directors declares itself in agreement that the matter should be put off until legislative action can be taken or until the end of the war; the board, however, in principle argues for the exclusion of Jewish retirees."[77] Along with the 11 Jewish members who belonged to Allianz's retirement fund at the turn of the year 1939/1940, a handwritten document from the same period lists a total of 19 other Jewish persons. These persons received as retirees or as their widows or widowers monetary payments from Allianz that did not stem from the Allianz pension fund (AVK) but from other retirement arrangements. When Nazi Germany began to plunder the assets of the Jewish population with increasing radicalism in 1938, the finance agencies took a closer look at Allianz's Jewish retirees. After the Night of Broken Glass on November 9, 1938, the officials partially froze their accounts or deducted monies directly from the retirement payments, as in the cases of Franz Heymann and Wilhelm Lewes in Munich, Gertrud Salomon and Johanna Mietzel in Berlin, and Fanny Nagel from Dortmund. In these cases, the finance agencies instructed the retirement fund managers to pay the benefits to the chief finance president until the person was reported dead. The 11th Decree of the Reich Citizenship Law, passed in November 1941 by the Reich government to expropriate the assets and goods of deported and emigrated Jewish citizens, mandated in Paragraph 10 that all retirement benefit entitlements should cease the moment they lost or gave up their citizenship. The law also declared that all Jewish citizens whose usual residence was or had been moved abroad would lose their citizenship.[78]

Office building of the Reich Aviation Ministry headed by Hermann Göring. A meeting took place here on November 12, 1938, three days after the Night of Broken Glass, at which top state and party representatives discussed serious measures for exploiting the Jewish population. Eduard Hilgard gave a presentation at the meeting as the head of the Reich Group for Insurance.

The attacks on the Jewish population reached a new dimension in 1938. During the course of the year, the German state passed 300 laws, decrees, declarations and clauses that increasingly restricted the rights and freedoms of those who were discriminated against, and destroyed the foundation of their material existence. On the Night of Broken Glass, the Nazi Party and government authorities let loose their functionaries and thugs to murder, steal, burn and plunder the Jewish population and their property – not counting the annexed Austria, there were at the time still around 235,000 Jewish citizens in Germany. In 1933, there had been around 500,000 Jews living in Germany.[79] The pogrom went on for several days in some places: at least 400 people died in the first night, whilst an unknown number of people died afterwards in prisons or in the concentration camps (Dachau, Buchenwald, Sachsenhausen), where almost 30,000 Jewish men were taken. Others took their own lives in despair. Around 1,400 synagogues and prayer halls were vandalized or destroyed, around 7,500 shops plundered. Joseph Goebbels, who had given the go ahead in a speech in Munich's old city hall on the evening of November 9, noted the following in his diary: "The Führer wants to turn to very sharp measures against the Jews. They will have to clean up their shops themselves. Insurance will pay for nothing. Then the Führer wants to slowly expropriate the Jewish businesses and give the owners paper documents that we can devalue any time."[80]

The Reich Propaganda Minister's diary entry foreshadowed much of what would transpire in the next days and months and what for Allianz and some other insurers would become a critical, defining situation and a moral challenge that they did not prove to be up to. Just one day after the Night of Broken Glass, Eduard Hilgard, in his function as the director of the Reich Group for Insurance, addressed a letter to all of the sections of the Business Group Private Insurance in which he called for a coordinated and unified response on the part of all insurers to the regulation of the pogrom damage and noted among other things the following: "It is not possible at this time either to even roughly estimate the true size of the damage or to conclude whether the damage qualifies for compensation under the insurance conditions." This became the line of argumentation that would be played out in the course of tedious negotiations on who and what was to be compensated and to what extent. The next morning, the office of Hermann Göring, who at this time was the dominant politician for economic policy in Nazi Germany, ordered Eduard Hilgard to appear at a meeting in Göring's office in the Reich Aviation Ministry. When he arrived there, Hilgard was led into a conference room where the leading officials of numerous ministries, the police and the SS, including Reinhard Heydrich, the director of the Reich Security Main Office, and Kurt Daluege, the director of the uniformed police, sat alongside Göring and Goebbels. In all, almost 100 people were assembled.

Those present at the meeting discussed a series of drastic measures that the government then put into legislative form within the shortest time possible. They were aiming for a complete and final elimination of Jewish citizens from the world of trade, commerce and public life as well as for the expropriation of their ownership of businesses, properties, valuables and stocks and bonds. Ultimately, the persecuted were forced to pay the so-called Jewish Atonement Tax amounting to the horrendous sum of 1 billion marks. The damage of the Night of Broken Glass, according to one of the conclusions drawn at the meeting, had to be paid by the victims. The Decree for the Restoration of the Appearance of the Streets around Jewish Enterprises (Verordnung zur Wiederherstellung des Straßenbildes) was passed on the same day and forced Jewish owners of small businesses and apartment buildings to pay the repair costs themselves and concluded with the following statement –

which was very important for the insurers: "Insurance claims from Jews of German nationality will be confiscated in favor of the German Reich."[81] Göring had summoned Hilgard to appear at the meeting because he hoped to gather information from him about whether foreign currency revenues could be generated for the state through the reinsurance contracts with foreign insurance companies. The claims of the insured Jews, Göring announced, would pose no problem for the insurance industry since he could nullify them by decree. Hilgard did not see much hope of raising foreign currency and instead explained: "This is the way things are, there are three types of insurance we have to deal with, and in fact it doesn't relate to riot insurance or tumult insurance, but rather to regular fire insurance, regular glass insurance and to regular burglary and theft insurance. The insured [...] are partly Jews, partly Aryan. In the case of fire insurance, which makes up the largest part, we are dealing with mostly Jews. With the warehouses, the owners, the Jews, must assume the damage; with the synagogues, naturally also, aside from the damage to the neighbors that was caused as the fires grew out of control." Hilgard's statements, only partially documented, lead one to conclude that he had hoped to free the insurance companies from paying for the damage. In any case, however, Hilgard had a different solution in mind than the one Göring had initially proposed that would utilize his power to make a ministerial decree. Hilgard apparently favored a solution that would somewhat preserve the insurance industry's integrity: the companies would pay and therefore demonstrate that they stood by the contracts concluded with Jewish customers. The Nazi government would then confiscate the paid sums and return the money to the insurance companies in a way to be determined in the future.

Even if this wish was never realized, Hilgard and state officials in the Reich Economics and Justice Ministries who were loyal to him did succeed during the long and difficult negotiations in helping the insurance companies to avoid paying large amounts.

Ultimately, the Nazi government directed its anti-Semitic logic in the following manner: all claims of non-Jewish insured parties as well as those of Jews with non-German citizenship had to be paid. The latter was a concession to the insurance industry to prevent its image suffering in the international markets. On the other hand, the state nullified the claims of Jewish customers who were German citizens and appropriated them for its own purposes. Hilgard brought Hans Goudefroy into the negotiations to act as the legal expert. They argued that it would be too much to ask the community of insured persons to pay for the repair of property damage incurred on the Night of Broken Glass through their premium payments. After all, the official state view was that the Jewish population had provoked the pogrom and that therefore they also had to pay for the damage. Using this type of argument, Hilgard entered into negotiations with state offices that finally ended in October 1939. Total property insurance damage was estimated at around RM 50 million, of which the lion's share of roughly RM 46 million was attributed to Jewish insured clients with German citizenship. This sum was negotiated since the state had confiscated this amount and could have done as it pleased with it.

During the course of the long and complicated negotiations, in which many political considerations and the interests of the insurers – but never the interests of the clients who actually suffered damage – were discussed, the amount to be paid to the state was first reduced to RM 23 million (January 1939), then to RM 6.5 million and finally to RM 1.5 million (July 1939). On October 14, 1939, the Reich Group for Insurance actually did transfer RM 1.3 million to the state treasury.[82]

In his study on the history of Allianz in the Nazi period, Gerald Feldman documented how the directors of Isar-Lebensversicherung (ISAR Life Insurance) petitioned the insurance supervisory agency and the Reich Economics Ministry one week after the Night of Broken Glass and formally requested that they be allowed to withhold from their Jewish customers the payment of the surrender value of their canceled life insurance policies.[83] Isar was founded in 1936 by several German and Swiss primary insurers and reinsurance companies in order to take over and secure the German assets of the Viennese Life Insurance Company Phoenix, which had collapsed. Lebensphönix (Phoenix Life) had been one of the largest life insurers in Europe. Its spectacular collapse, the creation of ÖVAG to take up its portfolio in Austria, and coverage of its clients' claims were hot topics across Europe and touched on the question of the credibility of the whole insurance business.[84] Paul Riebesell and Max Eckert, the directors of Isar, saw themselves as managers of a rescue operation that was now in peril. Their success was "threatened by the events of the last days, since the insurance portfolio of Isar was comprised to a large extent, estimated at as much as 20 to 25 percent, by non-Aryans. Although the number of surrender requests at Isar increased greatly in the last few years, now there are so many of them that the worst fears for the future existence of our company seem to be coming true."[85] They requested that a law be passed that allowed them to refuse to pay the cash surrender value, but to offer instead that they be exchanged for premium free insurance policies. Although the authorities refused Isar's request, the procedure illuminates a further field of conflict between the insurers, the National Socialist state and insured Jewish customers.

The marginalization and plundering and finally the deportation to the death camps affected the treatment of the life insurance policies of Jewish customers. According to Feldman's research, it is important to differentiate between two forms of expropriation of the assets of insured Jewish customers. The Jewish customers lost the vast majority of their life insurance capital through indirect expropriation. By contrast, direct expropriation first gained significance when the deportations began in autumn 1941.

A growing number of Jewish life insurance customers experienced indirect expropriation because they had grown poorer from 1933 and felt forced to liquidate their life insurance assets in order to sustain themselves or to finance the costs of their planned emigration out of Germany. They let their current life insurance policy either be reduced to zero benefits or canceled the policy prematurely. Since, in life insurance contracts, the calculations of premiums and benefits of both parties are made under the premise that the agreed upon life of the contract – 20 years was the usual period – be fulfilled, the value of the life insurance policy, and thus the originally hoped for gains decreased when the policy ended before this date, both for the customer and for the insurance company. When the policy was sold, the insurer usually per contract only paid the cash surrender value, which was derived through some complicated calculations.

From 1938, Allianz also felt how the radicalization of the anti-Semitic policies affected their Jewish customers. The value of the surrendered life insurance contracts grew from almost RM 14 million in 1937 to more than double that amount, RM 39 million, in 1939.[86] Absolute figures for the portfolio of policies for Jewish clients cannot be determined, since the sources usually contain no clear information that leads to direct conclusions concerning the insured's religious confession nor whether the Nazi state classified a specific insured party as a Jew according to the racial criteria established in 1935. Allianz holds documents on almost 2 million historical life insurance contracts, the majority of which comprised of the typically rather sparse files for industrial life insurance policies for less than RM 2,000. At Allianz Leben, the average life insurance sum of an industrial life policy amounted to RM 1,025. To nonetheless gain information concerning the situation of its Jewish customers, Allianz decided in 1997 to allow auditors to investigate in detail a sample of almost 70,000 policies. They uncovered around 6,300 policies that had probably belonged to Jewish customers. The insured sum of these ordinary life insurance policies amounted on average to around RM 15,000. They discovered also that the number of existing policies only slightly decreased through 1937. Only in 1938 did the number of policies sink dramatically, so much so that in 1939 there were only 800 policies remaining. Another sample of policies belonging to Allianz Leben – in other words, excluding the policies belonging to Frankfurter Leben, which was taken over in 1929 and involved more Jewish clients – shows that up to 1940 more than 90 percent of these policies were canceled by the owners themselves.[87] They thus exchanged their existing insurance contracts for hard cash, which they needed more urgently since the Night of Broken Glass to pay various special expenses like the Reich Flight Tax, which they were forced to pay to emigrate, and to make their contributions to the Jewish Atonement Tax.

A Berlin attorney requested in a letter from October 28, 1938, that Allianz calculate the cash surrender value of his then existing life insurance policy for RM 50,000 that he had owned for 14 years. He was now, he wrote, like all Jewish lawyers without a license since these had been revoked and thus unable to estimate whether he could in the future afford the premium payments. Now, he would like to cancel the contract and requested that the cash surrender value be transferred to a blocked account "because I need the money for the atonement tax on the Jews."[88]

In contrast to this indirect sort of expropriation, the state engaged in direct expropriation in the form of the Gestapo or the fiscal administration and canceled the insurance contracts. The Nazi dictatorship had already – on July 14, 1933 – created the legal basis for this in the Law for the Repeal of Nationalization and Recognition of German Citizenship as well as in the Law for the Seizure of Assets of Enemies of the People and the State of July 14, 1933.[89] Both laws threatened politically critical persons and naturalized Jewish immigrants from Eastern Europe who had come to Germany after the fall of the German Empire in November 1918 with the potential loss of their German citizenship. In addition, these laws allowed government offices to seize and confiscate their assets. The Gestapo, for instance, informed Allianz in spring 1939 that the citizenship of an attorney from Munich who had emigrated to Australia had been revoked. His assets were being seized, which is why Allianz had to pay the cash surrender value to the respective tax office in Berlin. Such and similar cases multiplied as the regime expatriated ever more Jewish citizens. Their names were published regularly in the Reichsanzeiger, the regime's national bulletin. Until the start of the war, the Business Group Private Insurance passed the names on via newsletter to the insurance companies, which then checked whether the named persons were to be found in their records and informed the appropriate authorities. The life insurance policies of Jewish customers that still existed after 1940 were then – at least the majority of them – canceled at the request of govern-

Life insurance policy of a Jewish Allianz client with an insured sum of RM 5,000. The policy was made inactive (no further payments) in 1935. The client emigrated to Beirut. In accordance with the 11th Decree of the Reich Citizenship Law, Allianz Leben registered the policy with the tax authority, which did not, however, cancel the policy. The policy was finally paid out to its owner in 1952.

ment authorities. A new legislative basis was established for this on November 25, 1941, when the above-mentioned 11th Decree of the Reich Citizenship Law was passed. With this legislation, the government revoked the German citizenship of all Jewish-Germans living abroad and expropriated everything they owned, including their insurance policies. Hidden behind the phrase usual residency abroad was the fact that for most Jews at that time this included deportation to a concentration camp or a ghetto outside the borders of Germany. The decree was thus already a component of the organization of the genocide on the Jews. The 13th Decree of the Reich Citizenship Law that became effective on July 1, 1943, made the expropriation complete with the terse announcement: "After the death of a Jew his wealth is forfeited to the Reich."[90] Banks and insurance companies were already obligated in accordance with the Eleventh Decree to check whether their clients residing abroad were Jewish. How compliant Allianz was in this obligation can only be ascertained in individual cases. In many cases the deportees themselves had to transfer their life insurance policies in writing to the Reich League of Jews. The Nazi agencies abused this institution – whose staff acted under existential duress – to expropriate the assets of the deported

quickly and unbureaucratically. And sometimes, Allianz was spared the task of searching for their expatriated customers. For instance, in April 1942 they sent a premium payment invoice for a life insurance policy to the address of a textile factory owner in Munich who had last paid his premiums in 1940. His lawyer, who was only allowed to represent Jewish clients at that point and therefore was forced to call himself a consultant, clarified the matter for Allianz: "I have to inform you that Mr. Israel G. was allocated to the deportation from Munich on November 20, 1941, in a deportation train; whereupon his assets are declared as forfeited to the German Reich."[91] Now, Allianz proceeded as the decree prescribed. The chief finance president in Munich canceled the policy and Allianz paid the cash surrender value of RM 2,820.10 on August 7, 1942, to the treasury. Mr. G. was deported to Kaunas and was murdered there on November 25, 1941. He was 44 years old.[92]

War, Peace, Reconstruction

In 1939, Allianz was full of optimism: it built, grew and posted more profits than ever before. In Berlin, the experienced architect duo Karl Wach and Heinrich Rosskotten, who had built Allianz's branch office building in Cologne in the style of the New Objectivity (Neue Sachlichkeit) in 1933, guided the con-

New construction projects: on Mohrenstraße in central Berlin a monumental administrative building was constructed for Allianz Leben; the new branch office in Greater Berlin was to be located on the Runder Platz that was to be laid out not far from Potsdamer Platz (left). The project was halted after the beginning of the war.

struction of two monumental projects embracing the Nazi mania for the gigantic. Within the framework of Albert Speer's plans to redesign Berlin, the duo created a new head office building that was to take up an entire street block itself for Allianz Leben. In addition, close to Potsdamer Platz an entirely new neighborhood was planned around the spacious Runder Platz that was to be built.[93] For Allianz's Greater Berlin branch, an office building containing 220,000 cubic meters was to be erected here.

The Allianz newspaper reported in richly illustrated articles about how Allianz was now growing in areas that had been foreign lands shortly before: photos showed images from Austria where Allianz together with Munich Re forced the takeover of the Allgemeine Versicherungs-Gesellschaft Phönix as well as its shareholders the Generali and Creditanstalt and in 1939 changed them into Wiener Allianz (Viennese Allianz). It also printed maps of the annexed Sudetenland, where Allianz took over the portfolios of the Prague-based Slavia-Versicherung in 1939. And finally, it printed reports on the occupied region that Nazi Germany had established called the Protectorate of Bohemia and Moravia.[94] Eduard Hilgard described the principle behind this growth in 1940 in a newspaper article, borrowing the well-known principle from colonial history that "trade follows the flag."[95] The September 1939 issue of the Allianz newspaper reported enthusiastically in word and image about the "magic of Danzig" where the German Army had just invaded; the October issue was covered by a map of Poland, which Germany had just attacked, thus setting off World War II. The issue only contained eight pages, all of which were devoted to the themes of insurance and war, and announced besides, under the headline "For the last time …," that the newspaper would not be allowed to appear during the war, since "the usage of newsprint should be reduced to a minimum." The next issue appeared exactly ten years later in October 1949.

And the figures for Allianz's 49th year of business – the preparations for the 50th anniversary were already almost completed – showed solid business development: with premium revenues at almost RM 220 million, reserves standing at almost RM 200 million, and a total (including all Allianz concern branches) insurance portfolio of RM 5.1 billion, Allianz had reached record heights. Only profits stagnated, which politically at least was not a bad thing, as it could then be argued that Allianz had subordinated its interest in profit to the good of the community of the insured and the state.[96]

The Nazi regime had an ambiguous relationship to private property, to private industry and to the value and principles of a capitalistic, profit-driven management of business. Since 1936, National Socialist economic policy had aimed to arm Germany to make it ready for war as quickly as possible and to make the country as autarkic and independent of the import of major raw materials as possible. Following an argument with Hermann Göring, who as the appointee for the four-year plan implemented the guidelines of these policies, Hjalmar Schacht resigned from his post as Economics Minister, which he had taken over from Kurt Schmitt in 1935. For one thing, he was upset because Hitler gave the inexperienced Göring free reign in matters of economic policy so that the economics ministry grew more marginalized; and secondly, he found the autarky strategy to be irrational, naive and inflationary. In a letter to Göring in the summer of 1937, he attempted to explain to Göring that lasting economic results could not be produced by political will and an increase in money supply alone, adding: "You can neither bake bread nor cast cannons out of paper."[97] Economic policy was directed from above and left little doubt that businesses in Nazi Germany were expected to follow the directives of politics. The regime did not refrain from using forceful methods to effect its desires. In a totalitarian state, however, it was often enough to merely remind businesses that force was a possibility. In actuality, forceful measures were rarely undertaken, since often "even National Socialist economic policy-makers recognized that private businessmen who cooperated voluntarily managed their companies generally more efficiently than those just taking orders."[98] The longer the arguments concerning nationalization of the insurance business and the role of the publicly chartered companies lasted, the more convinced Hilgard and the supporters of private insurance became that their room for negotiations was limited and that they needed to prepare to defend their businesses. In addition, they maintained their political contacts to Göring and the Nazi Party, utilized the politically correct rhetoric of the Third Reich, and emphasized as much as possible their loyalty to the regime.[99]

It was clear to the top management of Allianz how important it was to protect the company from populist accusations – for instance, that because of the size of the concern, it was unwieldy, inefficient, and wasted its customers' money.[100] However, those in charge had fundamentally restructured Allianz in the period of mergers for such political and also business management reasons. Even in peacetime, ten years after the last large merger of the Favag companies and parallel to expansion in Austria and in the annexed Sudetenland, Allianz had begun to restructure in order to become simpler, more efficient and less expensive. As a largely visible sign of this, the boards in 1940 decided to return to the more concise original name of the concern – Allianz – and to drop the additional names pointing to the Stuttgart companies taken on after the merger of 1927. The board of directors also asked the shareholders to approve a plan that would restructure the hierarchy of the concern. Under the title of Frankfurter Versicherungs-AG (Frankfurt Insurance Corporation), Allianz grouped together all the companies it had founded in 1929 in the course of the Favag scandal or taken over together with Munich Re (Neue Frankfurter, Hammonia, Providentia) and integrated this group along with the Wiener Allianz into the concern. Karlsruher Leben and Berlinische Leben thereafter formed an interest group with the Frankfurter.

The second large project of the year dealt with Allianz's relations to Munich Re, which was now, after the departure of Wilhelm Kißkalt in 1938, headed by Kurt Schmitt. Since 1921, when the last association agreement with Munich Re (formulated by Kißkalt and signed by Kurt Schmitt for Allianz) went into effect, Allianz had not only grown and developed considerably, but had also become more aware of its power and thought more about its independence. "For years now," Schmitt wrote in a file in 1937, "the relationship between Allianz and Munich Re has become problematic, in fact, both financially and also in respect to shareholdings."[101] Although both sides recognized how very much they had profited from their close cooperation, relations still deteriorated. Allianz considered the dependence of Munich Re as a burden and in light of the considerable reinsurance expenses found it inappropriate. Mistrust grew. Secretly, Allianz had been buying up its own shares for years in order to prevent even more shares being "acquired by Munich Re, because it then would [threaten to gain] a shareholding majority,"

Ernst Rasche, a director of Allianz, confided to the Reich Supervisory Office for Insurance.[102] Not only the mistrust but also mutual misunderstandings increased. In a twelve-page letter from April 3, 1938, Hans Heß, trying hard to stay calm, attempted to explain his view of the history of relations between the two enterprises, outlining especially the contributions Allianz had made; the beginning of his letter is revealing: "As I read through your remarks the first time, I was almost shocked that we could have such different viewpoints between us about these contexts." In the subsequent pages he worked through the history of the jointly completed takeovers and "set straight" who should really receive the praise.[103]

Schmitt sent a first draft of a new association agreement to Heß on April 23, 1940. During the following months a contract was worked out that was then signed on November 11, 1940, by Hans Heß, Eduard Hilgard, Paul Lux, Rudolf Schloeßmann and Hans Goudefroy for Allianz and by Kurt Schmitt and Alois Alzheimer for Munich Re. The signatories recalled their common roots, invoked the tried and trusted partnership and renewed the bonds of their cooperation for another 50 years. The document contains conditions pertaining to the mutual and equal contribution of capital up to a maximum of 30 percent and to mandatory personnel ties – the chairmen of the board of directors of both companies had to belong, alongside three other board members, to the other partner's supervisory board and a new shared council to the board of directors was created. Other conditions listed in the document included the fact that each company had to contribute 50 percent of the capital to the establishment of new firms and takeovers and that Munich Re had to participate in Allianz's domestic and foreign business, owning 30 to 50 percent of the shares. It also contained rules for reinsurance rates, internal accounting procedures and for arbitration proceedings in cases of conflict. This contract placed the partnership on a new foundation. Wilhelm Kißkalt, during Munich Re's supervisory board meeting in April 1940, expressed his relief that his original concerns that the company would lose its independence by requiring the principle of equality in rights to cross-holdings were, in fact, unfounded. In relation to Allianz, Munich Re would change, in the words of the minutes, "from mother to sister."[104]

When, in 1940, Allianz finally commemorated its 50th anniversary, the planned celebrations for the employees were canceled. The head office organized a celebration in Berlin in which the former employees who were drafted to serve in the German Army were briefly honored, a two-volume historical study appeared, a one-hour film about the history of Allianz was presented, and the employees received a bonus. The war presented Allianz with of course completely new problems, but the economic development of the business, contrary to the expectation that the special risks of war activities would destroy the foundation of insurance activities, was at first surprisingly good. Total premium revenues grew continuously up to 1943, only briefly interrupted by a short drop in the first year of the war in 1940. Decreases due to the war seen in transportation insurance, in liability insurance and above all in automobile insurance, which was the booming insurance branch in the 1930s, were balanced by increasing revenues in fire insurance, burglary and theft insurance and machine insurance. Allianz clearly profited from the war economy: industries important to the war experienced a boom; their insurance needs increased as well. Allianz Leben, especially, reported amazing figures. Its premium revenues climbed from 1939 to 1942 by around 35 percent, the number of newly signed life insurance policies rose by around 30 percent even though the price of the premiums rose by 3 percent and the guaranteed interest rate was reduced to 3 percent. A growing number of war fatalities, military as well as civilian, caused the payments to customers to climb from RM 77 million to RM 148 million. For the fiscal year 1943, Allianz recorded its highest pure profit in its history, RM 7.7 million.[105]

But not only the war economy drove Allianz's growth. What had only proceeded with difficulty in times of peace proved to be especially dynamic in the war. Max Surner, an important management figure in the foreign department for many years, looking back, gave his personal view of what had happened at that time: "With the start of the war the situation changed fundamentally. At first there was a period of stagnation, since aside from a few neutral countries, relations to our foreign business friends were interrupted. With the success of the German war machine, foreign operations were shifted from 1940 on to a completely new foundation. The occupation of the neighboring Western European countries made it impossible for British insurance companies, which had had a great deal of trade in the region for decades, to continue to do business. A vacuum arose that the domestic companies were not in a position to fill. From the German side […] measures were undertaken to mobilize the German private insurance industry to fill the void. Allianz played a decisive role in this process."[106] Needless to say, the German insurers who "followed the flag" enjoyed considerable political advantages in comparison to the domestic insurers in the occupied countries. Allianz's activities increased noticeably in these areas. Paul Lux and Hans Goudefroy wrote in November 1942 to Alois Alzheimer that the foreign premium revenues had tripled within a single year by 1941.[107] The board of directors of Allianz and Munich Re were willing to use the opportunities

presented by the military successes of Nazi Germany, even though their ambition sank with the shift in the course of the war after 1942, and the gold-
rush feeling subsided.[108]

Allianz and other German insurers operated less aggressively in their
expansion in the Western European countries – above all, in France, Belgium,
Holland, and Luxembourg – than they did in the East. Munich Re and to a
lesser extent Allianz as well as their Swiss partners Union Rück and Swiss
National had done business with customers in the Western markets for
decades. Hilgard traveled to France in September 1940, where he succeeded
in activating old contacts to guide discussions with the leaders of the French
insurance association and the supervisory authority. It also proved to be
advantageous that Gerd Müller, member of the board of directors at Allianz
Leben, had performed his war duty as a military administrative councilor in
France and had thus gathered some competence in insurance matters so that
he could supply Hilgard with information. At the same time, Kurt Schmitt
was negotiating with the head of the Reich Supervisory Office for Insurance.
Under discussion was the question of the legitimacy of getting assigned trusteeship in the administration of the portfolios that had until then belonged to
foreign insurance companies. The British companies alone had controlled a
market share of almost 50 percent. Allianz succeeded finally in taking over the
portfolios of a total of 18 French and international insurers in Alsace and Lorraine to administer in trust. In addition, Allianz was also busy building up a
management team for France in its own name that would offer almost all
types of property insurance; it also built up its investments in the company La
Préservatrice and indirectly also in the insurers La Cité and La Minerve.[109] In
the end, however, Allianz, like all the other German insurance companies
active in France, was not successful in completely appropriating the assets
thus administered in trust because the negotiations with the French authorities dragged on and were ultimately never concluded. The worse the war progressed for Germany, the more entangled things became in the French market: the amount of damage due to acts of sabotage grew constantly, and French
employees in the companies and in the administrative agencies were increasingly disinclined to work cooperatively with their German occupiers as they
hoped with growing confidence for the defeat of the Germans. In Belgium,
where 16 German companies received a license, and in the Netherlands,
where Allianz operated via domestic agencies, the development was similar.

While Allianz was not, for the most part, successful in the Southern
European market, in countries like Romania, the occupied countries of
Yugoslavia, Greece and Slovakia or the Reich Protectorate of Bohemia and

Brochure advertising life insurance for soldiers in the German Army (1936).

Moravia – it received no concession to do business in these places – it was able to do business in Poland. After the German invasion in September 1939, the country was divided up: parts of Upper Silesia, the region Danzig-West Prussia and the Reich region of Wartheland formed by the Nazi occupiers were integrated into the Third Reich and Germanized with brutal consequences; the other occupied Polish areas were grouped into the General Government (Generalgouvernement); areas of Eastern Poland became parts of the Soviet Union until the Germans attacked it.

Allianz and Allianz Leben established branch offices in Poznań and in Katowice.[110] Both were active as trustees for numerous Polish companies (Warschauer Versicherungs-Gesellschaft AG, Generali Port-Polonia, Patria) and for the portfolios of the British company Prudential. This had worked especially well since Munich Re had held interests in the three Polish companies and Wilhelm Arendts, the director-general of the Bayerische Versicherungsbank (BVB), which belonged to Allianz, had, in the context of his war service, been responsible in the administration of the occupied areas for allocating trusteeships. BVB also had a concession for the General Government, as did the Italian RAS.[111] In this context, the German insurance companies worked together with the HTO, the Head Trusteeship Office East (Haupttreuhandstelle Ost) created by Hermann Göring. Their task was to seize the assets of the Polish state and to expropriate Polish private enterprises, and prepare the transfer of their assets and operations to German companies. The Polish and Jewish inhabitants were systematically robbed by the HTO. In the beginning of 1942, the HTO definitively transferred the provisionally administrated businesses, including insurance companies, to the companies that had operated them in trust until then. The life insurers were to only fulfill the contracts belonging to German customers; the rights of the Polish and Jewish customers were no longer valid. Nonetheless, these policies from the prewar period had to be paid out by the German insurers, but these payments were then officially confiscated and the money – be it the cash surrender value or the contracted insurance sum – went to the HTO and not to the customers.

In February 1940, the police chief in the industrial city of Łódź, SS officer Johannes Schäfer, declared a portion of the city a ghetto. In the following months, over 150,000 Jews were forcibly quartered there. Allianz's director of the regional office in Łódź at that time, Dr. Hübner, concluded the first insurance policies as soon as July 1940 with the head of the ghetto administration. First, Allianz insured the transport of sewing machines into the ghetto where the residents were forced to sew uniforms for the German Army; then it insured the cloth stored in the ghetto used for the uniforms. As the risks to be covered grew greater, the ghetto administration office located in Poznań passed the insurance contracts on to a consortium made up of several insurers. For instance, fire insurance contracts for damage of up to RM 40 million for goods and raw materials owned by the German Army also stored in the ghetto were handed over to the consortium. Allianz, like Iduna-Germania, held a 20 percent share of the consortium, and the remainder was divided up among nine other insurers. Allianz's request to be allowed to inspect the ghetto to be able to better estimate and thus tax the fire risks was denied. The deputy director of the ghetto administration, Friedrich Wilhelm Ribbe, explained this decision to the Allianz agent in July 1941: "The estimation of the risk is seen now as before by me to be favorable because the eldest of the Jews places a guard to keep watch constantly, day and night, in each work room and also has an interest in being able to work because this is the only possibility that the Jewish community has to continue to survive."[112]

These are two examples of a whole series of deals that brought Allianz to the sites of Nazi mass crime. Other examples are the fire insurance contracts made between the Bayerische Versicherungsbank (BVB), as part of a nine-company consortium, and the SS and police chief in the Krakow district to cover the buildings, equipment, and goods stored on the grounds of the forced labor camp of Plaszow. Three other businesses owned by Allianz and Munich Re belonged to the consortium, as well as the Italian RAS and the Aachener und Münchener Versicherungs AG. The deals that Allianz's Berlin sub-director, Max Beier (1889–1945), acquired through his excellent contacts to the SS brought Allianz and BVB even closer to the places where human slavery and mass murder were being carried out. The insured customer in this case was the Deutsche Ausrüstungswerke GmbH (German Equipment Works, DAW), owned by the SS. It operated workshops in the concentration camps where prisoners were forced to produce furniture, clothes and metal goods for the SS and for use in the camps themselves. Between autumn 1940 and winter 1944–45, Beier concluded numerous insurance contracts through Allianz and BVB, for instance, for fire and theft protection for the DAW buildings on the grounds of the Dachau, Buchenwald, Ravensbrück, Sachsenhausen, Stutthof, Neuengamme and Auschwitz concentration camps. For the insurance policies on the buildings and goods in the Dachau and

The Allianz Zeitung reports on the occupation of Poland after Germany had begun the Second World War with its attack on its Eastern neighbor. The cover photo of the final issue shows, according to its caption, "the most important economic districts in the newly acquired areas."

Auschwitz concentration camps, there are also surviving documents concerning Beier's inspection visit to Dachau and records of the visits of two employees from the Kattowitz branch office to Auschwitz.[113]

When on February 2, 1945, Max Beier received the news from an SS office that some of the insurance contracts he had negotiated would not be extended, but rather a different consortium would receive the commission, Allianz was well on its way to falling apart. The next day, February 3, 1945, the head office in Berlin suffered its third and most devastating bomb attack. The bomb shelter located underground below the new Allianz Leben building, where hundreds of people had taken shelter, was partially damaged, leaving 31 persons, 17 of whom were Allianz employees, dead. For the fiscal year 1944, no further annual reports could be generated. 1943 was the first war year in which the number of employees dropped; it was listed as 16,030, but this included many employees who had either been conscripted to military service or were in other ways obligated to the state. Of the 15,598 employees on record in 1944, 8,700 had been called up.

The ratio of conscripted employees varied at the company's various locations between 40 and 60 percent of those who had worked during peacetime. Since the beginning of the war, the company had replaced them as much as possible with temporary workers, including many women and former retirees. In fact, the number of employees available dropped further from year to year. Clemens Maiholzer estimated the number of employees killed as soldiers or as civilians or reported missing in the war at around 12 percent of the employment level of 1939, or roughly 1,500 persons. To combat the personnel shortage and to balance out the rationing of work materials and constant interruptions in operations, costs were cut everywhere: workflows were simplified or completely eliminated, forms were shortened, advertising was for the most part prohibited, the only newspaper to appear through 1943 was that run by the DAF, Der Allianz-Adler. In addition, customers enquired less about insurance policies, and in 1944 the premium revenues sank noticeably for the first time. After 1943, the effects of the bombings were felt in the offices in the larger metropolitan cities. The minutes of department head meetings at Frankfurter Versicherungs-AG from the year 1944 read like those of a crisis management team. In many places the actual business rapidly became secondary. In March, the buildings in Frankfurt were heavily damaged. The branch offices in Cologne, Hamburg, Magdeburg, Dresden and Berlin were hit particulary hard by bombings. As the Red Army advanced, Allianz had to evacuate its offices in Königsberg and Breslau. Foreign business was no longer existent, and foreign assets were confiscated just

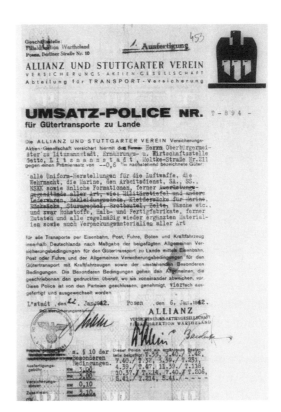

Allianz policy for insuring the transport of uniforms produced by prisoners in the Łódź ghetto. The mayor signed the document prepared by Allianz on January 22, 1942.

as they were in Soviet-occupied Germany. Even such a personality as Heinz-Leo Müller-Lutz, known for his boundless energy as director of the organization department in Frankfurt, seemed resigned: "In the last weeks, work has become increasingly meaningless. Contact with the branch offices was worsening and has now been completely cut off."[114] April 21, 1945, a week before Easter, was the last workday for the remaining employees of Allianz in the main office in Berlin; business was then suspended for 30 days.

The fate of Allianz was up in the air: many offices had been closed, the remaining employees were on the verge of scattering throughout the country, the circulation of money had come to a stop, communications suffered many interruptions, premium revenues collapsed to about one-third of the previous year's amount, and a large portion of the business capital was lost in the collapse of Germany. Allianz Leben, for instance, had invested RM 1 billion (of a total RM 1.9 billion) in bonds and securities in a government that would soon no longer exist, and its next-largest investments were mortgages and small loans.[115] What was that all worth now? Who was supposed to run Allianz? Ru-

Kurt Schmitt and his lawyer Oscar Maron during his denazification proceedings. Pictured here before the Starnberg denazification court on September 16, 1947.

dolf Schloeßmann had retired in winter 1944–45; Hilgard resigned at the beginning of 1945 from all of his offices and was, like August von Finck, politically compromised; Schmitt had been one of Hitler's ministers; Paul Lux, once seen as the future star of Allianz, died in 1943 after a gall bladder operation; and Hans Heß was 64 and experiencing health issues. Nothing was certain.

The American military government gave Frankfurter Versicherungs-AG permission on May 11, 1945, to start up business operations again. In Hamburg, the British agencies had already granted permission to start on May 7. On May 18, 1945, 250 Allianz employees met in the courtyard of one of the damaged buildings of the head office in Berlin for the first time since the weapons had gone silent. Gerd Müller, who would later become chairman of the board of Allianz Leben, had posted a note announcing that everyone should meet there on this day. Four days later, Allianz was given official permission to resume work. Allianz employees were also busy starting up again in Munich, Cologne, Stuttgart and even in areas in the Soviet-occupied zone, where, however, in 1946 it became clear that private insurers would have no future.[116]

A lot of things had ended; much was destroyed, much was lost and uncertain, and yet many employees were already gathering to start it up again. The people in liberated Germany were, however, the same ones who had been there before May 8, 1945, the day the war ended in Europe. The Allies who now occupied Germany and were establishing military governments had heard, experienced and seen much while they were fighting to bring down the National Socialist state; they now posed many questions about

Destroyed branch of Frankfurter Versicherungs-AG on Hermannstraße in Hamburg.

Hermannstraße   18.6.44

responsibility and guilt. Each Allied power handled these questions in its zone differently. In general, the aim was to investigate National Socialists and punish them for their crimes. In the process, many questions arose that would shape the emerging system of denazification: Who had been a Nazi? How could that be determined? At what point did the simple Nazi Party member, of which there were, according to party records, around 8 million before 1945, become a person who had made himself guilty of committing a punishable crime? How should such persons be punished?

On July 15, 1945, Allianz dismissed 56 employees due to their membership in the Nazi Party from the total of 552 workers who were on the payroll in the head offices of the group companies in Berlin at that time. During the first months after the end of the war, Hans Goudefroy, Gerd Müller and Clemens Maiholzer formed a provisional management team for the Berlin Allianz administration until Hans Heß took over as director in Berlin at the beginning of 1946. At a meeting of the provisional team on July 23, Goudefroy reported that the Americans had issued a directive ordering that all persons who had entered the Nazi Party until 1933 were to be dismissed or, respectively, not be rehired. They had to fill out a 131-question survey – this would become the instrument and symbol of the denazification process. Soon, other regulations followed, especially for influential people in the business world whose wealth could possibly be placed in fiduciary trusts, and general regulations for civil servants and for the whole of private industry.[117] At the head office in Berlin, Clemens Maiholzer established a denazification committee that discussed and reviewed the dismissal of 60 employees who were determined to be guilty in a total of 15 hearings by 1949. The majority of the top managers at Allianz were also investigated by their local denazification courts: Hans Goudefroy was exonerated; Gerd Müller, Hans Heß and Alfred Haase were never Nazi Party members. Wilhelm Arendts, the director of the Bayerische Versicherungsbank (BVB), was dismissed from his post and at first classified as incriminated (offender), but after further investigation was finally exonerated in 1948. Alfred Wiedemann, the director-general of Frankfurter Versicherungs-AG, was also initially classified as incriminated by the local denazification court but later, after an appeal, achieved a reduction to the less incriminated category (lesser offender) and had to pay a fine and court expenses. Eduard Hilgard was judged to be a major offender (Hauptschuldiger) in his proceedings, above all for his role in the Reich Group for Insurance. He, too, was able to achieve a reduced verdict upon appeal two years later. As a simple fellow traveler (follower), he only had to pay a small fine. Finally, Kurt Schmitt's denazification proceedings turned out to be his final act. In 1945, the American authorities dismissed him from all of his posts and indicted him. His case dragged on for a number of years during which he was prohibited from working and also, in the early stages, imprisoned on two occasions. There were also plans to indict him in one of the subsequent Nuremberg trials, but this never materialized. The court responsible for Schmitt's case in Starnberg classified him as a major offender in 1946, although this was later revised to less incriminated. Two years later, after numerous stages, he was reclassified as a fellow traveler after he had at one point actually been exonerated, a decision which was then overruled. He paid a small fine and also had to pay some of the legal expenses. Kurt Schmitt died in 1950 of cancer; he was 64 years old.[118]

"The first weeks following the currency reform are now behind us. There is no doubt that we are better off after the monetary cut. The food situation has improved, one can buy more, people take more pleasure in their work, the industrious are no longer seen as the idiots; in short, conditions have changed decisively and almost abruptly in many respects. To this extent, the currency reform has shown itself to have been not only urgently needed, but also successful. [...] The insurance industry has been especially hard hit by the currency reform. All that is left now are the employees and their manpower and the customers. Everything else has to be created anew or restored. The challenges facing us are many and difficult."[119] With this editorial written in August 1948, the directors of Frankfurter Versicherungs-AG hoped to give their agents courage and to motivate them to make new acquisitions. After all that had happened, the task did seem truly daunting. A few

3. 1933–1948 Allianz: The Nazi Years and Reconstruction

Paying out the per capita sum of DM 40 to the citizens of the Western occupation zones on June 21, 1948.

weeks before, on Sunday, June 20, the Western Allies had implemented the Currency Act, the Emissions Act and the Transition Act, bringing the currency reform to life. Even though this did not solve all the problems at once – for instance, the unemployment rate in West Germany rose from 3.5 to 12 percent by the beginning of 1950 –, the currency reform marked a significant turning point in the postwar period.[120]

Only after the end of the war did the dire consequences of war really set in in Germany. Before then, the German population had been privileged with the spoils of war at the cost of the inhabitants of Nazi-occupied Europe. Now, hunger and the bitter cold bore down on the Germans; millions of refugees and expellees had lost their homes and all of their possessions and sought shelter. The authorities rationed food supplies as they had to do throughout Europe; each person in Germany was allotted 1,000 calories.[121] The problem was not only the shortage of food items, gasoline, heating materials, clothing, and living space. What really stood in the way of an economic recovery, was the hopeless currency situation. The Third Reich had generated RM 380 billion in domestic debt to finance the war, that is to say, borrowed from its own citizens, banks, insurance companies, and other businesses; in addition, the burden on the occupied countries was estimated to be around RM 170 billion. By the end of the war, there was around RM 70 billion in circulation. This amount far outweighed the value of the real goods that remained in Germany. Only the strict regulation of prices and wages along with official rationing of the food supply hid the actual monetary depreciation.[122]

So legen wir die Gelder unserer
Versicherten an:

wertsicher und wertschaffend

*Excerpt from an
advertising brochure
by Allianz Leben
from the year after
the currency reform.
It advertises with
pictures of the life
insurer's investments
for the reconstruction
of the destroyed
country.*

Consequently, the Allied forces, especially the Americans, demanded a cut and a new beginning.[123] The currency reform fulfilled exactly this in a radical manner. Social considerations, which the German representatives broached in the preparatory stages, had to take a back seat. The specific power relations in the first years before the founding of the two German states made this possible: "Through the authority of the Allied Forces it was possible to push the reform through; a democratically elected government would have probably been toppled by such an attempt."[124]

What happened after June 20, 1948, left an imprint on the collective memory of an entire generation. Each person was entitled to 60 Deutschmarks (DM) from the newly created Bank deutscher Länder (Bank of German States); in a first step DM 40 were paid out. The next day, the Deutschmark was named the official currency and the once empty shelves in the shops filled again with goods. Most significant, however, was that all the owners of RM-denoted securities were more or less dispossessed: the assets of banks, of Nazi institutions, of public enterprises, of cities and of local communities were wiped out; for all the other cash assets the rule was that they were to be exchanged at a 10 RM to 1 DM ratio. This held also for debts, with the exception of those of the German Reich, which were not exchanged. The creditors, including Allianz, Allianz Leben, and all the other companies of the group, would have to go empty-handed at first. The creditors were granted compensation claims. In Allianz's opening balance statement after the currency reform, dated June 21, 1948, these claims were listed at an exchange value of DM 260 million.[125] All running costs such as salaries and pensions, as well as wages, retirement payments to the social insurance providers, rents and taxes were exchanged at the rate of 1 RM to 1 DM. Ultimately, after further additional regulations went into effect, all large credits were exchanged at a rate of 100 RM to 6.50 DM.[126] This was especially hard on those receiving private retirement payments, that is, all those whose entitlement to benefits were not covered by public institutions, but rather lay in the hands of private insurers. In other words, craftsmen and the self-employed suffered the most. Their claims were also exchanged at a ratio of 10 to 1. Dealing with life insurance policies proved to be especially difficult: according to the reform laws the premium reserves were also to be exchanged at a rate of 10 to 1, liquid cash assets were nullified, and the value of mortgages as well as real estate was uncertain. For these, as mentioned, compensation claims were granted, which, however, at first were not liquid and only yielded a small return in interest. The companies then recalculated the insurance sums of the existing life insurance policies according to a conversion chart drawn up by Hans Parthier, a member of the board at Allianz Leben. The owners of policies that had already been running for many years lost the most as the contributions paid in RM were now valued much lower. The value of the total sum insured of all contracts at Allianz Leben dropped from RM 6.8 billion in 1944 to DM 1.8 billion in 1949, the year the two postwar German states were founded.

That the life insurance branch nevertheless soon played a significant role in Allianz's recovery – and that of the insurance industry in general – owes much to the fact that the government in the new Federal Republic of Germany passed legislation helping to lessen the losses suffered by the owners of whole life insurance policies and private retirement funds.[127] Needless to say, the currency reform, which at first was only effective in the Western occupation zones since the Soviet military administration could not come to an agreement with the other Allied Forces, widened the gap between the East and the West. The Soviet authorities had already nationalized the private insurance within its sector in 1945–46. The immediate Soviet response to the currency reform was to block all access into West Berlin. The Cold War intensified; Germany, Europe and the world thus entered into a phase of constant conflict between the two antagonistic blocs.

ALLIANZ-
VERTRETER
ALS
BERUF

1948–1970

THE ECONOMIC MIRACLE
AND UNLIMITED GROWTH

As the Mercedes 300 was finally spotted on November 25, 1954, on the Königinstraße, the relief among the gentlemen of Allianz must have been great. Director-general Hans Goudefroy had waited many long years for this moment. At last, the day of the opening ceremony for the new head office in Munich-Schwabing on the edge of the English Garden had arrived. And stepping out of the official Mercedes as the guest speaker was the chancellor of the Federal Republic of Germany, Konrad Adenauer, who had come to Munich as part of his election campaign. He hardly needed to campaign in front of this audience. Instead, he showered compliments upon those present: "[…] We live in a very restless and very dangerous time […] But you, your activity and the activity of the other insurance companies contribute in very great measure to giving thousands of people a feeling of reassurance and security because in your hands they know their future is secure. In this respect, the insurance companies, and you leading the pack, my dear gentlemen, fulfill an important task, big and valuable, particularly in our time."[1] It was truly a moment of triumph. After years of waiting, of working in temporary circumstances spread across many locations both in and outside of Munich, the staff of the head office once again finally had a building that they could rightfully call a proper headquarters. It had been a long and arduous journey getting there.

	The idea of moving the corporate head-
A New Corporate	quarters was first documented in Novem-
Headquarters	ber 1945. Dr. von Nastvogel in the legal de-

partment, however, clearly rejected such considerations because he believed that "the future German center of power will be located in Berlin [...] The thought of moving the company has already lost a good deal of its timeliness because the zone division has been significantly loosened by permission for unrestricted postal traffic within the Reich."[2]

This view, though, quickly turned out to be mistaken: quite the contrary, the "zone division" grew dramatically more pronounced and the "German center of power in Berlin" was soon just a distant dream. On December 9, 1948, during the Berlin blockade by Soviet occupation troops, when the Western part of the city could only be reached by air, the Allianz board of directors met in Wiesbaden where a part of the central administration had moved. The decision was to be made at this meeting about where the second main office after Berlin should be located. In nearby Bad Nauheim, Hans Heß and his close colleague Alfred Haase lived, both of whom were members of the board. They wanted to get all of Allianz to move to Wiesbaden and Frankfurt and had gotten the board to pass a resolution to this effect in April 1948.[3] The opposing faction on the board was comprised of Franz Bohl, Kurt Schmitt's cousin, Hans Wilhelm Dümmler, and Hans Herbert Wimmer. The last two had been negotiating since August 1947 with the lord mayor of Munich, Karl Scharnagl. Scharnagl had been quietly informed of the situation by the Bavarian Finance Ministry and had been asked to come up with an appropriate accommodation on the part of the city administration.[4] When Dümmler and Wimmer explained to Scharnagl that Munich had been selected as seat of the corporate headquarters in the West, he got down to work. He listed seven "most urgent measures [...] that must first be carried out for the transfer of the Allianz company to Munich." He understood what was at stake: "In light of the great economic significance that the transfer of Allianz has for the city of Munich, the greatest possible acceleration and initiative is called for."[5] His plan to make office space available for Allianz was successful. More and more Allianz staff members moved bit by bit from Berlin to Munich so that, by the time of the decisive meeting, more than three times as many worked in Munich as in Wiesbaden.

But the decision had not yet been made. Heß's close associate, Eduard Hilgard, lobbied explicitly for Munich. "[...] I would like to point out what under some circumstances could, in my opinion, be a deadly threat that

Federal Chancellor Konrad Adenauer gave a speech at the opening of the new Allianz head office in Munich in 1954.

could push our Allianz out of the state of Hesse, and, indeed, will very likely threaten us soon. Hesse is, as everyone knows, the most socialist of all the Western zone [federal] states. This fundamental attitude alone should keep us from placing our headquarters in this very state that is so unfavorably disposed toward private business. But you know just as well as I do that Hesse in its constitution has just set its sights on socializing the insurance business. Not even in some minister's declaration but in the Basic Law of the state, which after all is enacted in order to be followed."[6] Heß bitterly countered these fears: "The board members who are for Munich point, among other things, at 'Red Hesse'. None of us know what the political circumstances will be in the future. I have always opposed this view with the idea that I am more afraid of the Bavarian extremists than the Hessian Social Democrats. I know that some gentlemen smile at this, but twenty years ago some smiled at the fact that I had already perceived the rise of a great threat that then unfortunately destroyed Germany."[7]

The meeting of the board of directors on December 9, 1948, had been convened for the sole purpose of coming to a decision. What had happened since October 5, when Hans Goudefroy had taken a "wait and see" stance in a letter to his colleague Horst Schiemann and simultaneously affirmed his preference for Frankfurt? A whole bundle of reasons came together to make a speedy decision seem advisable, and perhaps even first made one possible. First of all, Hans Goudefroy had been appointed the new chairman of the board of directors by the supervisory board and had thus become Hans Heß's successor. Now that he held the reins, he could bring about a decision. In addition, the Berlin blockade made it daily all too apparent what it meant to have the headquarters in that city. The three members of the board who had remained in Berlin certainly would have relayed their first-hand experiences to their colleagues. Third, by the end of the year, all compensation claims had to be submitted. These were debt register claims against the public coffer that were meant to close the gap on the asset side of the balance sheet that had arisen because the claims against the German Reich had not been recalculated into Deutsche Mark (DM) when the currency reform took place.[8]

Goudefroy allowed all the arguments for the one or the other region to be reiterated. The negotiations with representatives of the three cities and the condition of company-owned real estate – in Frankfurt as well as in Munich, Allianz had large subsidiaries with representative main offices – had led to the conclusion that it would be easiest to make sufficient office and living space available for the staff in Munich. Most staff members likewise saw slight advantages for Munich in the negotiations with the states of Hesse and Bavaria. Although both states made the same promises, namely, to treat Allianz in the matter of the compensation claims like West German companies, in Hesse this promise still sat on the finance minister's desk, whereas in Bavaria the entire cabinet and the budgetary committee of the state parliament had also already affirmed it. In addition, in segments of Hesse's SPD, which appointed the minister president in the SPD/CDU coalition, plans for socialization and codetermination really were being circulated that were a thorn in Allianz's side. Frankfurt's advantages lay in other areas. "Without a doubt, Frankfurt's central location speaks for it. Furthermore, the proximity of government agencies, because we can probably reckon with Frankfurt becoming the seat of the federal agencies."[9]

When the vote was taken, a clear picture finally emerged. Haase and Berlin director Johannes Mühlbauer were the only ones who voted for Frankfurt; everyone else voted for Munich. When the vote to move the administrative headquarters was repeated with the assumption that office space could be made available under the same conditions as in Munich, Horst Schiemann, who resided in Wiesbaden, and the two Munich residents Hans Wilhelm Dümmler and Hans Schmidt-Polex changed their votes in favor of Frankfurt. Hans Goudefroy, who had only just moved to Wiesbaden

Hans Goudefroy, Alfred Haase, and Gerd Müller shaped Allianz in the 1950s and 1960s (front row from right to left).

from Hamburg, where he had run a branch office since 1946, voted both times for Munich. With this, the board had reached its decision, which also turned out the way Goudefroy had wished. After all, although nothing is known about Goudefroy's motives, a reading of the minutes of the meeting and other relevant documents gives one the impression that he was first and foremost interested in an unequivocal decision and voted for Munich for pragmatic reasons.

The board of directors had made its decision, yet the shareholders still had to resolve to amend the company's articles of association in the general assembly. As a result, the supervisory board took on an important role. Its chairman since October 26, 1948, though, was Hans Heß, who, according to Goudefroy, "did not [have] the intention of asking the supervisory board to agree to the decision of the board of directors. On the contrary, he will instigate a showdown on the supervisory board."[10] In this, however, Goudefroy misjudged his predecessor – perhaps because Heß felt a responsibility toward "his" Allianz and thus wished to preserve unity between the board of directors and the supervisory board, or because Goudefroy, in a letter of December 13, 1948, supported Heß's position in a dispute between Hans Heß and Kurt Schmitt that lasted until Schmitt's death.[11] In any case, Hans Heß did express his own position in a letter to all members of the supervisory board but simultaneously asked them to agree to the board's resolution.[12] Almost all of them lined up behind this opinion and voted for Munich, with the exception of Waldemar Freiherr von Oppenheim.[13] The general

The Maillot estate stood on the site of the present-day head office until 1945. It was also called Rosipal Villa after its long-term owner.

assembly then unanimously resolved finally on January 27, 1949, to change the statute.[14]

A New Head Office

"The company supports the firm Allianz Insurance Corporation and has its headquarters in Berlin and Munich." Such was the wording of the amended sentence in the company statutes. The Berlin office quickly became irrelevant; by contrast, although Munich housed the headquarters, by no means could all the staff at this point actually move there. The department for machine insurance moved in May and the Allianz pension fund in early August 1949 from Berlin to Wiesbaden; the liability and accident departments had already been located in Stuttgart for some time.[15] In Munich, the headquarters were spread out in various buildings. Among other things, some Allianz staff were guests in the office space of the Bayerische Versicherungsbank, whose director-general Dümmler gave up part of his corporate housing for this arrangement.[16] In 1949, Allianz began not only to rebuild destroyed residential buildings but also began construction of new housing in Munich that was intended primarily to benefit its staff.[17] At about the same time, the search began for suitable property for a

Partial view of the head office from the English Garden.

new administrative building; a central but also quiet location as well as a good layout were the principle concerns. Properties on Leopoldstraße, Brienner Straße, and on Karolinenplatz came under consideration. Yet, the most attractive property by far was located on the edge of the English Garden, Munich's largest city park, and accommodated the ruins of a destroyed villa from the 19th century, the so-called Rosipal Villa. The property owner – the congregation of the Merciful Sisters of St. Vincent de Paul – at first categorically rejected the idea of selling. Only when the auxiliary bishop Johannes Neuhäusler as well as the order's superior Karl Nißl joined the negotiations did Allianz succeed in acquiring the property in May 1951.[18] After an architectural competition, Allianz decided on the plan by architect Josef Wiedemann, who was in the process of developing a name for himself in the destroyed city of Munich with his painstaking reconstruction of the Odeon, which once housed a renowned concert hall and today is part of the Bavarian Ministry of the Interior. Later, Wiedemann was responsible for the reconstruction of the arcades of Munich's Court Garden, the Victory Gate, and the Glyptothek (a museum of antiquities) on the Königsplatz. He also designed the subway station there, yet, also built a controversial department store on Munich's Marienplatz in the 1970s. Wiedemann competed for the Allianz contract with Alexander von Branca – later designer of the art museum, the Neue Pinakothek – who wished to erect a high-rise on the edge of the English Garden. The judging panel ranked both designs in second place and did not award a first place prize. Allianz responded with caution, not wishing to provoke anyone: "Branca's design for a high-rise, in the end, had no chance against Wiedemann's plans, in which he drew up more a palace than an administration building out of reverence for Schwabing and the English Garden."[19] From today's standpoint, the building was a success. Nothing is reminiscent of the proverbial insurance palace; the furnishings, large parts of which are still original, come across as classically dignified and by all means tasteful; all together, it forms a symbiotic relationship with the surrounding park landscape. Today, the head office of Allianz is regarded as a successful piece of 1950s architecture and is sought out by architecture classes for teaching purposes. At the same time, the building still continues, after more than sixty years, to serve the purpose for which it was erected.[20]

Allianz Pensions

From 1954, Allianz once again had a center. The danger some had evoked that it would break apart had not come true. At the same time, however, it was important for the company to maintain or restore its inner peace. When Allianz staff retired, according to the will of their bosses and with the help of their employer, they were to have an appropriate pension. Goudefroy expressed this in these words: "Whoever devotes his life's work in an insurance company to creating security for working people against dangers and uncertainties must be able to expect that his employer will assist him in building up a certain security against the most serious danger, namely, of being left with nothing in old age." In order to guarantee this, the Allianz Pension Fund (Allianz Versorgungskasse, AVK) was (re-)established in 1924, although it was transformed into a mutual insurance association in 1940 at the behest of the Reich Supervisory Office for Insurance and for tax reasons. This change in its legal structure, however, would turn out to be a great disadvantage after the currency reform. Benefits could still be paid out, but not all of them were complete: small pensions were paid in full, monthly sums of over DM 100 were paid out at 75 percent, and everything that exceeded DM 1,000 was paid at 50 percent, which in the AVK in 1948 affected precisely 18 pensioners, or 0.4 percent of all recipients.[21] Nonetheless, the AVK pensions, which were legally part of a mutual insurance association, were viewed by the state as insurance benefits. And for these the exchange rate in the currency reform was 10:1. This would have meant that pensioners, but also those who would retire in the following few years and had been paying into the AVK for a long time, would have had to reckon with miserably small pensions. Thus, former Allianz staff would have found themselves in the same pathetic situation as hundreds of thousands of other Germans who had departed the workforce. Whoever had not been able to save during his working years was dependent on the support of his offspring in his sunset years. The legal pension did not replace one's salary but at best protected one from falling into misery. And a couple of marks more from the Allianz pension that had shrunk to a tenth of its size would hardly have made life (or survival) any easier for people at the end of the 1940s.

The pensions of those who were able to submit their claims not to the AVK but directly to the Allianz companies, on the other hand, were exchanged at a 1:1 rate. These so-called contract pensioners primarily consisted of ex-staff members of companies that had been taken over in the great mergers of the 1920s – such as the Stuttgarter Verein and the Frankfurter Versicherungs-AG (thereafter the Frankfurter) – who had been too old or for some other reason had not been able to join the AVK and whose pension entitlements had, however, become a part of the merger agreements. This affected above all former managing staff. This, of course, had plenty of potential to spark social unrest as it could have given rise to the impression that the leadership circle took care of itself but deprived the army of em-

A motif from the matchbox campaign advertising life insurance.

ployees of its modest income. Consequently, even before the currency reform, the view that had come to dominate was that all pensioners had to be treated equally. Internally, in the works council, but also in talks with government offices and supervisory agencies, Allianz made it clear that it felt obliged to pay out the complete pension benefits and not just the sum of 10 percent to which they had been reduced, and then it did this as well. Allianz explained its action as a consequence of the guarantee it had given the members of the AVK in 1925, which contractually stipulated that Allianz would take over the responsibility of paying out pension benefits if the AVK for whatever reason was unable to pay the planned amount.

Three test cases heard before labor courts – since lost – that gave legal certainty to Allianz's position, as well as protracted negotiations, were necessary to persuade the Bavarian Finance Ministry to accept the exchange rate of one Reichsmark (RM) for one DM for the AVK pensions as well and to grant compensation claims of a certain size for this. Translated into numbers, this meant that just about a third of the pensioners received up to DM 50 a month in addition to their legal pension, which amounted to the sum that an apprentice at the Bayerische Versicherungsbank received in 1948 in his third year.[22] 26 percent received between DM 51 and DM 100, and another 13.5 percent got DM 101 to DM 150. These sums, which may appear paltry today, certainly would have at least secured a subsistence income for many pensioners.

As salaries began to rise with breath-taking speed during the phase of economic growth that set in at this time, the entitlements of the AVK members automatically rose as well; these were tied to the salaries and thus to the workers' future pensions. Whereas the staff naturally did not wish to dispense with their certified rights, the management worried whether Allianz would survive. The specter of being unable to pay the benefits hung threateningly like the Sword of Damocles over the company.

A whole series of measures was enacted to solve the problem. These were negotiated by a commission consisting equally of members of the management and the works council, the so-called Commission of Ten, in 1952: all pensioners were to receive their full benefits again, the AVK was closed to new members, Allianz's guarantee was eliminated, and the Allianz Pension Fund was established. As its benefits were no longer directly dependent on salary but related to contributions, higher salaries only made themselves felt when contributions increased, without Allianz bearing high supplemental costs. When the two funds once again merged into the AVK in 1962, the reform of the state-run pension system in 1957 had fundamentally altered the basis of pensions in general. Whereas the Allianz pension had previously been conceived of as the entire retirement income for a worker, which could not exceed 70 percent of the worker's last paid gross salary, its principle function now was to supplement the significantly increased state pension.[23]

	Much, much faster than anyone thought
The Clients Come	possible, Allianz's premium revenues re-
with Their Cars	covered. In 1949, property insurance pre-

Much, much faster than anyone thought possible, Allianz's premium revenues recovered. In 1949, property insurance premiums had already reached prewar levels, and life insurance, as well, which had temporarily suffered from a loss of trust on account of the currency reform, was soon experiencing a boom. Where did the growth come from? How could it be that in a country that stood in ruins, where people were starving and freezing, they would so quickly awaken again to their need for insurance protection? On May 23, 1949, the Federal Republic of Germany was founded; with a social market economy, it was to follow a liberal economic policy. The starting situation for economic recovery was surprisingly good: war destruction and dismantling by the Allies had not weakened West German capital stock decisively, and the army of millions of highly qualified refugees and displaced persons from the former German settlement areas and from East Germany seemed to provide an apparently inexhaustible workforce. When the Korean War then began in June 1950, tying up the production capacities of other countries with war goods, it triggered an export boom of unprecedented scope in Germany. By 1952, exports increased by 200 percent, providing for self-sustaining economic growth, a phase of economic prosperity that lasted until 1973 with only brief interruptions. Within a few years, the economy enjoyed full employment and real incomes tripled by 1973. This ushered in increased car ownership as well: in 1949 there were only 368,377 officially registered personal automobiles; by 1970 this figure had increased to almost 13 million.[24] Insurance policies were needed for all of these cars. Thus, automobile insurance, which had already been important before, now developed in many ways into the key branch of the insurance business. In 1949, Allianz premium revenues for property insurance reached almost DM 170 million, around DM 65 million of this from the car business, or more than 38 percent. The second largest branch, fire insurance, took in about DM 28 million in premiums, or less than half as much. Allianz managers expected continuing increases in revenues because car ownership in the Federal Republic, although it had once again reached the level of 1938, still amounted to only

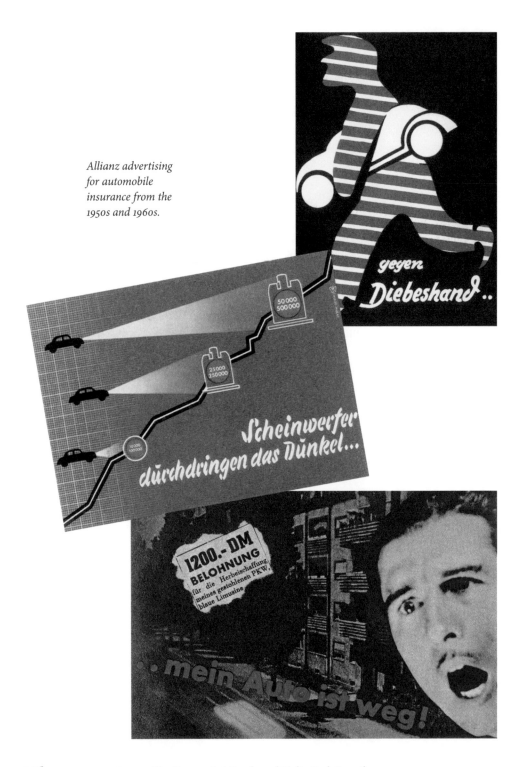

Allianz advertising for automobile insurance from the 1950s and 1960s.

17 people in a thousand owning a vehicle. By comparison, 56 out of 1,000 residents in England owned a car. But even the most optimistic probably did not foresee this dynamic developing to the extent it did. Carried by broad swathes of the population taking on car ownership, automobile insurance experienced an unanticipated boom. Whereas Allianz in 1950 had drawn up just about 660,000 policies, this figure rose by 1960 to over 2.5 million and by 1970 to about 4 million. The increases in premium revenues are even more impressive: they climbed from the aforementioned DM 65 million per year in 1949 to more than DM 1.2 billion by 1970. This amounted to more than 50 percent of property insurance premium revenues coming from automobile insurance.[25]

This distribution of business was not unusual; the picture was similar at other property insurance companies. At the Frankfurter Versicherungs-AG owned by Allianz, the proportion was even 5 percent higher, arising from a unique sales channel that Rudi Mehl and his good contacts to the Volkswagen factory had developed for the company. Mehl founded the Volkswagen-Versicherungsdienst (VVD: Volkswagen Insurance Service) in 1947, which sold automobile insurance policies with the help of Volkswagen dealers; in 1970, it contributed more than 20 percent of the premiums from this branch with around DM 89 million.

As liability insurance for automobiles was obligatory, it drove millions of future car drivers into the agencies of insurance companies starting in the early 1950s. Often, this was their first encounter with an insurer, so this branch opened doors to further business. After all, once the car owners had gotten to know the insurance agent as a serious businessman with whom one could insure one's car, it was logical for them to consider other insurance offers favorably. Consequently, the total number of property insurance policies at Allianz rose from about 3.8 million in 1950 to 8.2 million by 1960 and even to 12.8 million by 1970. In this year, there were approximately 67 million property insurance policies in Germany in total. High growth in workers' real incomes paired with high savings rates also led to meaningful growth in life insurance. When one considers that the 61 million West Germans in 1970 had taken out over 53 million life insurance policies, it becomes clear that by this time at the latest, insurance had become a mass business. This development inevitably affected Allianz's corporate design and advertising.[26]

Sag' es heiter, Du kommst weiter! (Say It with Cheer, and You'll Keep on Going!) Up to this point, advertising at Allianz had looked mostly like this: one showed gloomy pictures of burned houses, wrecked cars, or people who had had accidents. Dark figures sneaked around the houses and made off with other people's belongings. Another strategy was to print dense texts with serious and boring information about insurance protection. Allianz turned to people with warnings and a raised index finger to persuade them to take out insurance policies. Yet, a fundamental change started up in the early 1950s that was very decisively shaped by two people: the first was Hansjörg Dorschel, the son of an Allianz director from Stuttgart, who in no way wished to follow in his father's footsteps but rather to become a successful artist. The other was Walter Kappes, who had been an advertising manager for Allianz Leben since 1941, had been in charge of the Allianz newspaper since 1950, and at the start of 1952 replaced Arnold Hartung as the advertising manager for Allianz; Hartung had held the position for many years.[27]

In 1953, Walter Kappes was supposed to come up with advertising materials that could effectively raise awareness of the problem of underinsurance without costing a great deal of money or labor. To achieve this, he decided to embark on a new path, making enquiries with 15 well-known caricaturists, such as Manfred Schmidt, who had invented and drawn the master detective Nick Knatterton comic strip, and Gerhard Brinkmann, who, using cartoons, had made the following slogan famous: "Darauf einen Dujardin" (After that, a Dujardin), which advertised brandy by that name. The commissioning of the artists had a sensational effect. They were to "represent the concept, the essence or the consequences of underinsurance visually, and in the most amusing way possible." The sketchers took up pen and paper with great enthusiasm and developed entirely different solutions. If one flips through the drafts today, however, one cannot help but get the impression that not all of the artists were up to the task. Is it possible that this was because they did not believe that Allianz could handle very much humor? Nevertheless, Allianz did actually use some of the motifs for an advertising campaign and many others at least for staff training and thus utilized humor consciously and in a targeted way in advertising for the first time, with its self-selected Motto "Sag' es heiter, Du kommst weiter!" (Say it with cheer, and you'll keep on going!)[28]

Shortly after the first drafts had been published in the company newspaper, Allianz Zeitung, Allianz, on April 15, 1953, gave the go-ahead for an advertising campaign of unprecedented scope. Brochures, posters, official seals, advertising templates for agents, press events, and anything other than typical forms of advertising were purposefully used to familiarize people with a new insurance branch: travel weather insurance, which protected travelers in the case of too much rain at their vacation destination. The color motion picture "Wenn Kluge reisen" (When clever people travel) was the focal point of the campaign; the Allianz Zeitung reported – likewise printed in color this once – that it was quite popular and quoted one enthusiastic spectator: "It delights the eye with the colors, the ear with the sweep of the words and the music, the heart with the hilarity of the plot, and occupies one's mind with its persuasive presentation of something exciting and new."[29] A modern spectator might not be quite so ecstatic, yet the film still makes people laugh after more than 60 years. Along with their policy, customers received a chart for entering the daily precipitation. For practical purposes, it also included the telephone number of the German Weather Service, which Allianz had assigned to determine the official measurements. Nonetheless, the enthusiasm about the many calls from travelers plagued by rain who hoped to get a refund from Allianz may well have been rather limited.

The staff were sensitized to the subject by means of extensive reporting in the Allianz Zeitung and training memos and events. The travel weather insurance advertised in this manner turned out to be a real sales hit, exceeding esti-

This is how advertising graphic artist Ulrik Schramm illustrated under-insurance.

mates for premium revenues of DM 600,000 for the first year and doubling the following year. However, losses (DM 2.3 million) also increased in the same time period by a factor of thirty, and Hans Goudefroy emphasized that "one obviously [could] not simply continue to take losses of such magnitude." He suggested a change but did not call the new branch into question in principle, which certainly had to do with Allianz's strategy of introducing travel weather insurance to pursue other aims. In 1953, the news

Pamphlet for the film with which Allianz advertised travel weather insurance.

magazine Der Spiegel was already reporting that the possibility of making a profit from these insurance policies might not have been Allianz's top priority in this case. "Allianz makes no secret of the fact that it regards travel weather insurance as a means to its general insurance purposes, as a calling card for its agents, as a so-called treat. 'Afterwards, it is easier to talk about other things. Our representatives have a better starting point.'"[30]

The effect of the advertising for travel weather insurance was considerable. At a 1955 conference of international insurance companies that likewise offered or wished to offer such insurance, having been inspired by Allianz, Heinz-Leo Müller-Lutz, who had developed and now directed the travel weather insurance sector, reported on the great interest it generated in the German public, and gave two reasons for this:

"1) Rain is a fundamental occurrence that enters into things quite often and cannot by any means be avoided, regardless of how cautious one is. Everyone recognizes the certainty that it will rain. In this case no one can say: I don't need insurance; nothing happens to me as I am so cautious.

2) In the case of other insured events, an unpleasant, damaging event must first take place, such as an accident, fire, theft, robbery, or murder. This is not the case in travel weather insurance. Although rain is wet and annoying, it is otherwise harmless."[31]

It is possible that the new branch really did open the door to additional clients and stimulate business in other branches. Yet, premium revenues from travel weather insurance did not rise as easily as had been hoped, even though the company managed to reduce losses by raising the premiums. And despite Allianz advertising ever less for this branch, public interest in it persisted. It was so high, in fact, that the Verein Südwestdeutscher Zeitungsverleger (Association of Southwest-German Newspaper Publishers) recommended that its members "instruct the editorial departments, in the interest of advertising revenues, to discontinue any sort of editorial advertising for travel weather insurance as well as for commercial enterprises in general. [...] The insurance companies also have explained quite plainly that they did not need to utilize their allotted advertising budgets for travel weather insurance because the daily press as well as illustrated magazines had done a wonderful job of providing free advertising for them."[32] Nonetheless, interest in taking out such an insurance policy sank steadily, certainly due, in part, to Allianz tightening the requirements for making a claim. For example, it was not long before one could only take out a policy in one's place of residence and not in the vacation destination, and a waiting period was introduced between the signing of the policy and the start of its validity. After that, the number of policies sold dropped by 1966 to a mere 3,000. Germans simply avoided the "annoying" but "harmless" rain by traveling increasingly to the Adriatic Sea, to Italy or Yugoslavia, instead of to the Black Forest or the North Sea. The year after that, Allianz finally discontinued the sale of travel weather insurance.[33]

Hoffentlich Allianz versichert (Hopefully Covered by Allianz) The travel weather insurance branch had given Allianz a powerful boost in popularity. Walter Kappes, however, was not yet satisfied as the Allianz eagle was "by no means as well known as, for example, the Erdal frog, the Mercedes star, or the pelican of the Günther Wagner company."[34] To change this, Allianz arranged a competition among the staff in 1957 that aimed to replace the advertising slogan used up to that point: "Allianz – das Bündnis auf gegenseitigem Vertrauen!" (Allianz – the league of mutual trust!) The response was tremendous: the staff came up with about 2,000 suggestions, 30 to 40 of which utilized the concepts of protection and security. From these ideas, Allianz then finally developed the slogan "Das Zeichen für Schutz und Sicherheit" (The sign of protection and security), which was always to be combined with the Allianz eagle. Six of the amateur slogan writers were awarded DM 375 each in prize money, which at that time was still DM 39 more than punched card operators earned monthly in their third year in the punched card division of Allianz's Frankfurt branch office. Yet despite all these efforts and costs, the new advertising slogan did not catch on, not least because an unbeatable competitor turned up totally unexpectedly. In the same September 1957 Allianz Zeitung edition that announced the winners of the competition, the advertising slogan "hoffentlich Allianz versichert" (hopefully covered by Allianz) could be found beneath a rather bleak black-and-white drawing of a fully loaded delivery truck.[35] This inconspicuous saying, combined with small, bright pictures, would, in the following years, raise the Allianz eagle to a level of familiarity that would overshadow at least the frog and pelican.

Perhaps the aforementioned Hansjörg Dorschel had flipped through the pages of his father's Allianz Zeitung at home and seen the drawing of the delivery truck. Perhaps he also envisioned a man weighed down by luggage with a tremendous beard or a burglar with his booty in his sack tiptoeing away – two drawings that were printed in later editions. Perhaps he thought to himself, "I can do that better!", and sent his drawing to Walter Kappes. And then again, perhaps it was only a coincidence; after all, it was not only the advertising director of Allianz who got mail from this Stuttgart art academy graduate. However it may have come about, Walter Kappes was, in any case, delighted by Dorschel's humorous stick figures. And there was a new means of advertising that was perfect for the design: matchboxes. In April 1958, four different motifs appeared on 5 million matchboxes: a fireman, a boy who had shot out a window pane, an injured person in a wheel-

One of the first motifs from the matchbox campaign from 1958.

chair, and a burglar. Up until this point, only the brand names "Welthölzer" and "Haushaltsware" had adorned matchboxes. Now, they had suddenly become "a considerable venue for advertising that has the advantage of being carried directly into the home."[36] Allianz wanted to profit from this, and was able to. And the success was tremendous. The motifs went through several editions. Dorschel designed several more motifs, which were soon displayed on posters, as slides, and in other forms of advertising. At the end of 1958, the animation studio Reiner Film made the first film versions, which agents could order for the movie houses in their neighborhood. The ads in the cinema impressively showed off the new direction of the campaign: short and thus reasonably priced ads that drew attention with humor and were thus supposed to familiarize viewers with Allianz and its agents.

One burglar in Berlin had some particularly cynical fun with this campaign, leaving a matchbox adorned with the burglar motif at the crime scene. Fortunately, it turned out that the family silver stolen by the thief could be replaced. The victims had insurance for household contents – with Allianz no less.

Hansjörg Dorschel continued to draw his figures for many years and later developed Allianz's corporate design. For decades, he remained one of the most important designers of the company, rendering his father's initial concern over his choice of career unfounded. The advertising slogan "hopefully covered by Allianz" continues to be used to this day. Whereas, in the beginning, Allianz used the slogan as one of many and combined it at first with Dorschel's pictures and other phrases, it soon completely dominated Allianz's advertising. It was a decisive factor in making 90 percent of adults in Germany familiar with Allianz by 1965.[37]

The Company Undergoes Change	In 1997, the editorial staff of the Allianz Journal published a brief commemoration, as was usual at the time, of the former chairman of the board of directors

Heinz-Leo Müller-Lutz, who had died on May 17 at age 84. Otto Ladner, who had previously been the closest colleague of the honored man, was outraged: "My dear Ms. S., the abovementioned obituary is so pathetic that I as a former colleague and director of the business administration department cannot refrain from saying something."[38] Probably no one at Allianz had expected such a strong reaction to the obituary of a board member who had been retired for almost 20 years. At first, it was explained as a consequence of the fact that Müller-Lutz "[was] Mr. Ladner's foster father, and for L[adner] there has never been anyone greater at Allianz."[39] The chairman of the board of directors at Allianz, Henning Schulte-Noelle, was of a different opinion. Although he wrote a diplomatic reply to Mr. Ladner, internally he made it clear that Ladner's remarks were "actually right."[40]

Who was this man who could unleash such a storm so many years after leaving the company? His last file memo pertaining to "departing service," which he sent to his boss, director-general Wolfgang Schieren, two days before Christmas Eve in 1977, provides a first impression of his personality: "On December 30, 1977, the undersigned ended his work for Allianz. All of his tasks have been completed or open dates have been transferred to the responsible department leaders. Dr. Adolff has been informed about all important questions. The work station has been cleared. The unused vacation can be canceled."[41] Schieren, indeed, scribbled a note to the effect that Müller-Lutz also showed up for work on December 23 and 27. He probably also would have liked to show up on January 2 of the following year even though at that point he was already in his 66th year. His departure from ac-

Heinz-Leo Müller-Lutz changed Allianz in his 43 years of service like no one else of his era.

tive service was not entirely voluntary. It is not an overstatement to say that his departure ended an era at Allianz. For thirty years his name had stood for systematic and well-considered rationalization efforts. Müller-Lutz experienced three chairmen as a member of the board of directors. The effects of his work certainly were most impressive under Wolfgang Schieren, although the foundations for this had already been established under Schieren's predecessors, Hans Goudefroy and Alfred Haase.

Heinz-Leo Müller-Lutz was born on August 10, 1912, in Darmstadt; he completed his Abitur (high school diploma) in 1930 and, after completing a degree in economics went on to receive a doctorate in the economic and social sciences in 1934. That same year, he started as a volunteer at the Neue Frankfurter Versicherungs-AG (New Frankfurt Insurance Company), a subsidiary of Allianz, and rose there to become the sales manager and deputy board member by 1949. In early 1951, he transferred as deputy board member to the sales and marketing division of the general management of Allianz in Munich.[42]

Müller-Lutz carried out his first big plans for rationalization after the war still from Frankfurt. As the other branch offices of Allianz were still implementing the so-called block policies only with great hesitation, the

Frankfurt branch began systematically selling standardized insurance certificates in 1949. Agents received a block with a certain number of preprinted policy forms that they were able to fill out directly with clients. The offices that managed policies then only had to take care of the accounting for these, which significantly reduced administrative costs and effort. The insured, in turn, benefited from the fact that the insurance protection began immediately upon signing the policy.

The idea was not new. As early as the 1920s, Allianz had experimented with block policies for types of insurance that had short terms, such as baggage insurance and animal insurance, but also for simple fire insurance. The concept was now to be extended to other segments. At the Frankfurter, the method was tried at first on so-called people's accident insurance, the success of which proved Heinz-Leo Müller-Lutz right. Despite the resistance of the various departments, accounting, and company inspectors, and with the widespread approval of the agents, the organizational department, which was responsible for the project, managed to push the expansion of block policies through for 1950. Now the Frankfurter began, for example, to use block policies to sell household contents and private liability insurance.[43]

To make the new product popular with both the office and sales staff, Allianz created the fictional Fräulein Block Policy. In training films, she explained how block policies worked and reported on the increasing success of the new procedure. In addition, Allianz put her likeness on seals and other forms of advertising. Her popularity even brought her truly to life. At staff events, she and her troop of dwarfs that embodied the various insurance lines, as well as a javelin thrower likewise brought to life who sang vocal numbers, provided good entertainment. After shifting his career from Frankfurt to Munich, Müller-Lutz tied the block policy – whose further development for all of Allianz was now entirely up to him – to his next big project: the aforementioned travel weather insurance. It was intended not least to give the block policy an additional boost. As already more than half of the new policies were drawn up in this form in 1953, Allianz created its own divisions for processing and administration, thus breaking for the first time with its rigid structuring of office duties along various insurance lines.[44]

In 1954, Müller-Lutz finally found the position from which he could transform Allianz in the way he wished: he was appointed as the director of the newly founded business administration department (Betriebswirtschaftliche Abteilung, BWA) directly by the chairman of the board of directors of Allianz. In this department, all "questions that have up to now been addressed

Two Allianz seals with Fräulein Block Policy as the motif.

under the heading of 'factory'" were to be reviewed and coordinated according to the wishes of Hans Goudefroy, who saw this as the new department's most urgent task. Goudefroy was dreaming the old dream of generating similar "production conditions" for the insurance business that industrial companies had with their assembly-line production. Otto Ladner was also to work in this department and, in accordance with this aim, further develop the block policy. Müller-Lutz, however, wanted more. He also added the punched card department to his business administration unit and created a special area for rationalization measures of every sort. He reserved general operational planning for himself.[45]

First, though, the new department had to be firmly established, for which two years were set aside. Meanwhile, Müller-Lutz and his colleagues took lengthy trips, including a two-month study trip to the U.S., the lauded land of the insurance business, as well. Consequently, the head of Allianz Leben, for example, was able to report that the life insurance premiums paid per capita were 16 times as high as in Germany. Müller-Lutz, moreover, also realized that rationalization was already much more advanced in the U.S. than in Germany and that America and the American insurance companies in many ways should serve as models for Allianz.[46] But one thing endlessly fascinated Müller-Lutz: the progress in data processing that he had seen in

Hans-Willy Schäfer, the long-term head of the computer center, sitting before Allianz's mainframe large computer (IBM 650, opened).

America. A few years after the First World War, the great era of punched cards had begun at Allianz. More and more data were transferred to them in rooms designed for this purpose, with the help of hand punched card machines that were operated mostly by young women, the so-called punched card operators ("Locherinnen"). Millions and millions of these punched cards now had to be transported, stored, punched, copied, sorted, and analyzed. In America, Müller-Lutz discovered so-called electronic brains that were just beginning to compete with punched card technology. At the start of 1956, IBM delivered the IBM 650 to Allianz, making it the first European insurance company to utilize a mainframe computer. The IT age had begun.[47] From computer generation to computer generation, the computer center took over more and more of the tasks of the punched card divisions. Whereas the IBM 650's computing capacity had largely been taken up solely with statistical analyses, in 1961, insurance portfolios began to be stored on magnetic tapes. Now, the tabulating machines that had needed to be "fed" by punched cards and up to this point had carried out the majority of calculations were finally rendered obsolete.

Many Allianz workers first became acquainted with computers at the end of the 1960s when terminals were installed at work stations. This was made possible by a third, much more powerful generation of mainframe computers. With the help of these screens – connected by dedicated lines to the mainframe – employees were able to access insurance policy data online. In December 1983, Allianz Leben in Stuttgart acquired the first PC: an IBM PC/XT with at least a 10 MB hard drive. The old and the new existed side by side for a long time: up until 1988, one last data processing job was managed by means of punched cards.

In 1954, data processing was only one portion of the total operations that Müller-Lutz would extensively review. After four years of activity, however, he became somewhat disillusioned. So in October 1958, it was Goudefroy who seized the initiative and gave Allianz's reform efforts a boost with his speech before the innermost leadership circle. First of all, he pointed to one of the "fundamentals of the structure of our Allianz family," namely, the concentration of administrative tasks among the general management and the decentralization of sales, beginning with the branch offices. Then, he described the tasks that had been managed in the previous years and impressively elucidated the changes since 1938 by relating the growth in premium revenues: in 1957, with DM 190 million, the Frankfurter had taken in more premium revenues than all of Allianz had in 1938. The structure that Allianz had used since the end of the First World War and which had always proved effective up to that point was to be discussed in a commission under the leadership of Goudefroy himself. In front of the directors of the branch offices Goudefroy became, totally against his nature, even a bit melodramatic, if one can trust the manuscript of the speech, in concluding with the assertion: "It is our destiny-determining task of the next years." The reactions of the branch heads were not recorded, but this assertion must have engendered a lively discussion afterward. The commission was founded and its first project was quickly put into practice: to process simple transactions, Allianz founded "standard departments." Then, the work of the commission slowed down considerably, perhaps because resistance within the company was too great or because business continued to boom so that there was not enough pressure for reform. At the beginning of October 1961, Goudefroy became seriously ill, so the main driver of changes was absent. Alfred Haase, the Number Two at Allianz as head of the sales department, first took over management temporarily and then was appointed as the new boss after Goudefroy's death in December 1961. All the same, Haase managed to actually introduce the directorates, or board divisions, that had been repeatedly approved by the board of directors. As an additional administrative level below the branch offices, these board divisions took over tasks from these offices and allowed Allianz to grow within the structure it had used up to that point. Consequently, the commission discontinued its work.[48] Ernst Meyer, Haase's successor as the chairman of the board of directors, suggested that such a commission be utilized again four years later. Müller-Lutz was its chair this time. After a year of elaborate economic studies on topics such as the job market, population development, income development and use, traffic and monetary transactions, the commission members presented their suggestions to board of directors members Haase and Meyer: "The structural commission is of the opinion that a [...] significant simplification could be achieved if [...] for the management of the portfolios and the processing of claims [...] management and regulatory collectives were established."[49]

To assess the significance of this suggestion, one must consider how Allianz was structured at that time. Allianz Leben, the life insurance company, was largely independent, with its own computer center and branches that were often located in different cities from Allianz's branch offices. The property insurance branch was populated by various subsidiary companies such as the Globus Versicherungs-AG, the Assecuranz-Companie Mercur and the Union, Allgemeine Deutsche Hagelversicherungs-AG (a hail insurance company). Moreover, Allianz had sales agreements with companies that fell within the sphere of influence of Munich Re, a reinsurance company, such as the Berlinische Leben (Berlin Life Insurance Company) and the Hamburg-Mannheimer Versicherungs-AG. If someone was interested in taking out a policy with Allianz, he could do this to some extent with agents from three, four, or five competing companies. In Bavaria, he would land at the agency of Bayerische Versicherungsbank (BVB). Or perhaps there was an office of the Frankfurter next street over? If he was a Raiffeisenbank customer, he could obtain Allianz policies right there. Or if he was already a customer of Berlinische Leben or Hamburg-Mannheimer, he could take out an Allianz property insurance policy with their agents. Müller-Lutz and the structural commission clung to the principle of competing sales because one of Allianz's axiomatic principles was that two separate sales organizations were more successful than one common one. Alfred Haase also made it absolutely clear that the Frankfurter, as an independent company, was not up for discussion. Nevertheless, the commission did regard the doubling of the office work as superfluous, as every Allianz branch office had a Frankfurter branch office right across from it. Such doubling of structures was eliminated when the management collectives were introduced in 1971. The changes came at the right time because the new structure was started in the less economically prosperous 1970s; without any further big changes, the company could focus on other, more important things.

Müller-Lutz's closest colleague, Otto Ladner, knew exactly whom Allianz had to thank for its competitive advantage at that time. One can agree entirely with his assessment of Müller-Lutz when he said of him, "He was one of the most significant personalities of postwar history for Allianz, who deserved to have his actions described more thoroughly. He belonged to the generation that contributed decisively to reconstructing the company after the collapse and as the board of directors member responsible for the business management and data processing department transformed Allianz into one of the most progressive and modern service companies in Europe. The maxim of rationalizing operations always stood in the foreground of his work."[50]

On the Way to Becoming Allianz Staff

It is hard to imagine just how gloomy conditions in Germany were after the currency reform: "Ten million refugees and expellees, four million war victims, invalids, widows and orphans, 3.4 million people bombed out of their homes, two million evacuees, and 1.6 million late returnees; moreover, six million DPs (displaced persons) along with 13 million soldiers being reintegrated and the glaring discrimination against millions by the currency reform engendered problems that seemed to escape any sort of even halfway satisfactory solution."[51]

The unemployment rate was 11 percent, which often translated into bitter need for the almost 1.9 million persons so affected and their families. By contrast, those who had a job at Allianz in 1950 could count themselves among the lucky. Although the salary was often rather modest, it was paid out in the new currency, enabling employees to purchase what they needed most. Nonetheless, in the few years after the currency reform, there was at first an overabundance of employees at Allianz. One followed the principle that (male) returnees among the prisoners of war, refugees, and expellees from the East should be offered a position. Yet, because premium revenues, for example, in the life insurance branch, left something to be desired, there were too many workers, especially for office work. Therefore, those who had only worked for the company for a relatively short time were to be laid off. Random checks in the records, however, show that it was very often the women who were let go. In addition, Allianz instituted a hiring freeze in

One type of open office plan at Allianz in Stuttgart (around 1960).

August 1949, which reduced the number of workers by April 1950 by 142. At Allianz Leben, there were even 820 fewer office workers three years after the currency reform. It was not long, though, before business began to thrive, and the workload increased. The management handled this primarily with rationalization measures as the total costs in the personnel-heavy, service-oriented insurance industry were shaped very largely by personnel costs.[52]

Nonetheless, five years after the end of the war and two years after the currency reform, Allianz employees did not wish to wait any longer. Whereas workers in Germany overall were earning one-and-a-half times the salaries they had earned before the war, salaries in the insurance business had only risen by 15 percent. When the contents of the pay packet didn't add up, then the prestige of being an insurance official, which had paled in the meantime, no longer compensated for it. As a result, the Deutsche Angestelltengewerkschaft (German Employees Union) and the union Handel, Banken und Versicherungen (Trade, Banks and Insurance) canceled the wage agreement and demanded a considerable wage increase. Via the Employer Association Allianz offered a one-time payment in the fall of 1950, but the employee negotiators rejected it as it was too low. Goudefroy commented on this in the board of directors meeting in the tone of an aggrieved patron: "If our offers, with which we have shown our goodwill, were rejected, we should refrain from paying our offered benefit." After all, Goudefroy explained, "granting a raise without having the financial statements in front of us [would constitute] a leap into the darkness." Finally, an agreement was reached for a transitional payment of DM 100, which, incidentally, was postponed to the coming January.[53] The reason Allianz so categorically rejected a pay raise was, aside from the high portion of personnel costs in its total costs, the open question of benefits: Rising wages would immediately drive pension claims further upward. The solution was to have the wage increase codified as not entitled to pension benefits in the agreement with the unions. In the wage agreement of January 17, 1951, negotiators on both sides agreed under these conditions to a 10 percent wage increase. This set a trend for the coming years. By now at the latest, it must have become clear to the management staff that salaries would no longer be determined just by them but that the employees wished to have a say. The prosperous economy, the worker shortage that soon ensued, and the negotiating savvy of the unions led to the wages increasing significantly over the next years as well. Between 1950 and 1970, wages almost quadrupled, whereas the cost of living index in the same time period rose merely from 100 to 157.[54]

In addition, employees enjoyed the benefits of being able to go on vacation for reasonable prices in company-owned vacation homes, borrowing reading materials from company libraries that were soon set up, and spending free time playing sports in Allianz sports clubs with their colleagues. The company canteens provided staff with a substantial lunch, even a meal for a special diet if needed, always at very moderate prices. On the other hand, working on Saturdays was already long part of the routine. When the German Federation of Trade Unions (DGB) made the five-day workweek the focus of its demonstrations on Labor Day in 1955 and 1956 with the slogan "Saturday, Daddy belongs to me," the children of Allianz workers got their fathers' undivided attention on only 13 Saturdays a year. The insurance industry reduced working hours much more slowly than other branches. And other insurance companies that did not adhere to the federation's demands even used their shorter working hours as a competitive advantage in the struggle to attract employees, who were in ever shorter supply. The unions and employers finally agreed in December 1956 to a schedule that would make sure that insurance employees, too, would have more free time: at first, from February 1957, they got two Saturdays off a month with a 45-hour workweek, and in March 1960, when working hours were further reduced, they at last had all their weekends free. After further work-hour reductions in the 1960s, the workweek was set at 40 hours in 1973.[55]

At the end of the 1960s, Allianz workers had set working hours. Work began at 7:30 a.m. After 8¼ hours and a half-hour lunch break, they could leave the office at 4:15 p.m. Apparently, workers were occasionally not as punctual as the management would have liked as indicated by the urgent request of personnel director Rudolf Wilhelm Eversmann in a board of directors meeting that his colleagues "in all departments work toward punctual shift starts as otherwise renewed punctuality checks, in which names will be written down, will be necessary." But the times were changing because many employees had long since regarded the rigid working hours as burdensome. And so the management declared shortly thereafter that it was ready to test out flexible working hours. At first, only the workers at the branch office in Frankfurt and in the head office in Munich were able to enjoy the new freedom, but soon all the other locations followed suit. Most of the over 24,000 Allianz employees were probably quite happy about this new flexibility. With this figure, Allianz employed more than three times as many people in 1970 as in 1950.[56]

Codetermination in the Company	The editorial staff of the magazine Unser Adler (Our Eagle) had seen the signs of the times: under the headline "The Discovery of the Employee" in 1958, it described the

emergence of a new style of interaction within the company. The article in the employee newspaper for office workers described a notable attempt at rationalization in Hawthorne, Illinois. It had turned out that "taking care of human relations" in business could increase productivity just as much as what one expected from classic rationalization measures. From this, the author concluded: "Every employee ought to be aware of the problems of his company so that he can follow along and do his part to share responsibility in what happens in the company." It can no doubt be assumed that this statement was not published without the approval of a board member.[57]

It had been a long road for insurance employees, progressing from the 19th-century official to the member of the "company following" in National Socialism before becoming a "modern" employee. In the early 1950s, Allianz employees enjoyed some codetermination on all levels of the company whenever their interests were concerned: in the Allianz Pension Fund, in company health insurance matters, as works council members. Finally, they

The cafeteria at the branch office in Cologne in 1966.

even were preparing to take on voting positions on the supervisory board. By secret ballot and with a simple majority, the works council could elect supervisory board members. The prospect of this sort of company codetermination, however, caused quite a stir on the management level. After all, the supervisory board not only had to approve transfers of Allianz stock but also appointed members of the board of directors and formulated the employment contracts of these board members. Management certainly did not wish to share this knowledge with the employees. The chief legal officer Rudolf Wilhelm Eversmann found an elegant solution to this problem: even before the supervisory board met again, a working committee was formed including the two chairmen of the supervisory board and the representative of the majority stockholder. This circle, comprised of Hans Heß, the banker Karl Butzengeiger of the Bayerische Vereinsbank, and Alois Alzheimer of Munich Re, was, in future, to take over the "processing and regulation of all questions that pertain to the interests of members of the company board of directors." As no representatives from the works council were appointed to this committee, this would prevent employees from acquiring information about, for example, the board members' pay.[58] When the first supervisory board meeting in accordance with the new bylaws then took place in the fall of 1951, the employee representatives were absent, thus missing out not only on a tasty dinner in the Restaurant Walterspiel in the Four Seasons Hotel. The minutes of the committee meeting of the day before succinctly noted: "The elections for the works council members who are to be appointed to the supervisory board of the company have not yet taken place so that the supervisory board meeting of November 7, 1951, will convene without works council members."[59] About a year later, on October 31, 1952, though, the time had come: Hans Heß welcomed Max Scholber of Munich and Ernst Wansch of Cologne as employee representatives to Allianz's supervisory board; it was the first time employees had been represented in this body since 1933.[60]

The Works Constitution Act of 1952 expanded the participation of employees to one third and gave them equal legal standing to the other members. This led among other things to them getting paid like the representatives on the ownership side. In addition, the entire staff now elected their representatives for the supervisory board. It would soon become apparent that the management and the supervisory board members who had been appointed before would not be able or willing to deal constructively with the self-confidence of the new generation of employee representatives. From the beginning, the new "colleagues" were perceived as troublemakers who took positions away from the "real" supervisory board members. This was because the supervisory board was supposed to be expanded to include Friedrich Flick and Fritz Gummert of Ruhrgas AG. On account of the new law, however, it actually had to be reduced in size.[61]

Alfons Hooffacker, a member of the supervisory board and works council of the BVB, was elected to the new supervisory board as well. He had already made waves there that had drawn Goudefroy's attention to him.[62] On the Allianz supervisory board, Hooffacker repeatedly demanded that the employee representatives be included in the new working committee. As Allianz's legal department also regarded the categorical exclusion of the employee representatives as objectionable, the committee was disbanded in 1956; the responsibility for drawing up the contracts of members of the board of directors was then transferred to the chairmen of the supervisory board, all of whom belonged to the investment side of things. Hooffacker did not achieve his aim, but he was apparently not discouraged by defeat, and there were plenty of other areas for him to get involved in. After the pension reform of 1957, he wanted to make sure that the Allianz Pension Fund benefits would be reduced as little as possible, and he vehemently attacked the management. The employees of the BVB thanked him for these efforts with dream results in the works council elections. In 1957, he was elected with 838 of 910 ballots cast – by far the best result. All of the works council members of Allianz and of Allianz Leben, however, distanced themselves from Hooffacker over the course of the year and wished to prevent him getting reelected by providing a list of competing candidates. In the end, three of the four competing candidates were elected to the supervisory board – and Alfons Hooffacker as well. Nonetheless, he had gone too far in his campaign in the eyes of the managers by dropping comments about colleagues. Allianz accused him of repeatedly disturbing the peace of the company and fired him without notice from the supervisory board of Allianz five days after his reelection. After the case was heard in court, a compromise was reached, and on January 20, 1960, Hooffacker left the supervisory board for good.[63] Allianz did not look to itself to find the reason for the quarrel, as a BVB note from 1961 proves: "The processes that led to the dissolution of the employment contract stood in the context of the functions that Mr. Hooffacker had taken on as the works council chairman and employee representative on the supervisory board, and for which he did not find the appropriate standards." If one looks at the remarks of Allianz's chief legal officer Jürgen Mirow of 1972, however, when it was expected that Hooffacker would attend Allianz's annual general meeting as a shareholder, one gets the impression that it was rather Allianz's managers who were unable to find the appropriate standards for working with self-confident works council members: "One must be able to tolerate unpleasant stockholders. The current heads of the supervisory board are also [...] fully capable of dealing with a stockholder like Hooffacker and, in the worst case, of making use of their domiciliary right."[64] The sovereignty that these words convey reflects the new objectivity in the cooperation between management and works councils in the 1970s. Both sides had accepted codetermination as an integral part of West Germany's economic make-up, and one that had secured harmony in society. "The strong economic growth, which satisfied interests on both sides, naturally made it much easier to reach a consensus. The Federal Republic became a model state of 'social partnership.'"[65]

Allianz Agents

Allianz had been waiting for men like this: Willy Pempeit came from East Prussia where he had already sold insurance policies as a sideline before the war. In 1947, he returned from war captivity and was trained by the Frankfurter to be a regional inspector at age 44 in Stuttgart. In Heilbronn, he once again built up the inspection service and managed with the help of about 60 agents to make it into the "circle of great sales agents." In the fall of 1951, Pempeit took over the general agency in Heilbronn and achieved membership in 1952 and 1953 in the Heß Club, the highest distinction for Allianz agents.[66]

The Heß Club, named after long-term Allianz head Hans Heß, had come into being in 1949 when the Big Life Club and the Big Advertiser Club were combined. Agents accepted into this circle had reached the pinnacle of their careers. In this club, the most successful agents met once a year, jointly celebrated their successes and were praised by the heads of Allianz. After all, the company owed it primarily to them that it managed already in 1949 to bring in premium revenues for property insurance that were almost as high as before the war. With the help of its broadly branching sales organization, Allianz was able to support sales by pointing out the importance of insurance with centrally directed advertising and making people aware of Allianz. But it was the agents, above all, who turned these people into actual contractual clients. They convinced people of how important it remained or had once again become to be insured.[67]

And so it is not surprising that the agents with strong self-esteem – almost all of whom, at least among those who worked full-time, were men – also entered into the negotiations with Allianz. In order to assert their interests more effectively, they founded, first of all, the so-called Hausvereine, or agents' clubs, once again. These were associations of agents on the level of branch offices that had already existed in the 1920s. They quickly noticed, however, that the heads of the branch offices did not always possess the necessary authority to resolve the conflicts they wished to address. Consequently, on October 16, 1956, envoys of the various agents' clubs founded the interest group of the agents' clubs of the Allianz companies, which became the most important point of contact for all questions related to sales in the following years.

There were plenty of things to discuss. For example, the pension scheme had to be worked out. Sales agents could become members of the Allianz Pension Fund as early as 1940, but once it was closed, at first no further agents could be accepted into Allianz's pension plan. This had to do with tax considerations, for one thing, and also with a new law that gave agents the right to receive compensation if they gave up their portfolios. As Allianz did not wish to be asked to pay twice, it demanded that agents give up their demand for compensation if they wished to contribute to the pension plan. The agents, on the other hand, saw no relation between the pension plan and compensation payments and tried, in consultation with Allianz, which paid

Inside view of an Allianz agency in Buende, Westphalia.

the costs of the trial, to provoke a test case. The Federal Supreme Court (Bundesgerichtshof) decided in favor of Allianz on May 23, 1966.

The creation of a benefits plan for the agents was officially announced a year before at Allianz's 75th anniversary celebrations. The pensions promised correlated to the insurance portfolios the agents themselves had built up. Agents had to submit a written declaration that they were relinquishing any claim to compensation payments of the same amount. It had taken a long time to find a solution for the agents. Again and again, Goudefroy and Haase had had to comfort the sales agents. In the end, though, both sides were equally satisfied. The interest group put it as follows in a brochure for its 25-year anniversary: "Today, it can be said that the Allianz agents are included in one of the best benefits plans that has ever existed in the German insurance industry."[68] At first, the workday for agents hardly changed at all. Administrative tasks and the collection of insurance premiums took up a lot of time. Although Allianz repeatedly ran new series in the Allianz Zeitung on how to rationalize a modern agency, it was up to the agents themselves to take up these suggestions if they wished. Erwin Herz decided to take a different path. He had Allianz Leben collect the premium payments for life insurance policies directly. Herz was the most successful general agent in

Munich, having brought in the most new life insurance business in the previous two years of all agents; he praised this procedure of direct collection in the highest terms in an article in the Allianz Zeitung in 1957 and concluded his remarks with some advice: "Based on my experiences, I must recommend that every colleague allow the company to collect the ordinary life premiums directly. I, for one, would in any case fight tooth and nail if one wanted to burden me with it."[69]

Nevertheless, there was a simple reason that direct collection remained limited to ordinary life policies. Among this circle of clients, bank and checking accounts were already widespread, in contrast to typical small life insurance clients, who for the most part still gathered their monthly savings sum in their Allianz home money box. Most agents bristled at the thought of giving up premium collection, despite Erwin Herz's glowing words. Larger agencies allowed clients to pay their premiums in their offices, or established their own accounts into which the policyholders could transfer the money. Many part-time agents stuck with collecting the premiums themselves until well into the 1970s because they believed that this enabled them to maintain good contact with their clients.

In cities, especially, an agency's sales were important for establishing contact with customers. Ads with fluorescent lighting, like the ones familiar to us from particularly exposed locations such as the Europahaus in Berlin in the 1930s, now turned up not only at branch and regional management centers but also at larger agencies. When these agencies were accommodated in shops, more attention was paid to making the display windows attractive. Allianz offered smaller agencies the so-called Lightboy, a small box upon which one could mount a transparent pane with an advertisement that could be lit up from behind. This was a comparatively simple and reasonably priced form of illuminated advertising.[70] Allianz Leben made illuminated advertising of an entirely different sort available to its agents from 1948: slides that agents were able to have screened in local cinemas in order to advertise for Allianz and above all also for their own agency. The first slide that was distributed since spring 1948 portrayed a small girl in the foreground playing with a dollhouse with a young woman in a bridal gown in the background, her train functioning as a rug for the girl. This image was accompanied by the slogan: "Girls become brides, so take out dowry insurance early on." Above the Allianz logo, there was still room for the name and address of the agent. As the slide was well received, other motifs were quickly added – for example, advertising for education insurance with a boy in the foreground and a scientist bent over a microscope in the background.[71]

In the 1960s, Allianz became increasingly interested in display window advertising in the agencies (outside view of an Allianz agency in Bremerhaven).

Allianz began to utilize films in its advertising beginning in 1951. First, it produced the training film "Einst und Jetzt" (Once and Now), which was to inform the staff about block policies with the help of the eponymous Fräulein Block Policy. A little later, the first advertising film appeared, "Der schützende Adler" (The Protecting Eagle), which still appealed to clients' fears: drab colors predominated, and spectators may have grown pale watching it in light of the dangers, illnesses, accidents, catastrophes, and other calamities that could seek them out and endanger their lives and which they should protect themselves against by taking out insurance with Allianz as quickly as possible.

Other film strips – now humorous – rapidly followed, such as the above-mentioned film "When Clever People Travel" and the sketch that was reminiscent of comedian Heinz Erhardt about a housewife cleaning her windows whose bucket falls on the feet of a neighbor passing by. From today's standpoint, these first advertising films were rather stolid in their storytelling. They generated – simply by means of their length – considerable costs for individual agents. Accordingly, the wish for shorter material that would, thus, be more affordable for smaller agencies was quickly expressed.

Matchbox advertising fulfilled all the criteria of short, pithy and humorous advertising. After the resounding success of the first years, the Allianz Zeitung euphorically reported the following under the headline "Matchbox Advertising Comes to Life": "Something has happened! By means of the ten million matchboxes that have now come into families from individual sales, the advertising slogan 'Hopefully covered by Allianz' has now practically become an idiom, especially among large and small matchbox collectors. But doubled lasts longer, the advertising department said, bringing the images to life with the help of an animation studio."[72]

In order to counter sales agents' reservations and criticism about new ideas and changes, Allianz called the Rationalization Commission Sales Service into being in 1962, comprised of agents and staff members of various departments. Its task was to discuss rationalization questions for sales and to offer solutions. Agencies were to be managed as simply and economically as possible. In order to spread these ideas broadly and quickly among the agents, a newsletter was also distributed at regular intervals with information, for example, about agency management, application forms for car insurance, the standardization of preprinted application and insurance certificate forms, as well as advertising and informational materials. The new institutionalized ways of fostering cooperation complemented the rather informal talks at the Heß Club conferences and improved Allianz's cooperation with independent sales agents.[73]

The Little Man and Life Insurance

Fritz Otten was absolutely exotic. The 80-year-old had been working for 30 years as an Allianz agent and was blind. Nevertheless, he was repeatedly invited to closing conventions of the branch office in Hamburg. He was given the opportunity to give away his secrets of success in two extensive articles in the Allianz Zeitung. One thing he remembered particularly well was a visit two years after the currency reform from a farmer who had recently returned from a prisoner-of-war camp: "In 1950, a farmer came to me to cancel his insurance policy for RM 10,000. […] Asked about the reasons, he said that the insurance had become worthless as a result of the currency devaluation. By contrast, he welcomed the fact that the pension agencies had not devalued the pensions and would continue to pay the pensions in Deutschmarks. I explained to him that the insurance had been valued up to DM 7,000. (I use the term valued up in this case rather than the term devalued.) In this, he had to take into consideration that the premiums of the last years had been paid out of almost worthless money. Most recently, the annual sum was worth just about a pound of butter. [...] If that was the case, he said, then he wanted to top the policy off to the full sum."[74]

It is no wonder that Allianz made plenty of room for this man in its company newspaper because he seemed to have a ready solution for the difficulties that the life insurance business was encountering in West Germany after the currency reform. As mentioned above, the currency devaluation reduced insurance sums for life insurance rather significantly in some cases. Many customers, consequently, saw no reason to maintain their life insurance policies and switched them over to noncontributory policies or canceled them altogether. As a result, Allianz's premium revenues dropped in 1949 to DM 96 million, falling to the level they had been at in 1928. New business was hardly imaginable at first. People had other concerns besides thinking about how to prepare for their old age. If they thought about the future, they asked themselves whether the currency would remain stable. Agents spread out and explained what the currency reform meant for clients in concrete terms. This did not only pertain to life insurance policies; the contracts for some property insurance policies also had to be changed. The little new business that did come in derived primarily from clients who were topping their life insurance benefits off to their original levels.[75]

But by 1950 already, premium revenues and the overall state of insurance increased slightly, which could be attributed above all to a rise in the number of industrial life insurance policies being taken out. The economic recovery contributed to a trend that would shape the state of things for many years to come. Segments of the population that had not previously been able to even consider setting a sum aside every month now had some wiggle room, due to the steady pay raises, to take out wealth-accumulating insurance policies. For example, in 1956, more than 50 percent of customers taking out industrial life insurance policies were workers purchasing an average insurance benefit of DM 1,360. The new clients, as a rule, had not had any negative experiences with life insurance and were thus easier to persuade about the opportunities such policies presented. Agents were advised, for example, to tell prospective clients about the millions Allianz had paid out in the 1930s year after year for policies that had matured.[76]

From the mid-1950s, the dynamic emerged, however, less from exploding numbers of new industrial life insurance policies than from higher insured amounts for ordinary life insurance. The Old Savers Law, which doubled the cumulative amount saved up in a life insurance policy if it had

With this cinematic ad, agents could make viewers aware of their agencies in a targeted way.

been taken out before 1940 up until the currency reform, as well as dividends Allianz once again introduced in 1954, further strengthened customers' trust. Two years later, the insurance amounts at Allianz Leben added up to the prewar level with over DM 5 billion; by 1961, it had doubled to DM 10.7 billion and continued to grow to DM 35.6 billion by 1970. The average insured amount by that time had already risen to DM 8,000.[77]

New Investment Principles

Year in and year out, insurance companies collect more or less large sums of money. At Allianz Leben, for example, in 1970, the premium revenues amounted to DM 1.4 billion. If one adds the investment income to this, the sum rises to more than DM 1.9 billion. For this year, the total surplus was almost DM 400 million. Stockholders of Allianz Leben received more than DM 5 million, of which Allianz Versicherungs-AG was one of the principle ones and added more than DM 200 million to the over DM 600 million in total that Allianz invested in 1970.[78]

Traditionally, these monies flowed into the company's own real estate and mortgages. This was also the case in 1949 when Allianz established that there was a shortage of capital and a strong desire for credit from all segments of the economy and from the insured. Of the DM 83.7 million that Allianz had for investing in 1948/1949, DM 46.5 million were put into mortgages – more than half of the sum – and another DM 8.3 million went into property. With this traditional investment strategy Allianz accommodated the state's interests as it was hoped that impending financial regulation could be avoided. Yet already in the early 1950s, the head of Allianz Leben, Gerd Müller, complained about the low interest rate of the mortgage credit and announced that the bulk of loans would be made to industries and for other tangible assets. Allianz proudly reported on the many new construction projects that were supposed to alleviate the housing shortage of the postwar period. Internally, by contrast, there were grave doubts about these projects as it was feared that the increased construction costs could completely undermine the profitability of the newly constructed housing. Consequently, the company preferred to purchase properties that had already been built, at least for a time.[79]

Thereafter, however, Allianz maintained both its mortgage business and its purchasing of property. As the many new staff hired in the following years needed many offices, Allianz not only erected a new head office in Munich but also a high-rise office building in West Berlin, intended not least as a political symbol. Moreover, it built office buildings in Essen, Hamburg, Kiel, Nuremberg, Cologne, Stuttgart, and Düsseldorf, among others. Mortgages also remained a very important investment vehicle for many years. In 1970, Allianz Leben had about 30,000 mortgages worth DM 1.46 billion in its portfolio, which comprised about 18 percent of its total investments. New funds, though, were seldom invested in this sort of loan. These were replaced by promissory notes, which made up almost half the total assets in 1970. These were debts comprised of credits to large companies and the public sector, which were used to finance infrastructure projects, as well as for acquiring and processing raw materials.[80]

German exports experienced a long-lasting boom after the Korean crisis of 1950. It was financed by industrial loans from banks and insurance companies, whereby Allianz once again discovered the value of investing in shares of corporations. This investment vehicle had played a very subordinate role in the previous years. During the National Socialist years, Allianz had at first reduced its share of stock because the regime had restricted stock trading on account of its financial policies. After the war and the currency reform, the few papers that Allianz held largely lost their value. In 1939, the valuation of Allianz Leben's stocks comprised about 5 percent of the investments and included shares in life insurance companies, in a real estate subsidiary, as well as in preference stock in the German National Railway. After the currency reform, only the pitiful sum of a little over DM 40,000 remained. From 1948, though, Allianz Leben raised the ratio of stocks in its portfolio continually until 1958 when it reached its highest level at over 13 percent and DM 173 million. One might think that the reason for this development lay in the rapid increase in stock prices as the stock index DAX, calculated retrospectively, rose from 12.93 to 534.09 points, repeatedly doubling its value within one year, between 1948 and 1960. However, since these were unrealized gains, they were not accounted for in the budgets but increased the hidden reserves. Thus, the increase was based primarily on the increased acquisition of stocks.[81]

In contrast to Allianz Leben, the Allianz Versicherungs-AG held stock not only in insurance companies but also in industrial enterprises, such as the Vereinigte Stahlwerke (United Steelworks), before 1945 as well. In the 1950s, however, Allianz Versicherungs-AG grew markedly more interested in stocks. Perhaps it was an attempted hostile takeover – in the course of which an Allianz director-general, Hans Goudefroy, appeared on the cover of the news magazine Der Spiegel for the first and still only time – that turned managers' attention more to shareholding. At that time, August von Finck tried to gain a dominant influence on Allianz by buying shares. August was the son of Allianz founder Wilhelm von Finck, the owner of the bank Merck, Finck & Co. August had held the office of supervisory board chairman until he had been fired in 1945 after the end of the war for having been a Nazi Party member. After the end of the denazification proceedings, which were discontinued in 1949 because of amnesty being granted, he wished to take up his earlier positions as the chair of the supervisory boards of Allianz and Munich Re again. When this was denied him, he began to have front men buy up Allianz shares and, in 1954, left the supervisory board of Munich Re, which he had joined again in 1950. When the conflict escalated in the fall of 1954, von Finck even tried to prevent Chancellor Adenauer from visiting the new Allianz head office. Der Spiegel reported on this with a title story that went into detail about the now public dispute. Although von Finck's approach disturbed Goudefroy, the latter did not – at least officially – fear a takeover. This was because, for one thing, Munich Re's capital stock

One of the first new construction projects of 1949 on Brandenburger Straße for employees of the headquarters relocated to Munich.

share was too high, and, for another, banks and industrial enterprises had forged a consortium whose support gave Allianz security. Thus, it could ward off the attack even before it was to be waged in a special general meeting in January 1955. From Allianz's perspective, the cross holdings with Munich Re and its good relations with the banking world had worked beautifully.[82]

In 1955, von Finck relinquished his newly acquired shares in exchange for a block of shares in the Stahlwerke Südwestfalen (Steelworks of Southern Westphalia), a successor of the Vereinigte Stahlwerke (United Steelworks) that had been disbanded by the Allies; Vereinigte Stahlwerke had been the largest mining concern in National Socialist Germany. Allianz traded its shares in this and other mining companies in 1954 for shares in the successor companies Stahlwerke Südwestfalen and Hüttenwerke Siegerland (the Siegerland steel mills). These constituted Allianz's first industrial holdings in the postwar period, along with papers it held for the machine-tool manufacturer Schiess.[83]

These two components – industrial shares and cross holdings – comprised Allianz's investment strategy for almost the next 50 years. In economics, the phrase "Germany, Inc." was coined to refer to this strategy, which was defined as "close personal and capital interrelationships of large German companies."[84] After all, Allianz was not the only company that was interested in industrial shareholdings; the large German banks had already been doing it for much longer. Beginning in the 1950s, the insurance companies Munich Re and Allianz, on the one hand, and the Deutsche Bank, on the other, formed the core of "Germany, Inc." And so it is not surprising that Goudefroy joined the supervisory board of the largest German bank in 1957. Alois Alzheimer, director-general of Munich Re, represented both companies on the supervisory board of the Dresdner Bank. In exchange, Carl Goetz represented Dresdner Bank and Walter Tron represented the Deutsche Bank on Allianz's supervisory board; the Dresdner Bank had long since taken over the role of being Allianz's principal bank from Merck, Finck & Co., and the Deutsche Bank was slipping into a similar role.[85]

At this point, the deep intertwining of large German corporations resulted in "the company managers at the very center of this network of interrelationships, 'Germany, Inc.,' being imputed with management capabilities that extended beyond the limits of their own company or group." At first, this automatic growth in power made Allianz visibly uncomfortable. Again and again, reports of new purchases emphasized that "these investments in no way are meant to imply that political influence [...] should be exercised over the companies." Allianz managers were only to take up supervisory board positions in companies in which Allianz's financial interests made oversight necessary.[86]

Even if Allianz clearly did not wish to take over any company function with its holdings, it had concrete ideas of how to make use of its proximity to industry. To this end, it enlarged the supervisory board – even though this meant that another employee representative would also join – and appointed Günter Henle of Klöckner Works and Ernst von Siemens of Siemens AG as representatives of two industrial companies in 1955. Two years before, Allianz, likewise, had founded a series of advisory boards for the purpose of nurturing relations.[87] In return, Allianz hoped to have an opportunity to become the insurer of the companies that these men represented with the help of the industrial department established for this purpose under the direction of Rudolf Freiherr von Seydlitz-Kurzbach.

The life insurer proudly announced that, by now, it held shares in 113 German companies. One failed investment shows how Allianz began to exhaust the "management capabilities" it had gained at the end of the 1950s. When it was offered a holding of 4 million shares in the Frisia refinery in Emden with the assurance that these shares would be bought back three years after the company became operational at a minimum price of 125 percent, it turned it down. Although the offer in and of itself was attractive, Allianz rejected it "in consideration of the existing interests of the large oil companies in Germany, such as Esso, BP, etc." This made it more difficult for a powerful competitor of the already established companies to emerge.[88]

Dealing with New Risks: The Dawning of the Atomic Age Throughout its history, Allianz has repeatedly proven to be a company that could ferret out new insurance needs and come up with offers for previously uninsurable risks. This has been the case in its liability insurance, which was far from being an established segment when Allianz was founded, as well as in its automobile insurance, and also in its aviation insurance. In the aviation segment, the risk was spread out with the help of the Luftpool (Aviation Pool) among many direct insurers. The American model of a pool of insurers was then taken up when the insurance industry ventured to cover the risk of the peaceful use of atomic energy.[89]

Since 1951 at least, Allianz has dealt with atomic energy issues. In that year, the Frankfurter Versicherungs-AG had the supervisory authorities grant permission to exclude atomic risk from construction all risk insurance. One of the leading nuclear physicists of Germany was invited to the third managers' conference in 1952 organized by Allianz's machinery insurance department to "familiarize [Allianz's] business associates [...] with current questions of operations and damage protection." In the hall of the German Museum in Munich, Professor Walther Gerlach spoke in a way that non-experts could understand about the discovery of and research into atomic energy. He concluded with this hopeful statement: "If people might realize that the power source of our sun, which builds and sustains our world, is atomic energy, then they will perhaps also understand that they must not be allowed to destroy this world and themselves with the same atomic energy."[90]

One finds this enthusiasm about the progress of science coupled with concern about whether humanity could handle this progress not only among responsible scientists like the "Göttingen 18." This group of well-known nuclear researchers, which counted Gerlach among its members, protested the plans of the German government to equip the newly created Bundeswehr (German Army) with nuclear weapons. Ambivalence could also be heard from within the insurance industry. Allianz definitely saw nuclear energy as a future business and was active in the atomic commission founded by the Association of the German Insurance Business (GDV) in 1955. Ernst Pohl, who was responsible for the machinery insurance division on Allianz's board of directors and chaired the atomic commission, rejoiced about the opportunities that atomic energy presented to insurers: "With this, the insurance industry has a unique opportunity to demonstrate its great significance to the national economy. That is, the atom not only boosts industry but contributes to animating thoughts of insurance among the big and small alike." The supervisory board of Allianz thought along similar lines, agreeing in 1956 "that the state should only be called in to the extent that the insurance industry is not able to cover the risks in question from within, so that state influence should be kept to a minimum." On the other hand, Pohl made it clear that "assessments that deny risk are in error." He was fully aware of the risk; after all, he predicted "that claims will rarely be made, but this rare case will require unusually high expenditures to remedy." Hans Goudefroy drew the following conclusion in the atomic commission for a worst-case scenario: "Such an extraordinary case would then be perceived as a national disaster, for which the state would have to intervene. That would not have anything to do with socializing the losses." The GDV shared Pohl's skepticism and cautioned against taking the "assertions about the absolute safety of reactors" too literally.[91] Two years after the atomic commission was founded, the public voice of the German insurance guild, the magazine Versicherungswirtschaft (The Insurance Industry), announced that the insurance industry was ready: "After concluding the necessary groundwork, the German insurance industry is now prepared to cover the risks associated with the construction and operation of nuclear reactors." In addition, the German Nuclear Reactor Insurance Association (DKVG) was founded as an insurance pool; it was not long before 81 companies – "all the significant [insurance companies] active in Germany" – had become members. The DKVG was also supposed to offer insurance coverage for legal liabilities arising from the construction and operation of nuclear reactors. However, the atomic law of 1960 established that the liability risk should be primarily carried by the state rather than by the private insurance industry. This state subsidy accelerated the commercial use of nuclear energy and enabled the insurance industry to concentrate on the risk of nuclear power plants as "normal" industrial enterprises. After that, "nuclear insurance" developed into "a conventional industrial business in the 1960s, which still involved considerable risks but which had, in the end, become manageable and calculable by means of special insurance solutions." At the end of 1969, there were, in all, six nuclear power plants operating in West Germany, and Allianz had drawn up insurance policies for them for erection, machinery, and transportation insurance. Moreover, Allianz was also involved in insuring nuclear power plants outside of Germany.[92]

In August 1949, all the members of the **The Difficulty of** board of directors and Allianz managers **Rebooting Inter-** received a circular with the following an- **national Business** nouncement: "Department director [Max] Surner takes on the newly created department for foreign business as of today." With this, Allianz began its international business for the third time in its then less than 60-year history, more or less from scratch. And as when it was founded and after the First World War, it set great store this time as well in the experience and competence of its "big sister" Munich Re.[93]

At first, the occupation authorities had prohibited any sort of international activity for German insurers. The Association of the German Insurance Business (GDV) did not want to accept this since the industry viewed itself as the defender of the principle of internationalism, particularly against the National Socialists' recently failed attempts at autarky. "It contradicts the fundamental idea of every insurance protection to the highest degree to restrict the insurers to the country in which they are located. In the long run, the insurance business can only be carried out successfully when the risks are distributed across as many countries as possible." The responsible parties found it particularly bitter that German industry had long been able to engage in importing and exporting again, even though the exporting industry was struggling to get going. Exports to the U.S. amounted to $47 million in 1949, of which $12 million was collected for scrap metal; Germany, for its part, imported goods worth $825 million. The premiums for protecting these transactions now had to be paid in foreign currencies, the GDV complained, because insurance policies could only be taken out with foreign companies.[94]

Apparently, the lobbying efforts worked because in April 1949, the military administration in the Western zone loosened the prohibition – first for insurance for transportation that crossed borders, and then later for reinsurance. Allianz was soon the first German insurance company to be able to pay for damage "in all important places in the world" in foreign currencies – something desperately needed in light of the foreign competition in Germany. And so, in the summer of 1952, the director of the transportation section, Karl Friedrich von Schlayer, reported to the board of directors "that the reconstruction of this branch has now reached a certain level." At that point in time, the last legal restrictions had also been lifted for the other insurance segments.[95] Martin Herzog led the negotiations on behalf of the insurance industry. He had joined the Reich Group for Insurance as a young assessor in 1937, where he worked closely with Eduard Hilgard. As an advisor on foreign matters, he had undertaken and documented trips into the German-occupied areas. For example, he had traveled to Hungary in the summer of 1944 and reported on the effects that the deportation of Hungarian Jews had on the Hungarian economy. After the war, he contributed to the formation of the GDV and finally joined Allianz in 1949. From mid-1951, he directed the foreign department and was a major player in the development of the portfolios in Belgium, France, and the Netherlands for which Allianz had assumed custodial control during the war. In addition, he participated in the London debt convention as a representative of the insurance industry. The London Debt Agreement declared, much to the delight of the German insurance industry, that bilateral agreements needed to be reached for the debts from private, international insurance transactions. Although Germany's negotiations with various countries lasted for several years, once they were concluded successfully they made it possible for German insurers to do business in these countries again.[96]

For Allianz, however, the primary question was what had become of its foreign subsidiaries. There could be no illusions about the ones located in countries within the Soviet zone as the insurance business there had been socialized. So what remained were Plus Ultra in Spain, Swiss National, La Pace in Italy, the South African Liberal, Bore in Sweden, and Wiener Allianz in Austria as well as smaller holdings in Turkey and Persia. Yet, what Goudefroy announced to his colleagues on the board of directors in 1953 did not sound very promising. Wiener Allianz appeared to be irretrievably lost; its shares were now held by the Italian company Generali and the Erste Allgemeine in Austria, neither of which appeared inclined to relinquish them to Allianz. The former subsidiary Wiener Allianz did, however, continue to use not only the name but also the Allianz eagle logo, "which could cause unpleasant mix-ups in [Allianz's] foreign business." Liberal's shares had been auctioned and then resold for a much higher price without Allianz having any prospect of receiving any of the auction profits. Swiss National wanted to seize the moment and dissolve its ties to Allianz and Munich Re. At Plus Ultra, it looked as though the remaining 48 percent of shares owned by Allianz and Munich Re might be sold. Only at Bore

In 1961, the Heß Club meets in Vienna: in the Rococo Hall of the Pallavicini Palace the most successful agents are honored.

"could a small silver lining be seen, although one would have to wait for it to materialize." But this glimmer of hope was also extinguished. After protracted and often disagreeable negotiations, Allianz only managed in the end to retrieve some portions of Plus Ultra, La Pace, and, against all expectations, also Wiener Allianz.[97]

Goudefroy's experiences in the negotiations prompted him to change his strategy: "The resumption of foreign business has proven to be very difficult. Detailed analyses have shown that it is not currently expedient for Allianz to take up foreign insurance directly but rather, it would be more attractive from a business perspective to participate in reinsurance internationally." Together with Munich Re, three English and eight Dutch companies, as well as a Danish one, Allianz founded the reinsurer Constellation Insurance Company in New York in 1954. When Goudefroy presented this to Allianz's supervisory board, he particularly stressed "the cooperation this created with a series of foreign friends, which will turn out to be useful for Allianz in other areas as well."[98]

Goudefroy was probably quite relieved to know that Allianz had now been accepted as a business partner by foreign companies once again; he hoped to push Allianz's international business forward in consequence. Nonetheless, of the many plans that Allianz pursued, for example, in South Africa, Persia, South America, and Lebanon, the only foreign cooperation it managed to establish was a small holding in the life insurer O Trabalho in Portugal and in Bimeh Pars in Tehran. The company had more success in the reinsurance branch. In 1957, Allianz purchased $ 2.4 million in shares in the U.S. branch of Munich Re that was formed in early 1956, and in 1959 it purchased a 41 percent stake in the Munich American Reassurance Company, a life reinsurance company, increasing this to 45 percent later on. Both times, Allianz at first considered taking up the direct insurance business as well. In 1956, the working committee of the supervisory board had even already agreed to this. In the end, after Goudefroy and other members of the board of directors had taken various trips to America, it was decided that the company would stick with reinsurance as "the costs [of acquiring an insurance company] would be extraordinarily high and would hardly be reasonably proportional to the achievable returns." In 1960, therefore, the key source of international premium revenues came from American reinsurance policies.[99]

Not until the Treaties of Rome were signed on March 25, 1957, did Allianz turn its attention once again to its own continent. Six countries – Belgium, the Netherlands, Luxembourg, France, Italy, and Germany – founded the European Economic Community (EEC). European integration was to be fostered by strengthened economic cooperation. In addition, to abolishing customs barriers and creating joint institutions and the conditions for the free flow of capital and people, the treaties also had another important aim – to secure the freedom for companies to provide services in the other countries. For this reason, the German insurance industry at first regarded the EEC more as a threat than an opportunity. "In the EEC area up to this point, the German market has been the most interesting. Thus, we will have to assume that more insurers from other EEC countries will come to Germany than German insurers will be able to build up a healthy business in the other 5 EEC countries," Goudefroy predicted in 1962. Allianz armed itself for the new tasks it expected to have in the context of the Common Market by amassing high reserves and increasing its capital stock.[100]

And at this point, it once again felt confident in its own neighborhood. It began renewing its relations with agencies in neighboring countries: in 1957 with the Belgian agency Deckers & Meckelbert, and in 1959 with its former Dutch business partners; it also opened a branch office in Paris that year. In Italy, as well, it founded another branch office besides La Pace, a majority interest in which it had acquired together with Munich Re in 1966. Whether this would develop into a healthy business could not yet be predicted in the 1960s, but the company did not wish to miss the opportunity that the Common Market offered.[101]

At first, there was one core Western European country missing in the EEC: the UK applied to join in 1961 but was rejected because of resistance from France. Allianz did not seem to mind this as it feared British competition and suspected that insurers on the island utilized unfair practices: "Theoretically, the English insurance market is nearly open without limits to foreign insurers; de facto, though, foreign companies cannot build a solid insurance business in the English market. This has to do, for one thing, with the mentality of the English, who prefer their own companies; for another, it relates to the market structure, which allows for specially agreed arrangements between competitors in a form that would be prohibited by German competition law."[102] A new generation of managers, including Wolfgang Schieren as the chairman of the board of directors and Detlev von der Burg as the director of the foreign department, would have to take the helm at Allianz before it would overcome these reservations concerning England. But that already marks another chapter in the history of the company.

Say "Ah... Lee... Ahnz"

Allianz. The company everybody knows... but can't pronounce. The people at Allianz give you the best in coverage and services. Every department is built on experienced personnel, and backed by a worldwide network of insurance expertise. The next time you need help on your preferred commercial accounts, call us. We're the experts you should know. *(Even if you can't pronounce our name.)*

Allianz 🏛

Allianz Insurance Company
A Center of Excellence
6435 Wilshire Blvd., Los Angeles, CA 90048
(213) 658-5000

January 23, 1978

1970–1990

- - - - - - - - - - - - - - - - - -

PATHS OF
INTERNATIONALIZATION

The first two postwar decades represent the fastest economic growth that Germany has ever experienced. For the broad masses of the people that meant full employment, and increasingly, a certain share in the prosperity. Thus, prosperity contributed substantially to the political stability of the young democratic state. But in the mid-1960s, this growth had already begun to grow fragile. The end of the boom was marked by an event that was apparent to everybody – the oil crisis of 1973. The subsequent recession required a fundamental change in economic policy: measures to stabilize the currency by means of a policy of high interest rates, consolidation of the budget, with tax concessions and stimulation of the labor market by countercyclical additional expenditures, and an increased proportion of the GNP as government revenue were the responses of the Bundesbank and politicians.

For Allianz, too, the uninterrupted growth that had stimulated its business for almost 25 years came to an end. The 1970s began with a slump in its core business, automobile insurance. The reasons lay in a change in consumer desires: the customers were harder to please and demanded superior products. The kind of clothing, vacation, or car that was considered a status symbol was what mattered. Together with the skyrocketing number of motor vehicles on the roads, this had a direct effect on Allianz's cost burden. On the one hand, there was a sharp increase in the numbers of accidents due to the mass motorization; on the other hand, the larger and more expensive cars raised the size of the claims and the repair costs considerably. Thus, automobile insurance generated losses for the first time in 1970. New strategies urgently needed to be developed, and in view of the

Germans make a virtue out of necessity and use the car-free Sundays to take a walk on the freeway.

worsening economic circumstances, foreign business increasingly came into consideration.

German firms had returned to the world markets astonishingly quickly in the 1950s.[1] This led to an increased demand for insurance benefits, which Allianz was hesitant to satisfy at first, but then it did so in the 1970s with targeted special offerings. While Allianz had profited from the economic upsurge in the first two postwar decades, as had the entire insurance industry, it had only with difficulty recovered a small part of its business in Europe. The re-entry ticket was at first transnational insurance coverage for German companies operating internationally, termed "German-linked business." In the course of the increasing worldwide presence of Allianz itself, this was joined by dealings with foreign clients, termed "Allianz-linked business."[2] In order to promote business with industrial clients, industrial departments had been established in the German branch offices as early as 1956. In the 1970s, these were upgraded and supported specifically by a "foreign department." That was the first step back into international business. But it was not until the mid-1970s that Allianz reinforced its activities abroad, after it had become clear that further takeovers in Germany would be almost impossible due to anti-trust regulations, and that no appreciable expansion could be expected in Germany; the limits to growth had been reached.

Change of Command and of Generations At the beginning of the 1970s, Allianz was undergoing a fundamental change. The most important positions in the board of directors had to be filled again, since the people responsible for the company's renewed ascent were retiring. Ernst Meyer, the head of the organization for the sales force, emphasized on May 13, 1970, in Mainz, at the final conference – the ceremonious honoring of the best branch office – that this would have to involve a change of generation, as well: "Our generation will be glad [if] the tracks leading to the future have not been blocked." For only then would there be "not a conflict of generations, but only a handover," namely "for a joint task intended for the long term."[3] The chairman of the board of directors for many years, Alfred Haase (1903–1972), was already over fifty years old when he took over the position on Februar 8, 1962, from his predecessor, Hans Goudefroy (1900–1961). Like Goudefroy and the two other men in the company's highest offices – Gerd Müller (1903–1975), chairman of the board of directors of Allianz Lebensversicherungs-AG, and Ernst Meyer (1908–1972) – he belonged to the generation of German reconstruction, which retired from the scene in the early 1970s.[4] This time, the turnover in the top echelon proved to have particularly pronounced effects, for both Haase and Meyer died in March 1972 and were thus no longer able to provide continued advice to the company. The two, like Kurt Schmitt and Hans Heß before them, were rare examples of continuity and harmony; together with Gerd Müller, in over 35 years of service, they decisively shaped Allianz in the early years of the Federal Republic of Germany.

At the final conference in 1970, Alfred Haase summarized that the company's development phase, during which exceptional things had been achieved, was now finished, but how Allianz mastered the 1970s was what really mattered. For the future, he predicted a substantial transformation of the insurance market. Improvisation, which had been indispensable in the immediate postwar period, would now have to be replaced by long-term planning, as well as systematic and foresighted adaptation to the changes in technology, the market, and the structure of society.[5] The company was well prepared, and the new members of the board of directors had been trained to think long term. They had all been apprenticed to the departing management team. Haase called on the executive committee of the supervisory board "to reduce the average age of directors by electing younger gentlemen into the board of directors." This would ensure that the change of leadership would indeed also be a change of generations.[6]

Wolfgang Schieren (1927–1996) became chairman of the Allianz board of directors on July 16, 1971, replacing Alfred Haase, who shifted to chairing the supervisory board. Formally, Schieren had already been "appointed for special responsibilities in support of the chairman of the board of directors" as a deputy member of that body on January 1, 1970.[7] But this did not take effect until the completion of his job as head of the branch office in Berlin and his move to Munich. In his new function, he was prepared by Alfred Haase for his succession until the summer of 1971. Haase proceeded in a similar fashion with Arno Paul Bäumer (1920–1997), who was appointed a regular member of the board of directors as of January 1, 1970, and became chairman of the board of directors at Allianz Leben on January 1, 1972. Bäumer succeeded Gerd Müller, and Ernst Meyer's responsibilities had already been assumed by Helmut Bossenmaier (1923–1994) on February 4, 1971.[8] In his last speech before a company assembly at the head office on July 19, 1971, Haase congratulated his successors, "particularly Dr. Schieren and Mr. Bäumer as [...] the bosses of our Allianz companies," and expressed his conviction that "[t]he right men have been selected, of whom we know that they bring the force and necessary strength for their responsibilities." This also applied, he said, to "the new head of organization, Mr. Bossenmaier, [...] he is also an old coachman who rose from the ranks at Allianz Leben."[9]

Now, the fortunes of Allianz lay in the hands of the next generation. All three of them were born in the 1920s and were part of the war-youth generation whose lives were shaped by their war experience. The drastic experiences of this generation, soon designated the "skeptical generation," included, besides working in the Labor Service, war, and wounds, also years as prisoners of war, being a mature student or trainee, and delayed entry into normal working life.[10] The new leaders shared these experiences, and saw themselves faced with a "self-assigned mission of civilian rebirth from the total defeat."[11] They were power-oriented and decidedly pragmatic, and thus embodied characteristics of their generation. With revised work methods and approaches, such as the introduction of systematic planning, and new structures, such as industrial divisions and the founding of a holding company, the new managers faced up to the crisis, and in this way ensured the growth and continuous success of the company.

Wolfgang Schieren, chairman of the Allianz board of directors (center) and Arno Paul Bäumer, chairman of the Allianz Leben board of directors (left) – here together with Helmut Bossenmaier – were the most important decisionmakers in the 1970s and 1980s.

Wolfgang Schieren, the seventh chairman of the board of directors in the company's almost 80-year history at the time, remained in office for more than 20 years, longer than anybody before or after him. His successor, Henning Schulte-Noelle, gave an assessment of Schieren's lifetime achievement in a eulogy: "To a great extent, Schieren was Allianz; the Allianz of the '70s, '80s, and early '90s was his creation. This far-reaching identity, this union of person and achievement, is the result of his absolute identification with his company, [...] which came together with one of the great entrepreneurial talents in this country."[12] Schieren began his training at the Cologne branch office on November 1, 1956, ushered in at first by a recommendation from Goudefroy.[13] After various positions in branch offices and in sales, he shifted to the organizational department in Munich in 1962, which he headed from 1964 on. He then proved his merits in two cases of "restructuring," first in 1965 as interim head of the Paris branch office, and from 1967 in the West Berlin branch office, with which he twice won the Javelin Thrower, the award for the best branch office – which was known as a springboard to higher positions. At the time, the weekly newspaper Die Zeit spoke, with respect to West Berlin, of a "forge for directors-general," since it was particularly difficult to be successful there because of its isolation.[14] Schieren obviously fulfilled the expectations of Alfred Haase, at whose "disposal for special responsibilities" he had been since 1970,[15] when he had just been appointed a deputy member of the board of directors. The press painted a cooler picture. "Developing performance analysis and long-term programs is Allianz boss Wolfgang Schieren's greatest passion." This aloof technocrat was as devoted to his management games as he made himself scarce elsewhere, and usually had one of his fellow members of the board of directors take his place, they wrote. "And the boss does not think much of public relations work, either. Typical Schieren saying: 'Don't report that we have made the largest profit in our history.'"[16]

Arno Paul Bäumer was quite different; on the occasion of his 65th birthday, the Allianz Zeitung said of him, "It is partly thanks to his colorful personality that the insurance business is so 'present' in public discussions."[17] He did not hesitate to introduce himself into the dialog between the insurance industry and politics, and was already making use of the tools of press relations consciously and willingly in the 1970s. He was publicity-minded, as Arno Surminski, a business journalist and authority on the insurance industry, vividly summarized the point. His assessment of Bäumer's work, "this man who is not always easy to get along with," at the end of Bäumer's career was this: "We know Arno Paul Bäumer as a man who represents the interests of the insurance industry with great commitment, who stands up for it unreservedly, even if it is not, or not entirely, right, and also does this with [perhaps not always entirely nice] methods, […]. As in other industries, there are […] rarely great characters. Bäumer is one of them. He was obsessed in a positive sense where insurance was concerned."[18]

Arno Paul Bäumer had never expected nor desired to ever become head of Allianz Lebensversicherungs-AG. For he was very well trained in many aspects of the property insurance business. He began his career in 1949, after graduating in law, in the liability insurance claims department of Allianz in Hamburg, and continued this, among many other stages, as head of the branch office in Berlin. He had lost a leg in wartime service, and a career was not a matter of course for him. Furthermore, he came to know marketing with Alfred Haase and Ernst Meyer, who were in charge of organization at Allianz in the 1950s and 1960s. And this is where his real interests lay. "Bäumer made no secret of the fact that he would have preferred to become the successor of his deceased mentor [Ernst Meyer]." He reflected on this later to the weekly Die Zeit as follows: I "protested […] for the first time in this company, where previously, I had always done whatever I was supposed to."[19] When he accepted in the end, he first trained in the departments of Allianz Leben, since, as he himself said, he knew practically nothing about life insurance. "After the questions came the shake-up," he wrote. In accordance with his self-concept, he shaped a new style of management – trying to persuade, not simply order – thus clearly disassociating himself from his predecessor's style, which was perceived as patriarchal.[20] Furthermore, he was, like Wolfgang Schieren, very open to the latest findings on business management and corporate planning. He also saw clearly the advantages of electronic data-processing, which was new at that time: for example, he backed the Management Information System (MIS), and supported the new listing of turnover and costs for sectors and branch offices finally introduced in the summer of 1979.[21] A small book from 1985 for Bäumer's 65th birthday gives a good overview of the multitude of stories surrounding him, conveying a mixture of fear, respect, and admiration for the man. "Thus, many people in the broad Allianz public know that Bäumer has a memory like an elephant, has a passion for work (given the worldwide importance of Allianz, the attribute 'workaholic' would be appropriate), seldom has time, is hardly capable of interpersonal sentiments, and in brief is 'hard as rocks'."[22]

Helmut Bossenmaier was also well prepared for his position. Besides know-how in the field of life insurance and in sales, he possessed a good network and the ability to handle irritating trainers.[23] In the eyes of Wolfgang Schieren, he was the ideal candidate for director of sales, even though Bossenmaier himself, who until then was in charge of the life insurance business in Stuttgart, was not pleased with his appointment to the board of directors of the Allianz Versicherungs-AG. This interesting parallel links him with Arno Paul Bäumer. Neither got the position he desired but, rather, that of their colleague. "None of your splendid predecessors came as close to the innermost nature of this organization as you. You are an organization man," Schieren's laudatory farewell speech to Bossenmaier put it on March 13, 1986. And he continued: "This organization, which in a good dozen years made Allianz the most important insurer in Europe, became [...] your life's work." Among his services, Schieren said, was to have ensured Allianz a lead in the market of tomorrow through the sales department. He had achieved this in particular by managing to lower marketing costs by four percent, thus coming close to the dream score he himself had set. Such cost optimization while improving quality in the organization inspired the greatest respect from Schieren, as he suggested several times in his farewell address.[24]

Schieren, Bäumer and Bossenmaier were exceptional talents in their positions, and embodied in widely differing ways power orientation and pragmatism. But although they laid the foundations for the lasting success of the company as a team, this could not conceal one fact: the era of a triumvirate was over. The strong man in the background was Wolfgang Schieren.

1970: Losses and Restructuring

When the change of command and of generations took place at the beginning of the 1970s, retiring chairman of the board of directors, Alfred Haase, was able to look back at a successful term of office. The company followed an unchallenged course of success in the 1960s. Haase's successor inherited a well-ordered house. That his last full working year, 1970, was marked by stagnation, due to the slump in automobile insurance – for the first time since 1945 – did not really disturb him. In his address to the company assembly at the Munich head office of July 19, 1971, he commented on his expectations for the future as follows: "I hope that the year 1970 was an isolated phenomenon, and that in the future, we will have enough of a grip on earnings again that we will not have to fall back on reserves that we have collected as a precaution during the years of prosperity."[25]

Ever more cars, ever more accidents: at the end of the 1960s, automobile insurance needs to be restructured.

In retrospect, that was definitely a misjudgment, for it was not a matter of a singular event, but of structural problems that made fundamental changes necessary. Circumstances had changed, and the solutions that suited the 1950s and 1960s could not simply be transferred to the 1970s. Although there was sufficient growth in the so-called ordinary business sectors, with increases of 20 percent, and in life insurance – thanks to the Third Asset Formation Act (Vermögensbildungsgesetz) – the profit situation in the various forms of property insurance, except accident insurance, had worsened alarmingly.[26] In the 1970 fiscal year, automobile insurance, fire insurance, and burglary insurance suffered severe losses.[27] The extent of this becomes clear in comparison with previous years: "Between 1960 and 1969, Allianz Versicherungs-AG achieved on average surpluses of about 3.5 percent of the premiums earned from the underwriting activities; for 1970, in contrast, the losses amounted to 8.2 percent of the premiums earned."[28] In automobile insurance alone, Allianz lost DM 154 million.[29]

Much depended on the new management team setting the right course. A fundamental change in thinking in the management was needed in order to master the problems. As immediate measures, the director of sales Helmut

Bossenmaier prescribed "restructuring, selection, and keeping desired risks" for the ailing lines of business in order to restore the balance between receipts and expenditures.[30] "The first thing Schieren did was to implement his clear realization that lower costs would be a matter of survival in the medium and long term. A thoroughgoing wave of rationalization measures swept through all areas; every job had to have a functional justification. Precise personnel plans took the place of a relatively relaxed personnel policy of the preceding boom years." And at the same time, the company was supposed to "reach the leading position […] long since achieved in other fields in the market for industrial insurance policies, as well."[31] This is, in brief, the broad principle for the 1970s that was announced to the staff by a circular in 1971.[32] The measures to restore profitability in the motor-vehicle and industry lines approached the problem from three sides: cost reductions, personnel reductions, and rationalization measures. In all three fields, they could base the measures on existing activities. This applied particularly in two sections: the largest and most important one since the Second World War, motor-vehicle insurance, headed from 1964 until 1973 by Werner Brugger (1908–2008), and business administration and data processing, headed by Heinz-Leo Müller-Lutz.

Restructuring Automobile Insurance Everything else was subordinated to reducing costs in order to preserve competitiveness. The main causes of the losses were the increase in the number of claims by almost 10 percent, and the increase in the expense of individual claims by more than 16 percent. In contrast, premiums had remained almost unchanged since January 1, 1965.[33]

Two rate increases, on January 1 and August 1, 1971, were the first measures taken to bring the premiums and the explosive growth in claims expenses into somewhat better balance.[34] Despite this, 1971 still incurred a loss, which according to the annual report was due to the fact that the amount of premiums brought forward from the previous year was still at the rate level of 1970. In addition, a further increase in the average expense of property damage was expected.[35]

In 1970, lawyer Werner Brugger was already at the end of his over forty-year career at Allianz. Since 1948, he had been entrusted in Munich with his life's work, the establishment and expansion of the automobile insurance business, and was thoroughly familiar with the problems of automobile insurance through his work in the Haftpflicht-, Unfall- und Kraftverkehrsversicherungs-Verband (HUK) (Liability, Accident, and Motor-Vehicle Insurance Association). Brugger refined cost-oriented and risk-oriented cost calculation, and promoted accident prevention and aid to victims of traffic accidents as part of his work in the association. In the 1960s alone, he introduced more reforms than there had been altogether since the existence of that line.[36] From 1963 on, Allianz achieved initial success with the no-claims discount.[37]

By 1970 at the latest, it could be seen that insurance instruments such as increases in premiums, premium refunds, and retentions alone were not enough to get a grip on the avalanche of costs. Additional measures were needed. Property claims were affected by wage increases in the repair shop sector and higher prices for spare parts, and injury claims were affected by rising expenses for loss of earnings and therapeutic treatments.[38] And in 1970, the number of accident-caused deaths, at more than 19,000, and injuries, at about 530,000, reached an absolute maximum, as well.[39] Claims settlement became more and more difficult, and Werner Brugger observed the tendency of the courts to award higher damages for pain and suffering in the case of serious injuries.[40]

Quick-service claims stations, the system of quickly assessing damage on site, becomes generally known at the latest after the Munich hailstorm of 1984.

Customer Service and Safety Research

Especially in the case of bodily injuries, it became apparent that the system of keeping costs down had to be supplemented with improved customer service, safety research on accident and injury prevention, as well as an optimization of the claims settlement procedure in order to be truly sustainable. The quick-service claims stations installed throughout the country in the 1970s blazed the trail for this. The new drive-in system, undergoing trials since 1967 at the Frankfurt and Hamburg branch offices, made it possible to handle the claims in a decentralized manner at the Allianz sites in Germany. In 1981, there were already twenty quick-service claims stations in the subsidiaries. Until then, claims adjusters had visited the claimants in order to inspect the damage and process the claim. Now it was possible to have the scope of damage determined and calculated immediately after the accident. Customers received a declaration guaranteeing that Allianz would assume the costs of repair, or a check payable to cash, so that they no longer had to advance the money. Claims adjustment was assisted by the up-to-date technology of the day, first by terminals linked to the central policy and claims files, and since 1976 by the Audatex system for computer calculation of the costs of car repairs. A year later, cost estimates could be retrieved from all Allianz data-processing centers by computer.[41]

The quick-service claims stations proved their worth in the case of a disastrous hailstorm in Southern Germany, known as the "Munich Hail," on the evening of July 12, 1984. Munich was at the center of the hailstorm, and within five minutes, more than 200,000 cars had been wrecked by hailstones, some of them as big as pigeons' eggs. This caused property damage of about DM 800 million in automobile insurance alone. Over 50,000 claims had to be processed as quickly as possible.

The injured parties were informed of the rapid settlement at the two quick-service claims stations in Munich – soon supplemented by a third one in the suburb of Ismaning – via Bavarian Radio. Fifty technical claims adjusters from all over West Germany inspected, calculated, and settled claims for 300–500 vehicles per day per station on average, for four weeks. Thus, the company was able to manage the rush of claimants, making payments amounting to DM 180 million, and also received an entirely positive reaction from the press.[42] And even such a catastrophe was not able to spoil the 1984 business results – on the contrary, the good reputation of Allianz and its claims service were reinforced.[43]

Damage and safety research was given additional weight in 1971 by the

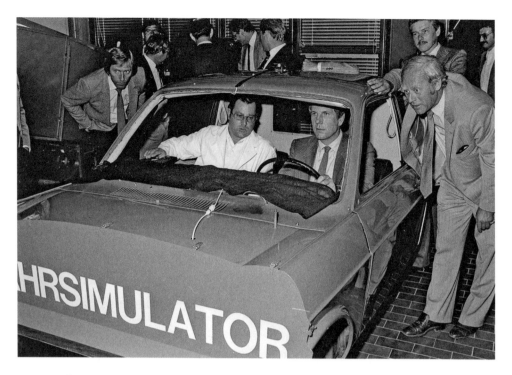

Minister of Transport Volker Hauff visiting the Allianz Center for Technology (1982).

establishment of the Institute of Motor Vehicle Technology at the Allianz Center for Technology (Allianz Zentrum für Technik, AZT).[44] The research work arose from practical problems.

Damage prevention had been discussed since the late 1960s for automobile insurance. In addition to the classical departments Automobile – Operation, and Automobile – Claims, the section Automobile – Technology as a separate department for motor-vehicle technology and traffic safety, was created under the direction of Max Danner (1930–1997). In parallel with claims settlement, technical solutions for handling insurance questions were to be developed here. The development of standards for repair methods and specifications for job duration, as well as the training of claims adjusters, were already among Max Danner's responsibilities before they were taken over by the AZT, which then had a staff of thirty. The department, and subsequently the AZT, became contacts for the automotive industry, specialist bodies, committees, and the media on the subject of motor cars and traffic safety. The initial successes of the research into repairs and the causes of accidents already became apparent in 1972, and two years later, the research results, such as the partial replacement technique and sectional repair or less expensive partial painting, were adopted in practice by automobile manufacturers and repair shops.[45]

It now became more and more important for the new institute to include non-technical factors in its work, as well – an expression of the trend to greater safety-consciousness. In 1956, when Ernst Meyer urged that the company must "apply [itself] to combating traffic hazards," which were usually caused, he said, by intentional or negligent disregard for the simplest traffic rules by "traffic upstarts," it still seemed as if "traffic education and propaganda remained practically without effect among adults."[46] At that time, Ernst Meyer had demanded stricter laws and penalties. Max Danner relied on persuasion. The topic of the seat belt revealed just how difficult this was and made the name of the Institute of Motor Vehicle Technology and its director known to a broader public, although he could not claim to have invented it.[47] A milestone on the way to more safety for motorists and sinking accident-victim figures was the obligation to wear seat belts, even though it was at first introduced only for the front seats, on January 1, 1976. As late as the 1980s, disregard for the obligation to buckle up was not prosecuted; the West German government relied on persuasion instead of punishment. Despite this, the number of serious injuries dropped continuously from the 1970s due to an increased percentage of people fastening seat belts.[48] In the early 1970s, Max Danner acquainted the Allianz staff with the research results of the HUK Association in the study "Sichere Autos …," based on the investigation of 10,000 accidents. The association demanded a set of measures, from headrests and safety steering columns and padded dashboards to safety glass. The focus returned to the seat belt again and again.[49] In 1983, he heated up the issue with his book "Gurt oder Tod"[50] (Belt or Death). His information campaign even included Ministers of Transport. At a crash demonstration with dummies in the AZT in 1982, on the occasion of the visit of the then Minister of Transport Volker Hauff (1980–1982), the grave consequences for children in the rear seat not wearing seat belts of an impact at barely 50 km/h [= 30 m.p.h.] were demonstrated.[51] However, in a subsequent radio interview, Hauff could only bring himself to confirm that the Allianz Center for Technology had helped the legislature in the field of safety standards with important advice – but nothing happened. Danner kept up the pressure and intensified his efforts with Hauff's successor Werner Dollinger (1982–1987). This time, the minister himself was subjected to a crash at 15 km/h. Dollinger remained unhurt in the experiment but not unimpressed, because the dummy next to him, not buckled up, slammed against the windshield.[52] Despite this, fines for not wearing a seat belt were not introduced until years later. By 1996, the numbers of casualties in united Germany dropped to below 8,700, and had thus more than halved since 1970, when on the roads of West Germany alone around 19,000 people had died.[53]

The expanded safety research at Allianz in the 1970s made a major contribution to the continuous decline in numbers of accidents, injuries, and costs after 1970. In recent years, the AZT has directed increased attention to human behavior in traffic in a new field: "accident research and damage prevention."[54] Indeed, it had already been discovered in the early 1950s, in the first systematic analysis of traffic accidents published in the study "Wir und die Straße" by Ernst Meyer and Ernst Jacobi,[55] that drivers were the main cause of traffic accidents in more than 90 percent of the cases, far surpassing the 8 percent due to the road and 2 percent due to technical defects.[56]

Rationalization and Cost Management

Electronic data-processing (EDP) was another essential cornerstone of the cost-cutting program. Allianz profited in this critical phase at the beginning of the 1970s in particular from the rationalization efforts of the two previous decades, which were inseparable from the figure of Heinz-Leo Müller-Lutz (1912–1997): the man they called the "rationalization practician" headed business organization, data processing and system-planning divisions. Together with his colleagues Otto Ladner (head of the business administration department, BWA) and Hans-Willy Schäfer (head of the computer center), he succeeded in linking the latest developments in the fields of office equipment, work processes, and business organization, the marketing structure and EDP with the goals of rationalization of operations and reduction in costs.[57] This resulted in projects in the field of portfolio and file management, such as microfilming or hanging file cabinets; in office organization, such as trying out open-plan offices; or in EDP, such as the idea of the paperless office, or the replacement of the punched card by magnetic disks and other storage media. The latest EDP technology became the driver of changes, and made inexpensive and labor-saving administration of the vast quantities of data possible, thus making Allianz perpetually competitive.

The fact that data management at Allianz became faster and more effective with each new generation of mainframe computers led to more closely

Only with the help of ever more efficient computer technology, here the IBM 360 in the Hamburg branch, does Allianz manage to remain competitive over the long term.

interlinked development of operations and data processing. This allowed the workflows in the departments to be streamlined considerably. Very soon, the use of office technology also meant that among many of the employees, the delight in the new capabilities was mingled with skepticism about the innovations in their working environment, and concern about possibly losing their jobs.

The staff was informed about the far-reaching changes at first by means of pamphlets, and since the start of the ELIAS I (Electronic Integrated Allianz System) project by means of a regular supplement to the Allianz Zeitung, the Computerreport, in order to lessen their reservations about the rapid-fire changes. The huge volume of data, one of the company's assets, required technical innovations, for the systems on the market in the 1970s were not able to handle such orders of magnitude. In order to remain competitive in the long term, it was necessary to develop custom software for the management of the new ELIAS database. Since the introduction of integrated portfolio management with ELIAS, and with the help of IBM/360 mainframe computers in 1968, workflows could be made much more efficient. The hub of the new system was a central database that combined all the relevant information of an insurance policy. The portfolio of policies was stored on magnetic disks for the first time, so that the central card files of the specialist departments, which had been established in the branch offices, very rapidly became superfluous. The staff could now retrieve the information on individual policies by way of a terminal. Computerreport informed the staff about the changes in methods of data entry, about the new IBM 3740 data entry system of 1974, and the greatly improved working conditions it brought: noiseless work, desk-like data-entry workplaces, and the new storage medium, the magnetic disk instead of the punched card.[58] The conversion of payroll accounting to the new technology replaced 1,500 working hours by one hour's work at the computer, for example.[59] However, the other side of the restructuring efforts appeared here, as well: Allianz tried to get a grip on increasing labor costs by means of rationalization. The works councils did not accept this without opposition. In a letter, the Central Works Council Working Party criticized "current and future rationalization measures aiming at staff reductions," and demanded that they be slowed or shelved. The board of directors defended its actions at the meeting of February 9–10, 1976, in this way: "Preserving jobs is only possible if the costs remain within the cover that can be achieved with the premium. Besides, to date there have been for the most part no dismissals, but simply people leaving who have not been replaced."[60] In the following meeting of the board of directors, on March 8, 1976, Müller-Lutz complained that the unions were running an anti-rationalization campaign, and the Allianz works councils were joining in. Now, such measures, up to dismissals, were becoming more difficult, Müller-Lutz said, and it would no longer be possible "to carry them out silently" without further ado. They felt forced to engage in a dialog, and offered "information events and discussions," but "without concrete figures," to persuade people of the necessity of the staff cuts.[61] At Allianz, the technological progress of that time did not necessarily mean dismissals; it could also be retraining: for example, keypunch operators – a dying occupation – could be trained as data typists, who no longer punched the data into punched cards, but entered them by keyboard and stored them on a diskette.[62]

Looking back, the rationalization measures during Wolfgang Schieren's term of office are evaluated positively without exception. For he knew how, said Klaus Liesen, "to accomplish strict cost management with the necessity of severe cuts in staffing [...] without engendering major social conflicts."[63] Heinz-Leo Müller-Lutz reported, on the occasion of the 20th anniversary of electronic data-processing at Allianz, that in 1976, about 13,000 more office employees would have been needed if they had still been working at the productivity level of 1958. At that time, this meant a savings of DM 500 million annually. According to Müller-Lutz, the EDP costs amounted, by contrast, to a mere 5 percent of this sum.[64]

The bundle of cost-cutting measures took effect more quickly than expected: after two years of taking a severe course, Wolfgang Schieren was able to present a positive annual financial statement for 1972. The systematic selection of the risks also had a positive effect. But the shrinking life insurance business was still worrisome, and in Schieren's opinion, the consolidation had to be continued in the property insurance fields.[65] A hiring freeze made the restructuring measures even more effective, and the number of employees began to drop: "In property insurance, it declined from 1975 to 1976 by 325 to 9,879; for the first time in the history of the head office, the number of persons employed declined."[66] Not until 1977 did the years of decline in office and sales staffing levels come to a halt. The Allianz Zeitung reported in May 1978 that there was "barely any more staffing shrinkage:" "In the companies of the Allianz property insurance group, 14,947 people [and 44,177 freelance agents] were employed in the country at the end of 1977." This was only 1.2 percent less than in the previous year, it stated, which was considered "a sign that the adjustment of staffing levels to improved operational prerequisites that commenced in the autumn of 1971 is coming to a close for the time being." Moreover, the increasing number of new policies signed, and the increase in claims work was raising the need for staff.[67] Wolfgang Schieren officially announced the end of the cost-cutting activities in his end-of-year review for 1977. The reward for these efforts, he maintained, was job security and the competitiveness "for the immediately foreseeable future."[68]

In order to get a grip on the perpetual matter of costs over the long term, a systematic approach to business administration was required, with planning for the entire company and implementation monitoring, as well as the involvement of additional departments. The existing system proved to be insufficient, especially in the fields of managerial accounting, uniform bookkeeping, and statistics.[69] Sales head Bossenmaier was the first, in 1975, to begin preparing comprehensive planning data for sales. Müller-Lutz supported this systematic approach with the proposal to integrate the input of the estimated figures for new business and premium revenues in the data express service of the business administration department. This would give all departments access to this information. The reactions to Helmut Bossenmaier's project were positive: "The possibility, with the help of the planning data, to specify targets that can be compared to the actual development at any time, is generally welcomed. Dr. Schieren emphasizes that, in the current situation, it is becoming more and more necessary to be able to account for developments continuously."[70] The goal was to extend this approach successively to the entire business. The advocates included, besides Heinz-Leo Müller-Lutz, also Arno Paul Bäumer, who supported the introduction of integrated planning in combination with an EDP-based Management Information System (MIS), which provided data on actual turnover and costs for the management as an aid to decision-making.[71]

The new methods could only be introduced gradually, starting in 1977, because in Rudolf Eversmann's[72] administrative section, which was in charge of this, there was no consensus on whether the innovations were necessary at all.[73] Therefore, a proven expert from outside was engaged who had already given evidence of his business-management skills facilitating restructuring at Wacker-Chemie GmbH.[74] He was appointed Eversmann's successor on October 1, 1976, at first for the 'General Administration' section.[75]

Peter Adolff had his work cut out for him convincing people of the benefits of integrated corporate planning, of comparisons of planned with actual figures, of profit-and-loss statements during the year, and of the idea of profit centers. The heads of the branch offices were opposed to the innovations, as Rudolf Eversmann was. The spokesman for the opponents was the head of Frankfurter Versicherungs-AG, Prosper Graf zu Castell-Castell, who explained that they feared for their entrepreneurial independence if the branch offices were to be managed like profit centers. Peter Adolff later commented on the split in the board of directors over this question to Wolfgang Schieren: "It is true that there was never a consensus on the board as to how far they wanted to go with setting up these 'modern' management instruments. But there was agreement, after Mr. Eversmann's departure, that a step in this direction needed to be taken."[76]

At the beginning of 1978, the responsibilities in the board of directors were restructured, and all business administration tasks were collected into a specially created "super-section" aptly called the business administration section, headed by Peter Adolff. In addition to administration, accounting, and taxes, the sectors business organization, data-processing and data protection, and, after his departure on January 1, 1978, system planning from Müller-Lutz's department, were incorporated into this.[77] In 1978, Peter Adolff presented his concept for planning to all regional companies, in order to convince them that planning increased "the chances of survival of a company operating by a division of labor very substantially, by trying to foresee possible future developments, to depict them, and to coordinate our ideas about them throughout the company."[78] In this, Adolff saw himself in the tradition of the controller, whose main task was supposed to be providing information for management decisions.

By the end of 1979, the new form of planning, with the new overview of turnover and costs, had been accepted throughout the company. The "super-section" as described above existed from early 1978 until early 1980. The initiative to once again separate financial controlling and business organization came from Peter Adolff in a letter of November 12, 1979, to Wolf-gang Schieren.[79] In practice, it had turned out to be difficult to unite financial controlling and business organization within a single department, which should not both be in one person's hands. Therefore, an additional board of directors section, business organization (BO), was created, with the divisions data processing, system planning, and administration, headed by Rolf Landwehr, who was supposed to develop a new data-processing plan. The first step towards professionalization of the accounting and integrated corporate planning had been taken, and in the following years, it was extended gradually to the foreign subsidiaries obliged to report to the company.[80] In this way, modern financial controlling was introduced at Allianz.

Success in the Life Insurance Business

In contrast to automobile insurance, life insurance in the 1970s continued the successes of the sector during the days of the "economic miracle." Indeed, in the following decades, personal lines insurance experienced a positive boom. In 1990, Allianz was the market leader in the life insurance business both in Germany and in Europe, administering in Germany alone 7.7 million policies with an insured sum of DM 190 billion.[81] These figures increased continuously: in the year 2000, it was 9.3 million policies with an insured sum of € 199 billion.

In the 1970s, life insurance (1972), accident insurance (1974), and company pension insurance (1970) were index-linked. This meant that, like West German public old age pensions, their contributions and payments could be continuously adjusted to a person's income situation, so that when needed, the beneficiary's standard of living could be maintained. The growing popularity of these three types of insurance among the clients can be explained by various social developments. The most important impetus was the growing prosperity of West Germans since the late 1960s. This en-

Lebensversicherung,
speziell für Frauen

Sichern Sie sich.
Hier. Noch heute.

hoffentlich **Allianz** versichert

*In the late 1960s, life insurance
ads first targeted working women
as a client group. In the 1980s,
this had already become a
matter of course.*

abled ever broader groups of the population to make provision for the
"vicissitudes of life," from illness or occupational disability to old age, pensions, and death. This was accompanied by the termination in 1967 of the
ASS industrial life insurance policy, which no longer accorded with demand, and by the fact that, statistically speaking, every West German had a
life insurance policy in 1976. That provision of a different order of magnitude would be necessary was shown by the demographic shift that gradually became apparent beginning in the 1970s, with sinking birthrates and
rising life expectancy. It was predicted that the percentage of those over
sixty years old would rise from 21 percent in 1990 to over 35 percent in the
year 2030.[82] Furthermore, the generous social-welfare policies were accompanied by a positive explosion of expenditure between 1969 and 1974, fired
not least by the major pension reform of 1972. In the 1970s and 1980s, both
the expansion of the welfare state and the rapid aging of the population –
beside other factors, such as rising unemployment and stagnating rate of
employment – caused social-security expenditures to skyrocket. The percentage of the total population who were pensioners over sixty rose to
15.6 percent. The impending excessive aging of society caused hitherto un-

known problems of financing public old age pensions. Contrary to assertions by politicians (Norbert Blüm, Minister of Employment and Social Affairs: "Pensions are safe."), massive cuts in the system that had been expanded as late as the 1970s became necessary already in 1992, with the Pension Reform Act. Sinking payments and rising contributions to the state pensions – between 1977 and 1989 from 9 percent to more than 18 percent of one's gross income – were supposed to slow the cost trend for the long term. The crisis in the social-security system left a financing gap that the citizenry had to bridge as individuals. In the 1980s, it was gradually recognized that government old age insurance needed supplementing by private provisions, for example, by a private life insurance policy and company pensions. Thus, general societal developments as well as government incentives and subsidies encouraged the undreamed of boom in personal insurance at Allianz.[83]

After 1945, Gerd Müller led Allianz to a leading place among European life insurance companies in a short time. He also led the way in modern in-

To overcome West German citizens' skepticism about investment funds, dit developed a board game to explain the Concentra Fund.

vestment policy, and established life insurance as a form of saving for long-term provision and wealth accumulation among broad classes of society. His section was restructured when it passed to his successor, Arno Paul Bäumer. Asset management was hived off from the more and more differentiated life insurance business. For the next eight years, the new head of finance, Klaus Götte (born 1932), was in charge of all asset management for the life and property insurance business.[84] He was also one of the first members of the board of directors to be brought in as an expert from outside. Since 1968, he had worked in the finance department of Friedrich Krupp GmbH. The principle of lifelong loyalty to the company, which until then had applied to the great majority of the members of the board of directors, was breached for the first time in this case.

The most important products of Allianz Lebensversicherung in the 1970s were wealth-accumulating life insurance (1), fund-linked life insurance (2), and in-house old age pension schemes for corporate clients (3).[85]

(1) The first experienced excellent growth rates after the Third Asset Formation Act (Vermögensbildungsgesetz) had included it in the catalog of state-subsidized wealth-accumulation benefits: in the first quarter of 1971, new business amounting to DM 4.5 billion was underwritten – more than 80 percent of the new business for all of 1970. In that same period, all other life insurers together earned DM 10 billion, in comparison. Gerd Müller predicted at the beginning of 1971 that the pronounced growth in mass income would encourage people to save on a long-term basis, and to make private provision.[86] He said this was an example of how legislative social-welfare measures benefited insurance work directly. Something similar was to be expected for the future of company old age pension systems.[87]

(2) Fund-linked life insurance, which Allianz has offered since April 1970, had to be publicized first. It took time until the skepticism of West Germans towards investment funds as a way to invest their money declined, because they still preferred to entrust their money to a savings account. And it was not only the skepticism of clients that had to be overcome at first. In 1974, Arno Paul Bäumer was sharply criticized by Gerd Müller – who was still active until mid-1974 in an advisory function and as a member of the Finance Commission – because he had spoken of the end of fund-linked life insurance in the press.[88] However, success came despite Bäumer's predictions to the contrary: in their first year already, the two new funds, Alleuropa and Allcontinenta, reached insured sums of DM 5.6 million, and rates of increase from the initial offering of 11.5 and

18.2 percent, respectively.[89] As the insurance companies did for fund-linked life insurance, the banks had to work to persuade West Germans about the benefits of equity funds. Deutsche Investment Trust (dit), the Dresdner Bank Group's investment company, succeeded in doing this in 1956 with the introduction of the first investment trust in Germany, the Concentra Fond. "On the first day of issue, Concentra proved to be a sales hit." With this, "the investment age dawned in Germany, too."[90] The Concentra game, specially developed for this purpose, was intended to help clients understand how investment funds function, and stimulate their interest in saving in an investment fund.

(3) Collective insurance policies were a particular success. Firms used them to establish an in-house old age pension system with the aid of a life insurance company. First called "collective insurance" and then renamed "group insurance" in 1956, the business with companies boomed as a consequence of the statutory provisions of 1974 on the vesting of company old age pensions. After twelve years, the Association of Life Insurance Companies was able to report a continuous upward trend: at the end of 1974, there were 1.34 million life insurance policies for company old age pension plans; at the end of 1985, there were 2.87 million. Indeed, the sums insured had increased 5.6 times.[91] In the late 1970s, Allianz also offered German companies operating internationally a wider service, and expanded its involvement in company old age pensions.[92] Four leading European life insurance companies – Allianz, the Dutch AMEV-Utrecht, the Belgian Royale Belge, and the British Eagle Star – joined together in the Area Benefits Network project to enable multinational corporate clients to provide company benefits in their respective countries. The goal was to combine the national collective insurance contracts of these firms into a worldwide risk network. Since more and more companies were operating abroad, the collaboration of the European insurers allowed them to serve entirely new client interests. In this way, multinational firms could offer their employees abroad, as well, a company old age pension plan, which prevented employees from being under- or overinsured and provided for equal treatment of staff in different countries to the greatest extent possible.

The life insurance sector grew ever more important in the following decades. It became the guarantor of continuous rates of growth. In order to ensure this success, IT applications custom-tailored to the needs of the life insurance business were developed.

This success enabled the life insurance company to retain a certain independence within the group. This independence was evident, for example, in the separate management of portfolios in the various branch offices of Allianz Leben. EDP was only one expression of this; other central functions also existed separately for the property insurance and life insurance companies; on the other hand, this led to losses in synergy. Allianz Leben was gradually integrated, beginning in 1972 with the field of investment, and then reinsurance and accounting with the so-called "integrated planning" (1976). These responsibilities were gradually shifted to Allianz Versicherungs-AG. But in the end, it was only with the founding of Allianz Deutschland-AG in 2006 that Allianz Leben was integrated on all levels.[93]

1977: A Corporate Identity for Allianz

The idea of corporate design began to develop in the 1970s. At that time, many firms created new symbols for themselves. For example, Dresdner Bank had a new logo created in 1972 on the occasion of its centennial, a triangle within a hexagon. Also called the "Ponto eye" after the head of the bank at that time, Jürgen Ponto, it was assumed to match the green stripe well.[94] Deutsche Bank also introduced a new logo in 1974, designed by the Stuttgart commercial artist Anton Stankowski and still in use, the "slash in a square."[95]

The step from company logo to "corporate design" was revolutionary; there was a need for action at Allianz. The director of advertising, Walter Kappes, was still relying on the successful humorous matchbox advertisements. But the incipient structural and strategic transformation of Allianz in the 1970s called for a change in its image. The opportunity for this came with the generation shift in the advertising department. The path was cleared when, in 1968, Ernst Benner succeeded Walter Kappes, who retired in October of that year. In Hansjörg Dorschel's eyes, the right moment had come: "I really started with this typography and corporate design thing because I told myself 'I don't want to be a joker all my life.'" Hansjörg Dorschel had already developed a corporate design for Bausparkasse Wüstenrot. He was able to introduce the decisive artistic impetus in this way: "First, I [...] collected forms [...] and then showed the collection to the board of directors, in order to demonstrate that for one procedure, in three different branch offices, five different forms were being used. Dr. Schieren was struck speechless when he saw that. And then I said, 'This is the point that we have to start from.'" The new design, according to Dorschel, was also supposed to give expression to "an organizational transformation."[96]

Since the summer of 1975, Allianz had been devoting more attention to

Rund um
Ihre
Sicherheit

Allianz 🏛

One of the caricatures
of the graphic artist
Gerhard Brinkmann
in the look of the new
Allianz logo from 1977.

the question of a new image. Until then, the significance of a uniform presentation had not been recognized in the company. The initiative for this
came from outside. Barbara Eichberger, of Ernst Benner's team, reported
on this: "Munich Re was the very first company that had worked with a
unified corporate image, and suggested it to the Allianz board of directors."[97] On the board of directors, Walter Rostock (1974–1982) was responsible for transportation and aviation insurance, and soon for the corporate
design, as well. He had switched from Munich Re to the Allianz board of
directors in 1974. Here, he sponsored a design competition, thus providing
the decisive organizational and material input for a corporate design. First,
two commercial artists were asked for designs. The graphic artist mentioned
above, Anton Stankowski, supplied a variation of the Deutsche Bank's
diagonal slash, but it was Hansjörg Dorschel's modified Allianz eagle that
was chosen. He later explained his design in this way: the logo is "a capital

that is of boundless value, [...] thinking at the time at the national level, I felt it right to follow a conservative track. And that proved to be right, too." In this, he was of one mind with the board of directors, apart from a few skeptics.[98]

The designer placed the eagle in a circle, and gave it softer contours. Together with Dorschel, a commission headed by Walter Rostock, which included, besides Ernst Benner, experts from the department of business administration, such as Luise Stepken, and the administration, was to develop a plan for implementing the project in stages.[99] In a decision model presentation, Walter Rostock formulated its task: this was to create a clear, uniform image for all Allianz companies that was both lasting and flexible for Allianz's technical design requirements. The design developed by Hansjörg Dorschel and Benner and presented in the autumn of 1975 had been revised in the meantime, he wrote. Furthermore, the results of psychological tests in selected groups had shown that Dorschel's suggestions generated positive associations, and thus were well received. Dorschel would demonstrate "the main constants of the new image," namely "the (once again) slightly revised eagle, and the Allianz trademarked logotype." In conclusion, he wrote: "Both elements combine in an optimum fashion the goals of, on the one hand, deviating as little as possible from the accustomed shape, because of its existing familiarity, while, on the other hand, finding more up-to-date and friendly details for the design."[100] The result was outlined in the Design Guidelines for a Uniform Image of the Allianz Companies, in which the font and color of the eagle and the brand name were specified for all uses, that is, from everything from letterheads, advertising brochures, and forms to illustrated advertising and agents' advertisements.[101] Only two other company logos, the Frankfurter eagle and the coat of arms of the Bayerische Versicherungsbank (BVB), were permitted in addition to the Allianz eagle.

For the first time, the importance of color for a corporate image was recognized. The guidelines state: "Strong clear colors characterize strong clear enterprises. The house color of Allianz is blue." Even color psychologists were cited, who had discovered that the color blue embodies respectability, reliability, discretion, prudence, and elegance: in short, everything that should characterize an insurance company. Allianz had already been using the color blue in its presentation for a long time. However, until the 1970s, the Allianz logo was done in black. One of the earliest known indications of a connection between the Allianz logo and the color blue is given by Rudolf Hensel in his festschrift for the 50th anniversary of Allianz in 1940. Referring to the company logo of 1922, he mentioned that "a new coat of arms" – alluding the first logo, the imperial eagle – had been introduced. The following remark is crucial: "This was joined by the new house flag, black, white, and blue, with the eagle (which now flies on the roofs of all our business buildings), and which also became the flag of our sports clubs."[102] This, however, was a light blue, which was combined with the black Allianz eagle, not the house colors specified in 1977, in two different hues of blue, the Allianz blue. The hue was varied for outdoor applications (Allianz Blue I, HKS 47) and for printed matter (Allianz Blue II, HKS 43), and sometimes supplemented with green and silver. In addition to the symbol and the blue hues, the Helvetica typeface belonged to the basic elements of the new design.

The changeover began with the refinement of the most important sales-promotion instruments: letterhead paper, business cards, policy applications, and all forms and damage reports. Barbara Eichberger and Elmar Siepe from the advertising department, and Hildtraut Feldmann, department head in marketing and sales promotion, worked on this for years.[103] Dorschel's approach of relying on the continuity of the company's symbol proved itself in practice. The results of a study conducted by the market-research department under Karl-Heinz Vogt confirmed that continuity paid off in every respect: 94 percent knew the Allianz image with a reminder, and 64 percent without; these figures were considered unbeatable.[104] Similar results were obtained for the Allianz eagle, symbol, and the advertising slogan "Hopefully covered by Allianz." "So the company was right in deciding not to go down a fundamentally new path in its new corporate image," the board of directors ascertained in March 1976.[105]

Since Ernst Benner had become head of the advertising department in 1968, the company had not only developed a new corporate design; in the insurance advertising of the 1970s and 1980s, there was also more emphasis on other topics. From 1969 on, there were new accident insurance leaflets that, with slogans such as "For the modern woman" and "A man of today," were addressed to independent-minded working men and women. And old themes of personal liability insurance, such as "If only I had …" – which had been reworked again and again since the 1930s – were now reinterpreted in the form of caricatures by the commercial artists Albrecht Steinert and Gerhard Brinkmann – the latter being better known under his signature "G. Bri".[106] In the 1980s, something completely new was introduced, the "Young People Program," a package of insurance for those starting their working life, targeting youths as a new client groups.

Nuclear Energy: Insuring a Radiant Vision of the 1970s

In 1976, Allianz reported proudly on its involvement as an international industrial insurer in an advertising brochure: "Marching along at the forefront of technological progress is always one party: the industrial insurer. The nuclear-powered research ship Otto Hahn is insured by Allianz, just like all German nuclear power stations, from Gundremmingen and Obrigheim to Biblis, currently the largest nuclear power station in the world."[107] Under the impression of the oil crises, West Germany counted euphorically on the new technology, and the insurance companies, as important partners, were convinced that they could calculate the technical risk. The experts at Allianz underpinned the business with systematic damage research in the field of nuclear engineering. Heinz Braun – from 1966 until 1987 managing director of the Center for Technology, and first deputy head, and from 1971 head of the engineering insurance branches – had acquired knowledge of nuclear engineering while working abroad for AEG for ten years. In 1979, he established the nuclear-engineering materials laboratory for examining weakly radioactive parts from nuclear power stations at the Center for Technology.[108] In the mid-1980s, for example, the lab handled an average of 60 to 70 commissions from nuclear power stations per year, of which roughly a dozen were analyses with radioactive samples. This amounted to about 10 percent of all the investigations performed at the Center for Technology per year.[109] Nuclear power was also a regular topic at the Allianz Technical Colloquia. Traditionally, Allianz insured what it could calculate. In the field of nuclear technology, this was mainly "nuclear plant insurance," consisting of the engineering insurance policies, the associated property insurance policy, and the liability insurance policy.

In June 1974, the fire, liability, and engineering branches established a coordination center for nuclear plant insurance, whose task was to deal with the clients and acquaint interested parties with the issue of insurance as early as possible.[110] Jürgen Feldmann was appointed to head it. The decision to take this step arose from the realization "that the insurance of nuclear plants" would be "of decisive importance for Allianz in the future." The coordination center bundled acquisition, customer relations, risk assessment, damage prevention, and claims adjustment across the types of insurance. This was necessary, among other things, because the three fields of insurance handled a very complex worldwide business:[111]

(1) The engineering insurance policies covered all engineering risks, from

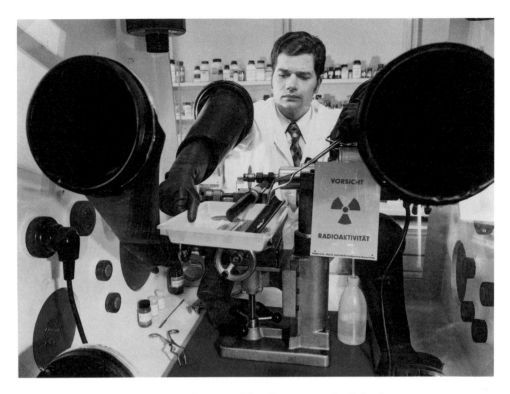

The Nuclear-Engineering Materials Laboratory of the Allianz Center for Technology was set up in 1979.

construction and erection to insuring machinery, against outages of machinery, and insuring the guarantees for machinery.[112]

(2) "The Associated Property Insurance for Nuclear Power Stations covers, besides the conventional fire risks, such as fire, lightning, and explosion, the nuclear-energy risks of the plant. These are in particular damage from accidental contamination within the plant, and also the very improbable melting of the reactor core."[113]

(3) A special feature was nuclear liability insurance, which covered damage due to nuclear impacts of the nuclear power station on the surroundings. Here, the complex provisions of the Atomic Energy Act applied, under which the owner of a nuclear power station was liable to third parties. In 1974, the amount of precautionary coverage provided via the nuclear liability insurance policy came to DM 120 million. The government was liable for any amounts exceeding this. As of March 1, 1977, the amount of liability insurance was raised to DM 500 million.[114]

Under the heading "More and more nuclear power stations," the readers of the company magazine learned in 1970 that Allianz had underwritten the erection all risk insurance for all West German nuclear power stations that had already been built or were under construction.[115] At that time, five power stations in West Germany and three abroad had erection all risk insurance from Allianz. In addition, four power stations had taken out machine insurance from Allianz in 1970.[116] In the following years, as a result of Allianz's increased activity abroad, Heinz Braun specialized his engineering insurance policies in insuring large export and construction commissions, especially of entire factories, or in cost-estimating major risks, which included the coverage of domestic and foreign nuclear power stations.[117] The main focus of insurance of nuclear power stations outside Germany lay in Europe, but Allianz also did business in the U.S. and South America.[118]

Since the mid-1970s, however, technological progress in the field of nuclear power in West Germany "faced not only technological and scientific limits, but also social barriers."[119] Nuclear power grew more controversial in public; the conflict over the power stations intensified. A possible escape of radiation was criticized, both in normal operation and due to accidents, earthquakes, terrorist attacks, airplane crashes, or acts of war. Questions of the transportation, as well as the interim and final storage of the radioactive material were debated heatedly. Slogans such as "Nuclear power? No thanks!" and "Let Gorleben live" shaped public opinion, which found expression in demonstrations and a variety of protests.

The people in charge at Allianz did not overlook the shift in popular opinion. In May 1977, the Allianz Zeitung wrote, "Nuclear power stations have fallen into disrepute. The start of construction has become the starting signal for demonstrations against the projects for the population of the areas concerned."[120] At the same time, the rejection of nuclear power in society became a focal point of a new protest movement. The Greens, a party founded in 1980 – and from 1998 until 2005 part of a government coalition – arose to a large extent as the political voice of this movement. The power-station accidents in Harrisburg (1979), Chernobyl (1986) and Fukushima (2011) also contributed substantially to the spread of anti-nuclear attitudes among the populace.

After the accident in Harrisburg, in which Allianz was involved as the holder of the associated property insurance policy and the nuclear liability insurance policy, the company newspaper set Allianz's broad strategy under the heading "Allianz will continue to insure nuclear power stations." An initial estimate in the summer of 1979 assumed that "in the most unfavorable case," Allianz "would have to cough up about DM 10 million" in the two types of insurance. But in the end, this would not alter "the positive attitude of our company:" "We continue to consider the use of nuclear power necessary, and will continue to provide the required insurance coverage to the suppliers and operators of nuclear power stations."[121] A good seven years later, the Chernobyl disaster – Allianz was not involved as an insurer – gave rise to a fundamental discussion in the insurance industry concerning the border-crossing effects of a severe reactor accident, to which little attention had been paid previously.[122] Despite this fundamentally new situation, Allianz stuck to its previous strategy. The positive assessment of the safety, and thus the insurability, of German and Western nuclear power stations was maintained.[123]

This attitude continues to govern Allianz's dealings with the topic today, and is based on its conception of itself as a globally active corporate group. German politicians, on the other hand, finally responded to the critical public attitudes and initiated the abandonment of nuclear power. The last nuclear power station is supposed to be shut down in 2022. The fact that the insurance companies, despite repeated expressions of confidence in the safety of the nuclear facilities, left the insurance of the nuclear risks largely to the state confirmed the misgivings of critics of these facilities, and functioned as an alarm for the public.[124] According to the sociologist Ulrich Beck, the increase in incalculable risks is associated with a decrease in the importance of private insurance, and the state becomes more and more the "reinsurer of last resort." Beck claims that this applies not only to the nuclear industry, but also to other areas of environmental, economic, and terrorist risks.[125]

In the last forty years, a sustained break with the enthusiasm for technology and unquestioning belief in progress of the preceding decades can be observed in Germany; to a large part, this is due to the public conflicts in the 1970s and the emergence of the environmental movement. In the end, this rethinking in society also evoked a rethinking in government and business.[126] One sign of the perception of these changes in society at Allianz was the founding of its Environmental Foundation, with an endowment of DM 100 million, on the Allianz centennial in 1990.[127] One of the first projects sponsored by the foundation was the Mauerpark. From 1992 on, a ten-hectare green strip was created along the demarcation line where the Berlin Wall and death strip used to separate the two Berlin districts of Prenzlauer Berg and Wedding.[128]

The View across the Borders: First Steps Abroad

Allianz began the 1970s ranked Number 16 in the world insurance market.[129] After 1945, it had operated mainly in Germany, and consequently was still far from the importance it had enjoyed abroad before the Second World War, not to mention the First. The share of foreign business in its total business was extremely small around 1970 – less than 3 percent. It was not until 1984 that it achieved a proportion similar to that of 1931, when 20 percent of premium revenues came from abroad.

In the 1970s, Allianz was the first German insurer to use a system of decentralized individual coverage of foreign risks on site. Thus, it was able to offer its German customers insurance coverage throughout the world even though it was not present everywhere. Its foreign business was based on a complicated combination of various involvements, with the emphasis on the European market. Furthermore, numerous people from a wide variety of departments were assigned partial responsibilities for the foreign business. International reinsurance was handled by Allianz in cooperation with Munich Re. Until the mid-1970s, international direct insurance was handled mainly in three ways: by the foreign subsidiaries in Spain (Plus Ultra until 1974), Italy (La Pace) and Austria (Wiener Allianz), by Allianz's own branch offices in Paris and Milan, and later in Spain and Holland, besides agencies in Holland and Belgium and in Chile for a time as well, and industrial business through cooperation with foreign insurance companies.[130]

In his last address to the annual general meeting on July 16, 1971, Alfred Haase was able to report that there was "only a small remaining technical loss" in foreign business for 1970, with an increase in premium revenues of almost 9 percent to DM 124 million. The reinsurance business in the U.S., consisting mainly of a joint holding with Munich Re in the Munich American Reinsurance Co., New York, had been especially successful, as in previous years. The focal point of the direct business was the branch offices for France and Italy. The former was headed from 1966 until 1986–1987 by Bernard Vitoux, the latter from 1966 until 1972 by Heinz Bremkamp. Under the direction of Vitoux, the Allianz branch office for France was transformed after 1966 into an engineering and industrial insurer, which was incorporated into the newly created Allianz France at that time in the course of the integration of RAS and Cornhill. In 1966, Bremkamp first assumed the management of La Pace Assicurazioni e Riassicurazioni S.p.A. of Milan, in which Allianz and Munich Re had a majority shareholding between 1935 and 1945, and since 1965, when the seizure due to the war ended. Its volume of business, financial basis, and position in the Italian insurance industry developed very positively after 1966. From 1966 to 1969, the year of the 50th anniversary of La Pace, the volume of business increased by 38 percent.[131] In parallel with this, Heinz Bremkamp gradually established the branch office in Milan, whose premiums volume amounted in 1971 to 2.1 billion lire, roughly DM 400 million. In June 1972, he handed over both positions to his successor, Detlev von der Burg, who had started in the legal department in 1962, and had been handling topics of the international – including Italian – insurance market and association work since 1966, as Ernst Meyer's assistant. The two Italian Allianz units, its branch office and La Pace, experienced similar problems in automobile insurance in the 1970s as did Allianz as a whole. After various concepts had been rejected, Detlev von der Burg developed a restructuring plan on the German model with new rates for large companies, with tightened restrictions, and with a head of the automobile insurance sector sent from Germany.[132]

One exception among the Italian insurance companies was Lloyd Adriatico, for even in times of crisis, it distinguished itself by achieving a substantially better ratio of claims to premiums. The firm was known for its innovative products: Ugo Irneri, the founder of what was created in 1936 as a mutual-insurance association named Sabauda di Assicurazioni, Lloyd Adriatico in Trieste, began by insuring church bells.[133] His son, Giorgio Irneri, who had in the meantime become his successor, introduced the 4R automobile liability insurance policy with a deductible in the mid-1960s, when the automobile had developed into a mass-market product. The deductible clause made the premiums unrivaled in price, which was vital in a market that often suffered from undercutting in the postwar period. An advertising campaign launched in collaboration with the magazine Quattroruote (Four Wheels) enabled the new policy to gain acceptance rapidly. The idea of selling the insurance policy via a magazine for motorists was such a success that the clients stood in line to apply for them. This anticipated the solutions of insurance companies in the 1970s, and showed one way of countering the crisis. In 1995, Allianz acquired Lloyd Adriatico from Swiss Re, and thus reinforced its presence in the automotive sector in Italy.[134]

Until 1972, Martin Herzog was the member of the Allianz board of directors responsible from Munich for all foreign business. Until the 1970s, the focus of his work was clearly on Europe and the markets of the European Economic Community. In order to provide urgently needed prospects for foreign business, in 1971 Herzog promoted the establishment of an Allianz foreign department.[135] This was intended to procure for German industrial clients "suitable insurance coverage and service for their risks abroad even in countries" in which Allianz did not operate. In this, it cooperated with Commercial Union, which possessed an international network of stations.[136] The impetus to acquire shares in Commercial Union was external: as part of a reform of company law in 1965, the relationship of the Allianz group to its subsidiaries had to be regulated anew in control agreements. The result was that the mutual shareholdings of Allianz and Munich Re of 30 percent each had to be reduced to 25 percent. Afterward, in 1966, Allianz exchanged 5 percent of the released shares it had held in Munich Re for similar shares in Commercial Union of London. In 1968, the holding was reduced from 4.8 percent to 3 percent.[137] The collaboration bolstered by the exchange of blocks of shares enabled Allianz to offer its clients the new approach of insuring their foreign risks via a correspondent company, as well. The experience of this internationally operating partner made it easier to meet the particular market requirements and legal norms of the respective country.

If Allianz did not want to rely solely on the cooperating companies, in the long run, it needed to open up new markets, and tie existing commitments more closely to the foreign department. The idea behind this plan was that foreign business should be controlled more tightly from Munich. So Martin Herzog had the situation in markets of interest to Allianz explored because more precise knowledge of the insurance business in these countries was needed in order to make strategic decisions from Germany. In contrast to today, in times of increasing networks, it was still relatively difficult at that time to obtain such specific information about geographically remote areas with greatly disparate economies. In order to acquire more skill and personnel, Herzog sent observers to learn from the local experts. As one of the first of these, Horst Fickel traveled to Latin America on two missions.[138]

Fickel had begun his career in 1953 as an apprentice in the transportation department of the Stuttgart branch office, and attracted Herzog's attention because of his knowledge of English, French, and Spanish.[139] In the postwar period, foreign languages did not yet rank very highly in German school education or businesses, so that it was very difficult to find suitable specialists to work abroad. Therefore, in 1961 Fickel was sent to Mexico for a year and a half, to Ajusco Compañia de Seguros Generales, a property insurance company founded in late 1959 by Munich Re and Allianz specializing in automobile insurance. Fickel got to know the market from the general managers Ernesto Warnholtz Sr. and Jr., who acted as brokers for the still manageable amount of business. After his return in the summer of 1962, Fickel described his market observations to the board members responsible for Ajusco, Martin Herzog and Karl-Friedrich von Schlayer; that autumn, there followed a slide presentation for the staff, announced in the company newspaper.[140] The broker Warnholtz remained Allianz's most important contact in Mexico during the 1970s, although in those years, the market did not offer good conditions for foreign investors.

In this, Allianz's associate Commercial Union, with its global presence, could help. At a meeting of the board of directors in October 1975, members complained that direct business was not possible "[f]or general legal and regulatory reasons;" but some German firms were doing extensive and allegedly good business, so German-Mexican collaboration with Commercial Union was being investigated in order for Allianz to make a fresh start in the Mexican market.[141] The motive for the cooperation agreement signed in 1977 with the La Comercial-Libertad Insurance Group was Mexico's cautious return to a free-market economy, which made the country more interesting for German industry again. Some 200 German-held firms, including the Volkswagen subsidiary Volkswagen de México, which was manufacturing the Beetle there, were potential clients.[142]

In 1969, Martin Herzog gave Horst Fickel his second assignment. During a three-month stay in Chile, he was to analyze the insurance companies Araucania and Germania, and the Allianz general agency, to investigate the possibilities of enlarging the business. Until then, the Allianz agency in Chile, with a staff of about 20 in Santiago de Chile, had concentrated on property insurance for private persons and small and medium-sized businesses. Herzog's notion for expanding the business was the following: Chilean risks underwritten in Germany by the branch offices in transportation, erection, and construction all risk insurance should be passed on to Germania or Araucania, to be insured in Chile.[143] On his way home, Fickel met with other cooperation associates, such as the director-general and majority shareholder of the Argentinian firm Plus Ultra, Louis D. Stueck, in Buenos Aires. Together with its associated partner Colon, this company, with which Allianz signed a formal cooperation agreement in 1978, ranked sixth among the Argentinian multiple-line insurers.[144]

However, the original goal of Fickel's journey was not achieved at first due to the political conditions in Chile. Not until 1981 did Allianz return to that country, with the complete takeover of a small local company under the name of Allianz Compañía de Seguros.[145]

Horst Fickel's South American experience resulted in a new field of

Hoffentlich
Allianz versichert

Well insured
by Allianz

Goed verzekerd
bij Allianz

Allianz,
seguridad
en seguros

Bien assuré
par l'Allianz

Bem segurado
com a Allianz

Assicurati bene!
Assicurati Allianz!

In allen Sprachen
ein guter Name für Sicherheit

In the 1970s, the Allianz world was focused on Europe.

activity for his employment. He switched from the industrial department in Stuttgart to Munich, and became the first head of the foreign department when it was founded in 1971.[146] The foreign department was an important step in adjusting the sparse network of Allianz branch offices, limited to Europe, to the needs for insurance and customer service of the German industrial clients who were ever more active abroad, so as not to lose them to the international competition. Since the late 1960s, West Germany had had a positive balance of capital exports, both in visible trade and in direct investment.[147] That made it more and more interesting for Allianz, both at home and abroad, "to achieve the leading position, long since reached in other types of insurance, in the market for industrial insurance as well."[148]

In addition, the expansion of business abroad resulted from the problem of lack of growth in West Germany, where Allianz had already run up against its limits in the mid-1970s. Even after 1970, foreign business, with only limited success at first, continued to be overshadowed by the domestic business. Martin Herzog, as "foreign minister of the German insurance industry" in general, and of Allianz in particular, was active in countless committees, and expanded Allianz's international connections and collaboration with foreign companies. He was supported in his work by the industrial departments in the head office and the branch offices, which were enlarged in 1974 as industrial business was upgraded. In addition, the heads of the transportation and engineering insurance departments were responsible for the foreign business of their divisions, and for specific countries that were specially assigned to them.[149] This was precisely the specialty of Karl-Friedrich von Schlayer (1951–1972), the head of the board section for Transportation and Aviation Insurance, and simultaneously the head of the Deutscher Luftpool (German Aviation Pool) from 1968 until 1972. With his work in international associations, as well as his experience abroad and language skills, he contributed to overcoming the "frontiers of national self-limitation" in favor of international collaboration.

Coordinated by the engineering insurance and liability insurance sections, Allianz offered a special insurance program to cover the risks involved in the export of turnkey industrial plants, for example complete steelworks or nuclear power stations, to over twenty countries. Fifty plant contracts were signed by 1975. The engineering insurance section accelerated the expansion of international business accordingly. After 1974, a focus was on the Arab countries: in 1975, a department for Saudi Arabia and two holding companies, Teheran Insurance Company (Bimeh Teheran) and Arab International Insurance Company in Cairo, were founded. In 1977, Allianz opened an office in the United Arab Emirates.

In Saudi Arabia, Allianz supervised more than just German business. It decided to maintain a local presence together with a Saudi partner in an agency from 1976 on, in order to provide support for a five-year infrastructure project in the country. Walter Rostock supervised the extreme risks of the major construction projects and industrial plant transactions together with the foreign and engineering insurance departments, and the industrial department, headed by Georg Mehl.[150] As the example of Saudi Arabia shows, people were working under pioneering conditions. This is illustrated by an advertisement in the Allianz Zeitung in 1977, a job offering for an insurance engineer for a new service center in the United Arab Emirates: "Are

The King Fahd International Stadium, opened in 1987 in Saudi Arabia, was one of the largest construction projects insured by Allianz (Source: Philipp Holzmann Werkfoto).

you looking for an opportunity in the Gulf? The oil boom is enlivening the Arabian Gulf. Would you like to work there?"[151] The requirements were at least three years of experience working in industrial insurance, a good command of English, and fitness for work in tropical climates. This showed very clearly the significance of the "human factor" for the success of business abroad. The company recognized that it would have to invest in employees if it wanted to succeed by means of customer service in industrial insurance. Applicants were promised "very thorough training." Successful employees needed to know not only how much premiums cost and other know-how, but also foreign languages, intercultural skills, and different mentalities, too.[152]

As in the central management positions, there was also a changeover of personnel in the handling of foreign business in the board of directors in 1972. Three of the four directors and heads of sections with experience abroad – the exception being Heinz Braun – left the company. Subsequently, nobody was assigned responsibility for foreign business in the board of directors. This was more than a changeover of generations. Foreign business became the responsibility of the boss.

After the restructuring efforts began to show initial success in Germany after two years,[153] Wolfgang Schieren personally began to concern himself more with foreign business. At the meeting of the Heß Club in London in 1973,[154] he remained at first quite in line with his predecessors. Before 1914, foreign business had provided a substantial share of the premium revenues, he said, but now in 1973, it did not amount to even 3 percent of the volume of business. Schieren promised "extreme efforts" to connect with the former successes.[155] That same year, Allianz became the largest European insurance company, which seems surprising in view of these figures. The company reached this position solely through its size on the domestic market, with a premiums volume of over DM 6 million from property and life insurance, thus also advancing into the group of the ten largest insurers in the world.[156]

Britain was the unmatched model at that point, where "two-thirds of the volume of premiums comes from abroad, above all from America, Canada, Australia," Wolfgang Schieren said at the London meeting of the Heß Club, and he expected that the British insurers would increase their involvement "on the European continent [significantly … given an existing] share of 5 %." In this context, he gave a new impulse for boosting foreign business: "The Allianz companies do not intend to operate throughout the world. Instead, they will select focal points in order to be able to provide insurance coverage to German businesses in their activities abroad, and they will follow European integration, for which they have been preparing themselves in recent years." They intended to improve their overall position in foreign markets substantially.[157] However, this could not be achieved by involving themselves in particular instances of industrial business originating in Germany alone; they needed to find a way to secure an adequate share of the international insurance market for the company by acquiring new business. This method of reinforcing foreign business first led the company to London, the hub of the international insurance business.

The Founding of Allianz International Insurance Co. Ltd., London

In 1974, Allianz took its first steps in the important British insurance market. What had still been a vision in 1972 was put into practice two years later. Hans-Jürgen Schwepcke, who had represented automobile insurance on the Allianz board of directors since 1972, was assigned to coordinate the preparation and implementation of the founding of Allianz International Insurance Co. Ltd.

in London as a wholly owned Allianz subsidiary. The "friendly relations with the house of Willis, Faber & Dumas and with Commercial Union" functioned as the ticket to the rather inaccessible British insurance market. Allianz International profited in 1974 from the partnership with one of the world's largest firms of brokers and underwriters: "Management and underwriting [of AI] are in the hands of Willis, Faber & Dumas."[158] The new company had the job of underwriting the business of the German clients, including the German industrial business. In addition, it participated in the special coinsurance communities of the British market, the so-called stamps, for the transportation, aviation, property, and engineering insurance business, with the focus on construction all risk insurance. This was because Allianz possessed worldwide experience in this field, which it wanted to introduce to the underwriting policies of Willis, Faber & Dumas.[159] This partnership and the close relations with Commercial Union helped Allianz International to become accepted as an associate member of the Institute of London Underwriters in 1975. Thus, the company could "now underwrite directly in transportation insurance, too."[160] In the spring

Allianz sent many of its insurance experts to Edward G. Marchant (center, wearing glasses), training manager of Willis and Faber, to familiarize them with the London insurance market.

of 1976, Ulrich Röder, the first Allianz underwriter for engineering insurance policies, was already demanding more personnel in order to be able to do more business.[161] After only three years, he already saw good chances for Allianz International "to become, at least in the engineering insurance field, one of the leading insurers on the London market."[162] The importance of the London insurance market is illustrated by the observation "that risks, which we are working our way towards directly in the Middle East with considerable difficulty, are often being dealt with at the same time by London brokers, as well." Allianz made use of this partnership, which lasted twelve years, to have its insurance specialists with little foreign experience train with the training manager of Willis and Faber, Edward G. Marchant.[163] With the purchase of the English insurance company in 1986, it emancipated itself from this partner, since the acquisition now finally brought the desired access to mass business, and industrial business was to be bundled at Allianz International.

Forced Expansion of Foreign Business

The change at Allianz from a cautious to forced expansion of international business was accompanied by a change in mentalities. Until the mid-1970s, the foreign business was characterized by improvisation and trial-and-error. From 1974 on, this changed. During the next ten years, various companies, some of them sizable, were founded or purchased, and work with holding companies was expanded to areas outside Europe. For example, Allianz not only entered the British market but also reinforced its presence in Austria, where it acquired Anglo-Elementar Versicherungs-AG in 1976, in addition to its decades-old connection to Wiener Allianz. The two Austrian companies provided about 16 percent of the overall foreign business in 1983.[164]

From 1974, Allianz also expanded its business outside Europe. Besides the U.S., Australia and South Africa, there were two focal points in particular: the Middle East and South America. One example of an ongoing involvement was the first substantial holding in a South American company, Allianz Ultramar in Brazil, in 1974. A year later, it had already acquired 40 German firms as clients for engineering and industrial policies, one of them being Volkswagen do Brasil. However, both regions were marked by economic and political instability, which made working there considerably more difficult. As in Chile, for example, the business in Iran also had to be interrupted or abandoned on account of the political conditions. Most

This picture of a cow-boy decorated AIC's first annual financial report of 1977.

ALLIANZ
INSURANCE
COMPANY

foreign business continued to be in Europe and the U.S., with its share of total premium revenues rising from 3 to 10 percent from 1971 to 1981.[165]

In this phase, Wolfgang Schieren began to exercise greater control over foreign business and developed plans to achieve two major strategic goals: a new structure of the group, and the internationalization of Allianz.[166] Foreign business was divided among a large number of people, and various markets were tested without clear structuring of the responsibilities or regions being visible initially. The chairman of the board of directors assigned the responsibility for different countries, or for different projects to the section heads, transcending the limits of the board members' functions in doing so. For example, Hans-Jürgen Schwepcke set up Allianz International in London. After a vacancy lasting three years, Detlev von der Burg was finally appointed to the international division in 1975. The board's minutes state: "The re-establishment of a board of directors division 'international business' has […] already been discussed. It is intended that von der Burg [...] be proposed as a deputy member of the board of directors as of January 1, 1975. [...] [It] is not intended that von der Burg be assigned immediately to handle all Allianz interests abroad. At first, the chairman of the board of directors will assign specific countries to him."[167] More and more divisions were now assisting in the expansion of foreign business. "The responsibilities for specific countries already assigned to individual members of the board will thus remain in force until explicitly altered."[168] The latter included, beside Heinz Braun and Hans-Jürgen Schwepcke, who headed the group's newly created overseas foreign division from 1985 to 1986, in particular Wolfgang Müller. Müller headed the liability section and was first in charge of various countries, such as Spain, and from 1985 on, he was in charge of the America division, and from 1987 on, of North and South America.[169] Other players, such as Klaus Götte, Walter Rostock, Rolf Landwehr, and later Uwe Haasen, were involved in the expansion of U.S. business.

The most important foreign involvement in the 1970s was in the U.S.[170] In the spring of 1976, Allianz founded a holding company, Allianz of America (AZOA).[171] It acquired an insurance company in October 1976, which was renamed the Allianz Insurance Company in Los Angeles (AIC). This company then obtained licenses to do business in all U.S. states but commenced business in January 1977 at first only in California.[172] The 1977 year-end summary emphasized this as being a milestone of foreign activities, which now had acquired "a new dimension geographically, as well."[173] Allianz pursued cautious business policies, but despite this, it already ranked number nine among the European direct insurers in the U.S. in 1977. Rolf Landwehr was the right "man in America" to implement these measured expansion guidelines: he had worked since 1954 as an accident specialist in the Hamburg branch office, and since 1971 as director of sales at Allianz Leben in Stuttgart. He was selected for these international responsibilities in part because of his foreign-language skills, which enabled him to act as a representative and vice chairman.

In order to score under the difficult market conditions, the newcomer did not concentrate on competing in prices, but on customer service, such as providing a rate quote within 24 hours and issuing a policy within 72 hours. Allianz celebrated its "Entry to America" with a press conference. President of AI, Frank Raab, had given this same title to a study on the prospects for a new company, which Allianz had obviously found convincing.[174] At first, quite basic matters had to be resolved: licences were obtained. By the end of 1976, the Allianz Insurance Company was licensed in California and five other states; staff was hired, and it became a member of the pool for insurers of nuclear risks "Nelpia" – with a maximum liability of $500,000 – and of the pool of transportation insurers; and it purchased an office building in Los Angeles and created its first printed forms.

In order to make its mark as a newcomer from Germany and distinguish itself from the many "Alliances" in the U.S., Allianz had a parrot introduce the company with the German pronunciation of its name: "Say 'Ah…Lee… Ahnz.' Allianz. The company everybody knows […] but can't pronounce."[175] Surprise and tradition – both aspects were played upon in the U.S. The first AIC annual report appeared with a picture of a cowboy in 1977. But after the introduction of the new corporate design that same year, the eagle and Allianz in blue displaced the parrot and the cowboy.[176]

At first, communication between Los Angeles and Munich was not easy because of the time difference, and "consisted mainly of telephone conversations between Dr. Landwehr and me [Wolfgang Schieren] at six in the morning." They took it good-humoredly: "That is somewhat unusual, but proves Frank Raab's claim that the distance between L.A. and Munich is no problem." Teletypewriters and air freight for the mail were intended to remedy the situation.[177] The concept was successful: by the end of 1977, AIC was

An office of the North American Life and Casualty Co. (NALAC), which, together with FULICO, represents Allianz's life insurance business in the U.S. since 1979.

already Allianz's third-largest foreign subsidiary, with premium revenues of about DM 15 million, and 51 employees who sold liability and workmen's compensation policies from their central open-plan office.[178]

However, AIC had to struggle against difficult market conditions from the beginning.[179] Between 1978 and 1984, the situation on the U.S. market worsened: a fall in prices due to the high rates of interest, a drop in premiums, an increase in the claims percentage, and underwriting losses were the result. That ruined many companies. In the mid-1980s, the rates of interest fell, causing many other firms to go bankrupt. AIC – with a turnover of $100 million in 1984–1985, it was one of the smaller companies – responded to this with cuts, reducing its business to California and New York, and abandoned the goal of becoming a "nationwide insurer." In order to operate throughout the country despite this, acquisitions seemed unavoidable.[180]

In 1979, two life insurance companies were purchased to supplement the property insurance business in the U.S. Klaus Götte played a major role in this; as the new chief financial officer (1972–1980), he was also responsible for the U.S. business.[181] Götte bought the Fidelity Union Life Insurance Company of Dallas, Texas (FULICO) – which specialized in individual universal life insurance policies and payroll-deduction policies – and the North American Life and Casualty Company of Minneapolis, Minnesota (NALAC), whose emphasis was on group life, health, and old age insurance, as well as the life reinsurance business.[182] In the early 1980s, the industry in the U.S. suffered from the huge increase in interest rates, which had a negative effect on endowment life insurance policies in particular, and forced the companies to put new, interest-oriented products on the market.

The structural changes in the U.S. life insurance business also caused the strategists from Allianz headquarters to become involved: in 1982, Arno Paul Bäumer, in his role as head of the largest European life insurer, sounded out the altered demand in the life insurance market in the U.S. at a meeting with the president of Prudential Life Insurance, which was probably the largest American life insurance company at that time. That same year, the journal World published interviews with nine board chairmen of leading European life insurance companies – including Arno Paul Bäumer – on the future of life insurance. Bäumer expressed his conviction "that life insurance products with elements of savings and security for long-term investments will have their place both in the protected space of the German market and on the world market, as well."[183] There would continue to be a demand from the lower and medium income groups. But it was not yet clear how the demand for traditional endowment policies would develop in the U.S. market. This depended on the rate of inflation, taxation, and customization of the product, as well as on the competition, and on whether the clients' interests lay more in short-term or long-term products, he said.

In order to adapt to the change in the market structure, in the 1980s the two American life insurers of Allianz, NALAC and FULICO, turned away from classical wealth-accumulating policies, "which often did not provide for any share in the profits [...] and thus gave the policyholders only an insufficient share in the increased earnings from interest."[184] Thanks to new, flexible products that offered attractive participation in profits, "such as the fund-linked single-premium annuity insurance" from NALAC, or the universal life policy from FULICO, a combined term insurance with a capital-accumulation function, they were able to hold their own in the difficult environment of the American market and diminish the exodus to other forms of investment.[185] In contrast to Allianz's property insurance business in the U.S., they earned solid profits until 1992 and were able to grow continuously. Growth from 1987 to 1992 amounted to almost 420 percent.[186]

In order to survive in the long term, in 1993 FULICO was merged with NALAC and renamed the Allianz Life Insurance Company of North America, Minneapolis, Minnesota, with a turnover of DM 4.1 billion.[187] It was hoped that amalgamating the management and forging new structures would reduce the costs generated by an expensive marketing system and the high level of customer service provided by the office staff. In the long term, the Allianz life insurance companies were successful, although the interest trend reversed in 1994. This made investment-fund-linked annuity insurance lose appeal; premium revenues fell by more than 30 percent. "Despite this, in 1995 Allianz Life earned almost 12 percent of the premium revenues in the group's life insurance and health insurance business [in the U.S.], and represented a market share of 0.7 percent in the U.S."[188]

Rolf Landwehr returned to Germany in late 1979. His death in August 1980, and the move by chief financial officer Klaus Götte to the Flick Group in December 1979, resulted in vacancies; for this reason, Götte continued to fulfil his obligations to Allianz even after leaving. Furthermore, the strongly increased business in the U.S. made a restructuring of the board functions essential. On September 12, 1980, all Allianz employees throughout the world were informed of the new structuring by a note from the management: "The importance and weight of our involvement in the U.S. make it necessary to establish a separate board function for this. Dr. Haasen will assume this responsibility, beginning immediately."[189] Uwe Haasen remained responsible for the U.S. until 1985, and then became head of Allianz Leben. His responsibilities in the U.S. covered the holding company founded in 1976, AZOA in Wilmington, Delaware, with the companies mentioned above, and the Underwriter Insurance Company (UIC).[190] The holding company made control from Germany possible, while the responsibility for the business remained decentralized in the hands of the companies.

In 1985, Allianz did about 55 percent of its foreign business on the American market. But in order to be really successful in the U.S., the business needed to be of another order of magnitude: the market power of Allianz in the U.S. was much too small. To grow substantially, Allianz had to buy up other firms. For Wolfgang Schieren, this was about as important as its involvement in London. It was not until 1991 – shortly before the end of his time as chairman of the board of directors – that the decisive step could be taken. But Fireman's Fund Insurance Company (FFIC), which was now acquired, generated the same difficulties that Allianz had experienced previously with its other U.S. property insurance business. FFIC had suffered a decline in gross premiums since 1987, amounting by 1992 to a 28-percent shrinkage of premium volume.[191] However, the purchase of this automobile and industrial insurer strengthened Allianz's position, placing it among the top twenty indemnity and accident insurers in the U.S.[192] FFIC ranked eleventh on the property insurance market, with a market share of almost 3 percent.[193] Together with the companies of Allianz of America (AZOA), Allianz now had a staff of 12,000 and premium revenues of DM 7.7 billion.[194] Since the company was focused on property insurance, with 80 percent of its business in this sector, it was strongly affected by all market fluctuations. These fluctuations determined positive or negative results much more strongly than Allianz was accustomed to in Europe, and made it difficult for the company to operate at a profit. Some fluctuations, in particular, resulted from natural disasters, fires, and special liability provisions in the U.S., such as the question of liability for damage resulting from asbestos. Another example is the burden of more than $ 22 billion imposed on insurance companies in 1992 by Hurricanes Andrew and Iniki and the riots in Los Angeles. The above-average cost ratio of 36 percent was also a cause for concern. From 1991 on, drastic cost-cutting measures were initiated, such as a staff cut of 1,400 from the original 10,350 employees at FFIC (as of 1990) within three years. While this did reduce administrative costs by $ 33 million, this was at first swallowed up by severance payments, costs of the restructuring, and a shrinking premium volume. To this day, the U.S. business of Fireman's Fund remains one of the headaches of the Allianz Group, so that it has since been decided that the wholesale insurance business of Fireman's Fund will be incorporated into the U.S. part of Allianz Global Corporate and Specialty (AGCS), Allianz's global industry insurer, while the business with corporate clients in property insurance in the U.S. will be re-organized under the brand Allianz. A decision on the future of the private-customer business has not yet been made.[195]

1985: Becoming the Allianz AG Holding Company

At the beginning of 1982, Wolfgang Schieren formulated his answer to the problems of the time, such as the economic downturn, gloomy prospects for the labor market, problems with sales in the economy, and what he considered excessive expenditures for social services. Summarizing, he said that "[…] we rationalized and […] cut costs, in order to preserve Allianz's competitiveness in the market" and that the next step had to be expansion of foreign business, so as "to catch up with the top group of leading international insurers."[196] Consequently, the idea of restructuring the Allianz Group gradually ripened in the 1980s.

That there was an urgent need to develop a strategy for the formation of the group had been demonstrated to Allianz repeatedly since the late 1970s. In 1979, the Aachener und Münchener Versicherungs-AG had established a holding company: the business of direct insurance was transferred to a wholly owned subsidiary, Cosmos Versicherungs-AG. The objective was at first to gain more freedom in the capital investment policies, as well as to separate the management of the group by the parent company, renamed Aachener und Münchener Beteiligungs-AG, from the day-to-day business of the property insurance company. So Allianz was "not the first insurance company to create a holding umbrella for itself," as the Frankfurter Allgemeine Zeitung commented later.[197]

Another impetus for founding the holding company came from ideas in the Bundesaufsichtsamt für Versicherung (BAV, Federal Insurance Supervisory Office) that amounted to a reform of the laws concerning its supervision of insurance.[198] These reforms involved the financing of holdings with equity capital, holdings in firms from other economic sectors (less than 25 percent), the principle of separation of classes of insurance, and the ban on non-insurance activities, which applied, for example, to the telecommunications repair firm Tela, in which Allianz held a 25-percent share. The restrictions in matters of asset investment and financing to which direct insurers would likely be subject in the future, such as detailed investment rules, prompted Allianz to make its plans. A newly established commission – consisting of the chief financial officer Marcus Bierich (1980–1985), the board member for business administration Jan Boetius, the finances and tax divisions represented by Breipohl and Ziegler, and Bernd Honsel for corporate planning – developed a structural model at its first meeting on July 15, 1983, that contained all the essential elements of the principles that were later implemented. It comprised a holding company with the tasks of managing holdings, intra-group reinsurance, non-insurance services, and the building business, and two holding companies for domestic and foreign insurance business.[199]

There was another factor, as well, namely, the failed takeover of the British insurance company Eagle Star. On June 1, 1981, after several attempts, Allianz, with the help of the banking house Morgan Grenfell, had secretly purchased 14.9 percent of the share capital of Eagle Star (20.4 million shares at a price of £ 59.2 million, that is, 290 pence per share), and at the same time made an offer for another 15 percent at the same price. In Britain, company law provides for holdings to be acquired in stages. By means of this secret action, Allianz increased its holding to 28.1 percent by June 9, 1981. However, they had not anticipated the vehement rejection by the chairman of the board and grandson of the company's founder, Sir Denis Mountain. He had already seen "no advantages for the Eagle Star shareholders" in 1980, and did everything he could to mobilize public opinion via the press against the purchase, viewed as an "unfriendly takeover," and later even prevented Allianz being represented on the board by a non-executive director. Even respectable papers such as the Times of London and the Börsenzeitung got involved in the clash with headlines such as "A shock to the system" or "Eagle versus Adler." In retrospect, the fact that Allianz nonetheless decided to make an offer for the remaining shares in October 1983 (at 500 pence per share) can only be understood as evidence that the British market was of great importance to it, and there were relatively few opportunities to expand there. This soon proved to be an absolute stroke of luck.

In November 1983, the conglomerate British American Tobacco Industries (BAT) responded to Allianz's takeover bid with a counter offer of 575 pence per share, which was supported by the Eagle Star management. Eagle Star adopted the same tactics as two years before: it shifted "the battle from the boardroom to the public arena," and rejected Allianz's "ridiculous offer" in advertisements.[200] By mid-December 1983, the two prospective buyers gradually raised the bid up to 675 pence per share, at which point

Allianz decided to drop out and offer to sell its share package to BAT. Shortly before the new year, they agreed on the sale, which was handled in early January 1984 via the new holding company Allianz Europe Ltd. in Amsterdam. This retreat from the bidding war brought what was a fantastic profit of £ 285.9 million at the time. This financial reserve was enormously helpful in other, friendly mergers that fitted in well with Allianz after the establishment of the holding company.

The crucial aspect of this failed purchase, besides the certainly significant monetary gain, was above all the gain in knowledge. For in the final phase of the takeover spectacle, the BAV had inquired "about the financing of the share of the purchase price attributable to [Allianz]." The BAV was of the opinion that "holdings in insurance companies are to be deducted from equity resources eligible for credit."[201] There were fundamentally different views on the form of financing major holdings, and in particular on taking up outside funds, between the BAV, on the one hand, and the Association of the German Insurance Business (GDV) and the insurance industry, on the other, which had the potential of hindering major operations substantially. This concerned in particular holdings in foreign insurance companies, so that if Allianz had taken over Eagle Star, a serious conflict with the supervisory authorities would have been likely.

This insight speeded up the conversion of Allianz Versicherungs-AG into a financial holding company. It rapidly assumed concrete form in discussions with the BAV from early January 1984 on. Many things had to be clarified, including the responsibilities of the holding company, the topic of reinsurance, endowment with equity capital, capital investments, real estate, and finally the name of the business, which triggered another discussion. The goal of "creating a structure for future investments [...] in the course of the expansion of its international activities that is also acceptable in the view of the BAV" was finally achieved in the summer of 1984, so that a resolution of the board of directors was adopted in August 1984, and of the supervisory board in December, approving the structural changes.[202] It took until June 27, 1985 for all the formalities to be completed: on that date, the annual general meeting voted for the restructuring, and the BAV granted the authorizations. The next day, on June 28, 1985, the restructuring officially went into effect upon entry in the commercial registers in Berlin and Munich.

Allianz Versicherungs-AG now did business as Allianz AG Holding, and the direct domestic business of the old Allianz Versicherungs-AG was transferred to a new wholly-owned subsidiary. This new subsidiary not only continued the use of the name Allianz Versicherungs-AG but also took over all the staff and the domestic establishments, and was linked to the holding company by a control and profit-transfer agreement. In addition, three corporate divisions with regional responsibilities were created on the holding level: Allianz Europa, Allianz Nordamerika and Allianz Übersee, for Europe outside Germany, North America, and other overseas areas. Detlev von der Burg took on responsibility for the Allianz Europa division, and Hans-Jürgen Schwepcke became the head of Allianz Übersee. The leadership of Allianz of America Inc., with a premium volume of DM 1.6 billion in 1984, was now assumed by Herbert Hansmeyer, since Uwe Haasen had shifted to Allianz Leben as chairman of its board of directors.[203] There were a few critical voices to be heard among the shareholders and clients, but in general, the restructuring met with approval. The business press was full of praise, called it a "masterstroke," and nominated Wolfgang Schieren, now head of Allianz AG Holding, as Manager of the Year for 1985.[204]

1985–1990: Changes in Allianz's International Business after Formation of the Holding Company

The founding of the holding company had the strategic goal of turning Allianz into a "more internationalized global group,"[205] for which a corresponding financial statement was presented for the first time for the 1989 fiscal year.

The future policy for foreign business was supposed to solve two basic problems: the existing foreign business was not big enough to be really effective, and Allianz lacked sufficient presence in many markets in the world. Most of Allianz's international companies were too small, and for this reason, company leaders wished to enlarge them through acquisitions into a size with which a better spreading of risks and good underwriting results could be achieved. In addition, they wanted Allianz to be present and profitable in all international markets. In Europe, for example, Switzerland was missing, in North America, Canada, and in Asia, Japan and the ASEAN markets. They wanted to offer clients a tight-meshed worldwide organizational network in the future such as they were familiar with from the world of finance.[206] This would prevent the danger of "sinking down to the status of a regionally-oriented insurer," as Wolfgang Schieren put it, and secure the future of the business.[207] It was only through the restructuring that the internationalization really got going. Instead of laboriously building newly established companies, the company purchased important international firms that already held a significant market position.[208] The most important additions were the two European insurance companies Cornhill in 1986, and RAS from 1984 to 1987.

After the sale of the holdings in Eagle Star, the Allianz board of directors had by no means abandoned its intention of acquiring an important company in the British insurance market.[209] With Allianz International alone, they would not be able to fulfill Wolfgang Schieren's idea of an expansion in Britain. Cornhill had already been Allianz's preferred option in 1974, and Hans-Jürgen Schwepcke regretted very much at that time that he had been just a bit too late when the influential partner in Allianz International, the Julian Faber family, sold its share in Cornhill to the British conglomerate Thomas Tilling Ltd.[210] In 1983, however, the British conglomerate British Tyre and Rubber PLC (BTR) acquired a majority interest in Tilling, and in October 1985 indicated that it was willing to sell Cornhill. After a memorandum of understanding was signed on January 22, 1986, and after approval by the supervisory authorities of both countries and the financing of the pur-

Allianz was finally able to gain a foothold in the British market with the Cornhill Insurance Company.

chase price of £305 million via Allianz Holdings Ltd. of Amsterdam,[211] the deal was concluded on April 17, 1986.[212] According to a note by Detlev Bremkamp, Cornhill was convinced that Allianz would be welcomed as the major shareholder by the entire management and staff. This was especially important, since Allianz wanted to avoid a situation such as it had experienced at Eagle Star at all costs.[213]

With Cornhill, established in 1905, Allianz took over a well-established medium-sized multiple-line insurer, with a staff of 2,400. It ranked tenth in Britain at that time and had a significant size in the market.[214] Cornhill's focus was on the mass business that Allianz was looking for, with earnings that had been well above average for the market for years.[215] Since 1967, it had been selling life insurance in the investment-fund-linked form, which accounted for about 10 percent of the premium revenues.[216] Automobile and property insurance were its two largest lines, and they had the typical problems of competition as in other European countries. Aviation and transportation insurance, on the other hand, also had problems but were seen as promising within the segment. A comprehensive sales organization served the clients in 41 branches and offices. Since Cornhill lacked a legal-expenses insurance policy, the business was supplemented with a specialized company acquired in 1986. As Cornhill took over in 1990, this specialized business has been known as Allianz Cornhill Legal Protection. A typically British feature was the health insurance policy for animals, named Petplan, which had been established in 1975 and was purchased by Cornhill in 1996. Since most British veterinarians promoted Petplan, the product is very successful among pet-loving Britons. In 2003, besides dogs, cats, and horses, about two million rabbits were insured, for example.[217]

At the time of the takeover, 15 percent of Cornhill's premium revenues came from foreign business in the U.S., Canada and France, with the emphasis on mass business.[218] Detlev Bremkamp, who had been responsible for Cornhill and Northern Europe on the Allianz board of directors since 1987, therefore analyzed Cornhill's foreign business immediately for possible synergy effects. In the U.S., Cornhill was active as a specialized automotive insurer, mainly in Illinois and Florida, with the American Ambassador Casualty Company of Chicago, purchased in 1978, he reported. Here, he did not expect any advantages from collaboration with Allianz's companies in the U.S.[219] In Canada, where business in Toronto and four other branch offices had been very bad during the past twenty years, things were different.[220] Cornhill also had branches in Australia and New Zealand, as well as agencies or subscription agents in Japan, Hong Kong, Belgium, Norway,

The merger with Riunione Adriatica di Sicurtà, whose business had traditionally been international in scope, was an important step on Allianz's path to becoming a global corporation.

Denmark, Germany, and the Netherlands.[221] Collaboration between Cornhill and Allianz did indeed develop very satisfactorily in the following years.

But even more significant than the takeover of Cornhill was the acquisition of Riunione Adriatica di Sicurtà, S.p.A. (RAS) in the years 1984 and 1987. This really marked the beginning of a new phase in Allianz's foreign business.[222] RAS, founded in 1838 in Trieste, which at that time was part of the Austrian empire, ranked second in Italy in 1984 after Assicurazioni Generali with a continuously growing market share, and controlled 69 insurance companies throughout the world. RAS operated in all lines of property, life, and health insurance. In life insurance, it achieved a market share of 10 percent in Italy and about 7.5 percent in automobile insurance in 1990.[223] Even more interesting for Allianz was the fact that RAS was "one of the insurance companies with the highest degree of internationalization" in Europe and the world. Of the roughly DM 4 billion in premium revenues in 1984, about 50 percent came from foreign business. Furthermore, the business was "very well diversified regionally," most coming from the European market, namely DM 1.6 billion, mainly from Austria, Switzerland, and Germany, "and then from markets that can be developed, such as France, Spain and Canada, and also to a smaller extent from regions that are of interest in the long term, such as Latin America and Australia."[224] In addition, RAS had been very active in the reinsurance business since 1840, and in 1917 gave "the first impetus for the creation of a reinsurance market in Italy" by founding the first reinsurance company, La Riassicuratrice.[225] Another special feature was its asset management segment, which had been built up since the 1970s by Ettore Lolli, president of RAS from 1967 to 1983, through various fund-management companies. This offered possibilities for increased development and networking of the insurance and finance sectors (savings, investments, and loans). This was an ideal supplement to Allianz's product range, where the asset-management sector was still in its infancy.[226]

Thus, RAS was ahead of Allianz in many ways at the time of the merger, and supplemented the latter's activities in foreign markets ideally, as well. This allowed unhoped-for synergies, which Allianz immediately began to exploit in 1987, together with RAS and Cornhill. European business was restructured, for example, by Cornhill taking over British Reserve from RAS. In addition, RAS was a company with "above-average earnings power and capital resources"[227] – which reflected the Italian insurance market of the late 1980s and early 1990s, which was one of the most dynamic in Europe. The innovations by RAS in many areas of industrial and retail business, and in the marketing of the "module programs" it already offered, comparable to today's bundled products, must also be included.[228]

RAS's remarkable degree of internationalization can be traced at a glance to the development of the company since its beginnings. Like Assicurazioni Generali and a few smaller Italian insurers, it originated in Trieste, an important intersection of commercial routes in Southeastern Europe. Its fire and transportation insurance business was internationally oriented from the start due to its location in this cosmopolitan, multicultural commercial center, and its seven founders were of different nationalities. From its first year of business, 1838, and throughout the 19th century, RAS established agencies in the major cities of the Austrian and Austro-Hungarian Empire and Italy, and moved into hail and life insurance. In the course of the 19th century, it expanded above all in Germany and Switzerland, and also in other countries of Central and Eastern Europe, as well as many others.[229] "It belongs […] to the few international direct insurers for whom foreign business plays just as important [sometimes even more important] a role as the domestic market." At the end of the 19th century, RAS added to its product range the still fairly young, growing lines of accident and liability insurance, and founded – following this trend – "its first subsidiaries: Interunfall in Vienna in 1890, and Assicuratrice Italiana in Milan in 1898 […]; in 1911 Protectrice Accidents in Paris was added."[230] During and after the First World War, RAS was caught "between the lines," as it were, since it served both warring parties, and its businesses in the collapsed Austro-Hungarian Empire suffered a sharp drop for a time. There was a greater focus on the Italian market.[231] Two of the most important presidents of RAS, the father and son Adolfo and Arnoldo Frigessi di Rattalma, headed RAS, first the father, then the son, from 1899 until 1917, in the interwar period, and in the first post-World War II years until 1950. "They built up the business in Eastern Europe, while at the same time setting the course for the expansion of RAS in Western Europe and overseas."[232] That was vital for RAS, since it lost its entire Eastern European business after the Second World War. This orientation westwards was shown in 1929, for example, when RAS crossed the Atlantic for the first time and established a separate division in Brazil. After the Second World War, it built up a new center of activities in the U.S., Canada, and South America with Venezuela, Peru, Colombia, as well as Australia, by the 1970s.[233]

Allianz's chance to acquire Riunione Adriatica di Sicurtà arose in July 1984 through an offer, similar to Cornhill later. In this case, the president of RAS's administrative council, Franz Schmitz, forwarded the offer by the largest shareholder in RAS, the Pesenti Group, which held a 38 percent interest via its holding company, Italmobiliare S.p.A. The Pesenti Group was in debt.[234] After a first working meeting in August 1984, the confidential preparations for the takeover began under the cover name "Mare," to arrive at a valuation of RAS as the basis for negotiations on the purchase price. This was difficult, because the president of Italmobiliare, Carlo Pesenti, thought that the discussions should be conducted without the knowledge of the RAS board of directors. This deprived Allianz of the possibility of obtaining detailed information about the business via contacts with the management, and it fostered a concern that was felt in all purchase negotiations after Eagle Star: the worry that they might not be welcome.[235] But in the end, it was Allianz's understanding of RAS corporate culture, and its willingness to make a quick decision that got its bid accepted over those of prominent rivals such as the American Insurance Group (AIG), or Assurances Générales de France (AGF), which would later become part of the Allianz Group, and the Zurich insurance company.[236] Friedrich Schiefer summed up the milestones of the purchase in an address to the supervisory board in February 1988: "[…] on October 28, 1984, we signed the contracts to buy 51.51 percent of the stock of RAS, […] which was adopted unanimously at the meeting of the board of directors on November 12, 1984. […] At that time, two blocks of shares were acquired, on the one hand, 13.51 percent from FIAT and, on the other, 38 percent from Italmobiliare, an Italian industrial holding company controlled by the Pesenti family. [...] Because of tax considerations of Italmobiliare, [...] the large block of 38 percent was transferred to us in three yearly stages. Since May 1, 1987, we possess the full 51.51 percent of the voting capital."[237]

According to the propositions negotiated during the sale, RAS was supposed to maintain its entrepreneurial independence, and not be made a plaything of superordinate corporate and financial strategies.[238] In the late 1980s, Allianz governed its relations with RAS by means of three bodies: the executive, foreign, and financial committees. In this way, the group implemented the principle of decentralization of the subsidiaries, which continued to use their brand names at the international level, as well. While RAS no longer celebrated its 150th anniversary in 1988 as an independent company, it did retain its own trademark and a clear conception of itself.

Yet, even before the takeovers of Cornhill and RAS in the mid-1980s, Allianz had made strides in foreign involvement after nearly a decade of effort. It succeeded in increasing the share of its foreign business, which had varied from 2.7 to 3.5 percent in the period from 1971 to 1975, to almost 19 percent in 1984, a proportion similar to that of the company's foreign business in 1913.[239] In 1986, the foreign share rose to 21.8 percent, thanks to the acquisition of Cornhill, and leaped to 36.4 percent in 1987 due to the complete takeover of RAS. This equated to a world turnover of more than DM 25.9 billion for the Allianz Group as a whole.[240]

The takeovers were tactical masterstrokes, and were usually the responsibility of only a few persons because of the desired secrecy. But what was much more important was the way the new acquisitions were successfully integrated and genuinely interlinked with the Allianz units after the purchase. RAS's business was very suitable for collaboration with Allianz. "In Italy, France, Spain, and Australia, Allianz is represented by smaller subsidiaries or branches, usually specializing in industrial business, while the RAS Group possesses companies in these countries that are considerably older, and also well established in mass business and in life insurance." Also, Allianz did not operate in Switzerland and Canada, and in Latin America only in Brazil and Chile, while RAS for its part was not represented in Chile. On the other hand, Allianz could offer RAS a valuable supplement in the form of Allianz of America in the U.S., where RAS had done relatively little business.[241]

Before the purchase of RAS, the breakdown at Allianz's foreign business was 60 percent in North America, 34 percent in Europe, and 6 percent in the rest of the world. Now, this ratio was almost completely reversed. The European business grew considerably in importance with a share of 65 percent,

North America dropped back to 31 percent, and the rest of the world followed with 4 percent.[242] And at the same time, the mergers initiated strong growth in foreign business, whose share had increased to almost 40 percent by 1988. After the purchase of FFIC in 1991, the total premium volume in the U.S. rose to DM 8 billion, so that the U.S. remained the largest single foreign market for Allianz. But the European market now consistently outplaced the U.S. market. In 1991, 63 percent of premium revenues came from Europe, 36 percent from North and South America, and 1 percent from the rest of the world.

The mergers with Cornhill and RAS soon had direct effects on the structure of the holding company: in 1987, "the Europe division […] because of the substantial amount of work servicing it, [was] divided into the Southern Europe and Northern Europe divisions." Southern Europe, the responsibility of Detlev von der Burg, consisted of the RAS companies and insurers and markets in France, Greece, Italy, Austria and Spain. Northern Europe, the responsibility of Detlev Bremkamp, combined the Cornhill companies and the markets of Belgium, the Netherlands, Switzerland and Great Britain. In addition, from 1987, after the retirement of Hans-Jürgen Schwepcke, Detlev Bremkamp headed the overseas division, which continued to exist. In the America division, under the auspices of Wolfgang Müller, North and South America were now serviced together.[243] South America had gained in importance due to the RAS subsidiaries. It was therefore removed from the overseas division and allocated to the America division.

The significance of the corporate divisions and the regions was emphasized, while that of the national companies declined further. Simultaneously, the structures in all countries were simplified by merging existing Allianz holdings with the acquisitions, or converting them into subsidiaries.

In the U.S. and Canada, the RAS, Cornhill and Allianz companies were not combined until 1992.[244] In Europe, the restructurings were initiated earlier.

In Italy, Allianz and RAS made use of the activities of RAS "at the interface between the insurance and banking businesses," and jointly established the RAS Bank S.p.A. in Milan in 1989, as well as the legal-expenses insurance company Allianz RAS Tutela Giudiziaria, which utilizes the sales networks of RAS and Allianz Pace.[245] Legal expenses insurance is one of the more recent inventions of the insurance industry, and was not authorized by the West German authorities until late 1968. Allianz founded a separate company for this in 1970. The above-average growth of this sector in the 1980s, with a 280-percent increase in the number of policies compared to

154 percent for Allianz business as a whole, was the reason for introducing it in those European subsidiaries that did not already have it in their portfolio.

In France, the situation was particularly complicated at first.[246] There were two French Allianz companies operating alongside three independent RAS units. This was changed between 1987 and 1989: all the companies, except the Cornhill companies that were yet to be incorporated, were integrated into the Allianz RAS Holding France. This was intended to enable better market penetration and lower administrative costs. "Despite this, the new Allianz France remained insignificant from the point of view of market share, with premium revenues of barely DM 500 million." The French insurance market continued to be shaped, on the one hand, by the three largest companies nationalized by the socialist government, which together had a market share of 46 percent, and, on the other hand, by public limited companies that were so closely embedded in French financial groups "that taking a holding in them seems hardly possible."[247]

But in the course of the preparations for the EU Single Market, the opportunity arose to break through this static situation when a pronounced process of concentration in the field of private insurance began in France. In September 1989, Allianz acquired the insurance holdings of the conglomerate Compagnie de Navigation Mixte (CNM) at a price of DM 1.9 billion. CNM was the majority shareholder in the insurance group Via/Rhin et Moselle and had come under severe pressure. This fifth-largest private insurance company, with a premium volume of about 8 billion francs, pushed the Allianz Group up into the top ten insurers in France. The new partners profited mutually from the now attractive size and from further possibilities of expansion, as well as from the international character of Allianz business, so that a rapid integration of Allianz/RAS France and the Via/Rhin et Moselle companies, under the new name Allianz Via Holding France, was agreed upon in 1990.[248]

The situation in Spain was similarly difficult: here five companies were operating, which were grouped together in 1988 in the newly created holding company Allianz RAS España, headed by Hans Falk-Bjerke. The two RAS companies, Cresa Aseguradora y Reaseguradora Iberica S.A. in Barcelona, and Adriática S.A. de Seguros in Madrid, competed for the retail business, as did the regionally active Ercos in Bilbao, acquired in 1988, and finally Allianz itself, with its small but profitable industrial insurer, Allianz Compañía de Seguros y Reaseguros, based in Madrid. The objective of the restructuring was to combine the business of the five companies legally and organizationally, so as to offer the entire product range in this growing mar-

The takeover of the French private insurer VIA/Rhin et Moselle made Allianz one of the largest insurers in France in 1989.

ket. The group already had a comparatively good position in the indemnity and personal-accident lines, but not in life insurance. This was supposed to be achieved by cooperation with the sixth-largest Spanish financial institution, the Banco Popular Español, on the one hand, by means of the pension-management company Europensiones S.A., founded in 1988, and on the other, by means of the life insurance company, founded in 1989, which was supposed to market its policies via the 1,600 branches of the bank. The role of the banks in Spain was fundamentally different from that in Germany; all major banks held controlling interests in insurance companies. Thus, Allianz profited in its experiment with sales via banks in Spain from the permeability of the banking and insurance sectors. It started in 1988 with a 3.4 percent market share and seventh place in Spain; one of the most attractive growth markets in Europe, Spain received an additional boost from its admission to the European Community in 1986.

Due to the clever takeovers and the successful integration of the companies acquired into the new holding structure, in the second half of the eighties, Allianz rose to become one of the strongest globally operating European insurance companies. In 1989, shortly before its 100th anniversary, Allianz drew up a world balance sheet according to new accounting rules, which listed 158 companies, of which 129 were foreign. This displays the special status of Allianz as a business with a high degree of internationalization. The foreign share of the group's total turnover now amounted to about 40 percent.[249]

<table>
<tr><td>The European Single
Market</td><td>Allianz had prepared itself for greater internationalization of its business by forming the holding company. But answers to the challenges of the EU Single Market,</td></tr>
</table>

planned for 1992, still had to be found. This was supposed to create "the largest uniform economic zone in the world, with the greatest purchasing power," with more than 320 million inhabitants.[250] In order to respond to the associated deregulation of the insurance market, which would abolish the trade restrictions, loosen state supervision of insurance, and introduce the freedom of establishment, Allianz launched the "Europe 1992" project in 1989. The focus of the work was on Germany as a business location, on the foreign competitors, on the potential for cross-border collaboration between Allianz companies, and the effects the new market would have on the structure of the financial services market in general.

"The deep-seated shock of the global depression [...] [imparted] a new dynamism to the process of European unification since the mid-eighties."[251] What had begun almost thirty years before with the Treaties of Rome was supposed to promote a gradual alignment of the social, economic, and monetary policies of the European countries.[252] This project experienced various ups and downs, and threatened to fail several times, before the member states agreed on an "obligation to establish the European Single Market" in February 1986, by the Single European Act (SEA). And it was high time for this, since "the relative interdependence with foreign countries" was increasing, without there being joint concepts for this.[253] Europe as an economic unit was in demand, but did not yet exist to the extent that was actually necessary. "The dynamics of globalization had made it clear that efforts by nation-states could no longer secure the maintenance of the standard of living achieved in Western Europe, much less generate a noticeable increase."[254]

The Channel Tunnel – a project of the century not only for the insurance industry – also had symbolic value representing the coming together of the continent.

Allianz was experiencing these developments directly, and preparing for the opportunities it expected from the new economic union. Allianz's Europe Commission, headed by Jan Boetius, the board member for business organization, was supposed to prepare the company for the new dimension of the single European insurance market. The European share of premiums amounted to 22 percent of the total volume of trade, and was now ranked third, behind the U.S. (39 percent) and Japan (25 percent). The point was for Allianz to maintain its leading role among European insurers. Allianz was the only European insurer among the ten largest companies in the world.[255] Increasing competition from foreign insurers – of which there were 4,600 in Europe – on the German market was to be feared. On the other hand, Allianz would obtain access to previously closed markets. And it was foreseeable that Europe would become an ideal field of business for many large corporations and medium-sized firms due to the new freedom of establishment for businesses, which in turn opened new fields of activity for the insurance industry. So the commission developed new strategic concepts, which provided for extensive modification of marketing and product strategies, as well as of the organizational structure. The governing idea of these considerations was to make the customer the center of attention.

Since 1987, the customer-oriented management structure had been tested in a five-year trial run at the Cologne branch office, known as the "Cologne Model," and from 1992, it was implemented.[256] The brochure "The European Single Market and Allianz's Response to It" presented the result of the study – even more customer orientation in a deregulated market – to the employees, as well. The goal of the reform was to abandon organization by lines of insurance, and to introduce a customer-oriented and market-based arrangement of responsibilities throughout the group, based on the customer groupings of industrial, commercial, and private customers.[257] With this formula, Allianz wanted to create lasting customer loyalty despite the new foreign competitors on the domestic market. The idea of "providing the customer with a fixed, and above all externally recognizable contact person" required a new organization of work processes and constantly confronted the staff with new tasks, such as advanced training in subject-matter knowledge, negotiating, data processing, and foreign language skills. The fact that there was practically no prototype for this re-organization was enough to make the "switch from pure back office work or from a specialist for one line to an industrial consultant with experience in other branches of insurance" difficult.[258]

Allianz helped to speed up Europe's geographical coalescence by contributing to insuring the two mammoth projects of the early 1990s, the Channel Tunnel, which connected Britain to the Continent in 1993, and the bridge over the Great Belt strait between the Danish islands of Funen and Zealand. Both structures were insured by international insurance consortiums, with the Allianz subsidiaries in London and Paris, respectively, playing major roles. For the bridge over the Great Belt, for example, a "Contractor's All Risks Policy" (CAR), was developed, custom-tailored to provide coverage for all relevant construction risks.[259] And the European Allianz life insurance companies from twelve countries were to be made fit for the Single Market through various workshops. The Allianz companies, which were represented in most E.C. countries, collaborated systematically in the hope of gaining competitive advantages in this growth segment and in the financial services sector, in particular. The experiences of RAS were a model for the latter.[260]

But when the Single European Market came into being, it received considerably less attention in the group than it deserved, despite its historic significance.[261] One reason was that, for Allianz, 1992 "was no longer an important date," as Wolfgang Schieren had said as early as 1988 in his speech at the annual general meeting, because Allianz possessed "the densest network of productive units in Europe," and was "largely equipped for the common European market."[262] And besides, the topic was overshadowed by other political developments: the dissolution of the Soviet bloc and the reunification of Germany, which opened up completely new, undreamt-of prospects for Allianz – a new growth market within Germany and in Eastern Europe.

1990–2015

- - - - - - - - - - - - - - - - -

THE INTERNATIONAL
FINANCIAL SERVICES PROVIDER

The years 1989 and 1990 marked the most significant political caesura of the late 20th century. With the reordering of the world after the fall of the Iron Curtain, a whole new dimension of global economic (and soon communicative) interconnection became possible. The Europeanization and globalization of the economy received a decisive push from the collapse of the socialist planned economies.[1] The reunification of Germany on October 3, 1990, fulfilled the nearly abandoned hope that the division of Germany could be overcome. In terms of economic policies, however, the phase of upheaval raised a number of questions. The union of the two Germanys' economies and currencies, which required exchanging money, a revision of the pension systems, privatization and legal adjustments – all presented serious challenges to the various historical actors.[2]

For Allianz, 1990 – the 100th anniversary of the company – was a crucial year in a number of respects. For all the awareness that great things had been achieved, the company wasn't content just to look back. Wolfgang Schieren's speech opening the festivities on March 9, 1990, was squarely focused on the future and the desire to shape what was to come. Along with his goals on the global market, Schieren sketched out a clear view of the potential of Eastern Europe as a market.[3] Even before the elections on March 18, he came out and declared that Allianz would be willing to organize an insurance industry necessary for the economic reconstruction of what was still the German Democratic Republic. He added weight to this statement with a certified investment in the monopoly insurance company of Hungary, Hungária. From March 1990, it did business as a private joint-stock company in which Allianz held a 49 percent share.[4]

Schieren's company anniversary address was something of a cross between a bequest and a call to recognize the entrepreneurial challenges of the future and to make the most of the chances afforded by freer and larger markets.[5] With the founding of the Deutsche Versicherungs-AG and the purchase of the U.S. insurer Fireman's Fund, Schieren's drive to shape the future also influenced his tenure as supervisory board chairman and left his successor with major tasks to master.

The anniversary was also the beginning of Allianz's environmental activism, which reflected the growing ecological awareness of the 1990s. The Allianz Environmental Foundation was established with a starting capital of DM 100 million. The idea behind the foundation was to engage in company projects and support external ones in the preservation of nature, wildlife and water, and land rehabilitation, as well as environmental education and communication. Since 1995, this has included the initiative Blauer Adler (Blue Eagle), which takes its name from the eagle in the Allianz logo and which together with Allianz agencies supports environmental initiatives undertaken by private citizens, institutions and associations. Often, children and young people are involved. The Benediktbeurer Gespräche symposia and the accompanying series of publications entitled "Diskussion" have been an institution since 1997. The first projects in 1993 – for instance the Spreewald biosphere reserve or the creation of a park on the site of the former Berlin wall – focused on Eastern Germany and were intended to encourage reunification on the level of environmental policy.[6] The establishment of the foundation can be interpreted as a reaction to the "largely failed expansion of the nuclear energy industry." As late as 1990, around two-thirds of all the energy research money spent in Germany went to nuclear power, but public attitudes were already changing. Former prestige projects like the High Temperature Reactor and the Fast Breeder nuclear reactor SNR-300 were canceled amid dwindling political support.[7]

Another major change in the company's anniversary year also helped set the course for the future. At a meeting of the board of directors on November 27, 1990, Schieren announced that he intended to resign on October 2, 1991, and join the supervisory board. Allianz employees learned of his decision in the first edition of the Allianz Journal in 1991. Simultaneously, his successor was officially announced far in advance: "To ensure continuity in the company leadership, the supervisory board has appointed Friedrich Schiefer (51), currently the director of the finance division on the board of directors of the holding company, as Schieren's successor effective October 2."[8] Schieren was at the "zenith of his power," commented the press. He

That which divided has fallen: the Berlin Wall in 1989 as a symbol for two worlds coming together.

was resigning nine months before the end of his contract "because the company was in excellent shape" and was submitting record profits of DM 1.2 billion in 1989. There was no topping that. Schieren, the press wrote, had made Allianz into "the largest European insurance company by a long way [...] and the sixth largest in the world." He had "increased premium income eightfold [...] to DM 32 billion a year" and had "formed Allianz into a company [...] that worked more internationally than any other firm in the sector." When Schieren took up the job, Allianz earned "2.7 percent of its revenues from abroad." In 1990, the year before he resigned, that figure was already 44 percent.[9]

There was no way of knowing at this point that the issue of Schieren's successor was not nearly as settled as it seemed. A few months later, in July

1991, Allianz and Schiefer suddenly parted ways. This was entirely shocking, and the way it was handled alone gave rise to various speculations in the press and among the general public. Even today, it remains unclear why Wolfgang Schieren "coldly ditched" his designated successor.[10] The press conjectured that Schiefer's increased self-confidence and his plans for Allianz were the reason for his departure. Yet, this cannot be confirmed from available sources. Nor could those involved be asked as both of them have died.

In his second attempt at finding a successor, Schieren decided to go with an in-house candidate who stood for continuity. Lawyer Henning Schulte-Noelle had already been considered as a potential candidate alongside Schiefer. Born in 1942, Schulte-Noelle was, like Schiefer, part of the postwar generation. He had joined Allianz in April 1975 as a legal expert with a focus on business and entrepreneurship and with considerable experience abroad; he had gradually worked his way up in the company from branch manager to sales and marketing director. In 1990, he had been involved in the company's most important big project, the founding of the Deutsche Versicherungs-AG, and as sales and marketing director he had been responsible in the steering committee for integrating and coordinating the company's sales and organization divisions.[11] On January 1, 1991, as part of the restructuring of the board of directors, he was made the head of Allianz Leben and, at the same time, a member of the board of directors of the Allianz holding company (hereafter: holding board).[12]

Allianz during the 1990s

In 1991, Schulte-Noelle took over a company that had a pronounced international orientation but that nonetheless, at its core, remained a German company. One of his top priorities was the continuation and expansion of the company's internationalization. It quickly became clear that size for its own sake was not in Allianz's interest. On the contrary, the numerous acquisitions had to be integrated into the company, and its mentality had to change. Schulte-Noelle's recipe for success was decentralized company leadership and global orientation. The projects he had inherited from his predecessor presented enormous challenges. The state insurance company of communist East Germany, for instance, had more than 12,000 employees, and Fireman's Fund, which had been acquired for DM 5.3 billion, had more than 10,000, which entailed enormous initial burdens and a loss of DM 1.8 billion. Expansion and integration could only succeed if variety and size could be used as advantages for the company.[13] That also meant that the new configuration had to be profitable.

In the first phase of his tenure, Schulte-Noelle thoroughly changed the company culture, and Allianz profited from doing away with patriarchal styles of leadership. This was necessary for long overdue developments in company philosophy, structure and external reputation to come about. Moreover, such changes could only become reality under a new generation. If the path of internationalization was to be successful, the structure of the company had to conform to international standards. The magic formula was "openness." Company structures were the first to be affected. Steering committees were internationalized. After a generation shift in the leadership of the Italian company RAS, Roberto Gavazzi was made vice-president of the Italian group and the first non-German member of a leading Allianz board. After the resignation of Detlev von der Burg, Gavazzi and Detlev Bremkamp headed the European sector. As of 1989, Gavazzi was responsible for Southern Europe, and Bremkamp for the North. From July 1993 to June 1997, Gavazzi was in charge of the entire European sector. As Allianz's first international manager and a representative of the company's most important foreign subsidiary from 1994 to mid-1997, Gavazzi was also a member of the holding board.[14] But until the founding of Allianz SE in 2006, he remained the exception. Afterward, this body, too, became more international.

Such personnel changes were aimed at exploiting the advantages of decentralized structures for a more effective exchange of ideas. The International Executive Committee, founded in 1997 and consisting of the Allianz board of directors and the chairmen of the boards of directors of group companies, was the next step toward intensifying intercultural exchanges and connections within the leadership circles of various companies. The directors of the Italian RAS, the Swiss ELVIA, the British Cornhill, the French Allianz Assurances, the Austrian Allianz Elementar, and U.S. Fireman's Fund and of Allianz Asia Pacific were all represented. That, in turn, increased the pace of internationalization of the Allianz Group.[15]

The International Executive Committee, founded in 1997, brings the group companies of Allianz closer together: RAS, ELVIA, Cornhill, Allianz Assurances, Allianz Elementar, Fireman's Fund and Allianz Asia Pacific take part.

Change in Allianz's Corporate Culture

One important aspect of Allianz's new corporate culture was a change in how it presented itself externally. Gradually, the company began to take a stand on social and cultural topics such as the environment and population demographics. The company and its chairman of the board of directors showed a heretofore unusual degree of presence on economic committees, in society and in the public sphere – for example, by helping to initiate a new museum of modern art in Munich and by chairing the board of the Allianz Cultural Foundation. Publicity, marketing and advertising were considered especially important. Parallel to the expansion of the company's international business and especially the establishment of the holding company in 1985, Allianz's PR work also began to change. Traditionally, company press officers had concentrated on press conferences about annual reports and on monitoring the media. As of 1955, this took the form of press reviews emphasizing business news and specific press releases on various topics. From 1962, systematic analysis of German newspapers and the development of regular contacts with trade journalists in Germany were added to the tasks of the company press officers. By the end of the 1980s, as the leadership of the PR division passed from the business journalist Hans Seyfried to Imai-Alexandra Roehreke, Allianz PR work was internationalized. Contact with foreign correspondents was intensified, press conferences were held outside Germany after major acquisitions such as RAS from 1984, and press documentation was expanded after international acquisitions.

This period also saw the beginning of Allianz cultural sponsoring. With the appointment of journalist Emilio Galli-Zugaro as director of corporate communications, a comprehensive communication strategy and management were gradually established. This was based on an entirely revised understanding of communications as an integral part of strategic business management. This proceeded in conjunction with the globalization of the company, and the internationalization and diversification of its interests and commercial sectors. PR branch offices were opened in Singapore and Washington, DC. Regular exchanges within the newly established global communications network, the so-called PRint Group (that is, PR International), ensured better connections among all Allianz communicators. The strengthening of foreign and financial business led to PR work being differentiated into national and international divisions; the national division focused more on insurance issues, and the international one on financial issues. Interest arose in issue management and media relations, and in 2001, work with new media with the establishment of Inter- and Intranet editorial boards, and in social media platforms was added. Among the most important developments in PR was crisis management and image construction. The latter, for example, was instrumental in Allianz's activities in the company's cultural and environmental foundations. Since 2012, both foundations have been located in the Allianz Foundation Forum on Berlin's Pariser Platz. The cultural foundation, established in 2000 with an endowment capital of € 51.1 million, encourages and initiates border-crossing cultural and educational projects in art, literature and music throughout Europe. At the center of all the foundation's activities is the process of uniting Europe. The discussion series "Speeches on Europe," which has been held in a number of European cities since 2006, publicly addresses a host of current European questions surrounding the issue of social responsibility. Henning Schulte-Noelle, architect Rem Kohlhaas and philosopher Peter Sloterdijk have been among the speakers. With the European Union's eastern expansions in 2004 and 2007, the spectrum of activities was widened to 18 predominantly Central and Southern European countries, for instance, with the extended literature project "European Borderlands." Together with the Mediterranean countries, the European margins have become a regional focus.[16]

Accompanying the changes in the company's self-concept was the establishment of a variety of Allianz foundations with various priorities. Among them are the Allianz Foundation for North America and the Allianz Direct Help Foundation. The latter coordinates immediate relief efforts using donations by Allianz employees and long-term activities by Allianz and its employees in relation to catastrophic events; for instance, terrorist attacks or tsunamis. The Allianz Foundation for North America is devoted to offering a better future to disadvantaged young people, primarily in the United States, but also in Mexico, where it cooperates with already existing projects. Moreover, the Allianz Children's Foundation in Germany has been supporting disadvantaged children there for almost twenty years.

Without doubt the most important example of proactive PR work is the company's treatment of its history under National Socialism. In 1997, Allianz was one of five European companies named in a class-action lawsuit from the United States, which accused the company of not having paid out on life insurance policies for Jews prior to 1945. There were also reports in the press that Allianz had been involved in insuring SS operations in the concentration camps.

The situation was grim. The Nazi years had been largely ignored in portraits of the company written after 1945. Gerald D. Feldman was hired in 1997 to research the history of the company in the Third Reich. He later commented: "There are limits, however, to adaptation and forgetting, and they were certainly reached when Allianz celebrated its centenary in 1990. Neither director-general Wolfgang Schieren nor the invited speaker on the occasion, the prominent journalist and Hitler biographer Joachim Fest, gave even a suggestion that Allianz might in any way have been implicated in the Third Reich."[17]

Allianz had difficulty coming to terms with its Nazi past, even after the Deutsche Bank presented a critical study of its past culpability on the occasion of that institution's 125th anniversary.[18] The news magazine Der Spiegel cited Schieren as telling his supervisory board that he wanted to postpone researching the company's Nazi past until its next major anniversary, i.e., in 2015.[19] But the issue couldn't wait that long. The first step toward a different approach to this most sensitive topic was made in 1993 with the establishment of the Allianz Center for Corporate History. In 1996, a permanent exhibit on the history of the company went on display, and at the opening, Schulte-Noelle explicitly announced that Allianz would begin to critically examine the most difficult periods in its history.[20]

A new management generation and public pressure in the U.S. were required for that process of historical investigation to begin. But once it did, Allianz acted comprehensively, confronting the topic in the media and communicating directly with victims and their families, for example, via a hotline, established in 1997, where people could get information about unpaid life insurance policies and receive offers of compensation. In a 1997 interview with Der Spiegel, Schulte-Noelle discussed his motivation for this sort of broad public clarification, saying "it would be intolerable for me personally if we still had money lying around that could be paid out to those who are entitled to it."[21] In order to answer the accusations raised against it, the company had to understand how people had worked in Allianz from 1933 to 1945 and reconstruct what had happened to the life insurance policies. In response Allianz hired an auditor to thoroughly check the life insurance policies in its own archives.

Already shortly after the Second World War, Allianz supported the compensation procedure for claims resulting from policies that were either prematurely terminated as an act of discrimination or directly confiscated by the state. To this end, the company searched for relevant files and began,

Peter Haas, grandson of Jewish agent Martin Lachmann, who was murdered in Minsk, Henning Schulte-Noelle and Prof. Gerald D. Feldman at the opening of the exhibition room on the history of Allianz during the National Socialist era in the year 2002.

at the behest of the Federal Republic of Germany, which regards itself as the successor to the German Reich, to calculate compensation amounts. Moreover, Allianz is a founding member of the Foundation "Remembrance, Responsibility, Future" initiated by German industry. Industry and the federal government each contributed DM 5 billion to the foundation established in the year 2000, which serves as a basis for clearing all claims against German businesses for their actions within the Nazi economic system. In this fashion, Allianz confronted its historical and moral responsibility for what it had done as a business during the Third Reich.

Finally, the company also commissioned an academic study on the history of Allianz during the Nazi period. Economic historian Gerald D. Feldman (University of California, Berkeley) carried out four years of research in European and American archives. In 2001, the results of this research were published in English and German. Feldman's book has since become a standard work in the history of insurance companies in Germany during the Nazi period.[22] The results of his research are also publicly accessible in the permanent exhibit in the Allianz Center for Corporate History and via a dedicated web page.

But Allianz's long-term, comprehensive involvement was not exhausted with the completion of the academic study or the payment made to the foundation. At a symposium on the subject of memory and corporate history, the director of the Allianz Foundation for North America, Christopher Worthley, remarked: "I would argue further that it is not enough for a company just to study its history; how it approaches history is just as important as whether it does so."[23] All of these activities can only be truly effective if they are long-term and directed toward the future. Just as some of the activities of the Foundation "Remembrance, Responsibility, Future" aim to combat the loss of historical memory of the Nazi era, for several years Allianz has tried to encourage dialogue between cultures with a guest professorship in Islamic and Jewish Studies at the Ludwig Maximilian University in Munich and the "Third-Generation Initiative." The latter is an exchange program for young Allianz employees and U.S. descendants of Nazi victims. The program reflects the company's awareness of its responsibility and its realization that a strong public presence and scrupulous transparency are essential for its own survival. Back around the turn of the millennium such an active and honest approach to potential threats to the company's reputation was by no means a given, but its significance increased with the financial crises in the years that followed. Crisis communication has become a new aspect of the company's PR work.[24]

The participants in the "Third Generation Initiative" of 2011 before the Brandenburg Gate: Allianz fosters dialogue between cultures since 2010 through an exchange program between descendants of Nazi victims and Allianz employees.

Affected as it was by political and social changes within Germany, Allianz's corporate culture was transformed both externally and internally. In 1989, the new global employees' magazine, Allianz Journal, provided an example of the significance attached to communication within the company.

Parallel to this, emphasis was also shifted in the realm of employee development. In the mid-1990s, Allianz's vacation homes were gradually closed since fewer and fewer employees were taking vacations with their work colleagues. What had been an expression of special appreciation for employees in the 1920s was an outmoded relic of the past. From that point on, Allianz began subsidizing a part of its employees' vacations. Earlier measures of promoting employee welfare were modified and refocused, although the core areas remain company pensions, health-care benefits and provisions for sales agents.[25] Allianz also seeks to support employees' further education and health, the latter by offering preventive medicine, sports clubs and healthy food in company canteens, which have of course changed dramatically since the 1920s. In Munich, for example, the distinction between restaurants for senior managers and canteens for general employees has been relaxed. In the 1920s, employees sat in long rows eating stew. As of the 1950s, they congregated at four-person tables in three "shifts." Since the

Change in Allianz's Corporate Culture

mid-1980s, meal times have been flexible and employees serve themselves. And as of 2001, modernizing emphasis has been placed on variety and standards such as the use of sustainably produced food. The company pays the canteens' costs for personnel and rent.[26] The "Free Table" initiative, which provided lunch free of charge for university students, including the writer Uwe Timm, in Allianz canteens from the 1960s to the 1980s, with some interruptions, even became a part of German literature.[27]

The continued education and training of both in-house office employees and sales agents commenced in 1919 with the publication of the company newspaper, the Allianz Zeitung. It aimed to inform traveling sales agents about the presentation of new advertising brochures and train them by using simulated sales talks and arguments. In the postwar era, the spectrum of further education and training was expanded to include new media such as training and company image films, sometimes produced by Allianz's in-house studio. Later years saw the establishment of systematic personnel development combined with the option of studying part-time at university. Today, Allianz employees are able to keep themselves fit for the changing challenges of a global corporation at the Allianz Management Institute, which was founded in the late 1990s. If Wolfgang Schieren stood for internationalization and a new business structure, Henning Schulte-Noelle embodied the change in corporate culture and mentality, which became the most effective instrument of internationalization and then globalization. Simultaneously, Allianz developed from a strictly hierarchical German insurer active on the international market into a truly international financial services provider.

The Process of Transformation in the 1990s

The steady growth of the early 1990s changed the company's prospects. Henning Schulte-Noelle developed five strategic goals that helped provide decisive impulses in the years that followed:[28]

(1) Allianz was to position itself among the top five providers in the major markets and as the leading one in special markets.
(2) Life and health insurance were to be rapidly expanded.
(3) Allianz was to become the leading foreign insurer in developing markets.
(4) Allianz was to take the lead in the international industrial insurance sector.
(5) Asset management should be made into a core company sector.

As the market leader in Germany, Allianz had already been confronted with the problem of market saturation in the 1970s, but the company had succeeded in further expanding both in Germany and in Europe. 1995 saw a series of mergers on the German and European insurance markets. The acquisitions of the ELVIA Group in Zurich, Lloyd Adriatico in Trieste and the Vereinte Versicherungsgruppe in Germany helped fill Allianz's blank spots on the European map. Just as the Deutsche Versicherungs-AG (which took over the portfolios of the former state insurance company of the German Democratic Republic, the Staatliche Versicherung der DDR) provided stimulus for further growth in Germany, the gradual integration of the Vereinte Krankenversicherung, today Allianz Private Krankenversicherung (APKV), became an engine driving the health-insurance business.

By far and away the most significant acquisition was the purchase of the Assurances Générales de France (AGF) in 1997. Its strategic importance was comparable to that of Allianz's investment in RAS in the early 1980s.[29] This acquisition received a great deal of attention in the press because AGF management first had to fend off a hostile takeover bid by Generali. This event demonstrated the importance of communication in complex takeover procedures.

An advertising calendar of Hungária Biztosító, the former Hungarian monopoly insurer, for comprehensive automobile insurance (1987).

The employee newsletter of the Vereinte Gruppe presented the new head office in Munich-Neuperlach on its front page in 1998.

The acquisition of AGF moved Allianz from the thirteenth up to the third spot on the French liability- and accident-insurance market, and the company became a pioneer in the expansion of the French life- and health-insurance markets.[30] AGF also bolstered Allianz's South American and Asian business.[31] Above all, though, the largest acquisition in the company's history represented a decisive step forward in Europe. Allianz became the leading insurer in nine of the eleven new EU member states.[32] It also changed the relationship between various insurance areas. After AGF was integrated in 1998, the percentage of European revenues rose by almost 10 percentage points (from 30.6 to 40.3 percent), while the percentage in Germany fell by 6 percentage points (from 51 to 45 percent) and in North and South America by more than 17 percent to around 14 percent. The figures in Asia and Africa in 1997 and 1998 were less than 1 percent, but they rose to 2.3 percent in 1999, and by 2003, under the new name Asia-Pacific and Africa, they were up to 5 percent.[33] In the years 1997 and 1998, business was clearly focused on Germany and Europe with significantly more than 80 percent of revenues coming from there. After the AGF acquisition, Allianz ranked among the top five insurance providers in 17 countries, thereby achieving one of Schulte-Noelle's five goals.[34]

The takeover of AGF required the entire corporation to be restructured.[35] From that point on AGF was responsible for France, Benelux, North and West Africa, the Middle East and South America while Allianz covered the remaining world regions. The presence of both companies in many European countries encouraged rapid reforms so as to profit from on-the-ground synergies. As had happened previously with the integration of Cornhill and RAS, subsidiaries in various markets were bundled together.

Allianz's partnership with RAS and AGF was underscored by the fact that both companies played a leading role and enjoyed commensurate responsibility within the Allianz Group. In Spain, the subsidiaries of both companies were merged into a jointly owned holding company. RAS and AGF were also involved in Allianz's joint venture with Banco Popular, which yielded a partnership in the life-insurance and retirement-fund market in Spain. In Portugal, AGF sold a 65 percent interest in Sociedade Portuguesa de Seguros (SPS) to RAS, and in Britain AGF passed on its rights to private- and commercial-insurance contract extensions to Cornhill. In addition, Allianz took over AGF's insurance contracts in Greece, Britain, Ireland, Japan, Canada, Poland and Singapore. In return, interests in the Netherlands and South America were transferred from Allianz to AGF.[36] In the late 1990s, Allianz turned its attention to markets in South America and Asia, where AGF played a major role in the insurance and asset business. Interesting synergies emerged. All in all, AGF allowed Allianz to attain a new dimension of internationalization that went far beyond just the insurance business.[37]

The purchase of AGF was both the zenith and the temporary end of Allianz's European insurer acquisitions until 2013. To achieve the strategic goals enumerated by Schulte-Noelle, Allianz needed to open up new ways of making its mark within the globalizing world economy. A strategically crucial decision was made in the background that marked the beginning of an all-important transformation process: the dissolution of the so-called Germany, Inc., the tight capital connection of industry, banks and insurers within Germany. This process commenced in the second half of the 1990s and was closely linked to Allianz's internationalization. In order to lay the groundwork for increased international activity, corporate structures in Germany had to be disentangled. This was carried out by selling off the joint interests of Allianz and Munich Re, Allianz's traditional fellow traveler, with whom Allianz shared joint insurance policies and established structures.

In his memorial speech for Wolfgang Schieren, who had died in 1996, Schulte-Noelle stated that in all of its major strategic corporate decisions, Allianz could count on "the trust and support of all major shareholders." He particularly stressed the loyalty of Munich Re, whose chairman of the board of directors Horst K. Jannott had also died young and who had been a "cordially and congenially connected partner." The tight connection between the two companies lasted until 1996. In the years that followed, Allianz and Munich Re "divorced," eliminating their jointly held insurance interests. This separation conformed to the model of corporate management, which as a rule Allianz held with property insurers and Munich Re with life insurance and reinsurance companies, and in which they were also represented in accordance with their respective capital stock.[38]

For example, Munich Re became the sole shareholder of American Re and increased its share in the primary insurer ERGO to 60 percent. In return, Allianz gained Allianz of America and a controlling interest of 50.3 percent in Allianz Leben. The restructuring made it possible to achieve new business goals without deploying liquidity and ensured, in the expectations of the two boards of directors chairmen, a better strategic position for both companies in Germany and the U.S.[39] It wasn't until Allianz could exchange its holdings with Munich Re that Allianz could take over the entire Vereinte Gruppe of Swiss Re, including Vereinte Krankenversicherung, which in turn, for anti-trust reasons, meant selling its market-leading health insurer Deutsche Krankenversicherung (DKV) to Munich Re. As a result of this transaction, Allianz acquired the Hermes Kreditversicherungs-AG.

Allianz and Munich Re were also traditionally connected by a common strategy of industrial holdings. Together with the major German banks, Allianz and Munich Re had insurance, banking and industrial holdings. From the 1970s these were selected according to their profitability and, in line with the company's double strategy, also became Allianz insurance clients.[40] The decision to disentangle this configuration was hastened by growing public criticism of the "Germany, Inc." phenomenon. The connections among corporations were the source of constant journalistic speculation and attacks. In this context, readers of the news magazine Der Spiegel in January 2000 were informed about the "Germany, Inc." phenomenon: "What's meant is the tightly woven network of banks, insurers and industrial corporations that has dominated the German economy for years, the system of interdependence that rests on mutual monitoring. The various entities

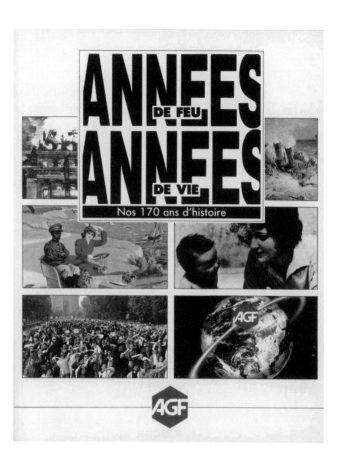

*In 1988, AGF published a
commemorative volume on the
history of the company and its
predecessors for its 170th
anniversary.*

know one another and share power."[41] Ultimately, the tax reforms of the
Social Democratic-Green coalition government spelled the end of Germany, Inc. The reforms, which were passed in 2000, allowed for the tax-free
sale of holdings. As a result, Allianz and Munich Re reduced their cross-holdings to less than 15 percent by 2003. The dissolution of the association agreement marked the end of a 103-year span of extremely close cooperation between the two companies. Nowadays, the two companies' joint holdings in
one another is less than 5 percent.[42] Financial means previously invested in
Germany were thus freed up and could be invested in the acquisition of
international insurance companies.

From Reunification to Global Player Status Foreign expansion opened up new business arenas, as had been foreseen in 1985 with the founding of the holding company. Three developmental strategies were of central importance in Allianz's foreign business in the 1990s: exploiting new markets in Eastern Europe as well as in Asia, and exploring the new business area of asset management. They unleashed a euphoria that far exceeded that of the 1970s.

In the wake of the political opening up of Eastern Europe, Allianz had begun the process of acquiring Hungária Biztosító in Budapest in 1989, and then took over the portfolios of the state insurance company of communist East Germany and acquired or formed new insurers in the Czech Republic, Poland, Romania, Slovakia and Russia. Hungary and Poland were the first of these countries in which insurance markets developed.[43] Political and economic reforms were the necessary preconditions for the economies to be restructured in accordance with free-market principles, for insurance to be privatized, and for insurance monopolies to be disbanded. In 1986, Hungary founded the new company Hungária from the state monopoly Állami Biztosító. Its starting capital consisted of guarantees for contracts for automobile, industrial and foreign insurance. This was a major signal. Hungária was converted into a joint stock company in which Allianz acquired a 49 percent share – it was the first major involvement by a Western European insurer in the Eastern European insurance market. The company started out with a segment of Állami's contracts and a part of its sales and marketing network with the commensurate market share. This was more than 40 percent in 1989 but has continually declined in the years that followed due to increasing competition.[44] Nonetheless, Hungária continues to occupy the leading position in the Hungarian automotive insurance sector to the present day.

Allianz's acquisitions in Hungary and the German Democratic Republic ran parallel to the integration of the two German states. In both cases, rapid, decisive action was essential. Wolfgang Schieren had put this insight into practice during his final acquisition, even though he was a representative of the "skeptical generation." The new supervisory board chairman Klaus Liesen said in 1996 in his memorial speech for Schieren: "He assumed that no one but Allianz could have shouldered the burden of the East German state insurance company [...] Here, Wolfgang Schieren acted not just as a visionary businessman. Personal emotions certainly also played a role [...] He understood this business involvement as a personal contribution to the success of German unity."[45] The example of the GDR state insurance company (Staatliche Versicherung der DDR) is paradigmatic for the plethora of challenges in the 1990s.[46] German reunification brought two societies together in the center of Europe that had to be harmonized in various ways in an enlarged republic.[47] Beginning on July 1, 1990, the GDR and the Federal Republic of Germany formed a single economy with a single currency.[48] Working together with the Treuhandanstalt, the East German trust agency responsible for the privatization of the former East German state companies, to establish the Deutsche Versicherungs-AG (DV), which took over the portfolios of the East German state insurance company, Allianz was both a mirror of and, as an employer, a driving force behind feverish development. In this emotionally heated atmosphere, Schieren demonstrated a keen sense for economic opportunities. His determination to realize this vision proved, earlier than expected, to be correct. After only five years, the DV was turning a profit, which secured a number of long-term jobs. Helmut Kohl's promise of blossoming landscapes in Eastern Germany sounded seductive, but enormous hurdles had to be cleared before Kohl's vision could become reality on an economic level.[49] "The Treuhand Agency was ordered by the Finance Ministry, to which it was subordinate, to prioritize speedy privatization ahead of restructuring," historians have written, "because the government believed private owners would make businesses profitable more quickly than a government office."[50] In contrast to a number of other takeovers, this was in fact the case with Allianz.

The crucial aspect of this success was the fact that Allianz and the East German state insurance company began coming together as early as November 1989. A series of meetings starting in January 1990 formed the basis for reaching rapid agreement about questions of cooperation and concrete projects to introduce the state insurance company to the free market. The process was accelerated by the effort of its deputy chief director, Günter Ullrich, who succeeded in January 1990 in convincing his superiors at the East German Finance Ministry of the necessity of working together comprehensively with Allianz. By this point, negotiations on a preliminary contract between Allianz and the state insurance company were already at an advanced stage, and it was signed in March 1990. When the deal was announced, the intended merger drew hefty criticism from Allianz's German rivals, who feared the creation of a monopoly and a violation of the principle of fair competition. All the plans they presented to political decision-makers foresaw splitting or even dissolving the state insurance company to allow as many West German insurers as possible to have a share in it.[51] That, however, was the opposite of what employees and managers of the state insurance company wanted. When agreeing to cooperate with Allianz, Ullrich's foremost concerns had been the future prospects of the company and its 12,000 employees. The preservation of the company and the greatest number of jobs possible was an explicitly stated goal of both partners and tipped the balance for the responsible GDR authorities to approve the founding of the Deutsche Versicherungs-AG.[52]

Nonetheless, considerable political assistance was needed to remove the remaining hurdles. Ultimately, on June 26, 1990, the monopoly state company was successfully transformed into a competitive joint-stock company, and its existing policies were transferred to DV, in which Allianz held a 51 percent share. But Allianz had to wait until July 1, the day monetary union went into effect, to start doing business. This was primarily due to the details of the treaty between West and East Germany, which created comparable conditions for the insurance industry throughout Germany. Only then could restructuring commence – an absolute necessity since two fundamentally different insurance systems collided with one another in this case. The former state insurance company had to be made competitive. New products had to be introduced, new offices acquired and equipped with modern accessories and computer technology, employees retrained with an eye toward the new products, and the sales force re-established from the ground up. Properties needed to be renovated, and business locations reduced to a level that made economic sense. In late 1991, Allianz bought the Treuhand's interest in DV for DM 440 million.[53]

By July 1, 1991, only nine so-called leading regional offices remained of what had been 200 local offices. There was no historical precedent for this mammoth restructuring. The process was something completely new. Consequently, experts from both the East and the West were appointed to the first board of directors, which was chaired by Ullrich and his deputy Michael Beckord, so that both perspectives could be used constructively from the very start. West German Allianz employees were assigned to help with the restructuring and new developments. This was a great challenge. The idea was to guide customers as seamlessly as possible into a "new world." Part of this initiative was the installment of 6,000 brand-new computers. Modernization and the simplification of various procedures quickly showed that the workforce of 12,000 employees was oversized. Restructuring and rationalization meant the elimination of almost 6,000 jobs between 1991 and 1993. A further 2,000 were eliminated by 1995. On the other hand, in the newly established sales force, Allianz created large numbers of new jobs for freelance agents – and their employees; there were more than 2,500 by 1995. That year, DV was already in the black. It would go on to become one of the most important employers in Eastern Germany in the years following reunification and would ultimately be integrated into Allianz in 1998. Two Eastern German Allianz branch offices were established in Leipzig and Berlin. They were directed by the two most important role models in the fusion of East and West. Ullrich, the head of the DV, took over the Leipzig branch, while his deputy Beckord assumed responsibility in Berlin.[54] In 1998, Renate Daniel-Hauser, the chairwoman of the DVAG works council, summarized the extraordinary cooperation between employee and employer representatives: "Over and above all the confusion, we always remained a team."[55]

Even today, northeastern Germany remains one of the most successful parts of Allianz Deutschland, which was reconstituted in 2006. Part of Allianz's success in Eastern Germany is based on the fact that the company continued to offer insurance products specific to the GDR. Expanded household contents insurance (erweiterte Haushaltversicherung) became a signature product, providing coverage for damage to household effects caused by natural hazards, which had not been available in the West.[56] This proved to be of existential importance to many clients whose policies were retained, albeit with adjustments to their premiums, when they were hit by the flooding of the Oder River in 1997 or the once-in-a-century flooding of the Elbe River in 2002.

Seen macroeconomically, reunification "widened the economic gap" between Germany and the other European nations. Germany became "more clearly than ever before the economic center of the region."[57] With its business in Eastern Germany and Eastern Europe, Allianz reflected this development.[58]

In the years that followed, Allianz became one of the leading international corporations in Eastern Europe. With its large market share in Hungary, Hungária is a paradigmatic example of rapid progress in the new, high-growth market of Eastern Europe.[59] The company's focus, accounting for over 50 percent of its business, is automobile insurance, but growth in its newly established life insurance branch reached nearly 100 percent in 1996 and 1997. In the meantime, Hungária is now wholly owned by and uses the name Allianz. Newly founded companies in the Czech Republic and Slovakia were comparably successful. Growth increased in 1995 thanks to car-liability insurance, and in 1996, after a three-year development phase, this sector was already profitable.[60] The advantage of founding new companies was that they allowed for greater consistency in building up a business, for instance, in the area of IT or the immediate introduction of Allianz cor-

Fuchs and Elster (fox and magpie) as mascots of expanded household contents insurance lasted beyond the GDR, just like the modernized sandman and the pedestrian walk sign figure.

porate branding. Gregor Linhof, the new Czech Republic company director, who had been a deputy director of sales and marketing in the 1980s, carried this out in exemplary fashion.[61]

In many Central and Eastern European countries, the new companies established themselves within a few years as leading providers of insurance and financial services. This was the case in Hungary, for example, in the pension fund sector, which featured cooperation between the Bausparkasse Schwäbisch Hall and the Tabarék Bank.[62] As success in Eastern Europe became increasingly visible, a corresponding adjustment of areas of responsibility within the board of directors became necessary. In May 1992, the divisional structure was reorganized, with the board division under Detlev Bremkamp being further differentiated into the corporate divisions Europe and Overseas, and Europe being divided into North, South and East.[63] Individual companies were initially joined together to form CEEMA (the area of Central and Eastern European Markets) and then in 2006 to form the sector New Europe. That allowed for the modernization of products and services as well as the bundling of reinsurance, financial administration, IT and communications.[64] The political upheavals in Europe also had unanticipated consequences for automobile insurance in Germany, as Allianz had to address an explosion in theft rates. In 1993, anti-theft insurance became a mandatory part of all comprehensive automobile insurance policies. The Allianz Center for Technology developed a profile of requirements for an electronic immobilizer that would not only protect a car from theft but also guarantee that its full replacement value would be paid if it should be stolen.

Allianz in Asia

Since the end of the 1990s the most important steps toward internationalization have taken place in Asia, not in Europe. During the 1990s, Allianz stepped up its internationalization efforts on that continent, pursuing the strategic goal of becoming one of the leading foreign providers on the booming Asia-Pacific insurance market. The mood at the company was buoyant.[65] During this period, Schulte-Noelle made crucial decisions that anticipated later international and global developments and still affect the company today. With that, he finally emerged from the shadow of his predecessor. In 1998, feeding off the enthusiasm of the AGF takeover the previous year, the decisive phase of Allianz's activity in Asia commenced. Allianz's foreign divisions were adapted to meet the dynamic changes on the international market, and the board of directors was expanded to include a division for Asian markets. In October 1998, Michael Diekmann was made deputy board member and took over the leadership of the new Asia-Pacific division, which had already been differentiated from Bremkamp's areas of responsibility in 1997 and which had been run provisionally by Schulte-Noelle.[66]

Because of unique aspects of this disparate economic region with its often serious hurdles to setting up businesses, Asian expansion had to be carefully prepared. A European insurer had to see success in the region as a long-term project, which is why Allianz's development in the Far East is a story of numerous twists and turns. All the way back in 1974, as Allianz entered the British and American markets, the company had investigated doing business in Japan. Tokyo Marine expressed interest in working together with German direct and reinsurers, but the negotiations, conducted with Munich Re, had not led to any concrete activity.[67] Nonetheless, the example of Japan did show how difficult it was to gain a foothold in the region and how quickly what had been achieved could be lost. Between 1976 and 1986, the share of the growing Japanese market in the global insurance economy went from 10 to 22 percent, but the country remained closed to business operations by outsiders until 1991. That year, Allianz became the first European insurer to open a legally autonomous property insurance subsidiary, Allianz Fire and Marine Insurance Japan Ltd., in Tokyo. Since 1986, the company had been present in the form of a sales agency and a branch office of the British affiliate Cornhill. It focused on offering property and casualty (P&C) insurance to German and European industrial clients in Japan.[68] But despite being celebrated as a milestone, this company was unable to fulfill expectations either in the property insurance sector, or later the life insurance sector.

During the 1970s, Walter Rostock had conducted the Asian negotiations for Allianz in the industrial sector. By the 1980s, Allianz pursued its interests in a more systematic fashion across the entire region of Southeast Asia. In the summer of 1982, Rostock took a trip throughout that part of the world to get to know the individual markets, the results of which were presented in his travel report to the board of directors that October.[69] The previous year, Allianz had succeeded in entering the Asian market with an affiliate in Jakarta and the founding of the subsidiary Allianz Insurance Pte. Ltd. in Singapore. Today, it remains one of the largest Allianz subsidiaries in Asia and works together with all affiliates and partners as an industrial insurer and reinsurance center.[70] 1996 saw the opening of the regional center of Allianz Asia Pacific in Singapore.[71]

At the same time, until the end of the 1990s, Allianz's Asian business remained in its infancy; the share of Allianz's total business in this region, soon to be renamed Asia and Africa, remained less than 1 percent.[72] It wasn't until 1999, when affiliates in Australia and South Korea were regarded as parts of this category, that the figure rose from 0.6 to 2.6 percent. How could the company succeed in overcoming the elementary economic, cultural and linguistic differences? In order to achieve true internationalization, more attention had to be paid to the unique characteristics of the various markets in Asia than elsewhere.

Initially, Allianz did business in Asia pretty much as it had earlier in the 1970s in South America. The company sent employees to the region, and success ultimately came down to their pioneering efforts. In 1985, Heinz Dollberg, then an employee of Allianz Leben, became one of the first people sent to Japan. He remained in Asia until 1990, although he had hardly anticipated taking this career path. In 1978, Dollberg had started working for Allianz in Stuttgart as a personnel officer and then for a number of years sold comprehensive commercial pension packages to internationally active German industrial clients for what was then the international life insurance department. In 1985, he became a trainee at Meiji Life Insurance in Tokyo, learned Japanese and built up an Allianz sales agency in the Japanese capital.[73] That year, he transferred to the newly established Allianz (AG), which from then on bundled Allianz's foreign business, and worked for its new head Detlev Bremkamp, who would manage Allianz's Asian operations until 1997. Dollberg recalls: "It was particularly difficult to gain a foothold in Japan. Knowing the language and the conventions was crucial since in the 1980s the country wasn't very international, and English wasn't widely spoken, which created problems, particularly in the public sector."[74] Continuity and language skills acquired on the ground were the keys to unlocking this market.

In 1988, Dollberg transferred to the Allianz sales agency in Hong Kong. The international flair of Southeast Asia's most important business hub made it easier to work there. The previous year, Bremkamp – in his double function as board member of British subsidiary Cornhill and as the new director of Allianz's overseas division – had opened up new offices for the agency and Cornhill Insurance Company (Far East) Limited. This was conducted in an entirely traditional manner with a feng shui master. Allianz's business in Hong Kong had been boosted by the 1986 acquisition of Cornhill, which had had a branch office in the city since 1983.[75] After Cornhill's integration, the subsidiary traded as Allianz Cornhill Insurance (Far East) Ltd. In the years that followed, Allianz's business, which focused on reinsurance for construction projects together with the Chinese company The People's Insurance Company of China (PICC), would make considerable progress.[76]

After returning to Munich in October 1990, Dollberg continued to work for Bremkamp in the overseas division's Asian section, which he would later direct. Over the course of his time at the overseas division, Dollberg prepared whole generations of managers for leadership positions in Asia, even though the difficult nature of the challenges there meant that not all of them would succeed.[77] Nowadays, the search for qualified talent, which is in short supply thanks to the furious economic expansion in Asia, is the central factor that determines the success of employee development.[78]

Between 1996 and 1998, Dollberg assisted Michael Diekmann from Munich, as Schulte-Noelle sent the latter to Singapore as the CEO of the newly founded regional center Allianz Asia Pacific. The time had come to start reaping the fruits of the work done by the individual mana-

Allianz advertising on the skyline of Hong Kong at the beginning of the 21ˢᵗ century.

gers Allianz had put on the ground there in the 1980s.[79] In 1996, the new leadership unit Allianz Asia Pacific was established in response to the above-average growth rate of 29 percent with revenues of DM 326 million in Asia and Africa.[80]

Diekmann arrived in 1996 in a Singapore that was economically booming, and he set about building up legal, training and communications staff.[81] Qualifications for employment were the ability to be a trustworthy partner and to bridge cultural differences. Previously, Allianz was mainly active in parts of Eastern and Southeastern Asia that already had existing insurance markets. Along with Japan they included Singapore, Hong Kong, Indonesia and South Korea (1999). The first subsidiaries were founded in Indonesia and Singapore. The early days were rocky, as the following example illustrates. In Indonesia, following the establishment of a representative office in Jakarta in 1981, it took until 1989 before Allianz Utama Indonesia could start offering industrial property insurance – and a further six years before the start of trade in life insurance. Nonetheless, Indonesia gradually developed into one of Allianz's key markets in the region. A network of more than 900 representatives and 21 branches was created. The changing role of the family amid massive social upheavals led the rise in demand for life insurance and, from 1997, retirement funds. The traditional multi-generational family was increasingly unable to cope with the task of caring for people in their old age.[82]

Allianz considerably expanded its activities in the region. In the latter half of the 1990s, Diekmann and Dollberg extended their reach to ASEAN states such as Malaysia, Thailand, Brunei and the Philippines, which were beginning to prosper and were poised to develop insurance markets. This was underpinned a few years later with cooperative agreements in Malaysia (2001) and Taiwan (1999) and holdings in the National Insurance Company in Brunei (1998) and Navakij in Thailand (2001). In addition, one of the most important company steps in the late 1990s was the takeover of the fourth-largest Korean life insurance company, First Life. After 1997, Diekmann's and Dollberg's activities profited from the acquisition of AGF and its vast network of foreign branches and international subsidiaries. This network provided crucial impulses not only in Asia, but South America as well. In conjunction with the coordination of AGF and Allianz in Asia, Diekmann's strategy of merger, restructuring and divestiture by a specially established integration steering committee attracted widespread support and proved a practical success.[83] It also brought Diekmann to the attention of Allianz's board of directors.[84]

The AGF property insurance subsidiary in Singapore and the Assurances Générales du Laos had already been integrated into the Allianz Group in 1998. That significantly increased the degree of internationalization of the entire Allianz Group and its incipient asset management business. Via acquisitions, Allianz doubled its business volume on the Asian and Latin American markets. The company's annual report in 1998 read: "This approach and portfolio […] complement the Allianz Group in ideal fashion. Together with AGF, we made progress toward reaching all five strategic goals."[85] This was especially true in the Asian market. Both credit insurance and assistance services played an increasingly important role in the Allianz Group, bolstered by AGF.[86]

Allianz's field of activity in the Asia-Pacific area continually expanded throughout the 1990s. By the new millennium, the company's radius extended from Japan to New Zealand and from Pakistan to the Philippines.[87] In 2003, Allianz was among the top three foreign insurance providers in Asia. Seven years later, the company was active in 15 countries, employed 14,500 people and serviced 21.5 million customers.[88] In 2013, Allianz only remained active in ten markets, doing € 7.2 billion in business and earning a profit of € 367 million in the process.[89]

During this phase of expansion, there were many avenues that were not pursued. There were also disruptions and delays, for instance, in Australia, Vietnam and China. Allianz's history in Australia is an example of highs and lows prompted by political developments; one consequence of these developments was that employer accident insurance was partially nationalized in 1986. In response, Allianz withdrew from Australia after a cooperation agreement had been reached with the Manufacturers' Mutual Insurance Company (MMI) and the sale of the Allianz Insurance Company Ltd. Sydney had been finalized. Ten years later, in 1995, Allianz re-entered the Australian market when Dollberg, armed with two checks for U.S.$ 50 million, acquired 15 percent of MMI. In 1999, Allianz completely took over MMI in Australia. Allianz withdrew from the Vietnamese market in 2006, seven years after taking the first steps there. Considering the economic development of the country today, that withdrawal would seem to have been premature.

One of the particularities of the Chinese market is that it takes an extremely long time to establish a business there. Numerous governmental regulations make it difficult for foreign investors to get involved, and Dollberg expected that it would take Allianz as many as fifteen years to turn a profit in China. The offices established in 1984 in Shanghai, Peking and Canton were initially just for show. As it began working in China, Allianz faced many of the same issues it had confronted in the U.S. in the 1970s – for instance, lack of name recognition in Asia. Another of Allianz's pioneers in Asia, the first CEO of Allianz Life in Shanghai, Benno von Canstein, tells the following story: the Chinese word for Allianz "An Lian" resembles the Chinese name for the Amway cosmetics company "An Li." Initially, the two firms were constantly confused, so that customers expected Allianz employees to sell make-up. A joint venture with the Dazhong Insurance Company in 1997 helped make the Allianz brand recognizable and speed up the licensing process. To that end, Allianz used the 2000 taxis of the Dazhong Group affiliate Dazhong Transportation Company as an advertising medium.

Allianz only commenced operations in China in 1997. The opening of the life insurance company Allianz Dazhong on January 25 of that year was a historic moment for Allianz as the first foreign life insurance company allowed to work in China since 1949. In China, foreign companies are only allowed to offer life assurance as a joint venture. In the 1990s, they could

In 1999, two years after the opening of a representative office in Seoul, Allianz takes over the life insurer First Life in South Korea, thereafter operating under the business name Allianz First Life.

hold a majority interest, while today parity is mandated. In mid-1997, Allianz was given a temporary operating license and the full one that fall. In early 1999, the newly founded Allianz China Life began doing business in Shanghai.[90] In 2005, Allianz left its partner Dazhong, which had proved to be too small, and formed a partnership with the China International Trust and Investment Corporation (CITIC).[91] In 2006, Allianz gained a high-caliber sales partner with the Industrial and Commercial Bank of China, Ltd. (ICBC). By means of a strategic investment, Allianz, together with Goldman Sachs and American Express, supported the ICBC in the largest public offering in history up to that point, securing long-term co-operation with the biggest bank in China. This investment was to reap rewards for Allianz in two respects. It was able to sell some of its shares in 2009 at a profit.[92]

In the last few years, Allianz has also done business, alongside its "normal portfolio," in specific regional insurance branches, such as the so-called full moon view insurance for the lunar festival in September 2013 and the sunshine insurance in Canton, which is offered by the Allianz property insurance company there.[93]

A particular success was the life and property insurance business opened in India in 2001 after six months of negotiations with the Indian business-man Rahul Bajaj. In only its second year, the Bajaj Allianz General property insurance company was already turning a profit. In 2013, Allianz increased

携手安联 尽享周全
Financial Solutions From A-Z

安联保险集团北京代表处
Allianz SE Beijing Representative Office

代表处电话: 010-6463 8052
Rep. office Tel: 010-6463 8052

中德安联人寿保险有限公司 (寿险业务)
Allianz China Life Insurance Company Limited

全国服务热线: 400-888-3636
Service hotline: 400-888-3636

安联保险公司广州分公司 (财产险业务)
Allianz Insurance Company Guangzhou Branch

服务热线: 800-830-8009
Service hotline: 800-830-8009

国联安基金管理有限公司
GTJA Allianz Fund Management Co.Ltd.

服务热线 400-700-0365
Service hotline: 400-700-0365

www.allianz.com.cn　www.gtja-allianz.com

Allianz ⑩
安联保险集团

Life insurance advertising is oriented around the image of the ideal family in China.

its activities in Turkey. Using acquisitions, it became the leader in this important market, where the property insurer Allianz Sigorta and Allianz Hayat ve Emeklilik conduct their business. The latter offers life insurance and retirement funds, an ideal sector for a country characterized by strong economic growth and a relatively young population.

Asset Management and Banking Operations

1997 and 1998 were key years for Allianz's development. In 1998, Allianz Asset Management GmbH (AAM) was founded. This founding was another important step in developing asset management as another independent area of operation, alongside the insurance and pension sectors.[94] Indeed, this was another of Henning Schulte-Noelle's five goals. As

Bajaj Allianz Life has been addressing Indian women with special insurance products for many years (2005).

Turkey has become one of Allianz's most important growth markets in recent years.

a result, Allianz expanded its business base, heightened its focus on third-party customers, and expanded its business line by offering asset management services with an emphasis on investment funds as well as pension fund investment services.[95] Allianz had been gaining expertise in this sector since 1922, when it first began to manage its clients' life insurance premiums as assets for wealth accumulation.[96] In the 1970s, it expanded its management of monies from industrial pension funds to the international sphere.[97]

This new business sector was also shaped by the rapid transformation of the financial services sector that commenced in the late 1990s and propelled Allianz in new directions. At the same time, Allianz's German operations were undergoing a fundamental shift, which also ushered in changes in asset and insurance management as well as in the existing investment culture. In Germany as in many other Western societies, average life expectancy had risen, while the birthrate had been declining for decades. To ensure their financial security after retirement, more and more clients had begun to invest in private pension plans. Traditional life insurance was no longer adequate, and the demand for other forms of investment for wealth accumulation was on the rise. Germany saw a substantial increase in demand for stocks. More and more clients began to demand new products, which global deregulation and the increasing networking of financial markets were offering in a variety of areas, such as financial derivatives.[98]

In the ensuing years, asset management operations underwent a significant transformation, which also resulted in a variety of acquisitions and cooperative agreements, many of which led to name changes. The 1998 founding of AAM led to closer connections among investment operations within the Allianz Group, but it also resulted in increased cooperation with external partners. One initial step in this direction was the partnership between Allianz and Dresdner Bank in asset management, which was launched in the same year.[99]

The collaboration with Dresdner Bank also spurred increasing debate regarding Allianz's bancassurance operations. To become a fully-fledged bancasurrance company, all Allianz needed to acquire at that point was a bank. However, as then finance director of the Allianz board of directors Diethart Breipohl remarked in 1998: "Bancasurrance is not one of Allianz's strategic goals, but active participation in the promising market of asset management is."[100] Initially, the asset management partnership with Dresdner Bank was based on the premise that both partners would maintain their own profile and prospective clients while benefitting from investments in information technology.

Likewise in 1998, Allianz further expanded its asset management business by integrating the investment activities of the RAS and AGF Group companies. From that point forward, credit insurance and travel insurance services assumed an ever greater role within the Allianz Group.

By 1997, capital investments had increased to more than DM 600 billion.[101] In the ensuing years, asset management became the key guarantor of ongoing growth. Initially, the area underwent rapid change. In accordance with its new importance, in January 2000, two years after the founding of AAM, a new board of directors division was created called asset management and other financial services with Joachim Faber at its helm.[102]

After the turn of the century, the most important changes at Allianz took place via acquisitions in the area of asset management. These acquisitions included two U.S. asset managers: PIMCO Advisors, acquired in 2000, and Nicholas-Applegate, acquired a year later. The largest spur to growth in this

Asien: von Tradition zur Boom-Region

Allianz RCM Oriental Income

Deutschlands globaler Fondsmanager.

Capital

Allianz ⑪
Global Investors

In recent years, Asia has become a main focus of investment for Allianz Global Investors (2009).

area was the acquisition of PIMCO Advisors (Pacific Investment Management Company Advisors), founded in 1971 by Bill Gross, Bill Podlich and Tim Muzzy and based in Newport Beach, California. For Allianz, PIMCO was the entry to the U.S. capital market, which was the world's largest. By the same token, PIMCO acquired access through Allianz to the European market. Allianz and PIMCO then joined forces in the Asia-Pacific region. The acquisition resulted in what was the sixth-largest asset management company worldwide, which together managed some € 1.2 trillion, including € 620 billion as capital investments for third parties.[103] The latter was a stronghold of PIMCO, which managed more than € 330 billion in such investments.[104]

This was reflected not least in the successful investment policies of the company's founder, Bill Gross. The two service providers each managed their operations separately. Today, PIMCO still operates under its own brand name. In the 2013 fiscal year, about 80 percent of the investments managed for third parties were managed by PIMCO.[105]

Allianz Dresdner Asset Management (ADAM) was founded after the purchase of Dresdner Bank in 2001. From 2002, ADAM also included dit (Deutscher Investment Trust) and RCM (Rosenberg Capital Management), Dresdner Bank's investment companies.

Although Allianz's and Dresdner Bank's collaboration in the area of investment was successful, the retrospective assessment of the purchase of Dresdner Bank is more sobering. With this purchase, Allianz abandoned its policy of maintaining a clear separation between its own activities and banking activities. Into the 1990s, Allianz maintained an unequivocal stance toward bancassurance: "The services provided by insurance companies and banks may overlap, but on the whole they should supplement one another. The issue of bancassurance, meaning the comprehensive provision of financial services of all sorts under one roof, is only a theoretical one for us. In the end, clients are looking for specialized expertise and experience, whether on the banking or on the insurance side. For this reason, we support the ongoing division of work between the various financial service providers."[106] Allianz's response to mergers between banking and insurance operations into what have been called federated providers – a move that had proven very successful in other European countries, among them Spain, France, Greece, Hungary and Italy – was to enter into cooperative sales partnerships with allied companies. Since the 1920s, these cooperation partners have included cooperative and Raiffeisen banks in Bavaria, the former Bayerische Hypotheken- und Wechselbank, and of course Dresdner Bank. Beginning in 1998, this collaboration was extended through the development of joint sales networks. In this respect, Allianz was following the successful bancassurance model established by RAS in Italy, and the French sales partner Crédit Lyonnais, which was based on the sales of insurance policies at the bank counter.[107]

The impetus for Allianz's purchase of Dresdner Bank in 2001 was the failed merger of the two major banks, Deutsche Bank and Dresdner Bank. For Allianz, the hoped-for benefits of the purchase – expansion of its product range and sales channels, along with improved business opportunities on the international capital markets – did not materialize. For the insurance and the bank, merging their two different operational cultures proved a struggle. Despite rigorous efforts at restructuring within what was at times a difficult financial environment, the companies did not manage to shift the banking operations with fungible expenditures and efforts from their strong product orientation to lasting customer orientation. Consequently, in the end, the plan to establish a new banking operation was abandoned. In 2008,

The American asset management company PIMCO introduces a new fund to the stock exchange in 2013: since 2000, PIMCO has been Allianz's most important partner in the financial services sector.

Allianz decided to sell Dresdner Bank to Commerzbank. This took place directly prior to the outbreak of the financial crisis, one week before the collapse of Lehman Brothers investment bank. In return, Allianz acquired from Commerzbank the capital investment company cominvest, which was integrated in 2009 into Allianz Global Investors (AGI), Allianz's renamed private investment company.

Within the board of directors, Paul Achleitner was responsible for takeovers and holdings. Before he joined Allianz, he had worked in investment banking. During his time working for Allianz, he oversaw the takeover of Dresdner Bank and the reduction of shares in Beiersdorf AG, as well as the purchase of a holding in the U.S. insurer The Hartford. Allianz invested $ 2.5 billion at the beginning of the financial crisis in October 2008 in shares of this company, which yielded a yearly total rate of return of about 15 percent through 2012. In spring 2012, Allianz sold a portion of this investment at a profit.[108]

Allianz's debut on the New York Stock Exchange did not achieve the hoped-for results either. To mark the initial listing of Allianz stock in New York on November 3, 2000, the historic New York Stock Exchange building was sheathed in blue cloth, signaling the slogan "Covered by Allianz." Henning Schulte-Noelle described the initial listing as "another important step toward a cosmopolitan and international enterprise."[109] As was the case for many other German companies such as Siemens and Deutsche Bank, the initial public offering in the U.S. was intended to serve as Allianz's point of entry into the U.S. capital market. The hope was that Allianz would profit from the enormous short-term successes to be achieved on the stock market. However, the move was also combined with significant effort and complexity. Allianz was required to conform to U.S. reporting standards and meet U.S. requirements for the transparency of business operations. To meet these standards, Allianz had already made the switch to International Accounting Standards (IAS) in 1997, and had disclosed its valuation reserves. In the ensuing years, however, it became apparent that the entrance into the U.S. stock exchange did not yield the hoped-for benefits on what is the world's largest finance market.

In 2009, Allianz decided to switch course. It fell to Burkhard Keese, then head of group financial reporting at Allianz SE and, after 2013, the chief financial officer on the board of directors of Allianz Deutschland AG, to explain the developments that led to this decision. In 2000, the initial public offering had served to demonstrate transparency to international investors. However, these transparency standards and the associated quality of financial reporting had since become the industry standard. As a result, it had become both feasible and advisable to focus on Frankfurt's Xetra platform.[110] Most Allianz shares continued to be traded in Frankfurt after the U.S. listing as well. Nine years after its initial public offering, Allianz elected to delist. Since 2009, the stock is no longer listed on the exchanges in New York, London, Milan, Paris and Zurich.

1999: A New Corporate Design

As the century drew to a close, Allianz realized it would need to update its public image and marketing to keep pace with economic developments in the second half of the 1990s as well as the group's increasing degree of internationalization. In 1999, a new group logo was developed to reflect the three business areas of insurance, retirement planning, and asset management. This was one of the most important tasks given to Michael Maskus, who had joined

Allianz's initial public offering in the U.S. – celebrated by cloaking the NYSE with Allianz banners on November 3, 2000 – did not lead to the hoped-for success in the largest financial market in the world.

Allianz in 1992 from Johnson and Johnson in Hamburg to become the new head of marketing. In an interview, Barbara Eichberger described her former colleague as a marketing expert who possessed a clear "concept of a unified image."[111] Given Allianz's plans to establish itself among the global competition, the move toward a unified design was long overdue. By the turn of the century, global competition was not merely a matter of products and services; it also required attention to corporate and brand communication. A new corporate design would heighten market interest. While maintaining a clear connection to continuity and tradition, it would conform to new market conditions and appeal to new client groups.[112]

The Cologne Institute for Market Research and Market Exploration was commissioned with evaluating the main design elements – the corporate seal, the signature color, and the font. The results showed that the Allianz brand name, the eagle and the signature blue color remained effective, and were perceived as "modern and up-to-date, especially by existing clients."

The color "evokes a sense of order, conscientiousness and seriousness." But the font required an update. According to the findings, "New fonts and improvements in text structure will aid in the communication of information both through conventional and new media."[113] However, these findings only applied to the German domestic market. Outside Germany, the response to the Allianz eagle was quite different. In the Asian cultural sphere, the logo was seen as out-of-date, bureaucratic and a sign of rigidity. The response among European neighbors was even more negative; in the Netherlands, France and Spain, respondents associated the eagle with the history of National Socialism. The message was clear: the logo would need to be changed to be effective on the global market.[114]

In redesigning the corporate logo, the task was to maintain balance between tradition and modernity. The advertising and design agency Claus Koch Corporate Communications was commissioned with "adapting the brand to international demands."[115] The eagle had to shed its feathers. The Düsseldorf agency revamped the 20-year-old logo, moving it a step further toward the abstract. The new logo was formed by a circle that enclosed three columns, in a loose reference to the international financial service provider's three core areas of operations – insurance, retirement planning, and asset management. This modified eagle was placed alongside an international group logo, which served as a subtitle for the independent logos of the subsidiary companies.[116]

The development is most easily recognizable in the form of the wordmark and the image in the "Allianz logo in the blue field at the top right."[117] This was supplemented by a photography concept that employed "images that capture movement and dynamism." The new design was rolled out in a variety of national and international media via brochures, film and TV advertising, annual reports, and staff and client magazines. The updated Allianz Journal appeared for the first time in 1997. It was followed by business reports and a revamped online presence, all in the new look.

The key challenge, however, was establishing the Allianz brand as a global player outside Germany. As Barbara Eichberger noted, a consistent market presence could only be achieved by incorporating all corporate divisions and all forms of media.[118] However, this was far more difficult to implement than it had been 20 years earlier. In this most recent revamp, the international group companies "were required to make a clear reference to Allianz in their business documents and advertising."[119] This could be achieved by including the subtitle "Part of Allianz Group," as was done in the case of the Fireman's Fund. At the same time, the company logo was to

Since 1999, Allianz has been advertising worldwide with its new logo.

become more adaptable through the use of a combination logo, as was first instituted in the Allianz Pace logo in 1997. In this combination logo, the new parent company was identified without abandoning the "Pace" brand name.[120] After Allianz acquired a share in Turkey's Koç, tough negotiations were held early on with the support of the foreign department in order to persuade Koç that their logo should also signal this collaboration in visible form. The debate surrounding the visibility and independence of the brand name finally resulted in the introduction of the first two-color double-branding. In 1998, Koç persuaded Allianz to introduce a red and blue logo, which was a combination of the two in-house colors. Koç also won the right to be listed first, under the new name Koç Allianz Sigorta A.Ş.[121]

On March 15, 1999, the first international advertising campaign was launched under the title "The Power on Your Side." It was the first international campaign featuring the newly designed logo and the "Allianz Group" logo, which had been introduced at the same time. The logo symbolized the group's new direction while combining a modern image with a successful corporate tradition. This campaign and communication concept had been developed by marketing specialists for the major companies. Their aim was to present a credible image of Allianz and its group companies as global players who combined international expertise with local competence and skills. In 1999, the campaign ran on television and in national and international print media.[122] Allianz's media presence now matched that of a global player. In 2007–2008, Allianz abandoned the group logo with its blue and gray color scheme, which was perceived as overly complicated. Nonetheless, the overall concept was preserved. The new "Moments" campaign, launched in 2007, utilized powerful, straightforward colors alongside the traditional blue.[123]

In 2009, in the middle of the financial crisis, Allianz launched its "One" global brand campaign, designed to present itself to clients as a solid and financially sound partner in difficult times. From that point on, the Allianz companies worldwide were to operate under a single name.[124] In the international campaign, the "One" concept did not envision customers only as a target group; instead, customers were portrayed as real individuals, who offered their own personal experiences, advice and insights.[125] In the Interbrand rankings, Allianz's ranking rose from $3.8 billion in 2009 to $4.9 billion in 2010. In 2014, it was named "Best Global Brand." Today, Allianz is once again emphasizing regional advertising campaigns. On a global level, Allianz continues to strengthen its public visibility through the Allianz Arena in Munich and sports stadiums in other cities, as well as through Formula 1 racing.

Allianz at the Start of the 21st Century

At the start of the 21st century, the asset management line and operations in Asia assumed increasing importance for Allianz. By 1999, Allianz already regarded itself as a global player offering financial services in more than 70 countries.[126] Due to its presence in so many different countries, Allianz found itself increasingly influenced by the "pull of globalization." As international connections and input grew ever stronger, global economic events and trends had a greater impact on Allianz as well. But the 21st century began with a "global shock" – the terrorist attack on New York's World Trade Center on September 11, 2001.

Terrorist violence was not entirely unknown in Germany. From the 1970s to the early 1990s, Germany had experienced the impact of terrorism with attacks by the Red Army Faction. With the murder of Alfred Herrhausen, the spokesman of the Deutsche Bank board of directors and a member

Performance.
Covered by Allianz Group.
Wherever you are. Whatever you do. The Allianz Group is always on your side.
For over 75 years we have successfully managed the assets of life insurance policy holders. This, together with the close cooperation of our global partners and the experience of our asset management team leads to improved long-term investment performance. It's no wonder then, that we are awarded with one of the highest ratings by Standard & Poors. Maybe that's why we insure more Fortune 500 companies worldwide than anyone else. Allianz. The Power On Your Side.
Allianz
Allianz Group. Europe's leading global insurer and provider of financial services.

The motif of the successful broker stems, like the Tsing-Ma Bridge in Hong Kong on p. 322, from the first worldwide ad campaign "The Power on Your Side," which ran between 1999 and 2002.

of the supervisory board of Allianz Leben, and the murder of Jürgen Ponto, head of the board of directors of Dresdner Bank and, from 1976, also the deputy chair of the Allianz supervisory board, the impact of terrorism had been felt within the company itself.[127] The result was increased emphasis on security along with heightened security arrangements, for example, at the group's headquarters, where building access control and visitor passes were introduced.[128]

However, the attacks on September 11, 2001, were of an entirely different order. Allianz was affected in a variety of respects: as an employer, as a tenant, as an aviation insurer, and as a building insurer. Nearly 2,800 people were killed during the destruction of the two World Trade Center towers. The material damage amounted to $ 32.5 billion.[129] But all Allianz employees were rescued out of their offices in the World Trade Center and neighboring buildings.[130] The terrorist attacks marked a profound rupture in the history of aviation insurance at Allianz. They also transformed the German market. Allianz increasingly began to assess risk independently of the Deutscher

Luftpool (German Aviation Pool). After the attacks, questions arose regarding the insurability of aviation risks in hull and liability policies with regard to acts of war and terror. Many insurers initially responded by canceling policies for such risks. In a number of countries, government guarantees were instituted as a temporary measure to bridge the insurance gap until premiums could be reassessed.

The attacks also had an impact on building insurance. But first, the U.S. courts needed to decide whether the destruction of the World Trade Center towers constituted one insured event, or two. This was decided in 2006, when the U.S. Federal Court of Appeals for the Second Circuit determined that it had been a single insurance event.[131] Allianz had initially paid a sum of $ 312 million to the buildings' tenants. In 2007, Allianz joined with six additional corporations to reach a settlement entailing a joint payment of a further $ 2 billion.[132]

In the 21st century, major loss events such as floods, tsunamis, hurricanes and earthquakes assumed greater public visibility. There were increasing indications that such catastrophes might also be a consequence of global climate change.[133] After the devastating tsunami in Southeast Asia in 2004, Allianz employees around the world came to the aid of the victims with donations, which were distributed through Allianz Direct Help, a foundation that had been already established in 2001. At the same time, it was apparent that such aid would not be sufficient; rather, ongoing assistance in reconstruction would be necessary.

Microinsurance policies are one means to help people affected by such events. Microinsurance policies encompass a variety of insurance forms, ranging from microsavings accounts to rain insurance, which allow individuals with low incomes to get coverage against risk and to build up assets. But how can customers be reached in countries with a poorly developed infrastructure? It will require innovative distribution concepts. In some areas, the telephone could replace the insurance agent, or the Internet. In Africa, for example, approximately 65 percent of adults own a mobile phone. In 2012, Allianz began working together with a telephone company to market mobile insurance policies in the Ivory Coast. Customers register with the insurer via their mobile phones and also conduct payment transactions by phone.[134]

To ensure an active response when confronted with new developments and risks during times of crisis, globally active enterprises like Allianz must understand and respond to megatrends. This is key to their ability to maintain control over their business prospects. To meet this challenge, in 2006 the group development division launched an initiative to identify the business models best suited to responding to worldwide social and economic developments.[135] The initiative identified the demographic shift and climate change as the trends that would be of paramount importance to Allianz.[136] These observations and insights will also help determine the creation and development of insurance products, retirement planning and asset management services for a variety of target groups in a variety of markets worldwide. In Western societies, customer needs will be influenced by an aging population and the rise of single-person households. In many regions of the world, families will feel the impact of climate change on their economic existence as farmers or small entrepreneurs. To address these and other changes, Allianz in Germany has expanded its range in the area of retirement planning, for example with the addition of the Riester pension (2001) – advertised by piggy bank "Waltraud." It has also further differentiated its range in long-term care insurance and property insurance, where additional targeted services – such as the accident insurance policy "Unfall 50plus" for elderly clients and the "Allianz Handwerker Service" to provide necessary handyman services also for elderly clients – have been introduced. In the 1990s, it had already developed accident insurance with premium refunds with wealth-accumulation and profit-sharing for long suppressed issues like invalidity and occupational disability.[137] To meet the needs of Muslim clients, Allianz is also developing a range of insurance and financial products that conform to the requirements of Islamic law.[138]

The Founding of the SE

In 2003, Michael Diekmann replaced Henning Schulte-Noelle as chairman of the board of directors of Allianz AG. After joining Allianz in 1988, Diekmann moved through a variety of positions in marketing and sales before he took over the Asia-Pacific regional division for Allianz in 1996, where he then – as previously described – also became a member of the board of directors in 1998 with responsibility for reporting to the board on this division.

Economic conditions at the time meant that prospects in the insurance industry were less than rosy; Allianz was undercapitalized and was still grappling with the effects of international natural catastrophes as well as the terrorist attacks of 2001. In addition, the company had embarked upon the challenge of integrating Dresdner Bank into its operations. In the 2002 fiscal year, Allianz posted a loss for the first time in its more than 100-year history; the loss amounted to approximately €1.2 billion.

Within the image:
A new perspective.
Allianz SE. So European.

Allianz becomes Societas Europaea.
A changing Europe requires a new perspective. As an international financial services provider we see our home market as a growth market. That's why we are taking this pioneering step to serve over 45 million European customers more effectively.
Find out more on www.allianz.com/europe

INSURANCE | ASSET MANAGEMENT | BANKING

Allianz ⑪

Since 2006, Allianz has been operating under European law as a Societas Europaea (SE).

When Michael Diekmann assumed his new position, his first task was to consolidate and to restore profitability. At the 2003 annual general meeting, Allianz agreed on a capital increase and a cost-cutting program. At the same time, Allianz developed a strategy under Diekmann's leadership that was publicized to employees under the name "3 plus 1." The strategy aimed to 1) protect and enhance the capital stock; 2) raise profitability; 3) reduce the complexity of processes within the group; and (plus 1) increase sustainable competitiveness and value.[139] The program reflected what Diekmann regarded as the key pillar to success: a company with positive morale required a leader who would devise and convey clear strategic goals while allowing staff room to implement their own ideas.[140] The cost management measures were accompanied by a withdrawal from some markets, among them a number of countries in Africa and Asia. In addition, Diekmann required that every group company provide a detailed budget that would include the payment of a dividend to the holding company.

Finally, a new leadership culture was to be instituted. One sign was the establishment of an e-mail address to send messages directly to the chairman

The board of directors of Allianz SE became successively more international and diverse: Helga Jung became the first woman in this executive committee.

of the board of directors. Another sign of change within Allianz was the intensity with which Diekmann sought to address criticism and to explain the group's strategy to clients, staff and investors. In the ensuing decade, these goals were implemented via direct meetings with sales agents, round table discussions with staff of the group companies (Diekmann forums), meetings with key investors, and teleconferences with the management boards of group companies. Among the particular areas of concern for Diekmann were issues such as sustainability, demography, and addressing reputational risks.

Allianz's consolidation measures took effect more quickly than expected. In 2004, Michael Diekmann reported to investors that Allianz had posted a profit of more than € 1.6 billion in fiscal year 2003. The risk situation had improved significantly, and the financial situation had stabilized.[141] However, structural factors continued to present an obstacle. In 2006, Allianz decided to strike a new course and adopt a new legal form. Allianz AG, which had held the form of a stock corporation under German law, merged with the Italian company RAS and adopted the legal form of a European company, a Societas Europaea or SE. The new legal form allowed for a simplification of structures and aided in cross-border management within the European domestic market. Mergers with group companies became simpler to undertake. Additionally, the supervisory board, on which employers and employees were equally represented, was reduced from twenty members to twelve, four of whom came from European countries other than Germany. The board of directors, too, became more international in its composition, with five of the eleven members now coming from outside Germany.[142]

These changes expressly included the maintenance of a high standard of equal codetermination, which had proven its value in Germany over decades. The existing representative bodies all the way up to the corporate works council were not affected by the founding of the SE. The European works council is comprised of employee representatives from 24 companies. Since October 2006, it has been headed by Rolf Zimmermann.[143] For the first time, non-German employee representatives held positions on a co-determined supervisory board.

Operations were also divided more strictly according to region, and into globally active companies. At the same time, Allianz simplified the group's structure by merging several national companies into a larger unit, as it did in Italy and Germany. What was probably the most radical re-structuring in the history of Allianz in Germany was when the nationwide operations in 2006 were combined into one company under the aegis of Allianz Deutschland AG. The reforms, which were intended to place a stronger focus on the customer and simplify in-house sales structures, triggered massive protests among staff and the works council. The reforms were to include a restructuring of the IT system and the standardization of data-processing within the framework of the Allianz Business System (ABS), the separation of office work and sales, and the closure of a number of sites. Taken together, these measures would result in the elimination of several thousand jobs. Many employees were concerned about their careers and livelihoods. Many were also dismayed by the top management's new approach to staffing, which they regarded as a breach of company culture. The works council also criticized the measures as the downside of globalization. The old truism that companies create more jobs in response to rising profits appeared at that moment as though it no longer applied.[144] Employee representative organizations and unions tried to stave off layoffs by holding demonstrations and protests.[145] Tough negotiations and confrontations were the result. Within what was then a very heated atmosphere, the dispute spilled over onto the pages of the staff magazine. Rolf Zimmermann, who was then works council representative in Frankfurt, submitted a letter to the editor describing the dismay of many who were affected by the reforms: "When highly profitable companies are destroyed and successful managers are removed from their positions, that also undermines the belief in the value of success; [it undermines the belief] that the constant assurances that make reference to Leadership Values and manage-

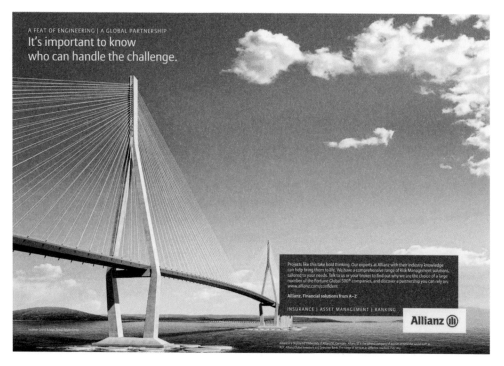

The motif from the "Moments" campaign depicts the Incheon Bridge in South Korea, whose total length is more than 12 kilometers. It was built between 2005 and 2009 and insured by Allianz.

ment guidelines were ever meant to be taken seriously; [and undermines the belief] that Allianz is a socially-minded employer that cares about the needs of its employees."[146]

Michael Diekmann, by contrast, insisted that this was precisely the time in which downsizing and structural change had to be carried out in Germany. Only by those means could Allianz reorganize and modernize from a position of strength. To do otherwise would be to wait until a crisis forced Allianz to take radical measures.[147]

After these disputes, Allianz in Germany experienced a long lean spell. The process of centralization radically transformed many areas of work. The streamlining measures were particularly painful in sites where central functions were moved to the head office. This included, for example, the removal of the branch head positions and the closure of Frankfurter Versicherungs-AG and Bayerische Versicherungsbank-AG in Munich. These reforms were seen as so radical that a number of managers, among them Reiner Hagemann, chairman of the board of directors of Allianz Versicherungs-AG, left the company.[148]

In the course of these measures, seven branch offices were converted into what was initially four fields of operation, with separate administrative units for the areas of operations and sales. Telephone and postal services were centralized, and letter post was henceforth digitized in the incoming mail center (PEZ). Ultimately, these changes played an important role in raising performance and profitability in the companies that made up Allianz Deutschland AG.

Within the insurance industry, globalization had resulted in increasing convergence of forms of sales and marketing, products and IT. This created the preconditions for additional streamlining of processes and for consolidating the group under a single brand. In 2006, the year that the SE was founded, Allianz began to further integrate its subsidiaries. In the first step, the Italian companies RAS and Lloyd Adriatico were integrated into Allianz S.p.A. Next, AGF was renamed Allianz France. Other international group companies followed.

In the next step, specialist companies with global spheres of responsibility were created. In 2006, corporate business was consolidated into Allianz Global Corporate & Specialty AG (AGCS), which now as well became a Societas Europaea. Credit insurance was consolidated under Euler Hermes S.A., headquartered in Paris, which had been founded in 2002. Euler Hermes S.A. was itself formed by the merger of the French credit insurer Euler and Germany's Hermes credit insurer, which were both members of the Allianz Group. Euler Hermes is the world's largest credit insurer, with more than 6,000 employees in over 40 countries. These companies are among the most important globally active business units, alongside the group's reinsurance company Allianz RE, which began in the 1980s as an in-house reinsurer and which, since the 1990s, has also worked for selected clients on the open international reinsurance market.

The interaction between the Global Lines and the local group companies also underwent refinement in accordance with the "collaboration" concept to create a comprehensive range of services for business clients and international groups. For example, Allianz Worldwide Partners was launched to develop comprehensive products and solutions for customers. Allianz Worldwide Partners is the integrated business to business to customer (B2B2C) entity for Allianz, and includes such lines as global assistance travel insurance, global automotive, and Allianz worldwide care.[149]

After founding the SE, Allianz also standardized activities within the group's corporate business. In 2006, AGCS was founded to serve as a new direct insurer for the corporate and transportation insurance operations. The company was created through the merger of Allianz Global Risks (AGR), which had provided industrial insurance services worldwide, and Allianz Marine & Aviation. Until that point, the two companies often served overlapping clients and business areas.[150] Cornhill's transportation and transportation reinsurance business and AGF's marine aviation transport operations had already been transferred to Allianz Marine & Aviation in 2002. Business operations from other countries were to follow. Most recently the U.S. subsidiary Fireman's Fund also saw the integration of the areas of ship and offshore insurance, and in 2015 its corporate customer business will be transferred to AGCS.[151]

These consolidations made it possible to consolidate and standardize areas such as IT, statistics, finance, and business operations. However, by themselves, streamlined structures and reasonable profits do not ensure success with customers. Local entities thus retain responsibility for direct customer contact. Underwriting, claims processing and customer management is still handled locally. The bulk of the business is generated by brokers, a practice which has its origins in the MAT industry. Today, AGCS has 3,500 staff in 60 countries, and has established specialist teams in 28 countries.

The standardization and centralization processes that underlie the successful path set out by the founding of the SE have also been extended to the creation of a globally active IT operation. This was defined within the target operating model (TOM) set forth within the "3 plus 1" strategy, announced in 2006. The initiative was based on the recognition that data processing is a key factor in global competitiveness, as had become apparent as early as the 1970s. As IT operations continued to industrialize and providers across the board gained access to tailor-made IT systems, this competitive pressure had continued to increase. To maintain its lead in this area, Allianz decided to bundle its capacities and standardize its disparate IT systems. In 2006, the separation of IT systems for life and non-life insurance operations was abandoned in Germany. By implementing the Target Operating Model, Allianz transformed its operation from one organized on a divisional basis to one in which customer focus was at the center of operations. In July 2007, Allianz employees began managing policies in the areas of property, life and health insurance on the unified Allianz Deutschland AG operating platform. This also entailed a restructuring of the workflow.[152] The model was initially tested in Austria, then introduced in Germany, and later implemented in other countries as well. It utilizes the technological advantages of digitiza-

Since 2004, Allianz has been offering special insurance solutions to low-income families. Today, Allianz is the leading provider of microinsurance policies with over 34 million insured.

tion in the incoming mail center and telephone systems to improve service standards for consulting and travel assistance.[153]

The concept was implemented in 2007 with the launch of ASIC (Allianz Shared Infrastructure Services). Between 2007 and 2010, ASIC gradually incorporated the regional IT units in Western Europe in order to improve service quality and data security. Friedrich Wöbking, head of the new international company, explained the concept: "In Western Europe, we currently have 26 smaller IT infrastructure units that utilize different technologies and products, which together serve the 15 Allianz subsidiaries." Because this model was inefficient, all IT units were scheduled for integration into ASIC. From its headquarters in Munich, ASIC would service the 15 Western European subsidiaries.[154] In 2010, ASIC was renamed AMOS, which is a central shared services company that delivers operational IT and non-IT services in

The Allianz Arena is a widespread motif in Allianz advertising in Asia.

the areas of purchasing, building and workplace management and internal consulting.[155] One key goal of AMOS is to ensure that Allianz can make optimal use of its worldwide scope and bundle the skills and talents of employees around the world.

Over the years, the insurance industry has become increasingly dependent on the Internet and the increasing digitization of other areas of life. This transformation has affected all areas of Allianz's operations, from sales and marketing to office work and data security. The purchasing habits of many customers have changed over the past years. Today customers obtain information online and increasingly purchase insurance policies online as well. The Allianz Group has already acquired a solid base of experience in this field. In 1997, RAS launched Lloyd 1885, Italy's first direct insurance unit. At first, Lloyd 1885 offered insurance via telephone. In September 1998, it was the first Italian insurance company to begin offering insurance online. In 1999, other Allianz subsidiaries began to follow, among them subsidiaries in France, Brazil, Colombia, Austria and Germany. Particularly in countries that lack an established sales network, online sales and marketing can be an attractive option. However, in countries where traditional sales structures dominate, such as in Germany, the initial response is often a skeptical one. This was articulated by Luca Pina, head of marketing for RAS, in the year 2000: "In a country where alongside mothers, pharmacists and clergy, the insurance agent is held in high regard, this new development represents a radical break."[156] After all, for many decades one of Allianz's major competitive advantages had been its nationwide and comprehensive sales network. But in this respect, too, the group changed to meet the changing needs of its clients. Allianz's special opportunity in this area may well be combining the tight-meshed sales network with the new Internet sales and marketing methods.

A Strong Community with a Future

For 125 years, one key factor in Allianz's success has been its ability to adapt to new circumstances and change with the times. Another equally important factor has been Allianz's ability to cope with crises, which is also a result of its early and ongoing commitment to sound business management. This commitment has also helped make the group astonishingly resilient in the face of the economic and financial crises that have emerged over the past 15 years. As Allianz has seen, a globally active enterprise will necessarily feel the impact of any crisis that is global in its scope. This was evident during the crisis of the New Economy in 2000; the economic turbulence that followed the terrorist attacks of September 11, 2001; the global financial crisis that began after the collapse of the subprime market in 2007; and the euro crisis that emerged in 2010.

In October 2008, only weeks after Lehman Brothers investment bank filed for bankruptcy, sending the financial markets into turmoil, Helmut Perlet, chief financial officer of Allianz at that time, assured the press that Allianz remained on a solid footing. According to Perlet, Allianz possessed "sufficient capital and a completely sound insurance business." He closed the interview with the statement, "No, we are not planning to institute a program of cutbacks."[157] One key reason for his confidence was Allianz's long-standing conservative investment policy – a policy that has not always been received well on the market.

Today, two key developments promise to have a substantial impact on the future of Allianz – globalization and digitization. In an online contribution dated August 5, 2014, Mohamed El-Erian, chief economic advisor for Allianz, described what he termed the "new face of globalization" after the 2008 crisis.[158] By 2014, he explained, the free movement of goods, services and persons – with the notable exception of the financial transactions that had precipitated the crisis – had already surpassed their historic highs. The trend toward comprehensive interaction and increasing integration across national borders was set to continue, he maintained. And it would be information that would continue to drive the process of globalization and growth. Global networking strengthens individuals, companies and corporations, he concluded, by accelerating the trend away from labor-intensive production processes and toward the knowledge-intensive goods that are associated with investment in research and development.

At the meeting of the supervisory board on October 2, 2014, Allianz also charted the course for its future personnel. The supervisory board members decided that Oliver Bäte would assume the office of chairman of the board of directors from May 2015 and, at the same time, asked Michael Diekmann to present himself as a candidate for the Allianz supervisory board elections in 2017. With these decisions, Allianz has remained true to its principle of maintaining continuity and utilizing the leadership qualities of experienced experts while at the same time trusting in the ideas and capabilities of a young generation of managers for shaping the company's future.

Today's economy and society is in the process of taking the next, decisive step beyond "classical" globalization, which has remained oriented toward national borders up to now. This step entails the globalization of information. Over the course of its 125-year history, Allianz, which was founded on February 5, 1890, as the Allianz Versicherungs-Aktien-Gesellschaft, has demonstrated an impressive capacity to master global political and economic developments, and respond with further growth. Endowed with this capacity, Allianz continues to set its course for the future.

NOTES

1890–1918 · The First Years and the First World War

1 BArch, R 3118/1409, sheets 3 ff.

2 Quotation: Georg Siebert, *100 Jahre Merck, Finck & Co.* (no place or year), p. 15. For simplicity's sake, the names Thieme and Finck will appear without the noble "von" in chapter one but with it in later chapters. Thieme was granted a noble title in 1914 by Bavarian King Ludwig III., see *Gesetz- und Verordnungsblatt für das Königreich Bayern* (1914), p. 118; biography on Thieme: Ludwig Arps, *Deutsche Versicherungsunternehmer* (Karlsruhe, 1968); Fink gained a personal noble title in 1905 and a hereditary one for his family in 1911, see *Gesetz- und Verordnungsblatt für das Königreich Bayern* (1905), pp. 519 f. and (1911), pp. 424, 752; Finck's biography: Bernhard Hoffmann, "Finck, Wilhelm Peter von," in: *Neue Deutsche Biographie* 5 (1961), pp. 150 f., URL: http://www.deutsche-biographie.de/pnd118687220.html, accessed on September 29, 2014.

3 Concerning the creation of Munich Re, see Martin Herzog, *Was Dokumente erzählen können – Zur Geschichte der Münchener Rück*, 6 vols. (no place or year [Munich, 1986–1992]) (unpublished manuscript, FHA), pp. 22 ff.

4 Quotation Thieme: *Wallmann's Versicherungs-Zeitschrift* 14 (1880), p. 827; quotation Ehrenzweig: Albert Ehrenzweig, "Deutschland. Geschichte des Jahres," *Assecuranz-Jahrbuch* 21 (1900), part III, p. 195.

5 Herzog, *Was Dokumente erzählen*, p. 101.

6 Liability legislation: *Deutsches Reichsgesetzblatt* (1871), pp. 207 ff.; and Ludwig Arps, *Auf sicheren Pfeilern. Deutsche Versicherungswirtschaft vor 1914* (Göttingen, 1965), pp. 63 ff. Lightning explosion: see records inventory of file 40122 Steinkohlenbauvereine des Dresden-Freitaler Reviers in: Bergarchiv Freiberg, URL: http://www.archiv.sachsen.de/cps/bestaende.htm?oid=09.01.03&file=40122.xml&syg_id=&obf2=, accessed on December 14, 2014; on Molt: Arps, *Versicherungsunternehmer*, p. 108.

7 ADVV annual report of 1886, p. 3; ADVV annual report of 1888, p. 3; minutes of the 14th annual general meeting on May 25, 1889, FHA, B 27/no call number, p. 9.

8 Discussion of Munich Re: Herzog, *Was Dokumente erzählen*, p. 101; on the founding: Wilhelm Kisch, *50 Jahre Allianz. Ein Beitrag zur Geschichte der Deutschen Privatversicherung* (Berlin, no year [1940]), pp. 1 ff., HADB, S 81; on Hammacher: Friedrich Zun-

kel, "Hammacher, Friedrich Adolf," in: *Neue Deutsche Biographie* 7 (1966), pp. 588 f., URL: http://www.deutsche-biographie.de/pnd116440619.html, accessed on December 8, 2014; distribution and later sale of the shares: "Aktienbuch der Allianz," FHA.

9 Stock corporations: Hans-Ulrich Wehler, *Deutsche Gesellschaftsgeschichte*, vol. 3: *Von der "Deutschen Doppelrevolution" bis zum Beginn des Ersten Weltkrieges 1849 bis 1914* (Munich, 1995), p. 86; letter from Merck, Finck & Co to the Deutsche Bank, September 6, 1889, HADB, S 81; investment capital rates: Allianz annual report of 1926; Kochstraße: Ludwig Arps, *Wechselvolle Zeiten. 75 Jahre Allianz Versicherung 1890–1965* (Munich, 1965), p. 26.

10 Walter Bayer, "Grundkapital, Kapitalaufbringung, Kapitalerhaltung," in: idem & Mathias Habersack (eds.), *Aktienrecht im Wandel*, vol. 2: *Grundsatzfragen des Aktienrechts* (Tübingen, 2007), pp. 708 ff.; Fritz Seidenzahl, *100 Jahre Deutsche Bank* (Frankfurt/Main, 1970), p. 31; Hans G. Meyen, *120 Jahre Dresdner Bank. Unternehmens-Chronik 1872 bis 1992* (Frankfurt/Main, 1992), p. 373; Commerzbank (ed.), *Die Bank – Dienstleister im Wandel der Zeit. 125 Jahre Commerzbank* (Frankfurt/Main, 1994), p. 322.

11 Insurance concessions: Arps, *Auf sicheren Pfeilern*, p. 55; new insurers: cf. *Neumanns Jahrbuch* (1925) and *Deutscher Versicherungs-Kalender* (1880) and (1892).

12 HADB, S 81; activities of von der Nahmer: Herzog, *Was Dokumente erzählen*, p. 92.

13 *Statistisches Jahrbuch für das Deutsche Reich* (1894).

14 Quotation: GStA PK, I. HA, Rep. 120, A XII 4, no. 19.

15 Arps, *Wechselvolle Zeiten*, p. 13.

16 Commercial register: fourth supplement to the *Deutscher Reichs-Anzeiger und Königlicher Preußischer Staats-Anzeiger* (February 7, 1890), no. 36; quotation: *Wallmann's Versicherungs-Zeitschrift* 23 (1888/89), p. 2358.

17 Quotation: letter from Thieme to Johansson, May 9, 1890; Martin Herzog, *Quellenedition zur Münchener Rück in 7 Bänden* (no pleace or year), vol. 1; idem, *Was Dokumente erzählen*, p. 108.

18 Arps, *Wechselvolle Zeiten*, p. 9; Andrés Hoyo Aparicio, "Economía, empresas y empresarios en el Santander de 1900," in: Manuel Suárez Cortina (ed.), *Santander hace un siglo* (Santander, 2000), pp. 30 ff., here p. 61; Johann Hanslik, "Genealogie der Versicherungsunternehmungen Österreichs," in: Wolfgang Rohrbach (ed.), *Das Zeitalter des modernen Versicherungswesens. Versicherungsgeschichte Österreichs*, vol. 3 (Vienna, 1988), pp. 1159 ff., here p. 1162; Berliner Gesellschaften: *Deutscher Versicherungs-Kalender für das Jahr 1892* (Berlin, 1891).

19 Barbara Eggenkämper, Gerd Modert, & Stefan Pretzlik, *Die Frankfurter Versicherungs-AG 1865–2004* (Munich, 2004); cf. also Chapter 2 in this volume.

20 Cf. Chapter 5 in this volume.

21 Herzog, *Was Dokumente erzählen*, p. 755; on Bruno Pohl: Arps, *Wechselvolle Zeiten*, p. 24.

22 Allianz annual report of 1890.

23 Wallich quotation: Hermann Wallich & Paul Wallich, *Zwei Generationen im deutschen Bankwesen 1833–1914* (Frankfurt/Main, 1978), p. 135; letters from Deutsche Bank to Finck, December 18, 1993, and Finck to Deutsche Bank, December 20, 1893 (quotation Finck), HADB, S 81; Kisch, *50 Jahre Allianz*, S. 12; Arps, *Wechselvolle Zeiten*, p. 33; von der Nahmer quotation: letter from von der Nahmer to Steinthal, November 4, 1895, HADB, S 81.

24 BArch, R 3118/1409; Arps, *Wechselvolle Zeiten*, p. 24; Herzog, *Was Dokumente erzählen*, p. 92; *Allianz-Zeitung*, special edition (May 1921); Rudolf Hensel, *40 Jahre Allianz. Ein Stück deutscher Versicherungsgeschichte* (no place or year [Berlin, 1930]) (unpublished manuscript, FHA, AZ 1.3/1), pp. 53 ff.

25 Construction file: LAB, A Rep. 10-02/7975; costs: in various annual reports of Allianz since 1895; Munich Re rentals: Allianz annual report of 1900; on von der Nahmer: Herzog, *Was Dokumente erzählen*, p. 32; further building history: *Allianz-Zeitung* 6 (1924), pp. 69 f.; *Österreichische Versicherungs-Zeitung* 22 (1895), p. 115 and 26 (1899), p. 187.

26 Wolfgang Kruse, "Industrialisierung und moderne Gesellschaft," in: Bundeszentrale für politische Bildung (ed.), *Dossier Das Deutsche Kaiserreich*, URL: http://www.bpb. de/geschichte/deutsche-geschichte/kaiserreich/139649/industrialisierung-und-moderne-gesellschaft, accessed on December 8, 2014.

27 For von der Nahmer: Ludwig Arps's notes on talks with Mr. Engelmann and Mr. Stolp as well as Karl Jego's records, Berlin, FHA, AZ 10/folder "Mitarbeiter, Personal- und Sozialwesen, Berichterstattung von Allianz-Pensionären;" Wehler, *Gesellschaftsgeschichte 1849 bis 1914*, p. 606; *Statistisches Jahrbuch für das Deutsche Reich* (1909), p. 270.

28 Ludwig Arp's notes on conversations with Charlotte Klatte and Mr. Witzke, Berlin, FHA, AZ 10/folder "Mitarbeiter, Personal- und Sozialwesen, Berichterstattung von Allianz-Pensionären."

29 Correspondence between Reich and Allianz, FHA, B 3/portfolio "Personalunterlagen 1901–1943," FHA, AZ 12.1/file "Gustaf Körner;" morning edition of the *Vossische Zeitung* (December 10, 1905), ninth supplement.

30 *Alltagsleben 1871–1914*, Internet page of the German Historical Museum, accessed on June 1, 2014, URL: http://www.dhm.de/lemo/html/kaiserreich/alltagsleben/index. html; "Rangordnung," supplement 6, FHA, B 27/file "Protokolle des Verwaltungsrats vom 25.5.1898 bis 19.5.1899."

31 "Anstellungsbedingungen und Dienstordnung für die Beamten des Allgemeinen Deutschen Versicherungs-Vereins," January 1, 1901, supplement no. 70, FHA, B 27/ file "Beilagen Nr. 1 bis 102 zu Band XXV der Aufsichtsrats-Protokolle vom 1.6.1900 bis 20.5.1901," p. 14.

32 Ibid.; letter from Emil Dohmann to Allianz, March 8, 1961, FHA, AZ 10/folder "Mitarbeiter, Personal- und Sozialwesen, Berichterstattung von Allianz-Pensionären;" Uwe Drepper, "Bodycheck und Zeitkontrolle. Eine Geschichte von Werktoren und Beamteneingängen," in: Burkhart Lauterbach (ed.), *Großstadtmenschen. Die Welt der Angestellten* (Frankfurt/Main, 1995), pp. 141 ff.; Ludwig Arps's notes on talks with Mr. Ullrich, FHA, AZ 10/folder "Mitarbeiter, Personal- und Sozialwesen, Berichterstattung von Allianz-Pensionären."

33 Conversation notes and letter from Charlotte Klatte to Allianz, March 12, 1961, FHA, AZ 10/folder "Mitarbeiter, Personal- und Sozialwesen, Berichterstattung von Allianz-Pensionären".

34 "Instruction betreffend die Abteilung und Leitung der Versicherungsgeschäfte," supplement no. 17a, FHA, B 27/file "Protokolle des Verwaltungsrats vom 25.5.1889 bis 19.5.1890;" letter from Köhler to Allianz, April 22, 1961, and letter from Nachstedt to Allianz, March 2, 1962, FHA, AZ 10/folder "Mitarbeiter, Personal- und Sozialwesen, Berichterstattung von Allianz-Pensionären;" Hensel, *40 Jahre Allianz*, pp. 59 f.

35 Telephone connection: Herzog, *Was Dokumente erzählen*, p. 59; *Verzeichnis der*

Theilnehmer an der Stadt-Fernsprecheinrichtung in Berlin (1892), p. 7; first typewritten letter: letter from Allianz to Deutsche Bank, Berlin, November 4, 1895, HADB, S 81; letter from von der Nahmer to Deutsche Bank, April 22, 1961, FHA, AZ 10/folder "Mitarbeiter, Personal- und Sozialwesen, Berichterstattung von Allianz-Pensionären," p. 5; pianist: letter from Georg Bauer to Allianz, April 2, 1961, ibid.; night course: Ludwig Arps's notes on talks with Mr. Engelmann, Berlin, ibid.

36 "Die proletarische Frauenbewegung 1871–1914," Internet page of the German Historical Museum, accessed on June 1, 2014, URL: http://www.dhm.de/lemo/html/kaiserreich/innenpolitik/prolfrauen/index.html.

37 Toni Pierenkemper, *Arbeitsmarkt und Angestellte im Deutschen Kaiserreich 1880–1913* (Stuttgart, 1987), pp. 198, 200; *Statistisches Jahrbuch für das Deutsche Reich* (1910), p. 14.

38 Letter from Elisabeth Branthin to Allianz, March 2, 1961, FHA, AZ 10/folder "Mitarbeiter, Personal- und Sozialwesen, Berichterstattung von Allianz-Pensionären."

39 Payroll lists: "Rangordnung," supplement 6, FHA, B 27/file "Protokolle des Verwaltungsrats vom 25.5.1889 bis 19.5.1890;" quotation: minutes of the 134th meeting of the administrative board on May 17, 1892, § 1092, FHA, B 27/file "Protokolle des Verwaltungsrats vom 23.6.1891 bis 24.5.1892;" "Anstellungs-Bedingungen und Dienstordnung für die Beamten des ADVV in Stuttgart," January 1, 1901, supplement no. 70, FHA, B 27/file "Beilagen Nr. 1 bis 102 zu Band XXV der Aufsichtsrats-Protokolle vom 1.6.1900 bis 20.5.1901."

40 "Anstellungs-Bedingungen und Dienstordnung für die Beamten des ADVV in Stuttgart," January 1, 1904, supplement no. 70, ibid.; letter from Emil Dohmann to Allianz, March 8, 1961, FHA, AZ 10/folder "Mitarbeiter, Personal- und Sozialwesen, Berichterstattung von Allianz-Pensionären;" quotation: presentation in the annual general meeting on June 10, 1904, supplement 86, FHA, B 27/file "Beilagen Nr. 1 bis 89 zu Band XXVIII der Aufsichtsrats-Protokolle vom 2.7.1903 bis 6.6.1904;" on Ms. Mohr: minutes of the 289th meeting of the supervisory board on January 8, 1904, FHA, B 27/file "Protokolle des Verwaltungsrats vom 2.7.1903 bis 6.6.1904."

41 GStA PK, I. HA Rep. 120 A XII 4, no. 21; Arp, *Auf sicheren Pfeilern*, pp. 359 f.

42 Herzog, *Was Dokumente erzählen*, pp. 120 f., 126 f., 155 f.

43 Germania: Arps, *Wechselvolle Zeiten*, p. 24; bicycle: idem, *Auf sicheren Pfeilern*, pp. 234, 360, and *Wallmann's Versicherungs-Zeitschrift* 33 (1898/99), p. 1993; special locks: *Wallmann's Versicherungs-Zeitschrift* 37 (1902/03), 1, p. 93.

44 Risks: Arps, *Auf sicheren Pfeilern*, p. 360, idem, *Wechselvolle Zeiten*, p. 24; approval burglary theft insurance: GStA PK, I. HA Rep. 120 A XII 4, no. 21.

45 Fides and Munich Re: Herzog, *Was Dokumente erzählen*, p. 116; Fides takeover: BArch, R 3118/1409; Herzog, *Was Dokumente erzählen*, p. 110; new direction: Allianz annual report of 1904.

46 Eggenkämper, Modert, & Pretzlik, *Frankfurter*, pp. 49 f.; Arps, *Wechselvolle Zeiten*, p. 49.

47 Concession: FHA, AZ 10/folder "Genehmigungsurkunden;" end of cooperation: Herzog, *Was Dokumente erzählen*, p. 110; figures from: Kaiserliches Aufsichtsamt für Privatversicherung (ed.), *Versicherungs-Statistik für 1913 über die unter Reichsaufsicht stehenden Unternehmungen* (Berlin, 1916); Harold Kluge calculated that Munich Re received about 10 percent of its premium revenues from Allianz until the First World War, at the same time, however, generating almost 38 percent of its profits from Allianz revenues: Harold Kluge, "Der Einfluss des Geschäfts der 'Allianz' auf die

Entwicklung der ‚Münchener Rückversicherungs-Gesellschaft' in deren ersten fünfzig Jahren (1880–1930)," *Jahrbuch für Wirtschaftsgeschichte* (2006), 2, pp. 217–46.

48 Quotation: *Münchner Neueste Nachrichten* (April 20, 1906), quoted from: Arps, *Auf sicheren Pfeilern*, p. 651; cf. also ibid.; Simon Winchester, *Ein Riss durch die Welt. Amerika und das Erdbeben von San Francisco 1906* (Munich, 2006), fatalities: p. 325, Los Angeles: p. 332.

49 Arps, *Auf sicheren Pfeilern*, p. 652; William Bronson, *Still Flying and Nailed to the Mast* (New York, 1963), pp. 85 ff.

50 Quotation: ibid., p. 85; "Report of the Special Committee of the Board of Trustees of the Chamber of Commerce of San Francisco," November 13, 1906, BArch, R 1501/117425.

51 Damage caused by earthquakes excluded: *Wallmann's Versicherungs-Zeitschrift* 40 (1905/06), 2, p. 2014; partial payments: "Die Rhein und Mosel-Gesellschaft zahlt," *New Yorker Handels-Zeitung* (December 4, 1909), BArch, R 901/16484; Archive of Munich Re, E-25/51; *Masius' Rundschau* 18 (1906), p. 224.

52 Figures and facts from: Tilmann J. Röder, *Rechtsbildung im wirtschaftlichen "Weltverkehr". Das Erdbeben von San Francisco und die internationale Standardisierung von Vertragsbedingungen (1871–1914)* (Frankfurt/Main, 2006); additional aspects: bankruptcy: report of the Imperial Supervisory Office, Berlin, October 11, 1906, BArch, R 1501/117424; other catastrophes: Arps, *Auf sicheren Pfeilern*, p. 653.

53 Quotation: *Wallmann's Versicherungs-Zeitschrift* 40 (1906/07), 1, p. 630; 11 million: Arps, *Auf sicheren Pfeilern*, p. 654, Röder, *Rechtsbildung*, p. 351; doubling of premiums: Arps, *Auf sicheren Pfeilern*, p. 656.

54 Quotation: "Reisebericht betreffend das Aufsichtsamt des Staates New York unter besonderer Berücksichtigung der Lebensversicherung, Berlin, den 1.4.1911," BArch, R 1501/117379; statistics for Munich Re: Geo Risks Research, NatCatSERVICEMR, quoted from Insurance Information Institute, Earthquakes and Tsunamis, URL: http://www.iii.org/fact-statistic/earthquakes-and-tsunamis, accessed July 9, 2014.

55 Quotation: Allianz annual report of 1905; 161,000 dollars: letter from Allianz to the Imperial Supervisory Office, Berlin June 23, 1906, BArch, B 280/12251; Allianz annual report of 1906.

56 Quotation: *Wallmann's Versicherungs-Zeitschrift* 41 (1906/07), 1, pp. 346 ff.; Arps, *Wechselvolle Zeiten*, p. 50; FHA, B17/folder "Feuerbranche Vertragskorrespondenz. Allianz Vers.-Akt.-Ges. Direktes Geschäft Allgemeines Berlin I;" on Hennig: *Allianz Zeitung* 5 (1923), p. 88.

57 On Bothe: cf. Handelsregisterauszug, BArch, R 3118/1407; conflict with the BVB: FHA, B 17/folder "Feuerbranche Vertragskorrespondenz. Allianz Vers.-Akt.-Ges. Direktes deutsches Geschäft Berlin I."

58 160,000: excerpt from a letter by von der Nahmer to Thieme, December 4, 1906, ibid.; mills, spinning works: von der Nahmer to Thieme, December 4, 1906, ibid.; serious risks: von der Nahmer to Thieme, April 15, 1910, ibid.; Sömmerda: von der Nahmer to Thieme, Berlin, October 7, 1910, ibid.

59 Herzog, *Was Dokumente erzählen*, pp. 129 f.; BArch, R 3118/1407; short biography of Siefart in *Allianz Zeitung* 5 (1923), p. 46.

60 Favag: see Chapter 2; quotation: Arps, *Wechselvolle Zeiten*, p. 45; Kisch, *50 Jahre Allianz*, p. 16.

61 General: Arps, *Wechselvolle Zeiten*, p. 55; Printing press industry: Arps, *Auf sicheren*

Pfeilern, p. 482; Herzog, *Was Dokumente erzählen*, pp. 116, 121 f., 125, 160; *Assecuranz-Compass* 16 (1908), 2, pp. 453 f.

62 Quotation: Kisch, *50 Jahre Allianz*, p. 16; departure: Arps, *Wechselvolle Zeiten*, p. 55; concession Switzerland: FHA, AZ 10/folder "Genehmigungsurkunden;" foreign figures: Kaiserliches Aufsichtsamt für Privatversicherung (ed.), *Versicherungs-Statistik für 1913 über die unter Reichsaufsicht stehenden Unternehmungen* (Berlin, 1916), pp. 360 f.; Barbara Eggenkämper & Gerd Modert, "Das Allianz Zentrum für Technik: Eine Geschichte der Schadenforschung," in: Dieter Anselm et al. (eds.), *AZT Automotive: Lösungen aus der Versicherungswirtschaft* (Munich, 2007), pp. 13 ff.

63 Correspondence in portfolio "Wiedes Papierfabrik Rosenthal in Blankenstein," FHA, B 17/folder "Feuerbranche Vertragskorrespondenz. Allianz Vers.-Akt.-Ges. Direktes deutsches Geschäft Berlin I."

64 Letter from von der Nahmer to Munich Re, March 25, 1908, and file note Fritz Thieme, Munich, April 16, 1908, ibid.

65 Marita Roloff & Alois Mosser, *Wiener Allianz. Gegründet 1860* (Vienna, 1991); Wolfgang Rohrbach (ed.), *Versicherungsgeschichte Österreichs*, vol. I–III (Vienna, 1988); more details on the merger history in the last years in company brochures: Marita Roloff (ed.), *150 Jahre Allianz in Österreich. Menschen machen Geschichte* (Vienna, 2010); *Veröffentlichungen des Kaiserlichen Aufsichtsamts für Privatversicherung* (Berlin, 1906), p. 12; quotation: letter from Schertel to Arps, Nuremberg, April 6, 1961, FHA, AZ 10/folder "Mitarbeiter, Personal- und Sozialwesen, Berichterstattung von Allianz-Pensionären."

66 Providentia: Kaiserliches Aufsichtsamt für Privatversicherung (ed.), *Versicherungs-Statistik für 1910 über die unter Reichsaufsicht stehenden Unternehmungen* (Berlin, 1912), pp. 38 f.; *Veröffentlichungen des Kaiserlichen Aufsichtsamts für Privatversicherung* (Berlin, 1909), p. 263; management of Providentia: *Assecuranz-Compass* 15 (1907), 2, p. 434; Manfred Knote, *Aus heiteren und düsteren Tagen entschwindender Zeit*, in: Herzog, *Quellen*, vol. 1; homepage of Knote family, accessed on July 20, 2014, URL: http://www.knote-familientag.de/; German assets of Providentia: Eggenkämper, Modert, & Pretzlik, *Frankfurter*, pp. 87 f; *Neumanns Jahrbuch* (1931), pp. 698 f.

67 Figures for agents: Hensel, *40 Jahre Allianz*, p. 34; overview of the Magdeburger Feuer agency from about 1895, FHA, B 28/no call number; "Auch eine Mission der Frau," *Monats-Zeitung der Stuttgarter Lebensversicherungsbank a. G.* 13 (1905), p. 1411.

68 The details on Mr. Reischert are based on the manuscript of a presentation Reischert gave on May 14, 1952, FHA, AZ 10/folder "Mitarbeiter, Personal- und Sozialwesen, Berichterstattung von Allianz-Pensionären."

69 Letter from Köhler to Arps, April 22, 1961, ibid.; Kissing: letter from Schertel to Arps, April 6, 1961, ibid.

70 On the small carriage, the then so-called "Chaisserl": letter from Mittermeier to Arps, March 23, 1961, ibid.; 6 marks: Schertel to Arps, April 6, 1961, ibid.; incomprehensible advertising: letter from Mittermeier to Arps, March 23, 1961, ibid.; machine insurance: letter from Köhler to Arps, April 22, 1961, ibid.; *Die Rote Fahne*, no. 119 (June 7, 1931).

71 Quotation: template of a letter to the shareholders, February 1906, FHA, B 17/folder "Feuerbranche Vertragskorrespondenz. Allianz Vers.-Akt.-Ges. Direktes deutsches Geschäft Berlin I;" circular of Allianz to the officials of Munich Re, January 1906, ibid.

72 Various letters between Allianz, Munich Re and C.H. Oehmig-Weidlich, in March 1907 and on October 8, 1908, ibid.

73 Wilhelm Kißkalt, *Erinnerungen an die Münchener Rück* (Garmisch, 1953) (unpub-

lished manuscript), p. 10 (in the holdings of the Allianz Center for Corporate History).

74 Amtsgericht in Berlin-Mitte, complete notarized copy from the commercial register, Berlin June 9, 1928, BArch, R 3118/1407, sheets 164ff.

75 Hensel, *40 Jahre Allianz*, p. 43.

76 Paul von der Nahmer in Paris: Herzog, *Quellen*, vol. 1, pp. 92, 229; foreign contacts: FHA, AZ 8/balance book I, sheets 3, 4, 7, 12; letter from Nachstedt to Allianz, March 2, 1962, FHA, AZ 10/folder "Mitarbeiter, Personal- und Sozialwesen, Berichterstattung von Allianz-Pensionären."

77 Kopenhagen and London: Arps, *Wechselvolle Zeiten*, pp. 13 f., 56; *Bericht des eidg. Versicherungsamts über die privaten Versicherungs-Unternehmungen in der Schweiz im Jahre 1896* (Bern, 1898), pp. XL, LVII; *Bericht des eidg. Versicherungsamts über die privaten Versicherungs-Unternehmungen in der Schweiz im Jahre 1897* (Bern, 1899), p. 118; *Bericht des eidg. Versicherungsamts über die privaten Versicherungs-Unternehmungen in der Schweiz im Jahre 1898* (Bern, 1900), pp. 77, 101, 118; *Bericht des schweizerischen Versicherungsamtes. Die privaten Versicherungs-Unternehmungen in der Schweiz im Jahre 1913* (Bern, 1915), pp. 87, 126.

78 Activities abroad: form letter from the Imperial Supervisory Office of 29 June 1909 with comment, BArch, B280/12251; on Schreiner: Herzog, *Dokumente*, pp. 91, 210 ff.; correspondence between Thieme, Schreiner, and Dietterle, January and March, 1909, FHA, B 17/folder "Feuerbranche Vertragsabteilung Allianz Berlin Ägypten."

79 FHA, B 17/folder "Feuerbranche Vertragscorrespondenz, Allianz' Überseegeschäft früher Association Siemssen & Co. Tientsin."

80 German-Chinese relations in the 19th century: Mechthild Leutner, & Klaus Mühlhahn (eds.), *Mission und Wirtschaft in interkultureller Perspektive* (Münster, 2001), pp. 20 ff.

81 Attachment to the letter of the German Consulate General of Calcutta to the Reich Chancellor, September 26, 1908, BArch, R 901/16498.

82 FHA, B 17/folder "Feuerbranche Vertragscorrespondenz, Allianz' Überseegeschäft früher Association Siemssen & Co. Tientsin."

83 Letter from Allianz to the Deutsch-Asiatische Bank, Berlin, March 11, 1915, ibid.

84 Thomas Mann quotation: Peter de Mendelssohn, *Der Zauberer. Das Leben des deutschen Schriftstellers Thomas Mann*, vol. 2: *1905 bis 1918* (Frankfurt/Main, 1996), pp. 1586 f.; Jörn Leonhard tells this story in his impressive monograph on the First World War: Jörn Leonhard, *Die Büchse der Pandora. Geschichte des Ersten Weltkriegs* (Munich, 2014). Allianz staff figures: Allianz annual report of 1914, p. 5; quotation and staff figures for ADVV: ADVV annual report of 1914, p. 1a f.; quotation Allianz: Hensel, *40 Jahre Allianz*, p. 45.

85 Hensel, *40 Jahre Allianz*, p. 44; Peter Borscheid, "Germany: Insurance, Expansion, and Setbacks," in: idem & Niels Viggo Haueter (eds.), *World Insurance. The Evolution of a Global Risk Network* (Oxford, 2012), p. 105; state support: "Bericht des Aufsichtsamts zum Versicherungsgeschäft im Ausland vom 17.6.1916," BArch, R 901/16497; Sweden, the Netherlands, Switzerland: Arps, *Wechselvolle Zeiten*, p. 67; Chile: Thieme to von der Nahmer, December 17, 1914, and excerpt from a letter by Fritz Dessauer, December 29, 1914, FHA, B 17/portfolio "Feuerbranche Vertragscorrespondenz Allianz Vers.-Akt.-Ges. Chile;" licenses in: FHA, AZ 10/folder "Genehmigungsurkunden."

86 Leonhard, *Büchse der Pandora*, p. 303; Ludwig Arps, *Durch unruhige Zeiten. Deutsche*

Versicherungswirtschaft seit 1914, vol. I: *Erster Weltkrieg und Inflation* (Karlsruhe, 1970), pp. 37, 133.

87 Quotation: Arps, *Unruhige Zeiten*, vol. I, p. 475; Hensel, *40 Jahre Allianz*, p. 45.

88 ADVV: Eggenkämper, Modert, & Pretzlik, *Frankfurter*, p. 121; letter from Köhler to Allianz, April 22, 1961, FHA, AZ 10/folder "Mitarbeiter, Personal- und Sozialwesen, Berichterstattung von Allianz-Pensionären;" quotation: *Annalen des gesamten Versicherungswesens*, August 15, 1918; Arps, *Unruhige Zeiten*, vol. II, p. 118.

1918–1933 · Crises, Rationalization, and Growth

1 John Maynard Keynes, *The Economic Consequences of the Peace* (London, 1920), p. 2.

2 Hans-Ulrich Wehler, *Deutsche Gesellschaftsgeschichte*, vol. 4: *Vom Beginn des Ersten Weltkrieges bis zur Gründung der beiden deutschen Staaten 1914–1949* (Munich, 2003), p. 241.

3 Grumbt's article was first published on November 23, 1918, in the *Schiffahrts-Zeitung*. Quoted here from the reprint in the *Zeitschrift für Versicherungswesen* (December 4, 1918), p. 352.

4 Allianz Versicherungs-AG annual report of 1918, p. 3.

5 See Ludwig Arps, *Durch unruhige Zeiten. Deutsche Versicherungswirtschaft seit 1914*, vol. I: *Erster Weltkrieg und Inflation* (Karlsruhe, 1970), pp. 182–228; Peter Koch, *Geschichte der Versicherungswirtschaft in Deutschland* (Karlsruhe, 2012), pp. 213 f.

6 Rudolf Hensel, *40 Jahre Allianz. Ein Stück deutscher Versicherungsgeschichte* (no place or year [Berlin 1930]) (unpublished manuscript, FHA, AZ 1.3/1), pp. 58–61.

7 Compare the statistics and explanations in: Gerald D. Feldman, *The Great Disorder. Politics, Economics, and Society in the German Inflation 1914–1924* (New York, & Oxford, 1997), pp. 81–5; on the perception of the inflation by Allianz and Munich Re: Hensel, *40 Jahre Allianz*, p. 50; Martin Herzog, *Was Dokumente erzählen können – Zur Geschichte der Münchener Rück*, vol. 2 (no place or year [Munich, 1986–1992]) (unpublished manuscript, FHA), pp. 420–49.

8 Wehler, *Gesellschaftsgeschichte 1914–1949*, p. 259.

9 On how dramatic the situation was: Mark Spoerer, & Jochen Streb, *Neue deutsche Wirtschaftsgeschichte des 20. Jahrhunderts* (Munich, 2013), pp. 88 f.

10 Allianz annual report of 1918, p. 5; Hensel, *40 Jahre Allianz*, p. 45; list of the companies merged in the "Allianz and Stuttgarter" group, Berlin, 1931, pp. 1–13; list of the foreign branch offices and subsidiaries of the Allianz und Stuttgarter Verein Vers.Akt.Ges., May 1931 in: FHA, no call number/folder "Allianz Beteiligungen;" Wilhelm Kisch, *50 Jahre Allianz. Ein Beitrag zur Geschichte der Deutschen Privatversicherung* (Berlin, no year [1940]), p. 135; Allianz annual report of 1933, p. 44.

11 "Viele Stimmen – nur eine Meinung," *Allianz Zeitung* 15 (1933), 6, p. 165.

12 URL: http://polunbi.de/inst/ullstein.html, accessed on December 8, 2014; Egon Bannehr et al., *Die Eule lässt Federn. Das Ullstein-Haus 1926–1986. Setzer, Drucker, Journalisten* (Berlin, 1996), pp. 39–58.

13 The documents in: Herzog, *Was Dokumente erzählen*, vol. 4; excerpt from minutes of meeting of supervisory board of September 7, 1917: ibid., p. 756; Peter Borscheid, *100 Jahre Allianz* (Munich, 1990), pp. 42 f.; how this relates to the relationship between Munich Re and Allianz: note by Kurt Schmitt, Allianz und Munich Re 1937, in: FHA, AZ 6/folder "Allianz Münchener Rück Gemeinschaftsvertrag."

14 Herzog, *Was Dokumente erzählen*, vol. 4; "Gemeinschaftsvertrag zwischen der Alli-

anz Versicherungs-AG in Berlin und der Münchner Rückversicherungs-Gesellschaft in München," Munich/Berlin, April 23/29, 1921, and appendixes: ibid., pp. 757 f.; FHA, AZ 6/folder "Allianz Münchener Rück Gemeinschaftsvertrag."

15 FHA, Wilhelm Kißkalt, *Erinnerungen an die Münchener Rück* (Garmisch, 1953) (unpublished manuscript), p. 10 (in the holdings of the Allianz Center for Corporate History).

16 FHA, NL 1/5: memo by Thieme, Munich, January 9, 1913.

17 Ibid., letters from Schmitt to Thieme, Munich, January 3, 1913, and April 6, 1913.

18 Kißkalt, *Erinnerungen*, p. 13.

19 Schmitt's post-1945 memoir contradicts the circumstances described here, based on the quoted letters and memos of Schmitt and Thieme, with regard to the events of his making contact with Thieme and starting at Munich Re. On Schmitt's biography see: Autobiographical notes by Schmitt from the period after World War II, FHA, NL 1/163; Gerald D. Feldman, *Allianz and the German Insurance Business, 1933–1945* (Cambridge, 2001), pp. 3–6; Wilhelm Arps, *Deutsche Versicherungsunternehmer* (Karlsruhe, 1968), pp. 165–79; Peter Koch, "Schmitt, Kurt Paul," in: *Neue Deutsche Biografie*, vol. 23 (Berlin, 2007), pp. 238 f.; on his later career during the Nazi period: Feldman, *Allianz*, pp. 60–105; Adam Tooze, *Ökonomie der Zerstörung. Die Geschichte der Wirtschaft im Nationalsozialismus* (Munich, 2007), pp. 96 f., 107 f., 111 f., 227 f.

20 On Schmitt's military service: Kißkalt, *Erinnerungen*, p. 15.

21 Eduard Hilgard, *Mein Leben in der Allianz* (unpublished manuscript) in: FHA, NL 2/7, p. 23.

22 FHA, AZ 3/folder "Dr. Wiedemann, Frankfurt," memo concerning 75th birthday of Dr. Wiedemann, Frankfurt, January 17, 1958; Ludwig Arps, "Heß, Hans," in: *Neue Deutsche Biografie* 9 (Berlin, 1972), p. 6; Feldman, *Allianz*, pp. 6–8; Gerd Modert, "Die Entwicklung der Frankfurter 1930 bis 1948", in: Barbara Eggenkämper, Gerd Modert, & Stefan Pretzlik, *Die Frankfurter Versicherungs-AG 1865–2004* (Munich, 2004), pp. 80 f.

23 Quotations in: Hilgard, "Mein Leben," p. 7; further description: ibid., pp. 3–10, 11 f., 16–21; "Direktor Eduard Hilgard 80 Jahre," *Unser Adler* (1964), 3, pp. 26–8; Feldman, *Allianz*, p. 7–10; FHA, AZ 3/folder Hilgard and others.

24 Allianz annual report for 1924, p. 10.

25 BArch, R 3101/17061, no page number, Kriegsministerium to the Reichskanzler, Reichswirtschaftsamt, Berlin, November 10, 1918, and annex: Stuttgart-Berliner Versicherungs-AG to Unternehmung Joh. & Karl Bauch, Stuttgart, September 3, 1918, "Versicherung gegen Schäden durch öffentliche Unruhen"; on Kurt Schmitt's negotiations with the Reich Supervisory Office on tumult insurance: Unfall-Versicherungsverband to Reichsaufsichtsamt für Privatversicherung, Berlin, Dezember 11, 1919.

26 Arps, *Unruhige Zeiten*, vol. I, pp. 150–2; financial figures in: Allianz annual report of 1920, pp. 22 f.

27 Koch, *Geschichte der Versicherungswirtschaft*, p. 219.

28 Allianz annual report of 1920, p. 8.

29 BArch, R 3101/17365, sheets 245 f., "Zur Beschlagnahme der Werte deutscher Versicherungsunternehmen in Amerika," *Berliner Börsen-Courier* (April 9, 1921); "Deutsche Versicherungsbestände in Amerika," *Frankfurter Zeitung* (April 30, 1921); American Consular Service to Reichswirtschaftsministerium, Berlin, May 10, 1922. In 1921, a total of $ 14.5 million had been deposited as surety by German insurers in the U.S. Of this, $ 450,000 was from Allianz, $ 400,000 from Favag, and $ 3.75 million from Munich Re.

30 Herzog, *Was Dokumente erzählen*, vol. 2, p. 366; Kißkalt, *Erinnerungen*, p. 14.

31 Feldman, *Disorder*, p. 5.

32 Allianz annual report of 1920, p. 8.

33 Michael Gold et al., *60 Jahre AGV 1950–2010* (Munich, 2010), pp. 9 f.; Sebastian Hopfner, *Tarifverträge für die private Versicherungswirtschaft. Kommentar*, 9th ed. (Karlsruhe, 2013), pp. 2 f.; "Angestelltenbewegung und Abbruch des Streiks," *Zeitschrift für Versicherungswesen* (January 14, 1920), pp. 14 f.; Herzog, *Was Dokumente erzählen*, vol. 2, pp. 376 f.

34 FHA, B 3.3/board of directors, transcript of the 6th management meeting, February 23, 1920, p. 1 f.; minutes of 38th meeting of board of directors, December 28, 1920.

35 FHA, B 3.3/supervisory board, minutes of meeting of supervisory board of BVB of March 16, 1920, p. 11.

36 For the most current survey of the overall development of Allianz structures until 1945, see: Borscheid, *100 Jahre Allianz*, pp. 44–77.

37 Allianz annual report of 1921, p. 6.

38 Hermann Habicht, *50 Jahre Hermes Kredit-Versicherungs-AG. Ein Beitrag zur Geschichte der Kreditversicherung in Deutschland* (Hamburg, 1967), pp. 16–24; Hensel, *40 Jahre Allianz*, pp. 76–9.

39 Herzog, *Was Dokumente erzählen*, vol. 4, pp. 846–52.

40 Hilgard, *Mein Leben*, p. 28; Stefan Pretzlik, "Vom Glasversicherer zum Frankfurter Konzern 1865–1929," in: Eggenkämper, Modert, & Pretzlik, *Frankfurter*, pp. 66 f.

41 BArch, 80 Ba 2/P 5784, correspondence between Kurt Schmitt and Eduard Mosler (proprietor of Disconto-Gesellschaft), Berlin, April 9, 1923, and copies of prior correspondence with Konsul Leiden.

42 FHA, B 3.3.1/2, minutes of supervisory board of BVB, January 19, 1924; report in: *Neues Münchener Tagblatt* (December 26, 1923).

43 The quotation from the 1923 annual report of the Hypobank explained in: FHA, 3.3.1/ no call number, Karl Ritter von Rasp, *Geschichte der Entwicklung der Bayerischen Versicherungsbank umfassend die Jahre 1856–1925*, Munich, May 1926 (unpublished manuscript), p. 101.

44 The letter from Kißkalt of December 18, 1923, quoted in: Herzog, *Was Dokumente erzählen*, vol. 4, p. 951.

45 See: "Erneute Ausdehnung der Allianz Gruppe," *Berliner Börsen-Zeitung*, evening edition (December 14, 1923); "Neue Großkombination in der deutschen Versicherung," *Frankfurter Zeitung* (December 15, 1923); "Bayerische Versicherungsbank AG, München," *Frankfurter Zeitung* (December 20, 1923).

46 *Allianz Zeitung* 3 (1921), 2, p. 3.

47 The document, a note by Kurt Schmitt of November 24, 1921, has not survived; however, an excerpt exists. The quote is based on this: Herzog, *Was Dokumente erzählen*, vol. 4, p. 965.

48 *Assekuranz-Jahrbuch* (1923), III, p. 19; quoted here from: Herzog, *Was Dokumente erzählen*, vol. 4, no page number; Steven C. Topik & Allen Wells, "Warenketten in einer globalisierten Wirtschaft," in: Akira Iriye & Jürgen Osterhammel (eds.), *Geschichte der Welt 1870–1945. Weltmärkte und Weltkriege* (Munich 2012), pp. 614 f.

49 *Neumanns Jahrbuch der Privatversicherung im Deutschen Reich 1925*, Berlin 1925, p. 449–51, lists under a specially included heading "Verzeichnis der Konzerne" a total of 37 corporate groups; on Schweizer Rück (now Swiss Re) see the information in: Peter Borscheid, David Gugerli, Harold James, & Tobias Straumann, *Swiss Re und die Welt der Risikomärkte. Eine Geschichte* (Munich 2014), pp. 379–98.

50 Description of sequence of events and quotations according to: Herzog, *Was Dokumente erzählen*, vol. 4, pp. 964–69.

51 Financial statement figures according to the *Assecuranz-Compass* 1920 for the year 1918, see: *Assecuranz-Compass. Internationales Jahrbuch für Versicherungswesen*, vol. 1 (Vienna, 1920), pp. 158–61, 194–6.

52 Hensel, *40 Jahre Allianz*, p. 137.

53 *Frankfurter Zeitung* (December 19, 1922).

54 *Allianz Zeitung* 4 (1922), 5, p. 1.

55 Ursula Büttner, *Weimar. Die überforderte Republik* (Stuttgart, 2008), pp. 57 f.

56 Hensel, *40 Jahre Allianz*, p. 64.

57 "Unsere neuesten Zweigniederlassungen," *Allianz Zeitung* (1923), 7, p. 79.

58 FHA, S 17.2/4 Minutes, twelfth meeting of the expanded board of directors on March 26/27, 1928.

59 Allianz annual reports of 1921, p. 7 and 1924, p. 12.

60 "Die Not der Zeit," *Allianz Zeitung* 5 (1923), 11, p. 139.

61 Description according to: Feldman, *Disorder*, pp. 759–63, 780–95; Büttner, *Weimar*, pp. 177–81; Harold James, "Die Reichsbank 1876–1945," in: Deutsche Bundesbank (ed.), *Fünfzig Jahre Deutsche Mark. Notenbank und Währung in Deutschland seit 1948* (Munich, 1998), pp. 44–54.

62 Allianz annual report of 1922, p. 9.

63 Quotation and explanations according to: Hensel, *40 Jahre Allianz*, pp. 108 f.

64 On Hilferding's role: Wehler, *Gesellschaftsgeschichte 1914–1949*, p. 247.

65 Hilgard, *Mein Leben*, p. 32.

66 BArch, 280/012242, sheets 10, 20, report on audit of Allianz Insurance Corporation in Berlin in regard to its foreign ties in fidelity insurance.

67 LAB, A Rep. 231/818, correspondence of Neue Frankfurter with Osram, containing: Frankfurter Allgemeine Versicherungs-AG, insurance policy no. 204586, glass insurance, "Allgemeine Versicherungs-Bedingungen für Glas-Versicherungen. Besondere Bedingungen (1924)".

68 Peter Borscheid, "Das Auslandsgeschäft der deutschen Versicherungswirtschaft 1870–1945," *Vierteljahrschrift für Sozial- und Wirtschaftsgeschichte* 88 (2001), pp. 311–45; the description is according to pages 332–7, in particular.

69 Kurt Schmitt, "Gegenwartsprobleme im Versicherungswesen," *Deutsche Versicherungs-Zeitung* (April 15, 1924), p. 93.

70 Heike Knortz, *Wirtschaftsgeschichte der Weimarer Republik* (Göttingen, 2010), pp. 115–25; Florian Pressler, *Der lange Schatten der Großen Depression. Geschichte der Weltwirtschaftskrise in den 1930-Jahren* (Bonn, 2013), pp. 126–32; Arps, *Unruhige Zeiten*, vol. II, pp. 3–13.

71 FHA, S 17.2/4, third expanded board of directors meeting, June 17–18, 1924, p. 11.

72 FHA, ibid.; fourth expanded board of directors meeting, October 14–15, 1924, p. 4; "Und neues Leben …," *Allianz Zeitung* 6 (1924), 1, p. 6 f.

73 Hensel, *40 Jahre Allianz*, pp. 59–62.

74 FHA, S 17.2/4, eighth expanded board of directors meeting, May 31–June 2, 1926, p. 12.

75 FHA, Technical Committee meetings, 1926–1931, here transcript of first meeting of October 20, 1926, p. 3 f.

76 For details see: Barbara Eggenkämper, Gerd Modert, & Stefan Pretzlik, *Bits and Bytes for Business. 50 Jahre EDV bei der Allianz* (Munich, 2006), pp. 36–42.

77 Allianz annual report of 1926, p. 11.

78 Kracauer's text quoted here from: "Auszug aus Siegfried Kracauer, *Die Angestellten*," in: Staatliche Kunsthalle Berlin and Neue Gesellschaft für Bildende Kunst (eds.), *Rationalisierung 1984*, exhibition catalog (Berlin, 1983), p. 223.

79 FHA, B 2.4.5/no call number, Branch Frankfurt: Favag to Else Heiss, March 30, 1928.

80 *Allianz Zeitung* 6 (1924), 1/2, pp. 1, 16. Möbius became fairly well known, mainly with commissions for monuments to German colonial history, and has more recently become the object of a critical consideration of traditions of commemoration of German colonialism. Many of his works were melted down during World War II. See for example URL: http://www.freiburg-postkolonial.de/Seiten/Zeller-Reiterdenkmal-1912.htm, accessed on December 8, 2014, and the study by the same author: Joachim Zeller, *Kolonialdenkmäler und Geschichtsbewusstsein: Eine Untersuchung der kolonialdeutschen Erinnerungskultur* (Frankfurt/Main, 2000).

81 Rudolf Hensel, "Amerika," reprint from *Allianz Zeitung* (Berlin, 1928), in particular the preface and pp. 103–14, first quotation p. 16. Second quotation: Hensel, *40 Jahre Allianz*, p. 217.

82 Chapter "Die Betriebskrankenkassen in der Weimarer Republik," in: Barbara Eggenkämper, Gerd Modert, & Stefan Pretzlik, *Mit traditionellen Werten die Zukunft gestalten. Die Landesverbände der Betriebskrankenkassen in Baden-Württemberg und Bayern* (Munich, 2008), pp. 67 f.

83 On sports and recreation, see: Borscheid, *100 Jahre Allianz*, pp. 99–103, including parts of the quotation from the *Allianz Zeitung*: "Die Gründung des Allianz-Sportvereins. Der Sport als Wirtschaftsfaktor," *Allianz Zeitung* 7 (1925), 5, pp. 79 f.; on the historical background: Büttner, *Weimar*, pp. 162–263, 331; Andreas Luh, *Betriebssport zwischen Arbeitgeberinteressen und Arbeitnehmerbedürfnissen. Eine historische Analyse vom Kaiserreich bis zur Gegenwart* (Aachen, 1998), p. 93 f.

84 Hilgard, *Mein Leben*, pp. 60–7; on the London conference: Alfred Manes, "Wiederauferstehung der internationalen Kongresse für Versicherungs-Wissenschaft," *Zeitschrift für die gesamte Versicherungswissenschaft* 27 (1927), pp. 1–4; idem, "Betrachtungen zum VIII. internationalen Kongreß für Versicherungs-Wissenschaft 27. bis 30. Juni 1927 in London," ibid., pp. 355–70.

85 Herzog, *Was Dokumente erzählen*, vol. 4, p. 958; memo by Kißkalt (Allianz ADV), October 20–21, 1922; Kißkalt to Schmitt, August 22, 1927, in: Herzog, *Was Dokumente erzählen*, vol. 4, no page number, as well as various correspondence between Kurt Schmitt and Wilhelm Kißkalt printed there after that.

86 Quoted as printed in: "Zusammenschluß Allianz …," *Zeitschrift für Versicherungswesen* (October 12, 1927), pp. 907–9; the first quotation in *Deutsche Versicherungspresse* (October 13, 1927), pp. 575–8; a comprehensive press review in: *Allianz Zeitung* 9 (1927), 11, pp. 173–5.

87 BArch, 80 Ba 2/P 5784, Mosler memo, Berlin, December 16, 1927.

88 FHA, B.1.12.2/2194, report by Gerhard Prüfer, head of proposals department at Allianz Leben, "Erinnerungen aus meinem Leben" (1980), p. 1 f.

89 FHA, B 1.1/973, Wilhelm Busekow, "Geschichte der ASS 1926–1951," *Monatsmitteilungen*, ASS special edition (January 1951), p. 3 f.

90 FHA, B 1.4/2165, Chronik ASS.

91 The quotation is by Georg Solmssen, banker of Disconto-Gesellschaft, according to: Gerald D. Feldman, "Die Deutsche Bank vom Ersten Weltkrieg bis zur Weltwirtschaftskrise 1914–1933," in: Lothar Gall, Gerald D. Feldman, Harold James et al., *Die*

Deutsche Bank 1870–1995 (Munich, 1995), p. 274; on the Favag scandal: Feldman, ibid., pp. 272–6; chapter "1929: Der Zusammenbruch der Favag und die Hintergründe eines Skandals," in: Eggenkämper, Modert, & Pretzlik, *Frankfurter*, pp. 11–39.

92 Ibid., p. 24. As remembered by Lauinger, quoted from: Borscheid, *100 Jahre Allianz*, pp. 69 f.

93 BArch, B 280/13299, p. 45, letter of Frankfurter Allgemeine Versicherungs-AG in Liquidation, July 14, 1939. Details see: Eggenkämper, Modert, & Pretzlik, *Frankfurter*, p. 34, 39.

94 Hilgard, *Mein Leben*, pp. 71 f.

95 HADB, memo "Frankfurter Allgemeine" by Eduard Mosler, Berlin, August 14, 1929, p. 2.

96 BArch, B 280/13264, report of the Reich Supervisory Office to the Economics Minister, Berlin, August 22, 1929, pp. 57–63. Cf. the assessment in: Feldman, *Allianz*, p. 22.

97 BArch, B 280/13264, Allianz to Reich Supervisory Office, re: Frankfurter Allgemeine Versicherungs-AG, Berlin, August 23, 1929, and annexes, pp. 86–110.

98 Cf.: Schmitt's arguments at meeting with the supervisory board of Favag with representatives of the Reich Supervisory Office at the Economics Ministry (RWM), where he mentions an immediate injection of capital by Allianz of RM 16–18 million: BArch, B 280/13265, record of a discussion at RWM, Berlin, September 27, 1929, p. 2.

99 Modert, "Die Entwicklung der Frankfurter," pp. 74 f.

100 Knortz, *Wirtschaftsgeschichte*, pp. 218 f.

101 Allianz annual report of 1932, p. 40; for membership statistics, see: FHA B 16, correspondence of Betriebskrankenkasse of Allianz, Berlin: BKK Berlin of Allianz to Bureau of Insurance of City of Berlin, Berlin, March 30, 1933. Comparative figures of BKK Berlin for 1931, of BKK Allianz Dresden 1939 and BKK Allianz Frankfurt/Main for 1932 and 1934 support this assessment. No other personnel statistics differentiating by gender have survived.

102 *Allianz Zeitung* 5 (1923), 4, p. 45.

103 BArch, DC 1/6979, Personnel file of ZKSK on Anna von Pritzbuer; *Allianz Zeitung* (1933), 6, p. 175; FHA, B 1.4/693, interview with director of department Narr "Postbote Berlin-München 1945" (ca. 1997); Konrad H. Jarausch, Matthias Middell & Annette Vogt, *Sozialistisches Experiment und Erneuerung in der Demokratie – die Humboldt-Universität zu Berlin 1945–2010* (Berlin, 2012), pp. 159 f. (vol. 3 of the six-volume *Geschichte der Universität Unter den Linden 1810–2010*).

104 Feldman, *Allianz*, p. 48.

105 *Allianz Zeitung* 1 (1919), 4, p. 1; the first quotation: *Allianz Zeitung* 1 (1919), 1, p. 1.

106 *Allianz Zeitung* 4 (1922), 5, p. 1.

107 *Allianz Zeitung* 4 (1922), 4, pp. 2 f.; on Haeselich: "Redaktionswechsel," *Allianz Zeitung* 15 (1933), 8, p. 229.

108 *Lebensblätter. Vierteljahreshefte der Allianz und Stuttgarter Lebensversicherungsbank* (1933), 4, p. 1; *Allianz Zeitung* 11 (1929), 3, pp. 54 f.

109 Karl Schulpig, "Wie mein Allianz-Adler entstand," *Lebensblätter* 33 (1937), 1, pp. 4 f.; "Wie unser Adler entstand," *Unser Adler* (1955), 2, no page number.

110 "Der Allianz-Adler als Warenzeichen," *Allianz Zeitung* 13 (1931), 11, pp. 262 f.

111 "Der Adlerhorst," *Allianz Zeitung* 13 (1931), pp. 19 f.

112 Ingomar Kloss, *Werbung. Handbuch für Studium und Praxis*, 4th ed. (Munich, 2007), pp. 31–7; on the history of its origins in the U.S., see the web site of the John W. Hart-

man Center for Sales, Advertising & Marketing History, URL: http://library.duke.edu/rubenstein/scriptorium/eaa/about.html, accessed on December 8, 2014.

113 Heading "Deutschland und Deutsches Reich (Zeitungswesen)," in: *Brockhaus Konversationslexikon*, vol. 5, 14th ed. (Leipzig, Berlin, & Vienna, 1894–1896), p. 163.

114 Borscheid, *100 Jahre Allianz*, p. 396. This also includes a comprehensive presentation of the history of advertising at Allianz up until 1990.

115 Alexander Schug, *"Deutsche Kultur" und Werbung. Studien zur Geschichte der Wirtschaftswerbung von 1918 bis 1945* (Berlin, 2011), pp. 133, 142.

116 Entry "Europahaus," URL: http://berlingeschichte.de/index.html, accessed on December 8, 2014; "Für alle Fälle," *Allianz Zeitung* 13 (1931), 11, pp. 263–6.

117 "Filmpropaganda," *Allianz Zeitung* 11 (1929), 4, p. 63.

118 "Zum Welt-Reklame-Kongreß und zur Reklameschau in Berlin," *Allianz Zeitung* 11 (1929), 9, pp. 167 f.; Alexander Schug, "Wegbereiter der modernen Absatzwerbung in Deutschland. Advertising Agencies und die Amerikanisierung der deutschen Werbebranche in der Zwischenkriegszeit," *WerkstattGeschichte* 34 (2003), pp. 38 f.

119 *Allianz Zeitung* 12 (1930), 5, p. 85.

120 Feldman, *Allianz*, pp. 39–50.

121 Uexküll's life is only documented in fragments. The most comprehensive outline is in: Martin Faass, *Martha Liebermann. Lebensbilder* (Berlin, 2007), pp. 90–3, 96–101; individual fragments in: Günther Brakelmann, *Helmuth James von Moltke 1907–1945. Eine Biografie* (Munich, 2007), pp. 200–3; Olaf Jessen, *Die Moltkes. Biographie einer Familie* (Munich, 2010), p. 357; Heinz J. Arnbrust, & Gert Heine, *Wer ist wer im Leben von Thomas Mann* (Frankfurt/Main, 2008), p. 288; Wladimir Nikolaevich Kokovtsov, *Out of My Past. Memoirs of Count Kokovtsov* (Stanford, 1935), pp. 75–7, 585–6; Hilgard, *Mein Leben*, pp. 67–9, 71.

122 FHA, S 17.2/4, minutes of 13th meeting of the expanded board of directors, November 8–9, 1928, p. 11.

123 Ibid., minutes of meeting of board of directors on May 8, 1930, p. 12; ibid., minutes of 15th meeting of expanded board of directors, November 5–6, 1929, pp. 16 f.

124 Hilgard, *Mein Leben*, pp. 68 f., 71.

125 The hazardous efforts to save Max Liebermann's widow are described in: Cecilia Lengefeld, & Annette Roeloffs-Haupt, "'Mir ist jetzt die Situation unerträglich geworden'. Martha Liebermanns verzweifelte Hoffnung auf eine Ausreise nach Schweden 1941–1943," in: Faass, *Liebermann*, p. 90–101; on Edgar von Uexküll's attitude towards the regime see, for example: Beate Ruhm von Oppen (ed.), *Helmuth James von Moltke. Briefe an Freya 1939–1945* (Munich, 1988), pp. 342 f.

126 "Personalien." An appreciation of Uexküll on the occasion of his 60th birthday on May 23, 1944. Materials from the files of Dr. Jürgen-Detlev Freiherr von Uexküll, to whom we wish to express our thanks for the information he provided already in the year 2000.

127 Lengefeld & Roeloffs-Haupt, "Situation," pp. 100 f., 103.

128 Werner Abelshauser, *Deutsche Wirtschaftsgeschichte 1945 bis zur Gegenwart* (Bonn, 2011), pp. 36 f.; Peter Borscheid & Niels Viggo Haueter (eds.), *World Insurance. The Evolution of a Global Risk network* (Oxford, 2012), pp. 104–9.

129 FHA, AZ 9/folder "Mitarbeiter-, Personal- und Sozialwesen. Berichterstattung von Allianz-Pensionären," report by W. Helms in a letter to Ludwig Arps, Nordenham 1961.

130 FHA, S 17.14/52, Lithuanian Lloyd; for the story of the Riga holding, see: FHA, S 17.14/51 I and II.

131 This only changed when the law releasing them was implemented in the U.S. in 1927. Cf.: Allianz annual report of 1930, p. 12.

132 On the Italian market see: Pietro Marchetti, "Le compagnie italiane e l'internazionalizzazione del mercato assicurativo: il caso Allianz," in: Paolo Garonna (ed.), *Assicurare: 150 anni di Unità d'Italia* (Rome, 2011), pp. 153–66, here pp. 157–62.

133 "England unterversichert – und wir?," *Allianz Zeitung* 14 (1932), 6, p. 159.

134 Data for Prudential and Allianz according to: *III. International Insurance Intelligence: An International Year Book of Insurance Companies' Accounts, 1931–1932*, pp. 429, 272 f., converted according to the rate of exchange given there of 1 pound sterling = 20 reichsmarks; the data on Metropolitan according to: *Assecuranz-Compass* (1930), pp. 1102 f.

135 FHA, S 17.2/4, minutes of meeting of board of directors on March 5, 1928, p. 3.

136 Allianz annual report of 1931, p. 6.

137 Hensel, *40 Jahre Allianz*, p. 317.

138 Extensive source documentation of the efforts by Allianz in the files of the Reich Supervisory Office and the Foreign Ministry: BArch, B 280/1441–1443.

139 BArch, B 280/1441, letter of the German ambassador in Vienna, Count Lerchenfeld, to the Foreign Ministry, Vienna, November 7, 1929.

140 "In Afrika," *Allianz Zeitung* 10 (1928), 4, p. 54.

141 "Aus Indien," *Allianz Zeitung* 15 (1933), 3, pp. 56–9.

142 "Nach Afrika: Indien," *Allianz Zeitung* 11 (1929), 2, pp. 21–2.

143 BArch, B 280/1443, sheets 59 f. and annex, Allianz and Stuttgarter Lebensversicherungsbank to the Reich Supervisory Office, Berlin, October 30, 1931.

144 FHA, AZ 10, Allianz holdings: "Liste der ausländischen Vertretungen bezw. Tochter-Gesellschaften der Allianz und Stuttgarter Verein Vers.Akt.Ges," May 1931.

145 BArch, B 280/1443, sheets 253–5 and annexes, German embassy to the Foreign Ministry in Berlin, Baghdad, September 5, 1936; Allianz and Stuttgarter Lebensversicherungsbank, foreign department, to Reich Supervisory Office, re: China, Berlin, November 12, 1936 (sheet 256).

146 BArch, B 280/12392, sheet 163, article in the Free Press of India, August 10, 1950, FHA, AZ 6/folder "Gemeinschaftsvertrag."

147 FHA, AZ 6/no call number, Gemeinschaftsvertrag; Paul Lux and Hans Goudefroy to Alois Alzheimer in Munich, November 17, 1942.

1933–1948 · The Nazi Years and Reconstruction

1 The reconstruction of Martin Lachmann's biography, which is only partially documented, is based on information offered by his grandson Peter Haas, who supplied Gerald Feldman with letters and photos for Feldman's study on the history of Allianz in the Nazi years. For further information, see Gerald D. Feldman, *Allianz and the German Insurance Business, 1933–1945* (Cambridge, 2001), pp. 135 f.; Frank Stern, "J wie Jude," *Allianz Journal* (2002), 3, pp. 40–2; see also Roxanna Noll, "Martin Lachmann" on the website: *Berlin-Minsk. Unvergessliche Lebensgeschichten*, URL: http://www.berlin-minsk.de/, accessed on September 29, 2014.

2 FHA/folder "Freudenburg/Lachmann," letter of Martin Lachmann to his daughter Ruth and his son-in-law Leopold Haas in Stockholm, Berlin, October 20, 1938.

3 Ibid., letter by Martin Lachmann to his son-in-law Leopold Haas, Berlin, October 26, 1938.

4 Ibid.

5 Chief Finance President of Berlin-Brandenburg, asset liquidation, file "Martin Michaelis Lachmann, Bln. Charlottenburg, Der Oberfinanzpräsident Berlin Vermögensverwertung-Aussenstelle," note of February 4, 1942, sheet 6, in: BLHA, Rep. 36A II/20903.

6 Death certificate of Standesamt I in Berlin of May 9, 1950.

7 URL: http://www.geni.com/people/Frieda-Fuchs/6000000024144968934?through= 6000000024144768137#/tab/media, accessed on September 29, 2014. Here one can find a copy of an undated newspaper article.

8 URL: http://www.stolpersteine-berlin.de/de/biografie/3367, accessed on September 29, 2014.

9 Michaela Melián, *Memory Loops, Mandlstraße 9*, URL: http://www.memoryloops. net/de#!/298/, accessed on September 29, 2014.

10 URL: http://www.bundesarchiv.de/gedenkbuch/de907497, accessed on September 29, 2014, compare to the *Gedenkbuch der LH München*, URL: http://www.muenchen.de/ rathaus/Stadtverwaltung/Direktorium/Stadtarchiv/Juedisches-Muenchen/Gedenkbuch/Biographisches-Gedenkbuch.html, accessed on December 9, 2014; the testimony there relies on the testimony given by the Haas family.

11 Martin Lachmann to Kurt Schmitt, Berlin, July 4, 1933, in: FHA, NL 1/2.

12 "Hugenberg's successors," *Basler Nachrichten* (June 30, 1933), in: FHA, NL 1/48; "Fear of Reprisals," *Times* (London, August 1, 1933): FHA, NL 1/68. The condensed survey of the history of Allianz in the Nazi years presented here is based on the findings of a research project led by Gerald Feldman from 1997 until 2001 and essentially follows Feldman's monograph published in 2001.

13 Christoph Strupp, "Beobachtungen in der Diktatur. Amerikanische Konsulatsberichte aus dem ‚Dritten Reich'," in: Frank Bajohr & Christoph Strupp (eds.), *Fremde Blicke auf das "Dritte Reich". Berichte ausländischer Diplomaten über Herrschaft und Gesellschaft in Deutschland 1933–1945* (Göttingen, 2011), pp. 95, 97.

14 Henry A. Turner, *Die Großunternehmer und der Aufstieg Hitlers* (Berlin, 1985), pp. 393–6; further: Feldman, *Allianz*, p. 92, and Ian Kershaw, *Hitler 1889–1936* (Stuttgart, 1998), pp. 566 f.; concerning Schmitt and von Finck, who are not mentioned by Turner, see Schmitt's rather vague and von Finck's rather detailed remarks in: NA, RG 260, OMGUS, FINAD, 2/58/3, and ibid. 2/47/4 (von Finck).

15 Feldman, *Allianz*, p. 64.

16 Gustav von Tein to Reich Minister of Labor Seldte, Berlin, March 30, 1933, in: BArch, R. 31.01/17078; Rudolf Beume to Seldte, Berlin, March 31, 1933, in: ibid.; note from the Reich Commissioner for the Prussian Ministry of the Interior, April 24, 1933, BArch, R. 31.01/17078; cf. Feldman's presentation in: Feldman, *Allianz*, pp. 61–3.

17 Ludolf Herbst, *Das nationalsozialistische Deutschland 1933–1945* (Frankfurt/Main, 1996), pp. 68–70.

18 From the reports of the SoPaDe, quoted in: Hans-Ulrich Wehler, *Deutsche Gesellschaftsgeschichte*, vol. 4: *Vom Beginn des Ersten Weltkrieges bis zur Gründung der beiden deutschen Staaten 1914–1949* (Munich 2003), p. 737.

19 For more details, see: Feldman, *Allianz*, pp. 50–9; the quotation and the presentation follow Eggerss's testimony in his interrogation by the American military authorities on August 17, 1947: NA, RG 260, OMGUS, FINAD, 2/56/10.

20 On this, see Turner, *Großunternehmer*, p. 182. Carlos Collado Seidel contends that money in the amount of several million RM was paid and uses as proof an estimate made years later in 2003 by Heinz Hermann Niemöller. Niemöller is the son of Pas-

tor Martin Niemöller. During his childhood and during the time of his father's persecution and imprisonment in a concentration camp, he was a neighbor and close contact of the Schmitts in Berlin Dahlem: Carlos Collado Seidel, "Vom Reichswirtschaftsminister zum Gegner des NS-Regimes. Der Wirtschaftsführer Kurt Schmitt: Financier Hitlers und des Widerstandes?," in: Detlef J. Blesgen (ed.), *Finanziers, Finanzen und Finanzierungsformen des Widerstandes* (Berlin, 2006), pp. 55 f. Feldman, who during the research project also spoke with Niemöller, draws the opposite conclusion. A manuscript of the conversation between Heinz Hermann Niemöller, Barbara Eggenkämper and Gerald Feldman in September 1997 is to be found in the Allianz Center for Corporate History.

21 Feldman, *Allianz*, p. 58.

22 Gideon Botsch, "Von der Judenfeindschaft zum Antisemitismus. Ein historischer Überblick," *Aus Politik und Zeitgeschichte* 28–30 (2014), p. 15.

23 Kurt Schmitt, "Erinnerungen, nach 1945," in: FHA, NL1/133, pp. 22 f.

24 BArch, former BDC, SSO Dr. Kurt Schmitt (7.10.1886): Schmitt's personnel file with the SS.

25 Compare Karl Rasche's path to the Freundeskreis. He was a member of the board of directors of the Dresdner Bank: Johannes Bähr, *Die Dresdner Bank in der Wirtschaft des Dritten Reiches* (Munich, 2006), pp. 478–80; on Schmitt: Feldman, *Allianz*, p. 104.

26 BArch, former BDC, SSO Dr. Kurt Schmitt (7.10.1886), PK Dr. Kurt Schmitt (7.10.1886), NSDAP membership file of Dr. Kurt Schmitt (7.10.1886); ibid., NSDAP membership file of August von Finck (18.7.1898), PK August von Finck (18.7.1898); ibid., NSDAP membership file of Georg König (2.6.1880); ibid., NSDAP membership file of Ludwig Neumüller (7.8.1884); ibid., NSDAP membership file of Wilhelm Arendts (6.2.1883), PK Wilhelm Arendts (6.2.1883); ibid., NSDAP membership file of Dr. Alfred Wiedemann (21.1.1883); ibid., NSDAP membership file of Dr. Hans Goudefroy (8.2.1900); ibid., Parteistatistische Erhebung Dr. Hans Goudefroy (8.2.1900); ibid., NSDAP membership file of Dr. Walter Eggerss (24.5.1890) (Eggerss left the party in December 1935); ibid., NSDAP membership file of Dr. Hans Schmidt-Polex (2.10.1900); ibid., NSDAP membership file of Dr. Gerd Müller (20.11.1903); ibid., NSDAP membership file of Martin Herzog (15.9.1909); ibid., NSDAP membership file of Eduard Hilgard (1.3.1884), Parteistatistische Erhebung Eduard Hilgard (1.3.1884).

27 Letter from Heß to Schmitt, Agnesdorf, November 8, 1945, p. 1, in: FHA, NL 1/20.

28 Feldman, *Allianz*, p. 79; interrogation of Edgar von Uexküll by the American military government, Tübingen, June 9, 1947, in: NA, RG 260, OMGUS, FINAD, 2/57/4; for a conflicting account of von Helldorf's biography see: Ted Harrisson, "'Alter Kämpfer' im Widerstand. Graf Helldorff, die NS-Bewegung und die Opposition gegen Hitler," *Vierteljahrshefte für Zeitgeschichte* 43 (1997), pp. 385–423.

29 Hans Heß's statement under oath, "Meine politische Einstellung, in Sonderheit zum Nationalsozialismus," Agnesdorf, August 5, 1945; interrogation of Edgar von Uexküll by the American military government, Tübingen, June 9, 1947, in: NA, RG 260, OMGUS, FINAD, 2/57/4.

30 Minutes of the 21st meeting of the expanded board of directors on May 10, 1933, p. 5, in: FHA, S 17.2/4.

31 *Allianz Zeitung* 15 (1933), 8, p. 214; for further commentary see *Deutsche-Versicherungs-Presse* (Berlin, August 31, 1933).

32 Alfred Zaubitzer, "Der Außendienst im neuen Deutschland," *Allianz Zeitung* 15 (1933), 8, p. 215.

33 Minutes of the 22nd meeting of the expanded board of directors on September 8, 1933, p. 4 f., in: FHA, S 17.2/4.

34 Ibid., p. 5.

35 Allianz annual report of 1933, pp. 6 f., 47.

36 Quotation from: André François-Poncet, *Als Botschafter im "Dritten Reich". Die Erinnerungen des französischen Botschafters in Berlin September 1931 bis Oktober 1938* (Mainz & Berlin, 1980), p. 180; the last quotation found in: Jean-Marc Dreyfus, "'… und dann wählen sie Männer wie Hitler zum Werkzeug ihrer Katastrophe aus.' Die Berichterstattung Botschafter André François-Poncets," in: Bajohr & Strupp (eds.), *Fremde Blicke*, p. 146.

37 Klaus Dietmar Henke, *Die Dresdner Bank 1933–1945. Ökonomische Rationalität, Regimenähe, Mittäterschaft* (Munich, 2006), pp. 12 f.

38 See further Schwede-Coburg's detailed presentation in which he criticizes private insurance's integrity and questions its raison d'etre: Schwede-Coburg to Hermann Göring, Stettin, June 15, 1938, letter and attachment: notes about the conditions in private and public insurance industry with reform suggestions from the regional leader and Chief President Schwede-Coburg, in: SM, 1458/1/94, p. 1–41.

39 "Die Versicherung muss verdienen. Direktor Hilgard gegen unsachliche Kritik," *Frankfurter Zeitung* (October 28, 1938); quotation from: Reich Treasurer Schwarz to Göring, Munich, July 12, 1938, in: SM, 1458/1/92, sheets 128 f.

40 Concerning the argument between Hilgard and Schwede-Coburg and the nationalization debate: Feldman, *Allianz*, pp. 159–89; on the denunciation of Hilgard and Hans Heß, which stemmed from Schwede-Coburg's letter to the Gestapo citing reports of them as homosexuals, cf. ibid, p. 183. The information is taken from Hilgard's testimony at his interrogation by the American military authorities; Matthes's testimony taken from: Willi Alfred Boelcke, *Die deutsche Wirtschaft 1930–1945. Interna des Reichswirtschaftsministeriums* (Düsseldorf, 1983), p. 141.

41 Press review of Allianz's annual financial report for 1937: *Allianz Zeitung* 20 (1938), 7, pp. 145 f.; compare the more neutral description of the results of 1938 in *Völkischer Beobachter* (May 7, 1939).

42 Concerning the capital investment behavior of Allianz and state regulations: Feldman, *Allianz*, pp. 150 f., 424.

43 Circular of the Reich Group for Insurance to all the insurance companies that belonged to it, Berlin, January 13, 1943, p. 2, in: GDV, RS/22.

44 Allianz annual statements of 1933, p. 42, 1934, p. 44, 1938, p. 46, 1939, p. 13 and 48.

45 *Die Versicherung. Organ für Versicherung, Hypothekenwesen und Geldwirtschaft* 13 (September 22, 1938), p. 377; Feldman, *Allianz*, p. 289; Rüdiger Hachtmann, "Chaos und Ineffizienz in der Deutschen Arbeitsfront. Ein Evaluierungsbericht aus dem Jahr 1936," *Vierteljahrshefte für Zeitgeschichte* 53 (2005), p. 48; DAF insurance policies: Rüdiger Hachtmann, *Das Wirtschaftsimperium der Deutschen Arbeitsfront 1933–1945* (Göttingen, 2012), pp. 190–260.

46 Minutes of the 23rd meeting of the expanded board of directors on May 4, 1934, in: FHA, S 17.2/4, p. 4.

47 "Die Weltgeltung der deutschen Privatversicherung," *Allianz Zeitung* 17 (1935), 6, p. 164; report: Max Surner, "Das Auslands-Geschäft der Allianz und der zweite Weltkrieg, nach 1949," in: FHA, S 17/14/53.

48 I follow here Feldman's presentation: Feldman, *Allianz*, pp. 106–49.

49 "Zum Jahreswechsel," *Allianz Zeitung* 16 (1934), 1, p. 1.

50 Richard J. Evans, *Das Dritte Reich*, vol. II/2: *Diktatur* (Munich, 2006), pp. 558 f.

51 Minutes of the 26th meeting of the expanded board of directors on October 29, 1934, p. 4, in: FHA, S 17.2/4.

52 "Dr. Ley vor 3000 Versicherungsangestellten," *Völkischer Beobachter* (February 5, 1936), p. 2.

53 "Unsere Betriebsversammlung," *Allianz Zeitung* 18 (1936), 3, pp. 47–9.

54 Further, see Barbara Eggenkämper, Gerd Modert, & Stefan Pretzlik, *Die Frankfurter Versicherungs-AG 1865–2004* (Munich, 2004), pp. 92–4.

55 Feldman, *Allianz*, p. 116.

56 Attachment to the form "Leistungskampf der deutschen Betriebe" for the year 1940/41, in: BArch, NS 5 IV/260, sheet 3.

57 Attachment to the minutes of the meeting of the department managers of June 22, 1937, in: FHA, B 2.3.1/59.

58 Feldman, *Allianz*, p. 113; on the mobilizing function of the DAF: Wehler, *Gesellschaftsgeschichte 1914–1949*, pp. 771–4.

59 Feldman, *Allianz*, p. 120–4.

60 Allianz and Stuttgarter Verein Versicherungs-AG, Organization Department to the branches of Greater Berlin and Branch Management of Königsberg, Berlin August 15, 1933, in: FHA, AZ 5.1/3.

61 Circular of the management: Stuttgart department to all branch offices, the department for Greater Berlin and BG Frankfurt and Munich on Hunting Liability Insurance, Stuttgart, March 9, 1937, with a copy of the contract with the Reich Association, in: FHA, AZ 7.1/9. Feldman's interpretation relies with all due caution, above all, on the transcripts of Georg Amend's testimony when he was interrogated by the occupation authorities. Amend was the son-in-law of the treasurer of the Nazi Party, Franz Xaver Schwarz, and worked initially as the director of the insurance subdivision of the Nazi Party treasury and after 1939 as director of the Reich Supervisory Agency for Private Insurance.

62 Evans, *Diktatur*, p. 455; on Allianz's charitable contributions: Feldman, *Allianz*, p. 78; Eggenkämper, Modert, & Pretzlik, *Frankfurter*, pp. 91 f.

63 Notes on the meeting with the Presidential Committee of the Reich Association for Private Insurance on September 19, 1933, in Baden-Baden, Berlin, October 31, 1933, in: GDV, RS/12, p. 11.

64 Evans, *Diktatur*, p. 588.

65 Special Expenses 1938, attachment to circular 52a of November 23, 1936, in: FHA, S 17.1/79; Allianz annual report of 1943, p. 2.

66 Concerning the Jewish employees at Allianz in the Nazi years, see Feldman, *Allianz*, pp. 125–38; Eggenkämper, Modert, & Pretzlik, *Frankfurter*, pp. 94–101.

67 Röse to Gehrke, Frankfurt/Main, April 21, 1933, in: FHA, B 2.4.5/145.

68 Freudenburg to Hans Heß, December 11, 1934, in: FHA, B 2.4.5/134.

69 Lux to Wiedemann, Berlin, October 5, 1939; various file notes and news items from Wiedemann to Lux from Oktober 1939, newspaper article and the wording of the Reich Court verdict in: ibid.

70 Handwritten letters by Erika Freudenburg to Mr. Pfeiffer, Allianz Retirement Office in Frankfurt, January 28 and March 20, 1945, in: ibid.; written notice by Charlotte Perzine, Erika Freudenburg's sister-in-law.

71 Feldman, *Allianz*, p. 127.

72 Eichbaum to Heß, Johannesburg, June 28, 1947, in: FHA, NL3/6.

73 Concerning the following see: *Das Schwarze Korps* (November 19, 1936), p. 14; fur-

ther: Feldman, *Allianz*, pp. 129–35; as well as: Eggenkämper, Modert, & Pretzlik, *Frankfurter*, pp. 97–100.

74 Feldman, *Allianz*, p. 132.

75 Quotation: Maiholzer to Bünger, November 17, 1939, in: FHA, O 1.4.2/31; process: Bünger to Maiholzer, Cologne, November 11, 1939, in: ibid.; list "Jüdische Pensionäre der Versorgungskasse," November 28, 1939, in: ibid.

76 Rossmann to Arendts, Munich, November 14, 1939, in: ibid.

77 Lux to Arendts, November 22, 1939, in: ibid.

78 Handwritten list "Jewish pensioners" undated, in: FHA, O 1.4.2/31; nationality: Joseph Walk, *Das Sonderrecht für die Juden im NS-Staat*, 2nd ed. (Heidelberg, 1996), p. 357; list of names and internal instructions of the Allianz pension fund: file note by Maiholzer, Gut Grochwitz, November 17, 1944, in: FHA, O 1.4.2/31.

79 Memorial Book of the Federal Archive: URL: http://www.bundesarchiv.de/gedenkbuch/einfuehrung.html.de?page=2, accessed on September 29, 2014.

80 Quoted from Feldman, *Allianz*, p. 163; concerning the Night of Broken Glass in detail: ibid., pp. 190–235.

81 RGBl. I (1938), p. 1581.

82 Feldman, *Allianz*, p. 231.

83 Ibid., p. 236; life insurance policies of Jewish customers and their expropriation: ibid., p. 236–76.

84 Marita Roloff, "Exkurs: Der Österreichische Lebensphönix," in: idem & Alois Mosser, *Wiener Allianz. Gegründet 1860* (Vienna, 1991), pp. 135–55. Isar was taken over by Allianz in 1994 as a part of the Vereinte Versicherungsgruppe.

85 Riebesell and Eckert to the Reich and Prussian Economics Minister, Munich, November 17, 1938, in: BArch, B 280/3867, p. 75.

86 Feldman, *Allianz*, p. 241.

87 Figures: ibid., p. 247–9.

88 Ibid. p. 251.

89 RGBl. I, (1933), p. 479 f.

90 Walk, *Sonderrecht*, p. 399.

91 Feldman, *Allianz*, p. 272.

92 *Biographisches Gedenkbuch der Münchner Juden 1933–1945*; *Verzeichnis der gewerbepolizeilich gemeldeten jüdischen Gewerbetreibenden in München*: URL: http://www.rijo.homepage.t-online.de/pdf_2/DE_MU_JU_gewerbe.pdf, accessed on September 29, 2014.

93 Allianz bought a plot of land (around 250 sq. meters) located on Mohrenstraße from a Jewish inheritance association for the building project. It paid around 600,000 RM which was approximately 15 percent above the average assessed value in 1935. A letter from Clemens Maiholzer to Albert Speer suggests that the owner agreed to sell under the duress of the circumstances—the sale took place in October 1938, and the owner had a large tax bill due. In 1945, the building was located in the Soviet sector of Berlin and thus was expropriated and not restored to Allianz ownership after reunification: letter Allianz Leben, Clemens Maiholzer to Albert Speer, Berlin October 17, 1938, in: LAB, R 4606/2785.

94 Elementarphönix: Roloff & Mosser, *Wiener Allianz*, pp. 240–7; Feldman, *Allianz*, pp. 292–5; the authors each point to the significance of political pressure in the takeovers of the shares of the Creditanstalt and the Generali; Sudetenland: Feldman, *Allianz*, pp. 302 f.

95 Eduard Hilgard, "Südostkurs deutscher Versicherungswirtschaft," *Südost-Echo* (Vienna, December 20, 1940).

96 Allianz annual report of 1939, pp. 56 f.

97 Christopher Kopper, *Hjalmar Schacht. Aufstieg und Fall von Hitlers mächtigstem Bankier* (Munich, 2006), p. 314.

98 Mark Spoerer, & Jochen Streb, *Neue deutsche Wirtschaftsgeschichte des 20. Jahrhunderts* (Munich, 2013), p. 162.

99 Hilgard's rhetoric: Feldman, *Allianz*, p. 279.

100 Reforms of 1940: ibid., pp. 278–89.

101 File note by Kurt Schmitt, 1937, in: FHA, AZ 6/no call number: Gemeinschaftsvertrag.

102 According to Kurt Schmitt in: minutes of the 251st meeting of the supervisory board of Munich Re, Munich, April 16, 1940, in: FHA, MR A 3.4/5.

103 Heß to Kisskalt, Bad Nauheim, April 3, 1938, p. 1, 8 f., in: FHA, AZ 6/no call number: Gemeinschaftsvertrag.

104 Feldman, *Allianz*, p. 286.

105 Allianz and Allianz Leben annual reports (1939–1943); surcharges and interest: Eduard Hilgard, *Die Allianz im 2. Weltkrieg* (unpublished manuscript), p. 26, in: FHA, AZ 1.3/2.

106 Max Surner, "Das Auslandsgeschäft der Allianz und der zweite Weltkrieg" (undated manuscript), in: FHA, S 17.14/53.

107 Lux and Goudefroy to Alzheimer, Munich Re, November 17, 1942, in: FHA, AZ 6/no call number: Gemeinschaftsvertrag.

108 Feldman, *Allianz*, p. 354.

109 Circular from the Organization Department of Allianz, Berlin, December 15, 1941, in: FHA, S 17.14/53; Allianz and Munich Re in the Second World War: Feldman, *Allianz*, pp. 345–443.

110 Ibid., pp. 395–409.

111 *Assecuranz-Compass* 51 (1943), p. 529.

112 From a letter Ribbe wrote to Allianz, quotation from: Feldman, *Allianz*, pp. 403–5.

113 Ibid., p. 405–15.

114 Reports 1944/1945, in: FHA, S 17.18/124.

115 Allianz Leben annual report of 1943, p. 8.

116 Clemens Maiholzer, *Die Berliner Allianz-Betriebe* (unpublished manuscript) (Munich, 1960), pp. 108 f.; Frankfurt: Eggenkämper, Modert, & Pretzlik, *Frankfurter*, p. 110; deprivatization: Barbara Eggenkämper, Gerd Modert, & Stefan Pretzlik, *Die Staatliche Versicherung der DDR. Von der Gründung bis zur Integration in die Allianz* (Munich, 2010), pp. 21–48.

117 Denazification: Paul Hoser, "Entnazifizierung," in: *Historisches Lexikon Bayerns*, URL: http://www.historisches-lexikon-bayerns.de/artikel/artikel_46003, accessed on September 29, 2014; Allianz: Maiholzer, *Berliner Allianz-Betriebe*, pp. 163, 183–215; Feldman, *Allianz*, pp. 444–538.

118 Verdicts: ibid., pp. 451–87.

119 "Liebe Mitarbeiter," *Frankfurter Nachrichten* 16 (1948), p. 41.

120 Wehler, *Gesellschaftsgeschichte 1914–1949*, pp. 970–2.

121 Ibid., p. 951.

122 Spoerer, & Streb, *Wirtschaftsgeschichte*, p. 206.

123 Christoph Buchheim, "Die Errichtung der Bank deutscher Länder und die

Währungsreform in Westdeutschland," in: Deutsche Bundesbank, (ed.) *Fünfzig Jahre Deutsche Mark. Notenbank und Währung in Deutschland seit 1948* (Munich, 1998), pp. 117–31.

124 Ulrich Herbert, *Geschichte Deutschlands im 20. Jahrhundert* (Munich, 2014), p. 597.

125 Financial report of Allianz Leben for the period from January 1, 1944, to December 31, 1949, with the opening balance in DM, p. 27.

126 Buchheim, *Bank deutscher Länder*, p. 130.

127 Peter Borscheid, *100 Jahre Allianz* (Munich 1990), pp. 205–9.

1948–1970 · The Economic Miracle and Unlimited Growth

1 *Allianz Zeitung* 28 (1955), p. 5.

2 Note for director Dr. Maiholzer, Berlin, November 19, 1945, FHA, AZ 10/folder "Schriftwechsel der Sitzverlagerung bzw. Doppelsitz der Allianz;" materials on the question of moving the headquarters can be found primarily here and in FHA, AZ 6/folder "Handelsregister Sitzverlegung."

3 Transcript of the meeting of the board of directors of December 9, 1948, in Wiesbaden, FHA, AZ 3/binder "Dr. Goudefroy Allianz-Mutter Vorstandssitzungen 1946–54."

4 Letter from Finance Ministry to Lord Mayor Scharnagl, Munich, June 18, 1947, BArch, B 280/12393.

5 Transcript of file note by Karl Scharnagl of August 5, 1947, FHA, AZ 6/folder "Handelsregister Sitzverlegung."

6 Letter from Hilgard to Heß, September 4, 1948, FHA, AZ 6/folder "Handelsregister Sitzverlegung."

7 Hans Heß to the members of the supervisory board, Wiesbaden, January 4, 1949, FHA, AZ 6/folder "AR-Protokolle Allianz 1946–1961."

8 Preference for Frankfurt: letter from Goudefroy to Schiemann, October 5, 1948, FHA, AZ 10/folder "Schriftwechsel der Sitzverlagerung bzw. Doppelsitz der Allianz;" Goudefroy to the chairman of the board of directors, minutes of the supervisory board meeting, October 26, 1948, FHA, AZ 6/folder "AR-Protokolle Allianz 1946–1961;" on compensation claims, see, for example: file note "Bemerkungen zur Frage des Sitzes der Allianz," December 3, 1948, Dr. B./He., FHA, AZ 6/folder "Handelsregister Sitzverlegung."

9 Minutes of the board of directors meeting of December 9, 1948, in Wiesbaden, FHA, AZ 10/folder "Schriftwechsel der Sitzverlagerung bzw. Doppelsitz der Allianz."

10 Letter from Goudefroy to Bohl, December 27, 1948, FHA, AZ 6/folder "Handelsregister Sitzverlegung."

11 Goudefroy to Heß, Wiesbaden, December 13, 1948, FHA, NL 3/8; on the dispute between Heß and Schmitt see: Gerald D. Feldman, *Allianz and the German Insurance Business, 1933–1945* (Cambridge, 2001), p. 439 f.

12 Letter from Heß to the members of the supervisory board, Wiesbaden, January 4, 1948, FHA, AZ 6/folder "AR-Protokolle Allianz 1946–1961."

13 See the letter in response by supervisory board members; Karl Butzengeiger's response was not preserved, FHA, AZ 10/folder "Schriftwechsel der Sitzverlagerung bzw. Doppelsitz der Allianz."

14 Minutes of the extraordinary general meeting on January 27, 1948, FHA, AZ 6/folder "HV-Protokolle Allianz 1929 bis 1957."

15 Direktionspost, Munich, March 18, 1949, FHA, AZ 5.1/6; circular from the board of directors, August 1, 1949, FHA, AZ 3/folder "Dr. Goudefroy Allianz-Mutter Vorstandssitzungen 1946–54."

16 Letter from Dümmler to Haase, October 16, 1970, FHA, AZ 3/folder "Dr. Dümmler."

17 *Allianz Zeitung* 22 (1949), p. 14.

18 FHA, B 23/folder "München Königinstraße 28 Bauvorhaben Ost bis 31.8.1953."

19 Gerd Modert, "Die Architektur," text for the exhibition curated by Barbara Eggenkämper, Gerd Modert, & Stefan Pretzlik, *Arbeitswelten gestern heute – 50 Jahre Hauptverwaltung der Allianz in München*, FHA, AZ 10/"Projekt 50 Jahre HV."

20 A current appreciation of the building and its creator can be found here: Reem Almannai & Florian Fischer, "The Essence of Things. Josef Wiedemann's Building for the Alliance Headquarters," *oase, journal of architecture, codes and continuity* 92 (2014), pp. 56 ff.

21 Quotation Goudefroy: printed report by Goudefroy of the annual general meeting of Allianz on January 25, 1955, FHA, AZ 6/folder "Merck Finck II 24.11.1954 bis 25.1.1955," p. 14; minutes of the meeting on January 8, 1952, and minutes of the meeting of the board of directors of the Allianz Pension Fund on January 29, 1952, FHA, B 15/folder "1341 AVK 1950–1953," sheet 10; on its self-conception: draft of an affidavit by Eduard Hilgard and letter from Maiholzer to Eversmann, August 11, 1951, p. 3, FHA, B 15/folder "134 AVK 1912–1952"; the last two folders contain copious material upon which the further exposition is based.

22 Martin Brugmayer, "Notizen und Auszüge aus meinen 'Erinnerungen'," FHA, AZ 10/no call number.

23 FHA, B 15/folder "134 AVK 1912–1952;" FHA, B 15/folder "1341 AVK 1950–1953;" minutes of the board of directors meeting of November 28, 1950, FHA, AZ 3/folder "Dr. Goudefroy Allianz-Mutter Vorstandssitzungen 1946–1954;" Ludwig Arps, *Wechselvolle Zeiten. 75 Jahre Allianz Versicherung 1890–1965* (Munich, 1965), pp. 165, 168; Peter Borscheid, *100 Jahre Allianz* (Munich, 1990), p. 138; Allianz Pension Fund annual report of 1990, pp. 22 ff.

24 The arguments about economic development are based on Hans-Ulrich Wehler, *Deutsche Gesellschaftsgeschichte*, vol. 5: *Bundesrepublik und DDR 1949–1990* (Munich, 2008), pp. 53 ff.; on car ownership figures: H. C. Graf von Seherr-Thoss, *Die deutsche Automobilindustrie*, 2nd rev. and exp. ed. (Stuttgart, 1979), pp. 634 f.

25 Minutes of the meeting of the expanded board of directors on April 24, 1950, FHA, AZ 3/folder "Dr. Goudefroy Allianz-Mutter Vorstandssitzungen 1946–54;" figures are derived from the statistical annual report of Allianz Versicherungs-AG of 1951, 1960, and 1970, FHA, AZ 2.

26 For detailed information on the Volkswagen Insurance Service: Heidrun Edelmann, *Vermögen als Vermächtnis. Leben und Werk der Stifter Christian und Asta Holler* (Munich, 2011), pp. 85 ff. and Barbara Eggenkämper, Gerd Modert, & Stefan Pretzlik, *Die Frankfurter Versicherungs-AG 1865–2004*, pp. 136 f., 145 ff.; the figures are derived from the statistical annual report of Allianz Versicherungs-AG of 1951, 1960, 1970 and 1971; the total number of policies was calculated from the number of policies at Allianz with its market share of 19 percent, FHA, AZ 2.

27 FHA, AZ 4/hanging folder "Walter Kappes;" *Allianz Zeitung* 23 (1950), p. 11.

28 Quote: Walter Kappes, "Humoristischer Wettbewerb bekämpft Unterversicherung," *Versicherungswirtschaft* 8 (1953), pp. 248 ff.; "Mit Humor gegen die Unterversicherung," *Allianz Zeitung* 26 (1953), pp. 18 f.; in the following years, Gerhard Brink-

mann illustrated countless ads for Allianz, see: Matthias Kretschmer, *Gerhard Brinkmann (1913–1990). Werbezeichnungen für die Dresdner Bank. Begleitheft zur Ausstellung* (Frankfurt/Main, 2008).

29 *Allianz Zeitung* 26 (1953), p. 65.

30 Figures: Allianz annual reports of 1953 and 1954, pp. 38 f.; quote: transcript of the meeting of the expanded board of directors of October 15, 1954, FHA, AZ 3/folder "Dr. Goudefroy Allianz-Mutter Vorstandssitzungen 1946–1954;" "Auf Regen folgt Geld," *Der Spiegel* 7 (1953), 17, p. 33.

31 Excerpt from the presentation by Dr. Müller-Lutz (Travel weather insurance conference on January 18–19, 1955), pp. 3 f., FHA AZ 7.6/archival box "Reisewetterversicherung, roter Band Tagung München, Anlage 3."

32 Attachment to circular no. 16/55 of May 4, 1955, Verein Südwestdeutscher Zeitungsverleger e.V., FHA, AZ 7.6/folder "Reisewetterversicherung (Presse)."

33 Statistical annual reports of Allianz Versicherungs-AG 1953 to 1967, FHA, AZ 2.

34 *Allianz Zeitung* 30 (1957), p. 134.

35 *Allianz Zeitung* 30 (1957), pp. 131, 134 f.; on Marion D.: FHA, B 2.4.5/file "Marion D."

36 "Eine zündende Werbung," *Allianz Zeitung* 31 (1958), p. 58.

37 *Allianz Zeitung* 38 (1965), 5.

38 Otto Ladner to the editor-in-chief of *Allianz Journal*, November 3, 1997, FHA, AZ 3/folder "Professor Müller-Lutz."

39 File note signed with "e" to the letter from Otto Ladner to Henning Schulte-Noelle of November 12, 1997, FHA, AZ 3/folder "Professor Müller-Lutz."

40 Remark to letter from Otto Ladner to Schulte-Noelle on November 1, 1997, FHA, AZ 3/folder "Professor Müller-Lutz."

41 Note for director-general Dr. Schieren, December 22, 1977, FHA, AZ 3/folder "Professor Müller-Lutz."

42 These facts are taken from: FHA, AZ 3/folder "Professor Müller-Lutz."

43 On fire insurance see the minutes of the meeting of the expanded board of directors on February 26/27, 1924, FHA, S 17.2/4, p. 8; FHA, AZ 19.1.1/vol. "Fünf Jahre Blockpolice," sheet 2, figures on block policies: FHA, AZ 19.1.3/1, sheet 249.

44 Attachment to letter from Müller-Lutz to Goudefroy on February 26, 1954, FHA, AZ 19.1.3/1, sheet 5.

45 Quote Goudefroy: note on conversation with Dr. Müller-Lutz of February 1, 1954, FHA, AZ 3/folder "Professor Müller-Lutz;" transcript of the meeting of the expanded board of directors on May 5, 1954, FHA, AZ 3/folder "Dr. Goudefroy Allianz-Mutter Vorstandssitzungen 1946–1954", p. 24.

46 Board of directors meeting on June 11, 1956, FHA, AZ 3/folder "Dr. Goudefroy Allianz-Mutter Vorstandssitzungen 1955 bis 1960;" transcript of the meeting of the expanded board of directors on May 5, 1954, FHA, AZ 3/folder "Dr. Goudefroy Allianz-Mutter Vorstandssitzungen 1946–1954," p. 8; letter from Müller-Lutz to Goudefroy, New York, October 15, 1954, FHA, AZ 19.1.3/1, sheets 172 f.

47 For detailed information on this: Barbara Eggenkämper, Gerd Modert, & Stefan Pretzlik, *Bits and Bytes for Business. 50 Jahre EDV bei der Allianz* (Munich, 2006); Alexander Metz, *Geschichte der Allianz-EDV/IT. Eine Chronik der DVZ/DVA/AGIS von 1926–2005* (Munich, 2005).

48 On Müller-Lutz's disillusionment: annual report of the business administration department 1957/58, p. 85, FHA, AZ 19.1.3/4; speech by Goudefroy to the branch managers: speech manuscript for the branch head conference on October 6, 1958, FHA,

AZ 3/folder "Ansprachen Dr. Goudefroy;" standard department: transcript of a meeting of the board of directors on April 7, 1959, FHA, AZ 3/folder "Dr. Goudefroy Allianz-Mutter Vorstandssitzungen 1955–1960;" on his illness: board of directors meeting on October 12, 1961, and report on the board of directors meeting of October 16, 1961, FHA, AZ 3/folder "Dr. Goudefroy Allianz-Mutter Vorstandssitzungen 1.1.1961 bis 31.12.1961;" Directorates: board of directors circular 1/62, February 1, 1962, FHA, AZ 19.1.2/vol. "Vorstandsrundschreiben 1962–1967."

49 Transcript of the 13th meeting of the structural commission on April 29/30, 1968, FHA, AZ 3/3, p. 9.

50 Otto Ladner to Henning Schulte-Noelle, November 12, 1997, FHA, AZ 3/folder "Professor Müller-Lutz."

51 Wehler, *Deutsche Gesellschaftsgeschichte 1949–1990*, p. 257.

52 Minutes of the meetings of the board of directors on March 7, 1950, April 24, 1950, and June 7, 1950, FHA, AZ 3/folder "Dr. Goudefroy Allianz-Mutter Vorstandssitzungen 1946–1954;" savings in personnel at Allianz Leben: minutes of board of directors meeting on October 25, 1951, ibid., p. 6.

53 Transcript of the board of directors meeting on October 25, 1950, FHA, AZ 3/folder "Dr. Goudefroy Allianz-Mutter Vorstandssitzungen 1946–1954," p. 6; transitional money: transcript of the meeting of the board of directors on November 28, 1950, ibid., p. 5.

54 Michael Gold et al., *60 Jahre AGV 1950–2010* (Munich, 2010); agreement: circular no. 1/51, January 18, 1951, FHA, B 3/folder "GD-Rundschreiben Personal und Verwaltung 13.1.1933–31.12.1964;" statistical annual report of Allianz Versicherungs-AG of 1970, FHA, AZ 2, sheet 106; downgrading: circular no. 37/49, FHA, AZ 5.1/6.

55 Gold et al., *60 Jahre AGV*, p. 33.

56 Quote: transcript of the meeting of the board of directors on March 3, 1969, FHA, AZ 3/folder "Vorstandsprotokolle ab 1968 bis 1969," p. 10; flexible working hours: *Unser Adler* 15 (1969), 6, 9, *Unser Adler* 17 (1971), 1; number of personnel: statistical annual report of the Allianz Versicherungs-AG of 1970, FHA, AZ 2, sheet 92.

57 *Unser Adler* 4 (1958), p. 50.

58 File note by Eversmann, Munich, February 20, 1951, FHA, AZ 6/folder "Aktienrecht, Arbeitnehmervertreter im Aufsichtsrat;" transcript of the 1st meeting of the working committee of the Allianz supervisory board on May 22, 1951, FHA, AZ 3/folder "Dr. Goudefroy Allianz-Mutter Arbeitsausschuss-Sitzungen 1951 bis 1956."

59 Transcript of the 3rd meeting of the working committee of the Allianz supervisory board on November 6, 1951, p. 11, FHA, AZ 3/folder "Dr. Goudefroy Allianz-Mutter Arbeitsausschuss-Sitzungen 1951 bis 1956."

60 Minutes of the supervisory board meeting on October 31, 1952, FHA, AZ 6/folder "AR-Protokolle Allianz 1946–1961."

61 Transcripts of the board of directors meetings on November 21, 1952, and April 16, 1953, FHA, AZ 3/folder "Dr. Goudefroy Allianz-Mutter Vorstandssitzungen 1946–1954," p. 5; transcript of the 6th meeting of the working committee of the Allianz supervisory board on October 30, 1952, FHA, AZ 3/folder "Dr. Goudefroy Allianz-Mutter Arbeitsausschuss-Sitzungen 1951 bis 1956."

62 Minutes of the supervisory board meeting on November 13, 1953, FHA, AZ 6/folder "AR-Protokolle Allianz 1946–1961;" in addition, a letter from the works council to Goudefroy, July 23, 1952, as well as other letters by Hooffacker, Goudefroy and others in June and July 1952, FHA, AZ 6/folder "Hooffacker bis zur Kündigung."

63 Minutes of the supervisory board meeting on November 13, 1953, FHA, AZ 6/folder "AR-Protokolle Allianz 1946–1961;" board of directors meeting on July 19, 1956, FHA, AZ 3/folder "Dr. Goudefroy Allianz-Mutter Vorstandssitzungen 1955–1960;" note signed by Graf Castell and Goudefroy, Munich, June 6, 1956, FHA, AZ 6/folder "Hooffacker bis zur Kündigung;" file note Graf Castell, Munich, December 6, 1955, FHA, AZ 6/folder "Aktienrecht, Arbeitnehmervertreter im Aufsichtsrat;" dismissal: file note Meyer, November 11, 1955, and file note from the legal dept., Munich, November 4, 1955, FHA, AZ 6/folder "Hooffacker bis zur Kündigung;" works council election: minutes of the election of the works council of the BVB of April 8, 1957, ibid.; Hooffacker's résumé: FHA, AZ 6/folder "Hooffacker nach dem Vergleich;" FHA, AZ 6/folder "Hooffacker nach der Kündigung;" FHA, AZ 6/folder "Hooffacker Kündigung I."

64 Quote BVB: letter from the BVB to the information center, February 16, 1961, FHA, AZ 6/folder "Hooffacker nach der Kündigung;" quote Mirow: Mirow to Schieren, December 13, 1972, FHA, AZ 6/folder "Hooffacker nach dem Vergleich."

65 Edgar Wolfrum, *Die geglückte Demokratie. Geschichte der Bundesrepublik Deutschland von den Anfängen bis zur Gegenwart* (Stuttgart, 2006), p. 86; Werner Abelshauser, *Deutsche Wirtschaftsgeschichte seit 1945* (Munich, 2004), pp. 352 ff.

66 *Allianz Zeitung* 25 (1952), p. 167; *Allianz Zeitung* 26 (1953), p. 158; *Allianz Zeitung* 30 (1957), p. 133.

67 "Die Grundgedanken, die Herrn Dr. Hess zur Gründung des Grosslebens-Klubs veranlassten, sind unverändert geblieben. Es geht weniger um die materielle Belohnung als darum, in besonders persönlicher Form unsere erfolgreichsten Mitarbeiter für ihre hervorragenden Erfolge zu ehren, ihren Ehrgeiz zu wecken und in ihnen das Gefühl der Solidarität und der Zugehörigkeit zu einer Gesellschaft von überragender Bedeutung zu stärken." "The basic ideas that drove Dr. Hess to found the Big Life club remain unchanged. It is less about material reward than about honoring our most successful colleagues for their outstanding successes in an especially personal way, to spark their ambition and to strengthen in them the feeling of solidarity and belonging to a company of remarkable meaning," circular no. 12/49 – Organization, Wiesbaden and Stuttgart, February 26, 1949, FHA, AZ 5.1/6; transcript of the meeting of the expanded board of directors on April 24, 1950, FHA, AZ 3/folder "Dr. Goudefroy Allianz-Mutter Vorstandssitzungen 1946–1954."

68 Circular on the new structure of benefits for full-time agents, February 3, 1965, FHA, AZ 5.4.1.1/folder "Neue Versorgung Rundschreiben I;" *25 Jahre Interessengemeinschaft. Eine Dokumentation der Allianz Hausvereine und ihrer Interessengemeinschaft*, p. 28; further information on benefits for representatives: Allianz pension fund annual report of 1990, p. 3.

69 *Allianz Zeitung* 30 (1957), p. 174.

70 An example of a display window ad: *Allianz Zeitung* 30 (1957), p. 184; Lichtboy: ibid., p. 191.

71 *Monatsmitteilungen der Allianz Lebensversicherungs-AG* (1948), 4, p. 3; *Allianz Zeitung* 23 (1950), p. 84.

72 *Allianz Zeitung* 31 (1958), pp. 184 f.

73 Short news items from the business administration department "Betriebswirtschaftliche Abteilung", 2, XI/1964, FHA, AZ 19.1.5.

74 Quote: *Allianz Zeitung* 34 (1961), p. 122; *Allianz Zeitung* 25 (1952), p. 59.

75 Allianz Leben annual reports of 1944/1949 and 1928.

76 Allianz Versicherungs-AG statistical annual report of 1956, FHA, AZ 2; *Monatsmitteilungen der Allianz Lebensversicherungs-AG* (1948), 7, p. 6.

77 Arps, *Wechselvolle Zeiten*, pp. 190 ff., Allianz statistical annual reports of 1956, 1970, FHA, AZ 2.

78 Allianz and Allianz Leben annual reports of 1970.

79 Allianz Leben annual reports of 1944/49; transcript of the meeting of the expanded board of directors on October 25, 1951, FHA, AZ 3/folder "Dr. Goudefroy Allianz-Mutter Vorstandssitzungen 1946–1954."

80 Allianz Versicherungs-AG statistical annual report of 1956, FHA, AZ 2, p. XII; Allianz Leben annual report of 1970, pp. 10, 24.

81 Table of yearly development of the German stock index DAX calculated back to 1937, URL: http://de.wikipedia.org/wiki/DAX, accessed on April 1, 2014; Allianz Leben annual report of 1958.

82 Files of August von Finck's denazification proceedings, Amtsgericht München now Staatsarchiv München; "Kampf um die Allianz," *Der Spiegel* 8 (1954), 51, pp. 15 ff.; on cross holdings, see, for example, transcript of the working committee meeting on July 3, 1954, FHA, AZ 3/folder "Dr. Goudefroy Allianz-Mutter Arbeitsausschuss-Sitzungen 1951 bis 1956;" on the syndicate contrast, see board of directors meeting on October 26, 1955, FHA, AZ 3/folder "Dr. Goudefroy Allianz-Mutter Vorstandssitzungen 1955 bis 1960;" FHA, AZ 6/folder "Merck Finck IV Verhandlungen über Separatio I + II 1955 bis 1959".

83 FHA, AZ 6/folder "Merck Finck IV Verhandlungen über Separatio I + II 1955 bis 1959;" transcript of the Allianz supervisory board meeting on December 10, 1954, FHA, AZ 6/folder "AR-Protokolle Allianz 1946 bis 1961."

84 Jürgen Beyer, "Deutschland AG a.D.: Deutsche Bank, Allianz und das Verflechtungszentrum großer deutscher Unternehmen," MPIfG Working Paper 02/4, URL: http://www.mpifg.de/pu/workpap/wp02-4/wp02-4.html [version of 29.03.2007 11:00], summary, accessed on January 5, 2015.

85 Note Dr. Wegener, February 19, 1954, FHA, AZ 3/folder "Dr. Goudefroy Allianz-Mutter Arbeitsausschuss-Sitzungen 1951 bis 1956;" transcript of board of directors meeting on April 18, 1957, FHA, AZ 3/folder "Dr. Goudefroy Allianz-Mutter Vorstandssitzungen 1955 bis 1960."

86 Quote on Germany, Inc.: Jürgen Beyer, "Deutschland AG a.D.," introduction; quote on influence: transcript of the meeting of the expanded board of directors on October 15, 1954, FHA, AZ 3/folder "Dr. Goudefroy Allianz-Mutter Vorstandssitzungen 1946–1954," p. 25; transcript of the working committee meeting on March 9, 1954, FHA, AZ 3/folder "Dr. Goudefroy Allianz-Mutter Arbeitsausschuss-Sitzungen 1951 bis 1956."

87 Transcript of the Allianz supervisory board meetings on November 3, 1955, and December 12, 1955, FHA, AZ 6/folder "AR-Protokolle Allianz 1946 bis 1961;" industry division: transcript of the meeting of the board of directors on June 11, 1956, FHA, AZ 3/folder "Dr. Goudefroy Allianz-Mutter Vorstandssitzungen 1955 bis 1960," p. 3 and supplement 2; transcript of the meeting of the board of directors on April 16, 1953, FHA, AZ 3/folder "Dr. Goudefroy Allianz-Mutter Vorstandssitzungen 1946–1954."

88 Transcript of the meeting of the board of directors on June 18, 1958, FHA, AZ 3/folder "Dr. Goudefroy Allianz-Mutter Vorstandssitzungen 1955 bis 1960," p. 13.

89 Cf. the very informative contribution by Christoph Julian Wehner, "Grenzen der Versicherbarkeit – Grenzen der Risikogesellschaft," *Archiv für Sozialgeschichte* 52 (2012), pp. 581–605.

90 The Frankfurter: excerpt from the transcript of the 18th meeting of the special commission for insurance supervision on March 9, 1951, in Weinheim, BArch, B 280/12389; the 3rd conference of Allianz managers, in: *Der Maschinenschaden* 25 (1952), pp. 57 f.; Walther Gerlach, "Technische Anwendungsmöglichkeiten der Atomversicherung," in: 3rd conference of managers on May 8 and 9, 1952, in Munich, convened by Allianz Versicherungs-AG, special printing of the presentations, FHA, B 9.

91 Future prospects: Goudefroy's list of key words for the board of directors meeting on June 11, 1956, FHA, AZ 3/folder "Dr. Goudefroy Allianz-Mutter Vorstandssitzungen 1955–1960;" quotations Pohl: Ernst Pohl, "Atomrisiko und Versicherung," *Versicherungswirtschaft* 10 (1955), pp. 548–50; GDV: GDV annual report 1957/1958, p. 67; quote supervisory board: transcript of the supervisory board meeting on July 10, 1956, FHA, AZ 6/folder "AR-Protokolle Allianz 1946–1961;" quote Goudefroy: Joachim Radkau, *Aufstieg und Krise der deutschen Atomwirtschaft 1945–1975* (Reinbek, 1983), p. 389.

92 Quote on the foundation: "Versicherungswirtschaft deckt Kernreaktor-Risiken," *Versicherungswirtschaft* 12 (1957), p. 155 and member assembly of the DKVG, in: ibid., p. 291; quote: Wehner, "Grenzen der Versicherbarkeit," p. 589; insurance policies at Allianz: *Allianz Zeitung* 43 (1970), 7/8.

93 Board of directors circular of Allianz Versicherungs-AG, Munich, August 1, 1949, FHA, AZ 3/folder "Dr. Goudefroy Allianz-Mutter Vorstandssitzungen 1946–1954."

94 Quote: GDV annual report 1948/49, p. 53; figures: "Wer von Deutschen kauft," *Der Spiegel* 4 (1950), 13, p. 31.

95 GDV annual reports of 1948–1951; law 36 brought further relief, especially for transportation and reinsurance: transcript of the meeting of the board of directors on September 27, 1950, FHA, AZ 3/folder "Dr. Goudefroy Allianz-Mutter Vorstandssitzungen 1946–1954;" quote "in all important places in the world:" Allianz Versicherungs-AG annual report of 1948/1952, p. 14; permission granted: letter from Bank Deutscher Länder to Allianz, Frankfurt, September 24, 1949, BArch, B 280/12388; quote Schlayer: transcript of the meeting of the board of directors on July 10, 1952, FHA, AZ 3/folder "Dr. Goudefroy Allianz-Mutter Vorstandssitzungen 1946–1954;" last restrictions lifted by Law of the Allied High Commision A – 15 of April 26, 1951, GDV annual report of 1950/51, pp. 23 ff.; AA, B 86/927.

96 On Herzog in Hungary: SM, 1458/104; letter to Wilhelm Zangen, December 3, 1952, FHA, AZ 3/folder "Herzog;" *Unser Adler* 18 (1972), p. 12; GDV annual report 1951/52, p. 30; bilateral regulation: AA, B 86/209; negotiations with Belgium: AA, B 86/695; with Belgium, the Netherlands, and Denmark: AA, B 86/1045; with Austria: AA, B 86482 and B 86/1025, with France: AA, B 86/189.

97 Transcript of the meeting of the board of directors on October 9, 1953, FHA, AZ 3/folder "Dr. Goudefroy Allianz-Mutter Vorstandssitzungen 1946–1954;" file note H. M. Huber, February 15, 1988, FHA, AZ 15.2/folder "Materialsammlung Ausland."

98 Transcript of the Allianz supervisory board on December 10, 1954, FHA, AZ 6/folder "AR-Protokolle Allianz 1946–1961."

99 Transcript of the board of directors meeting on February 11, 1955, FHA, AZ 3/folder "Dr. Goudefroy Allianz-Mutter Vorstandssitzungen 1955–1960;" file note H. M. Huber, February 15, 1988, FHA, AZ 15.2/folder "Materialsammlung Ausland;" note Herzog, June 24, 1957, FHA, AZ 3/folder "Dr. Goudefroy Allianz-Mutter Präsidialausschusssitzungen 1957–1961;" quote Goudefroy: transcripts of board of directors meetings on April 18, 1957, and June 18, 1958, FHA, AZ 3/folder "Dr. Goudefroy Allianz-Mutter Vorstandssitzungen 1955–1960;" minutes of the working committee meeting on July 9,

1956, FHA, AZ 3/folder "Dr. Goudefroy Allianz-Mutter Arbeitsausschuss-Sitzungen 1951 bis 1956;" transcript of the supervisory board meeting on November 11, 1959, FHA, AZ 6/folder "AR-Protokolle Allianz 1946–1961."

100 On the EEC: Gerhard Brunn, *Die Europäische Einigung von 1945 bis heute* (Bonn, 2004); quote: transcript of the meeting of the board of directors on August 13, 1962, FHA, AZ 3/folder "Vorstandssitzungen 1.1.1962 bis 31.4.1964;" transcript of the meeting of the board of directors on June 18, 1958; increase in capital: transcript of the meeting of the executive board on May 2, 1963, FHA, AZ 3/folder "Allianz-Mutter 1962 bis 1970 Präsidium."

101 Paris branch: *Allianz Zeitung* 33 (1960), p. 3; file note H. M. Huber, February 15, 1988, FHA, AZ 15.2/folder "Materialsammlung Ausland," "Die Allianz im Ausland."

102 Report of a board of directors meeting on August 13, 1962, FHA, AZ 3/folder "Vorstandssitzungen 1.1.1962 bis 31.4.1964."

1970–1990 · Paths of Internationalization

1 Harm G. Schröter, "Von der Teilung zur Wiedervereinigung (1945–2000)," in: Michael North (ed.), *Deutsche Wirtschaftsgeschichte. Ein Jahrtausend im Überblick* (Munich, 2000), pp. 351–82, especially pp. 365 and 380.

2 FHA, AZ 15.2/folder "Materialsammlung Ausland," "Die Allianz im Ausland," lecture (no author) to company insurance brokers on the occasion of the BVB meeting on April 12, 1988, p. 5.

3 *Allianz Zeitung* (1970), 7/8.

4 Cf. "Abschied in München und Stuttgart," *Unser Adler* (1971), 9, in this: "Generaldirektor Haase vor der Betriebsversammlung der GD am 19.7." (excerpt); life dates: Alfred Haase (1903–1972), Hans Goudefroy (1900–1961), Gerd Müller (1903–1975), Ernst Meyer (1908–1972).

5 "Abschlußtagung: Berlin wiederholt seinen Sieg. Allianz vor neuen großen Aufgaben," *Allianz Zeitung* (1970), 7/8.

6 FHA, AZ 3/folder "Allianz-Mutter, 1.1.1962–31.12.1970, Präsidium;" minutes of the meeting of the executive committee of the supervisory board of Allianz Versicherungs-Aktiengesellschaft on Friday, November 28, 1969, at 10 a.m. in Munich, p. 3.

7 Ibid., pp. 3 f.

8 Ibid. Cf. Allianz annual report of 1986.

9 "Abschied in München und Stuttgart," *Unser Adler* (1971), 9, in this: "Generaldirektor Haase vor der Betriebsversammlung der GD am 19.7." (excerpt).

10 Helmut Schelsky, *Die skeptische Generation* (Düsseldorf, 1957). Cf. address by Dr. Klaus Liesen, chairman of the supervisory board of Allianz AG, in: "*In Memoriam Dr. Wolfgang Schieren." Ansprachen bei der Trauerfeier in der Hauptverwaltung der Allianz AG, 1.3.1996,* Liesen uses the expression "skeptical generation" in connection with Wolfgang Schieren.

11 Bernd Weisbrod, "Generation und Generationalität in der Neueren Geschichte," *Aus Politik und Zeitgeschichte* 8 (February 21, 2005), pp. 3–10, here p. 5.

12 "*In Memoriam Dr. Wolfgang Schieren.*"

13 FHA, AZ 3/portfolio "Dr. Schieren, W. I.," contract correspondence, letter from Wilhelm Eversmann of October 19, 1956, to director Ludwig Schorling, Cologne, with the note: "Dr. Schieren is also known to Dr. Goudefroy."

14 *Allianz Zeitung* (1970), 7/8 and Hermann Bößenecker, "Tränen wie bei Wasch-

weibern. Arno Paul Bäumers dreißigjährige Allianz mit der Allianz," *Die Zeit* (May 28, 1976).

15 "Veränderungen im Vorstand," *Unser Adler* (1971), 3.

16 "Die Rollen sind verteilt: Spiegel-Report über die Allianz, Europas mächtigste Versicherungsgruppe," *Der Spiegel* 31 (1977), 50, pp. 107–20, here p. 120.

17 "Arno Paul Bäumer wird 65," *Allianz Zeitung* (1985), 1, p. 3.

18 Arno Surminski, "Assekuranz im Orwell-Jahr," *Zeitschrift für Versicherungswesen* (1984), pp. 610–4, here p. 614.

19 Bößenecker, "Tränen."

20 Ibid.

21 Ibid. Cf. FHA, AZ 3/folder "Aufzeichnungen Dr. Peter Adolff aus der Zeit von 1976 bis 1981."

22 "Geschichten über Arno Paul Bäumer," no date, no author, p. 23 (booklet prepared by employees for Bäumer's 65th birthday, FHA).

23 *Allianz Adler* (1971), 3.

24 Both quotes from the speech by Wolfgang Schieren on March 13, 1986, on the departure of Helmut Bossenmaier, pp. 1–7, here pp. 3 and 6, in: FHA, AZ 3.3/pendant file folders "Helmut Bossenmaier," partly quoted from *Allianz Zeitung* (1986), 4, p. 4.

25 "Abschied in München und Stuttgart," *Unser Adler* (1971), 9, therein: "Generaldirektor Haase vor der Betriebsversammlung der GD am 19.7." (excerpt).

26 "Abschlußtagung in Berlin: Frankfurt gewann den Speerwerfer," *Allianz Zeitung* (1971), 7/8, therein: report by Ernst Meyer, head of the organization department.

27 Allianz annual report of 1970, p. 6.

28 Ibid.

29 Ibid., p. 7.

30 Cf. *Allianz Adler* (1971), 12.

31 "*In Memoriam Dr. Wolfgang Schieren,*" therein: "Traueransprache Dr. Henning Schulte-Noelle."

32 Peter Borscheid, *100 Jahre Allianz* (Munich, 1990), pp. 77 f.

33 Allianz annual report of 1970, pp. 12 f.

34 FHA, AZ 3/folder "Sach/AR-Sitzungen, Schieren ab Juli 1971 bis 7.12.1972." Dr. Werner Brugger to the general secretariat re supervisory board meeting on November 26, 1971, supplementary report for automotive line.

35 Cf. Barbara Eggenkämper, Gerd Modert, & Stefan Pretzlik, *Die Frankfurter Versicherungs-AG 1865–2004* (Munich, 2004), note 70; Allianz annual report of 1971, p. 8.

36 *Allianz Zeitung* (1973), 11.

37 Allianz annual report of 1963, p. 7. Cf. also Eggenkämper, Modert, & Pretzlik, *Frankfurter*, pp. 140 ff.

38 Ibid., note 69.

39 Ibid., p. 140, and German Federal Bureau of Statistics (Wiesbaden, 2013), URL: https://www.destatis.de/DE/ZahlenFakten/Wirtschaftsbereiche/TransportVerkehr/ Verkehrsunfaelle/Tabellen/PolizeilichErfassteUnfaelle.html, accessed on September 9, 2014.

40 FHA, AZ 3/folder "Sach/AR-Sitzungen, Schieren ab Juli 1971 bis 7.12.1972;" Dr. Werner Brugger to the general secretariat re supervisory board meeting on November 26, 1971, supplementary report for automotive line.

41 Eggenkämper, Modert, & Pretzlik, *Frankfurter*, pp. 143 f.

42 FHA, AZ 15.2/folder "Material Jubiläum, Ressorts Inland." "Bericht Ressort Kraftschaden," Wolfgang Veit, of July 15, 1988, pp. 15–7.

43 *Allianz Zeitung* (1985), 1, p. 3.

44 Eggenkämper, Modert, & Pretzlik, *Frankfurter*, p. 140. Cf. on origins and responsibilities of the Allianz Center for Technology: Dieter Anselm, Barbara Eggenkämper, Gerd Modert, Stefan Pretzlik, & Heike Stretz (eds.), *AZT Automotive. Lösungen aus der Versicherungswirtschaft* (Munich, 2007), p. 27, and FHA, AZ 15.2./folder "Material Jubiläum, Ressorts Inland," Max Danner, "Das Allianz Zentrum für Technik – Institut Kraftfahrzeugtechnik, Rückblick und Ausblick."

45 Anselm, Eggenkämper, Modert, Pretzlik, & Stretz (eds.), *AZT Automotive*, pp. 27 f., and Federal Bureau of Statistics (Wiesbaden, 2013), p. 26.

46 Note for Director Eversmann on the minutes of the meeting of the supervisory board on November 15, 1956, in: FHA, AZ 6/folder "AR-Protokolle Allianz, 1946–1961."

47 Cf. Wikipedia entry, URL: http://de.wikipedia.org/wiki/Maximilian_Danner, accessed on September 29, 2014.

48 Allianz annual report of 1984, p. 14.

49 "Sichere Autos sind kaum teurer," *Allianz Adler* (1972), 6.

50 Max Danner, *Gurt oder Tod* (Percha & Starnberg, 1983).

51 *Allianz Zeitung* (1982), 11, p. 6.

52 Anselm, Eggenkämper, Modert, Pretzlik, & Stretz (eds.), *AZT Automotive*, pp. 27 f., and Federal Bureau of Statistics (Wiesbaden, 2013), p. 1 f.

53 Reiner Hagemann, "25 Jahre Institut KFZ-Technik im AZT, Festrede vom 27.11.1996, Ismaning" (manuscript), in: FHA, B9/"25 Jahre AZT."

54 Anselm, Eggenkämper, Modert, Pretzlik, & Stretz (eds.), *AZT Automotive*, p. 31.

55 Ernst Meyer & Ernst Jacobi, *Typische Unfallursachen im deutschen Straßenverkehr, dargestellt anhand einer statistischen Untersuchung*, 2 vols. (no place, 1961). The study became a fundamental work.

56 Cf. on this section: Anselm, Eggenkämper, Modert, Pretzlik, & Stretz (eds.), *AZT Automotive*, pp. 23–5, and Eggenkämper, Modert, & Pretzlik, *Frankfurter*, p. 140.

57 Ibid., p. 214.

58 Barbara Eggenkämper, "Die Vision vom 'aktenlosen Büro.' Von der Lochkarte zum Computer," in: Burkhart Lauterbach (ed.), *Großstadtmenschen. Die Welt der Angestellten* (Frankfurt/Main, 1995), pp. 228–48, esp. pp. 238–44; *Unser Computerreport*, supplement of the *Allianz Zeitung* (1969–1976), nos. 1–66, here nos. 32 and 43.

59 Barbara Eggenkämper, Gerd Modert, & Stefan Pretzlik, *Bits and Bytes for Business. 50 Jahre EDV bei der Allianz* (Munich, 2006), p. 75.

60 FHA, AZ 3/"Vorstandssitzungen Juli 1975–September 1976," minutes of the board of directors meeting on February 9 and 10, 1976, pp. 7 f.

61 FHA, AZ 3/"Vorstandssitzungen Juli 1975–September 1976," minutes of the board of directors meeting on March 8, 1976, pp. 1 and 5.

62 Eggenkämper, Modert, & Pretzlik, *Bits and Bytes*, pp. 74 f.

63 Speech by Dr. Klaus Liesen, chairman of the supervisory board of Allianz AG, in: "*In Memoriam Dr. Wolfgang Schieren*."

64 FHA, AZ 19.1/"20 Jahre BWA," speech by Prof. Müller-Lutz on April 1, 1976, see also Eggenkämper, "Lochkarte," p. 244.

65 *Allianz Adler* (1973), 12.

66 FHA, AZ 19.1/25, "BWA-Jahresbericht 1976 (XXIII)," p. 25, and Eggenkämper, Modert, & Pretzlik, *Bits and Bytes*, pp. 75 f.

67 *Allianz Zeitung* (1978), 6, p. 6

68 *Allianz Zeitung* (1978), 1, p. 3, and FHA, AZ 19.1.3/25, "BWA-Jahresbericht 1976 (XXIII)," p. 1.

69 FHA, AZ 3/folder "Materialsammlung Peter Adolff," note from Dr. Peter Adolff to Dr. Wolfgang Schieren of November 12, 1979, pp. 3 f. The idea of "establishing a modern set of instruments for corporate management on the model of the manufacturing industry" had already been discussed in the Allianz board of directors in 1973.

70 FHA, AZ 3/folder "Vorstandssitzungen Januar 1975–September 1976," minutes of the meeting of the board of directors on February 3, 1975, pp. 6 f. "The planning data for marketing were drawn up for the first time at the level of the head office for 1975 – as an experiment, and to gain experience."

71 FHA, AZ 19.1.3/25, "BWA-Jahresbericht 1976 (XXIII)," Müller-Lutz had been using the business indicators for a long time to plan cost control. Cf. Bößenecker, "Tränen" and FHA, AZ 3/folder "Materialsammlung Peter Adolff," report by Dr. Adolff (Sec. 2) to Dr. Schieren of November 21, 1979, p. 1.

72 "The Administration, Personnel, Pension Administration, Law, Taxes, and Social Facilities sections reported to him." Cf. *Allianz Zeitung* (1977), 5, p. 3.

73 FHA, AZ 3/folder "Materialsammlung Peter Adolff," note from Dr. Peter Adolff to Dr. Wolfgang Schieren of November 12, 1979, p. 4.

74 *Allianz Zeitung* (1994), 7/8 (Stuttgart regional edition).

75 Allianz annual report of 1976, p. 22, and: "In den Vorstand berufen," *Allianz Zeitung* (1976), 7/8, p. 3. Rudolf Eversmann's section was divided up among Franz Link and Peter Adolff. Peter Adolff was responsible for administration, accounting, and taxes. That included the subject of integrated planning.

76 FHA, AZ 3/folder "Materialsammlung Peter Adolff," note from Dr. Peter Adolff to Dr. Wolfgang Schieren of November 12, 1979, p. 10, quote on pp. 4 f.

77 Allianz annual report of 1976, p. 22.

78 FHA, AZ 3/folder "Materialsammlung Peter Adolff," presentation for the department directors meeting of Allianz Versicherungs-AG on October 4, 1978.

79 FHA, AZ 3/folder "Materialsammlung Peter Adolff," note from Dr. Peter Adolff to Dr. Wolfgang Schieren of November 12, 1979, p. 28.

80 FHA, AZ 3/folder "Materialsammlung Peter Adolff," note by Dr. Seitz of June 25, 1979, re definition of planning targets for international divisions, pp. 1–4.

81 Allianz Aktiengesellschaft Holding (ed.), *100 Jahre im Zeichen des Adlers* (Munich, 1991), p. 29; Allianz Leben annual report of 1990, and Allianz Leben annual report of 2002. The consolidation of the figures, including the life insurance companies abroad, was done in 1990.

82 Cf. Hans Georg Lehmann, *Deutschland Chronik 1945 bis 1995* (Bonn, 1996), p. 510.

83 Cf. on the pension system the corresponding sections in: Hans-Ulrich Wehler, *Deutsche Gesellschaftsgeschichte*, vol. 5: *Bundesrepublik und DDR 1949–1990* (Munich, 2008), pp. 264–7, Rudolf Morsey, *Die Bundesrepublik Deutschland, Entstehung und Entwicklung bis 1969* (Munich, 1995), pp. 187–8, and Wolfgang Beywl, *Soziale Sicherung* (Berlin, 1994), pp. 85 ff. Cf. especially p. 87 "... die Renten sind sicher!"

84 *Allianz Adler* (1972), 12.

85 "Monatsmitteilungen der Allianz Lebensversicherungs-AG," *Allianz Zeitung* (1971), 7.

86 "Monatsmitteilungen der Allianz Lebensversicherungs-AG," *Allianz Zeitung* (1971), 2.

87 "Monatsmitteilungen der Allianz Lebensversicherungs-AG," *Allianz Zeitung* (1971), 7/8.

88 FHA, AZ 3/folder "Vorstandssitzungen Januar 1973–Januar 1975," minutes of meeting of board of directors on April 30, 1974, p. 20.

89 Allianz Leben annual report of 1970.

90 Johannes Bähr, *50 Jahre dit. Aufbruch, Wachstum, Zukunft, 1955–2005* (Frankfurt/Main, 2006), pp. 12–4 and p. 20.

91 "Betriebliche Altersversorgung durch Lebensversicherung nach wie vor im Aufwärtstrend," *Allianz Zeitung* (1986), 11, p. 10.

92 *Allianz Zeitung* (1982), 10, p. 11.

93 FHA, AZ 3.3/portfolio,"Gerhard Rupprecht," Intranet message of Allianz Deutschland AG of August 19, 2014, "Allianz trauert um Gerhard Rupprecht," and FHA, AZ 15.2/folder "Material Jubiläum, Ressorts Inland," therein: Bernd Honsel, "Entwicklung der Allianz-Strukturen," p. 2.

94 Hans G. Meyen, *120 Jahre Dresdner Bank. Unternehmens-Chronik 1872 bis 1992* (Frankfurt/Main, 1992), p. 316.

95 Deutsche Bank, *Group Brand Communications* 2011: "Markengeschichte: Die Entwicklung des Deutsche Bank Logos," p. 3.

96 All Dorschel quotes: FHA, AZ 10/folder "Interviews," Interview Hansjörg Dorschel of December 28, 2004, p. 8 and p.12.

97 FHA, AZ 10/folder "Interviews," Interview Barbara Eichberger of February 3, 2005, p. 2.

98 FHA, AZ 10/folder "Interviews," Interview Hansjörg Dorschel of December 28, 2004, p. 10. At the meeting of the board of directors, Dr. Müller-Lutz took a critical position because of the enormous effort and the costs associated with this, and Rudolf Eversmann rejected the project.

99 FHA, AZ 3/folder "Vorstandssitzungen vom Juli 1975–September 1976," therein: minutes of the meeting of the board of directors on August 4, 1975, p. 6, and FHA, AZ 10/folder "Interviews," Interview Barbara Eichberger, Marketing/Advertising, of February 3, 2005, p. 2.

100 FHA, AZ 3/folder "Vorstandssitzungen vom Juli 1975–September 1976," minutes of the meeting of the board of directors on June 14, 1976, pp. 3 f.

101 FHA, AZ 11/folder "Gestaltungsrichtlinien für ein einheitliches Erscheinungsbild der Allianz-Gesellschaften, 1977."

102 Rudolf Hensel, *50 Jahre Allianz 1890–1940* (Berlin, 1940), p. 22.

103 FHA, AZ 10/folder "Interviews," Interview Barbara Eichberger, Marketing/Advertising, of February 3, 2005, p. 3, and *Allianz Zeitung* (1986), 12, p. 4.

104 *Allianz Zeitung* (1976), 6, pp. 2 f.

105 FHA, AZ 3/folder "Vorstandssitzungen vom Juli 1975–September 1976," minutes of the meeting of the board of directors on March 8, 1976, pp. 8–10.

106 Matthias Kretschmer, *Gerhard Brinkmann (1913–1990). Werbezeichnungen für die Dresdner Bank*. Begleitheft zur Ausstellung (Frankfurt/Main, 2008).

107 FHA, AZ 11/folder "Werbemittel 1976," Allianz Report International (1976), p. 6.

108 *Allianz Zeitung* (1977), 5, p. 2.

109 FHA, AZ 9/folder "Kernkraftversicherung," TV-Schaden, Koordinierungsstelle Kernenergie-Anlagen-Versicherung, Dipl.-Ing. Klaus Kaspar, "Versicherung von Kernenergie-Anlagen, Bericht über das Jahr 1986," Munich, April 1987, p. 15.

110 FHA, AZ 3/folder "Vorstandsprotokolle Januar 1973–Januar 1975," minutes of the meeting of the board of directors on May 27, 1974, p. 17.

111 FHA, AZ 9/folder "Kernkraftversicherung," letter from Heinz Braun to the department heads of engineering insurance and the engineering office of

engineering insurance of June 7, 1974, re coordinating office for nuclear plant insurance, p. 1, and letter from Dr. Opitz, Dr. Müller and Dr. Braun to the branch heads, director of the departments F., H., TV, members of the board of directors, directors of June 20, 1974, "Nuclear plant insurance," p. 1.

112 Allianz Leben annual report of 1970, p. 13.

113 Jürgen Feldmann, "Können Kernkraftwerke versichert werden?," *Allianz Zeitung* (1975), 2, pp. 2 f., here p. 2.

114 "Wie sind Kernkraftwerke in der Bundesrepublik versichert?," *Allianz Zeitung* (1977), 5, p. 4.

115 Jürgen Feldmann, "Immer mehr Kernkraftwerke," *Allianz Zeitung* (1970), 7/8.

116 *Allianz Zeitung* (1970), 7/8. The company also insured the transportation risk for "heavy parts," such as fuel assemblies, extended liability, and fire risk.

117 *Allianz Zeitung* (1976), 7/8, p. 9.

118 Feldmann, "Können Kernkraftwerke versichert werden?," p. 3.

119 Schröter, *Teilung*, p. 395

120 "Wie gefährlich sind Kernkraftwerke?," *Allianz Zeitung* (1977), 5, pp. 2–4.

121 "Die Allianz versichert auch künftig Kernkraftwerke," *Allianz Zeitung* (1979), 7/8, p. 4.

122 FHA, AZ 9/folder "Kernkraftversicherung, TV-Schaden, Koordinierungsstelle Kernenergie-Anlagen-Versicherung," Dipl.-Ing. Klaus Kaspar, "Versicherung von Kernenergie-Anlagen, Bericht über das Jahr 1986," Munich, April 1987, p. 14.

123 Dr. Wolfgang Müller, note for Mr. Reinicke and Dr. Seyfried of August 6, 1986, speech at annual general meeting by Dr. Schieren with draft text on the topic "Kernkraftrisiko nach Tschernobyl," in: FHA, AZ 9/folder "Kernkraftversicherung," therein: Interview for broadcast by WDR 1 of July 3, 1986, with Wolfgang Müller, in charge of liability insurance on Allianz board of directors.

124 Christoph Julian Wehner, "Grenzen der Versicherbarkeit – Grenzen der Risikogesellschaft," *Archiv für Sozialgeschichte* 52 (2012), pp. 581–605, here p. 605.

125 Ulrich Beck, *Weltrisikogesellschaft. Auf der Suche nach der verlorenen Sicherheit* (Frankfurt/Main, 2007), pp. 246 f. and p. 251.

126 Wehner, "Grenzen der Versicherbarkeit," p. 605.

127 John R. McNeill & Peter Engelke, "Mensch und Umwelt im Zeitalter des Anthropozän," in: Akira Iriye & Jürgen Osterhammel (eds.), *Geschichte der Welt 1945 bis heute. Die Globalisierte Welt* (Munich, 2013), pp. 495–502 and p. 514.

128 *Allianz Journal* 2 (1991), pp. 35–7, see also further initiatives in: McNeill & Engelke, "Mensch und Umwelt," pp. 357–534 and p. 514.

129 "Der Heß-Club tagte in Florenz," *Allianz Adler* (1970), 11.

130 Ibid. and "Zur Versicherung von Auslandsrisiken," *Allianz Zeitung* (1968), 6, and "Das Auslandsgeschäft wird ausgebaut," *Allianz Zeitung* (1975), 5, pp. 1–4.

131 "Fünfzig Jahre 'La Pace'," *Allianz Zeitung* (1970), 7/8, and "Dr. Bremkamp im Ruhestand – Nachfolger Detlev von der Burg," *Unser Adler* (1972), 7/8.

132 FHA, AZ 3/folder "Vorstandssitzungen vom Oktober 1976–Dezember 1977," minutes of the meeting of the board of directors on July 12, 1976, pp. 7–11. The alternative of merging the branches into La Pace, already considered here, did then occur after formation of the holding company and the purchase of RAS.

133 Ugo Irneri, *Cinquant'Anni Di Battaglie, Memorie di un Assicuratore* (Trieste, 1973), p. 49.

134 Ibid., pp. 100 f., and Pietro Marchetti, "Le compagnie italiane e l'internazionaliz-

zazione del mercato assicurativo: il caso Allianz," in: Paolo Garonna (ed.), *Assicurare: 150 anni di Unità d'Italia*. (Rome, 2011), pp. 152–65, here p. 163.

135 "Zur Versicherung von Auslandsrisiken," *Allianz Zeitung* (1968), 2.

136 FHA, AZ 3/folder "HV-Allianz Stenographische Protokolle vom 30.7.1958–18.7.1970, bzw. 8.8.1975," therein: speech by Alfred Haase to annual general assembly of Allianz Versicherungs-AG, Berlin-Munich on July 16, 1971, pp. 12 f., and: "Der Allianz Auslandsdienst," *Allianz Zeitung* (1971), 6. The Commercial Union Group has subsidiaries, branches, and agencies in about a hundred countries.

137 FHA, AZ 3/folder "Allianz-Mutter, 1.1.1962–31.12.1970," minutes of the meeting of the executive committee of the supervisory board of Allianz Versicherungs-AG on November 9, 1965, at 10 a.m. in Munich, pp. 1 f.; FHA, AZ 3.3/folder "Vorstandsprotokolle ab 1968 bis 1969," minutes of the meeting of the board of directors on July 1, 1968, at 9:30 a.m., p. 16, and described in detail in Borscheid, *100 Jahre Allianz*, p. 453.

138 FHA, AZ 10/folder "Interviews," transcript of interview with Horst Fickel of March 24, 2014.

139 FHA, AZ 3/portfolio "Horst Fickel," "Stuttgarter Verein Branch Office of Allianz Versicherungs-AG, transportation department, suitability report for October 30, 1954."

140 FHA, AZ 3/portfolio "Horst Fickel," note of July 25, 1962.

141 FHA, AZ 3/portfolio "Vorstandssitzungen 1975," minutes of the meeting of the board of directors on October 6, 1975, p. 14.

142 *Allianz Zeitung* (1978), 2, p. 4.

143 FHA, AZ 3/portfolio "Horst Fickel," note, Munich May 14, 1969, and letter by [Martin] Herzog and [Heinz] Schöttler [personnel department] to Horst Fickel of May 30, 1969.

144 Cf. *Allianz Zeitung* (1978), 7/8, pp. 3 f.

145 Cf. Allianz annual report of 1983, p. 23.

146 FHA, AZ 3/portfolio "Horst Fickel," letter from Horst Fickel to Heinz Schöttler on January 21, 1971, with copy to Mr. Herzog, and *Allianz Adler* (1972), 12, and FHA, AZ 3/folder "Herzog."

147 "Der Allianz Auslandsdienst," *Allianz Zeitung* (1971), 6.

148 "*In Memoriam Dr. Wolfgang Schieren*," therein: "Traueransprache Dr. Henning Schulte-Noelle."

149 FHA, AZ 3/folder "Vorstandsprotokolle Januar 1973–Juni 1975," minutes of the meeting of the board of directors on November 4, 1974, 9:30 a.m., p. 3.

150 FHA, AZ 3/folder "Vorstandssitzungen vom Oktober 1976–Dezember 1977," minutes of the meeting of the board of directors on November 3, 1975, pp. 21–4, and *Allianz Zeitung* (1976), 9, p. 6.

151 *Allianz Zeitung* (1977), 12, p. 4.

152 *Financial Times* (March 1, 1988), quoted from: FHA, AZ 15.2/folder "Materialsammlung Ausland," "Die Allianz im Ausland," talk (no author given) to company insurance brokers on the occasion of the Bayerische Versicherungsbank meeting on April 12, 1988, pp. 1–43, esp. p. 27.

153 *Allianz Zeitung* (1973), 6. The *Allianz Zeitung* headline read "1972 a year of stabilization."

154 "Dr. Hans-Hess-Club tagte in London," *Allianz Adler* (1973), 12.

155 Ibid. and *Allianz Zeitung* (1974), 9, p. 6.

156 Allianz AG (ed.), *Expansion Abroad*, imprint from Willis Faber plc, London, "Review," Summer/Autumn 1986, p. 19, and *Allianz Zeitung* (1974), 9, p. 6.

157 "Dr. Hans-Hess-Club tagte in London," *Allianz Adler* (1973), 12.

158 "Stapellauf der 'Allianz International' in London," *Allianz Zeitung* (1975), 5, pp. 5 f.

159 *Allianz Zeitung* (1977), 12, pp. 3 f.

160 FHA, AZ 3/folder "Vorstandsprotokolle Januar 1973–Juni 1975," minutes of the meeting of the board of directors on May 16, 1975, p. 7.

161 FHA, AZ 3/folder "Vorstandssitzungen vom Oktober 1976–Dezember 1977," minutes of the meeting of the board of directors on March 16, 1976, pp. 5 f.

162 *Allianz Zeitung* (1977), 12, pp. 3 f.

163 "Zu Gast in München: Wiedersehen mit 'Ted'," *Allianz Zeitung* (1981), 5, p. 9.

164 FHA, AZ 15.2/folder "Materialsammlung Ausland," file note by Dr. Zimmermann, foreign department, of February 19, 1985, "Allianz im Ausland," p. 4.

165 *Allianz Zeitung* (1981), 4, pp. 1–3.

166 *In Memoriam Dr. Wolfgang Schieren*," therein: "Traueransprache Dr. Henning Schulte-Noelle."

167 FHA, AZ 3/folder "Vorstandsprotokolle Januar 1973–Juni 1975," minutes of the meeting of the board of directors on November 4, 1974, p. 3.

168 Ibid.

169 *Allianz Zeitung* (1987), 1, p. 3.

170 *Allianz Zeitung* (1978), 1, p. 3.

171 Cf. FHA, AZ 3/folder "Vorstandssitzungen vom Oktober 1976–Dezember 1977," minutes of the meeting of the board of directors on July 12, 1976, p. 12, and Allianz annual report of 1976, p. 11.

172 FHA, AZ 3/folder "Vorstandssitzungen 1976," meeting of board of directors on October 22, 1976, U.S.A., Allianz Insurance Company, Munich, October 22, 1976, Allianz Insurance Company, press release, October 1976, p. 2.

173 *Allianz Zeitung* (1978), 1, p. 3.

174 FHA, AZ 3/folder "Vorstandssitzungen vom Oktober 1976–Dezember 1977," minutes of the meeting of the board of directors on June 14, 1976, pp. 8–12, and *Allianz Zeitung* (1977) 7/8, pp. 6 f.

175 FHA, AZ 11/advertisement collection.

176 FHA, AZ 13.1/box file "Auslandsgeschäft", portfolio "Wolfgang Schlink," "10 Jahre Allianz in den U.S.A. 10 Jahre German Linked Business," Los Angeles, April 1987, p. 3.

177 FHA, AZ 3/folder "Vorstandssitzungen 1976," meeting of board of directors on October 22, 1976, U.S.A., Allianz Insurance Company, Munich, October 22, 1976, p. 5.

178 *Allianz Zeitung* (1978), 1, p. 3.

179 *Allianz Zeitung* (1977), 7/8, p. 6.

180 FHA, AZ 15.2/folder "Materialsammlung Ausland," file note by Dr. Zimmermann, foreign department, of February 19, 1985: "Allianz im Ausland," p. 4, and ibid., "Strategievortrag von der Burg," October 20, 1985, p. 4, and Thorsten C. Kölmel, *Das Auslandsgeschäft deutscher Versicherungsunternehmen in den U.S.A.* (Frankfurt/Main, 2000), p. 205.

181 Cf. *Allianz Zeitung* (1978), 1, p. 4.

182 Allianz annual report of 1991, p. 47.

183 "Where is the insurance industry headed?," in: World. Peat, Marwick, Mitchell & Co., (1982), 3, pp. 24–32, therein: Arno Paul Bäumer, chairman, Allianz (Munich), p. 25.

184 Ibid., p. 25.

185 Allianz annual report of 1992, p. 25, and Allianz annual report of 1991, p. 47.

186 Cf. the evaluation in the following paragraph based on FHA, AZ 13.1/AZOA, "Quartalsberichte des Ressorts H6/außereuropäisches Ausland" for the North America region, therein: evaluation of the quarterly reports by Christian Maenz, "Lebensversicherung USA 1990–1994," and FHA, AZ 15.2/folder "Materialsammlung Ausland," talk by Zimmermann, "Auslandsgeschäft der Allianz," February 4, 1986, p. 5, and FHA, AZ 15.2/folder "Materialsammlung Ausland," therein: file note Dr. Zimmermann, foreign department, of February 19, 1985: "Allianz im Ausland," p. 4.

187 Allianz annual report of 1992, p. 25.

188 Allianz annual report of 1994, p. 32; as well as Kölmel, *Auslandsgeschäft*, p. 206.

189 FHA, AZ 3/folder "Vorstandsprotokolle Januar 1973–Juni 1975," minutes of the meeting of the board of directors on November 4, 1974, p. 3.

190 Cf. the overview in Kölmel, *Auslandsgeschäft*, p. 189. Ten years later, Allianz also owned the Jefferson Insurance Company of New York, the AIC, Fireman's Fund and Allianz Life Minneapolis.

191 Cf. the figures for Fireman's Fund based on FHA, AZ 13.1/AZOA "Strategische Standortbestimmung 1993," and "Quartalsberichte des Ressorts H6/Außereuropäisches Ausland" for the North America region, therein: evaluation by Christian Maenz, "Sachversicherung USA 1990–1994," and "Lebensversicherung USA 1990–1994."

192 *100 Jahre im Zeichen des Adlers* (Munich, no year), p. 37; the consolidation of FFIC occurred on January 1, 1991.

193 Cf. on all figures for Fireman's Fund in the following paragraph: FHA, AZ 13.1./AZOA "Strategische Standortbestimmung 1993," and "Quartalsberichte des Ressorts H6/Außereuropäisches Ausland" for the North America region, therein: evaluation by Christian Maenz, "Sachversicherung USA 1990–1994."

194 Kölmel, *Auslandsgeschäft*, p. 204.

195 Allianz SE annual report of 2014, and press release "Allianz stellt Firmenkundengeschäft in den USA neu auf" by Allianz Global Corporate & Specialty and Fireman's Fund Insurance Company, Munich/Novato, September 17, 2014, cf. URL: https:// www.allianz.com/de/presse/news/geschaeftsfelder/versicherung/140917_allianz-stellt-firmenkundengeschaeft-in-usa-neu-auf.html, accessed on September 29, 2014.

196 *Allianz Zeitung* (1982), 1, p. 3.

197 "Aachener und Münchener Versicherungs-Gruppe, Versicherer unter dem Dach einer Holding konzentrieren," *Handelsblatt* (December 15–16, 1978), p. 25, and *Frankfurter Allgemeine Zeitung* (June 4, 1985), p. 13, quoted from: FHA, AZ 10/"Sammlung Interviews," interview Bernd Honsel October 2005, p. 2.

198 Cf. *Zeitschrift für Versicherungswesen* (1983), pp. 134 ff., quoted from: FHA, AZ 10/ "Sammlung Interviews," interview Bernd Honsel October 2005, p. 2.

199 FHA, AZ 10/"Sammlung Interviews," interview Bernd Honsel October 2005, pp. 7 f.

200 "Der Schlagabtausch: A shock to the system," *The Times* (London) (June 8, 1981), p. 16, and: "Eagle versus Adler," *Börsen-Zeitung* (June 13, 1981), p. 6. Cf. the extensive press documentation FHA, AZ 15.2/"Presseberichte zu Eagle Star 1981–1985," three volumes, and a detailed description of this "takeover thriller" in Borscheid, *100 Jahre Allianz*, pp. 461–5, and: "Lächerliches Angebot," *Die Welt am Sonntag* (November 6, 1983).

201 FHA, AZ 10/"Sammlung Interviews," interview Bernd Honsel October 2005, p. 9, reference to BAV inquiry to Allianz of December 20, 1983.

202 FHA, AZ 10/"Sammlung Interviews," interview Bernd Honsel October 2005, pp. 3 f., p. 10 (quote), p. 12 and p. 16.

203 FHA, AZ 6/57, "Ein neues Kapitel Allianz-Geschichte ist aufgeschlagen," pp. 2, 4, and 9.

204 The reference to the nomination is to be found in: "*In Memoriam Dr. Wolfgang Schieren*," in the address by Henning Schulte-Noelle.

205 FHA, AZ 15.2/folder "Materialsammlung Ausland," talk by Zimmermann, "Auslandsgeschäft der Allianz," February 4, 1986, pp. 1–9, pp. 3 and 5; Allianz Holding annual report of 1985, p. 18.

206 Ibid., file note of February 19, 1985, Dr. Zimmermann, foreign department, "Allianz im Ausland," pp. 5 f.

207 FHA, AZ 3/portfolio "Hauptversammlung," therein: Wolfgang Schieren, "Interne Vorstandsvorlage zur Hauptversammlungsvorbereitung für das Geschäftsjahr 1972."

208 FHA, AZH 3.4.4/portfolio "Mehrheitsbeteiligung an der französischen Versicherungsgruppe Via/Rhin et Moselle," therein: "Auslandsstrategie."

209 FHA, AZ 13.2/"Dokumentation Übernahme Cornhill 1985–1986," "Dr. jur. Wolfgang Schieren an die Herren des Ständigen Ausschusses im Aufsichtsrat der Allianz Aktiengesellschaft Holding vom 21.1.1986," p. 1.

210 FHA, AZ 3/folder "Vorstandssitzungen Januar 1978–Dezember 1979," therein: expertise with minutes of November 13, 1978, "Überlegungen zur Weiterentwicklung des Allianz-Engagements auf dem britischen Versicherungsmarkt vom 26. 10. 1978."

211 Cf. FHA, AZ 13.2/"Dokumentation Übernahme Cornhill 1985–1986," memo of foreign investments department (Becker) of April 25, 1986, to Dr. Schieren and Dr. Schiefer, re acquistion of Cornhill Insurance PLC, London, by Allianz, pp. 1–4.

212 Cf. the detailed description of the purchase negotiations with Cornhill, BTR, Kartellamt in: FHA, AZ 13.2/"Dokumentation Übernahme Cornhill 1985–1986," and in Borscheid, *100 Jahre Allianz*, pp. 465–7.

213 FHA, AZ 13.2/"Dokumentation Übernahme Cornhill, 1985–1986," Detlev Bremkamp, note concerning Cornhill Insurance Company, here: "Gespräch Dr. Schiefer und Unterzeichner mit C. G. Borrows/General Manager am 29.10.1985 in München," p. 2.

214 FHA, AZ 15.2/folder "Materialsammlung Ausland," "Die Allianz im Ausland," talk (no author) to company insurance brokers on the occasion of the BVB meeting on April 12, 1988, pp. 1–43, here p. 13.

215 FHA, AZ 3/folder "Vorstandssitzungen Januar 1978–Dezember 1979," therein: expertise with minutes of November 13, 1978, "Überlegungen zur Weiterentwicklung des Allianz-Engagements auf dem britischen Versicherungsmarkt vom 26.10.1978." And on this Mr. Geller on August 9, 1978. The analysis by the foreign department of 1978 had already shown that the focus of the business was on types of non-life insurance, with the lines liability, automobile, FBU/MBU, accident, and property, and transportation and aviation.

216 Josef Kolb, "Die Allianz in Großbritannien. Am Nabel der Versicherungswelt," *Allianz Journal* (1990), 4, pp. 19–23, here pp. 22 f.

217 FHA, AZ 10/"Sammlung Interviews", interview Rüdiger Schäfer of June 27, 2013, pp. 4 and 5.

218 FHA, AZ 13.2/"Dokumentation Cornhill Übernahme, 1985–1986;" "Dr. Wolfgang Schieren an die Herren des Ständigen Ausschusses im Aufsichtsrat der Allianz AG Holding, 21.1.1986," pp. 2 f.

219 *Allianz Zeitung* (1987), 2, p. 3, and Julian Faber, *75 Years of the Cornhill* (London, 1980), pp. 21–5, here p. 25.

220 FHA, AZ 13.2/"Dokumentation Cornhill Übernahme, 1985–1986," "Detlev Bremkamp an Dr. Wolfgang Schieren vom 16.12.1985 betr. Cornhill/England," p. 2.

221 Cornhill had branches and agencies in: Australia (Melbourne with seven agencies), Canada (Toronto and four other agencies) and New Zealand (Auckland with five agencies).

222 Cf. Friedrich Schiefer, "Integration der RAS, Zwischenbericht an den Aufsichtsrat der Allianz AG, 24. Februar 1988," in: FHA, AZ 15.2/"Chronik, Dokumentation und Presseberichte Mehrheitserwerb RAS 1984–1987, München, 1989," pp. 1–35.

223 *Allianz Journal* (1990), 1, p. 21. In the period from 1988 to 1990 the proportion increased from 7 percent in 1988 to more than 9 percent in 1990.

224 FHA, AZ 15.2/"Chronik, Dokumentation und Presseberichte Mehrheitserwerb RAS 1984–1987, München, 1989," p. 1 and p. 4. The Canadian business did not go well; Allianz has withdrawn from Canada in the meantime.

225 Cf. Marchetti, "Compagnie Italiane," pp. 153–65, esp. p. 157. The reinsurance company La Riassicuratrice, founded by RAS in 1917, was later taken over by Assicuratrice Italiana.

226 Cf. ibid., p. 162, and FHA, AZ 15.2/"Chronik, Dokumentation und Presseberichte Mehrheitserwerb RAS 1984–1987, München 1989," p. 4.

227 "Riunione Adriatica di Sicurtà. Ein internationaler Partner für die Allianz," *Allianz Zeitung* (1985), 2, p. 3.

228 Josef Kolb, "Ein europäisches Haus in Italien," in: *Allianz Journal* (1990), 1, pp. 19–22, here p. 22.

229 Cf. Marchetti, "Compagnie Italiane," pp. 154 f. Cf. on the origins of the business Erminio Tedeschi, *Aufzeichnungen für eine Geschichte. Ras: 1838–1988* (Milan, 1990), and RAS (ed.), *Nel primo Centenario della Riunione Adriatica di Sicurtà (1838–1938)* (Trieste 1939), and *Allianz Journal* (1990), 1, pp. 19–22.

230 Quotes in: "Riunione Adriatica di Sicurtà," p. 3.

231 Cf. Marchetti, "Compagnie Italiane," p. 156.

232 *Allianz Journal* (1990), 1, pp. 19–21, here p. 21.

233 Cf. Marchetti, "Compagnie Italiane," pp. 158–60.

234 FHA, AZ 15.2/"Chronik, Dokumentation und Presseberichte Mehrheitserwerb RAS 1984–1987, München, 1989," pp. 1–35, here p. 5.

235 Ibid., p. 8 and pp. 11 f. In parallel, Allianz secured an option on the 13.5-percent share of the Fiat group in RAS, for a fixed price and an option fee of 200 lira per share until the end of 1984. Allianz was only interested in obtaining both blocks so as to secure a majority holding in RAS.

236 Ibid., p. 17. Thus, in October, they managed to persuade Pesenti Jr. that "due to its corporate philosophy, Allianz provides a better guarantee for the preservation of RAS's corporate structure than other foreign competitors."

237 Friedrich Schiefer, "Integration der RAS, Zwischenbericht an den Aufsichtsrat der Allianz AG," February 24, 1988, ibid., pp. 25 and 32.

238 Ibid., p. 23.

239 FHA, AZ 15.2/folder "Materialsammlung Ausland," file note of February 19, 1985, Dr. Zimmermann, foreign department, talk "Die Allianz im Ausland," p. 2.

240 Allianz AG Holding annual report of 1987, p. 9.

241 FHA, AZ 15.2/"Chronik, Dokumentation und Presseberichte Mehrheitserwerb RAS 1984–1987, München 1989," pp. 4 f., and the quote in *Allianz Zeitung* (1985), 2, p. 4.

242 Allianz Holding annual report of 1985, p. 18, and FHA, AZ 15.2/folder "Materialsammlung Ausland," talk by Zimmermann, "Auslandsgeschäft der Allianz," February 4,

1986, p. 3, and Allianz Holding annual report of 1987, p. 14, and 1988, p. 15: Europe's share was 80 percent (78 percent), that of the U.S. 20 percent (20 percent).

243 "Auslandsbereiche neu gegliedert," *Allianz Zeitung* (1987), 2, p. 3.

244 Allianz Holding annual report of 1992, p. 25.

245 The companies in Italy: La Pace, with a staff of 500, did business in 1990 as Allianz Pace. The holdings were: La Pace/Allianz Pace: Allianz and Munich Re 40 percent each, 20 percent Generali, cf. *Allianz Journal* (1990), 1, p. 22.

246 FHA, AZ 15.2./ "Chronik, Dokumentation und Presseberichte Mehrheitserwerb RAS 1984–1987, München 1989," p. 33.

247 Quotes: Allianz Holding annual report of 1989, p. 47.

248 Allianz Holding annual report of 1989, p. 48, and 1990, p. 9.

249 Allianz Holding annual report of 1989, p. 9. In comparison: before 1989 the world-wide group revenues were based on 23 consolidated domestic firms, which accounted for about 40 percent of the worldwide turnover. Cf. Allianz Aktien-gesellschaft Holding (ed.), *100 Jahre im Zeichen des Adlers* (Munich, 1991), pp. 1–72, here p. 55.

250 Ralph Bryan Habich, "Das 'Europa-Projekt' der Allianz: Auf dem Weg ins Jahr 2000," *Allianz Journal* (1990), 3, pp. 12–5, here p. 12, and Jörn Badenhoop, "Die Zukunft der Versicherungswirtschaft im europäischen Binnenmarkt," *Verwaltungsrundschau* 45 (1990), pp. 137–42.

251 Herbert, *Geschichte Deutschlands*, p. 1034.

252 Eggenkämper, Modert, & Pretzlik, *Frankfurter*, p. 219.

253 Schröter, *Teilung*, pp. 384 f. and p. 398.

254 Herbert, *Geschichte Deutschlands*, p. 1040.

255 "European Workshop on Industrial Business. Generalprobe für Europa," *Allianz Journal* (1990), 1, p. 8.

256 Hermann Busch, "Das Kölner Modell in der Praxis: Der Kunde im Mittelpunkt," *Allianz Journal* (1991), 3, pp. 24–6.

257 *Der europäische Binnenmarkt und die Antwort der Allianz* (no place, 1992), pp. 1–10.

258 Hermann Busch, "Das Kölner Modell in der Praxis: Der Kunde im Mittelpunkt," *Allianz Journal* 3 (1991), pp. 24–6, here p. 24.

259 "Eurotunnel – ein Jahrhundertwerk," *Allianz Journal* (1989), 1, pp. 36–9, and Joa-chim R. Stephan, "Sprung über den Großen Belt: Brückenschlag zum ver-einten Europa," *Allianz Journal* (1990), 3, pp. 46 f., and Busch, "Das Kölner Modell," p. 24.

260 "European Workshop on Life Business. Erste Schritte auf dem Weg in den EG-Bin-nenmarkt," *Allianz Journal* (1990), 4, pp. 11 f.

261 Herbert, *Geschichte Deutschlands*, p. 1034.

262 "Allianz AG/Ungetrübtes Verhältnis zur Deutschen Bank. Schieren: 'Europa 92 ist für uns kein Datum mehr'," *Handelsblatt* (October 6, 1988).

1990–2015 · The International Financial Services Provider

1 Gerhard A. Ritter, *Über Deutschland. Die Bundesrepublik in der deutschen Geschichte* (Munich, 1998), p. 245.

2 Harm G. Schröter, "Von der Teilung zur Wiedervereinigung (1945–2000)," in: Mi-chael North (ed.), *Deutsche Wirtschaftsgeschichte. Ein Jahrtausend im Überblick* (Mu-nich, 2000), pp. 410 f.

3 "Ansprache des Vorsitzenden des Vorstands der Allianz AG, Dr. Wolfgang Schieren," in: Allianz AG (ed.), *100 Jahre Allianz, Festansprachen 9. März 1990* (Munich, 1990), pp. 35–7, 41–5.

4 Ibid., pp. 41–5.

5 Ibid., pp. 45–7.

6 See Allianz Umweltstiftung (ed.), *Zehn Jahre Allianz Umweltstiftung* (Munich, 2000), pp. 3, 99, 109; URL: https://umweltstiftung.allianz.de/veranstaltungen/benedikt-beurer/index.html?mode-print, accessed on December 9, 2014.

7 Schröter, "Teilung," p. 396.

8 "Personalien, Veränderungen im Vorstand der Allianz Gesellschaften," *Allianz Journal* (1991), 1, p. 32.

9 Karl-Heinz Büschemann, "Rückzug auf dem Zenit. Allianz-Chef Wolfgang Schieren übergibt seinem Nachfolger ein kerngesundes Unternehmen," *Die Zeit* (December 7, 1990).

10 "Nur einer sagt, wo's langgeht," *Der Spiegel* 45 (1991), 32, pp. 84–6, here p. 84.

11 Barbara Eggenkämper, Gerd Modert, & Stefan Pretzlik, *Die staatliche Versicherung der DDR. Von der Gründung bis zur Integration in die Allianz* (Munich, 2010), p. 177.

12 *Allianz Journal* (1991), 1, p. 32.

13 FHA, AZ 9/493_1, press release from August 2, 1990; "Allianz erwirbt US-Versicherungsgruppe Fireman's Fund."

14 FHA, AZ 9/495, press release from July 23, 1993; *Allianz Journal* 2 (1997), p. 51; *Allianz Journal* (1997), 3, p. 51. In the run-up period to the acquisition of AGF, Gavazzi was the director of Allianz in France. After 1997, Dominique Bazy took over that post, and Detlev Bremkamp was given responsibility for the Europe I division in addition to Europe II, Africa and the Middle East. In 1997, responsibility for South America was transferred from Bremkamp to Herbert Hansmeyer and responsibility for the Asia Pacific section to Henning Schulte-Noelle.

15 See Allianz AG annual report of 1997, p. 8, as well as *Allianz Journal* (1997), 3, p. 51.

16 Allianz Kulturstiftung (ed.), *Allianz Kulturstiftung* (Munich, 2011), esp. pp. 2–3, 5, 79, 81, 83.

17 Gerald D. Feldman, *Allianz and the German Insurance Business, 1933–1945* (Cambridge, 2001), pp. 534 f.

18 Lothar Gall, Gerald D. Feldman, Harold James et al. (eds.), *Die Deutsche Bank 1870–1995* (Munich, 1995).

19 "Das 'Wagnis Auschwitz,'" *Der Spiegel* 51 (1997), 23, pp. 50–62, here p. 50.

20 URL: https://www.allianz.com/ns-zeit, accessed on December 9, 2014.

21 "Vom System vereinnahmt," *Der Spiegel* 51 (1997), 19, pp. 104–7, here p. 105.

22 Feldman, *Allianz*.

23 Christopher Worthley, "Confronting Trauma in Corporate History," manuscript from symposium: Memory and Oblivion, Representations of Trauma, Akademie Schloss Solitude, Stuttgart, June 5, 2004, pp. 1–15, here p. 6, FHA, AZ 9.

24 Emilio Galli-Zugaro, "Lost trust and the challenge for reputations," *Project M #11* (2012), pp. 37–9, as well as URL: http://projectm-online.com/global-agenda/risk/lost-trust-and-the-challenge-for-reputations, accessed on December 9, 2014.

25 Allianz Versorgungskasse annual report of 1990 offers a historical overview of 100 years of retirement planning, cf. FHA, B 15.

26 See FHA, AZ 3.3/folder "VS-Sitzung 10.12.79 bis 6.12.82," report of board of directors meeting of November 8, 1982, pp. 1 f.

27 See Uwe Timm, *Freitisch* (Cologne, 2011); Egmont Merte, "Begrüßungsrede zur Lesung von Uwe Timm aus seinem Buch Freitisch im Firmenhistorischen Archiv am 24.11. 2012," FHA, AZ 10.

28 The strategy was communicated to employees, shareholders and the general public in various ways in annual reports and company publications. See for example Allianz AG annual reports of 1996, p. 5, and 1998, p. 16.

29 Allianz AG annual report of 1998, pp. 16 f., 46 f.

30 Ibid., pp. 46, 16.

31 Ibid., pp. 16 f. In Asia, Allianz began in Shanghai and the Philippines. Thanks to AGF, it became active in Laos, South Korea and Malaysia, as well as Croatia, Bulgaria, Brazil, Argentina, Chile, Venezuela, Tunisia and Morocco.

32 Allianz AG annual report of 1998, pp. 46, 16 f.

33 See Allianz AG annual reports of 1997, p. 47, and 1998, p. 13. Overview of the shares in the revenues before and after the integration of AGF: Germany 51.3 percent (45.1 percent), Europe 30.6 percent, (40.4 percent), North and South America 17.6 percent (14 percent), Asia and Africa 0.4 percent (0.6 percent). Details for all companies involved in European markets: Italy 11 percent, (RAS, Lloyd and Subalpina) Switzerland 5.6 percent, Great Britain 4.0 percent, France 3.2 percent, Austria 2.5 percent.

34 Allianz AG annual report of 1998, pp. 16 f. The eight markets were Germany, Italy, Switzerland, Austria, the Czech Republic, Slovakia, Hungary and Indonesia. In 1998, they were joined, among others, by France, Spain, Greece and Chile.

35 FHA, AZ 3/folder "Vorstandsprotokolle, Januar 1997–Juli 1998," minutes of board of directors meeting of May 4, 1998, p. 13. After the AGF acquisition, two options were discussed. Ultimately, Detlev Bremkamp was made responsible for part of the European division, while the second part, which also included Northern Africa and the Middle East, was put under the control of AGF (Mansion) in Paris.

36 FHA, AZ 9/495_1, Allianz AG, Unternehmenskommunikation, press release from December 17, 1998, "Weitere Schritte zur Umsetzung der Partnerschaft von Allianz und AGF."

37 See Allianz AG annual report of 1998, pp. 91–5, "Die Veränderungen nach Erwerb und Integration der AGF."

38 FHA, AZ 10/"Sammlung Interviews," interview Henning Schulte-Noelle of April/May 2012.

39 FHA, AZ 9/495_1, press release from December 18, 1998: "Münchener Rück und Allianz ordnen Beteiligungen neu."

40 "Die Rollen sind verteilt," *Der Spiegel* 31 (1977), 50; "Nur einer sagt, wo's langgeht," *Der Spiegel* 45 (1991), 32, p. 32.

41 "Eichels Revolution," *Der Spiegel* 54 (2000), 1, pp. 22–5, here pp. 22 f.

42 Press release from Allianz AG of October 23, 2003, FHA, AZH 9/"Sammlung Pressemitteilungen."

43 Allianz BGZ Polska S. A. in Warsaw, a joint venture with the Polish bank BZG SA, began offering property insurance in Poland in 1997; later life insurance was added. Sales were made initially at some 1,300 BGZ bank counters and then via the newly established sales network.

44 Allianz AG annual report of 1989, pp. 18, 48 f.

45 See Dr. Klaus Liesen, chairman of the supervisory board of Allianz AG, in: "*In Memoriam Dr. Wolfgang Schieren." Ansprachen bei der Trauerfeier in der Hauptverwaltung der Allianz AG, 1.3.1996.*

46 See Eggenkämper, Modert, & Pretzlik, *Staatliche*, pp. 71–195.

47 Ritter, *Über Deutschland*, p. 194.

48 Schröter, "Teilung," p. 410.

49 Ibid.; see also Eggenkämper, Modert, & Pretzlik, *Staatliche*, p. 170.

50 Wolfram Fischer, Herbert Hax, & Hans K. Schneider (eds.), *Treuhandanstalt. Das Unmögliche wagen. Forschungsberichte* (Berlin, 1993). Cited in Schröter, "Teilung," p. 411.

51 See Eggenkämper, Modert, & Pretzlik, *Staatliche*, pp. 179–84.

52 Ibid., p. 183, and on the alternatives ibid., p. 177.

53 Ibid., p. 203; DVAG annual report of 1991, p. 5.

54 Eggenkämper, Modert, & Pretzlik, *Staatliche*, p. 206.

55 Ibid.

56 Ibid., pp. 200, 206 f.

57 Schröter, "Teilung," p. 414.

58 See *Allianz Journal* (2003), 1, p. 11.

59 Allianz AG annual reports of 1989, pp. 48 f., and 1995, p. 21: FHA, AZ 3/"Vorstandsprotokolle Januar 1997–Juli 1998," minutes of the board of directors meetings of Allianz AG on September 11, 1997, minutes no. 11, pp. 6 f.

60 Ibid.; Allianz AG annual report of 1995, p. 21.

61 *Allianz Zeitung*, supplement Allianz Munich (1980), 4, no page number. The introduction of corporate branding in the Czech Republic is excellently documented in: FHA, AZ 11/hanging folder "Allianz Tschechische Republik".

62 FHA, AZ 3/folder "Vorstandsprotokolle Januar 1997–Juli 1998," minutes of the board of directors meetings of Allianz AG on September 11, 1997, minutes no. 11, p. 6.

63 FHA, AZ 9/"Konzerngliederung," section structures of the Allianz Versicherungs-AG of 1984 and the Allianz AG of 5/1992; résumé Detlev Bremkamp as of 3/1992.

64 *Allianz Journal* (2006), 1, p. 22.

65 Allianz AG annual report of 1997, pp. 6 f.

66 *Allianz Journal* (1998), 4, p. 48. Background information: In 1997, Detlev Bremkamp was put in charge of both Europe I (Northern Europe including Belgium, Great Britain, Ireland, Luxembourg, the Netherlands, Austria, Switzerland, and Scandinavia) and Europe II (France, Italy, Spain, Portugal, Greece and Turkey together with Africa and the Middle East) divisions. In 1997, responsibility for South America was transferred from Bremkamp to Herbert Hansmeyer, and responsibility for the Asia Pacific section to Henning Schulte-Noelle – Michael Diekmann assumed responsibility for this area as deputy board member in October 1998. See FHA, AZ 9/"Konzerngliederung," section structures of the Allianz Versicherungs-AG of 1984 and the Allianz AG of 5/1992. Subsequently, responsibility for Bremkamp's foreign division was in constant flux. In 1998, Asia-Pacific was removed from his area, followed by the Middle East, Africa and Central and Eastern Europe. From then on, Bremkemp focused on parts of Europe, reinsurance and the new area Allianz Risk Transfer (ART), which primarily affected reinsurance.

67 FHA, AZ 3/folder "Vorstandssitzungen Januar 1974–Dezember 1974," report of board of directors meeting of August 5, 1974, p. 10.

68 Allianz Aktiengesellschaft Holding (ed.), *100 Jahre im Zeichen des Adlers* (Munich, 1991), p. 37.

69 FHA, AZ 3.3/folder "VS-Sitzung 10.12.1979 bis 6.12.1982," report of board of directors meeting of October 22, 1982, p. 6.

70 Allianz AG annual report of 1997, p. 49.

71 *Allianz Journal* (2010), 4, p. 54.

72 Allianz AG annual report of 1995 ff., esp. 1999, p. 12. The respective percentages of Allianz business done in Asia are as follows: 1995–96: 0.4 percent, 1997: 0.5 percent, 1998: 0.6 percent, 1999: 2.4 percent. Allianz AG annual report of 1997, p. 23.

73 FHA, AZ 10/folder "Interviews," interview Heinz Dollberg on January 16, 2014, p. 2. This concerned language and social conventions.

74 Ibid., pp. 2 f.

75 See *Allianz Zeitung* (1987), 4, p. 8.

76 On the situation of the Asian market in 1991, see Allianz Aktiengesellschaft Holding (ed.), *100 Jahre*, p. 37; FHA, AZ 10/folder "Interviews," interview Heinz Dollberg on January 16, 2014, p. 4.

77 *Allianz Journal* (2010), 4, p. 54.

78 Ibid., pp. 55 f.

79 See *Allianz Journal* (2003), 1, p. 12.

80 Allianz AG annual report of 1996, p. 38.

81 *Allianz Journal* (2003), 1, pp. 14 f.

82 See *Allianz Journal* (1997), 1, p. 9 and (2003), 1, p. 15.

83 The members of the committee were Henning Schulte-Noelle, Detlev Bremkamp, Diethart Breipohl, Emilio Galli-Zugaro, Antoine Jeancourt-Galignani, Yves Mansion, Dominique Bazy and Jean-France Debrois.

84 FHA, AZ 10/folder "Interviews," report Emilio Galli-Zugaro of August 6, 2014, p. 1.

85 Allianz AG annual report of 1998, p. 16.

86 Allianz AG annual report of 1997, p. 7.

87 *Allianz Journal* (2002), 1, p. 45.

88 *Allianz Journal* (2010), 1, p. 54.

89 FHA, AZH 9/"Sammlung Pressemitteilungen," press release of Allianz SE, March 11, 2014.

90 *Allianz Journal* (2001), 4, p. 54; *Allianz Journal* (2002), 1, p. 45; FHA, AZ 10/folder "Interviews," interview of Canstein of December 16, 2013, esp. pp. 1, 15–8.

91 Ibid., pp. 20–3.

92 Press release of the investor relations department, Allianz SE, January 27, 2006 and April 28, 2009, FHA, AZ 9/"Sammlung Pressemitteilungen."

93 FHA, AZ 10/folder "Interviews," interview of Canstein of December 16, 2013, supplemental letter of January 7, 2014.

94 Allianz AG annual report of 1998, pp. 16, 46 f., "Asset Management wird zum Kerngeschäftsfeld ausgebaut."

95 Allianz AG annual report of 1997, p. 54.

96 Allianz AG annual report of 1998, p. 12.

97 Ibid., p. 94; all told, it involved an investment volume of € 330 billion and aimed to offer clients a wide range of products.

98 Schröter, "Teilung," pp. 415 f.

99 Allianz AG annual report of 1998, pp. 94 f.

100 Ibid.

101 Ibid., p. 12 and Allianz AG annual report of 1997, p. 7.

102 In January 2000, Diethart Breipohl was replaced by Paul Achleitner as chief financial officer.

103 URL: http://www.pimco.com/EN/OurFirm/Pages/PIMCOTimeline.aspx., accessed on November 19, 2014.

104 Allianz AG annual report of 2001, p. 130.

105 Allianz Group annual report of 2013, p. 88.

106 Allianz AG (ed.), *100 Jahre Allianz*; including ceremonial address by Wolfgang Schieren, p. 51.

107 Allianz AG annual report of 1996, pp. 14 ff. Bancassurance, which is the sale of insurance policies at a bank, is very successful in most European markets. In Italy, the share of the insurance market carried out through banks was 19.2 percent. In 1996, France began marketing property insurance via the 2,000 bank counters belonging to Crédit Lyonnais. That same year, bancassurance operations commenced in many other European countries, including Portugal. In Spain, bancassurance operations began in 1998, while in Britain they began in 1996 at Cornhill.

108 Allianz Group annual report of 2008, p. 131, as well as the press release from the investor relations department, Allianz SE, April 17, 2012, FHA, AZ 9/"Sammlung Pressemitteilungen."

109 "Wall Street: Neue Ära eingeläutet," *Allianz Journal* (2000), 4, p. 6.

110 *Allianz Journal* (2009), 4, p. 18–20.

111 FHA, AZ 10/folder "Interviews," interview Barbara Eichberger, sales/marketing, of February 3, 2005, p. 10, and *Allianz Journal* (1997), 1, p. 11.

112 *Allianz Journal* (1989), 4, p. 10. Michael Maskus explained this to the employees as follows: "All major brands must change their appearance over time." For example, Shell modified its logo five times between 1904 and 1971. Similar changes were made at Daimler-Benz between 1909 and 1989.

113 *Allianz Journal* (1997), 1, p. 11.

114 Ibid. and *Allianz Zeitung* (1998), 12, p. 2.

115 FHA, AZ 11/folder "Materialien Barbara Eichberger," letter by Barbara Eichberger of March 13, 2013, to the Allianz Center for Corporate History.

116 *Allianz Journal* (1997), 1, p. 10. Diversity in public image is regarded as a weakness.

117 Ibid., p. 11.

118 Ibid.

119 Ibid.

120 *Allianz Journal* (1998), 4, p. 11.

121 Haydar Kazgan, *Koç Allianz, Cumhuriyet'in 75 Yillik Sigortacisi* (no place, 1998).

122 FHA, AZ 11/Corporate marketing brochure, Munich (ed.), "Allianz Group, The Power on Your Side," pp. 1–45, esp. p. 34 and looseleaf paper "Allianz Corporate Media Plan Germany".

123 FHA, AZ 11/Brochure "Brand Communication 2009, Allianz. Financial Solutions from A-Z," pp. 1–127, see esp. p. 13.

124 Ibid., p. 3.

125 Allianz Group annual report of 2010, p. 61, see esp. "Die Marke Allianz."

126 Allianz Group annual report of 1999, p. 21.

127 FHA, AZ 3/"Vorstandsprotokolle von 1978–1979," here: minutes of the board of directors meeting of March 12, 1979, p. 1.

128 *Allianz Zeitung* (1981), 1, no page number, title page of the Allianz Munich enclosure; *Allianz Zeitung* (1985), 6, no page number, enclosure Allianz Munich.

129 Tobias Straumann, "Der unsichtbare Riese. Die Geschichte von Swiss Re 1863–2013," in: Harold James (ed.), *Swiss Re und die Welt der Risikomärkte. Eine Geschichte* (Munich, 2014), p. 454.

130 *Allianz Journal* (2001), 4, p. 3.

131 Straumann, "Riese," p. 454.

132 Norbert Kuls, "Wiederaufbau kann beginnen. Allianz einigt sich im Streit um World Trade Center," *Frankfurter Allgemeine Zeitung* (May 24, 2007).

133 Gerhard Berz, *Wie aus heiterem Himmel? Naturkatastrophen und Klimawandel. Was uns erwartet und wie wir uns darauf einstellen sollten* (Munich, 2010); "Zunehmende und veränderte Wetterrisiken erfordern angepasstes Risikomanagement," Munich Re press information, Munich, October 20, 2014, URL: http://www.munichre.com/de/media-relations/publications/press-releases/2014/2014–10-20-press-release/index.html, accessed on November 17, 2014.

134 FHA, AZH 9/"Sammlung Pressemitteilungen," therein: press release of May 27, 2014, "Ein winziges Geschäft für einen riesigen Kontinent."

135 *Allianz Journal* (2006), 1, p. 17.

136 Ibid., p. 16.

137 See also *Allianz Zeitung* (1982), 10, p. 5.

138 *Allianz Journal* (2006), 1, p. 15.

139 "Strategie 3 plus 1," special issue of the *Allianz Journal*, published in November 2003.

140 *Allianz Journal* (1998), 4, p. 16.

141 Allianz Group annual report of 2003, p. 2.

142 *Allianz Journal* (2006), 1, p. 16.

143 Ibid.

144 Schröter, "Teilung," p. 402.

145 See Eggenkämper, Modert, & Pretzlik, *Staatliche*, p. 208.

146 *Allianz Journal* (2006), 1, p. 50.

147 Michael Diekmann, "Die Massnahmen sind leider absolut notwendig," press release of Allianz, Munich June 22, 2006, FHA, AZ 9/"Sammlung Pressemitteilungen."

148 See Eggenkämper, Modert, & Pretzlik, *Staatliche*, p. 208.

149 Allianz Group annual report of 2013, p. 57.

150 Allianz Group annual reports of 1998, pp. 94 f., and 1999, p. 36.

151 FHA, AZH 9/"Sammlung Pressemitteilungen," therein: group letter by Michael Diekmann of November 7, 2014, p. 1. See also Herbert Fromme, "Mann im Feuer, Allianz-Chef Diekmann räumt auf – sein Vertrag läuft bald aus," *Süddeutsche Zeitung* (September 13/14, 2014), p. 25.

152 Allianz Deutschland AG group annual report of 2007, p. 7.

153 Ibid., pp. 19 f.

154 FHA, AZH 9/"Sammlung Pressemitteilungen," therein: press release of April 27, 2007, "Allianz consolidates its IT infrastructure in Western Europe," pp. 1–4.

155 AMOS annual report of 2010, pp. 4 f.

156 *Allianz Journal* (2000), 1, pp. 28 f. See also Allianz Group annual report of 1998, p. 21.

157 "Schrottpapiere? Wir sind da sehr sauber," *Süddeutsche Zeitung* (October 23, 2008), p. 21.

158 El-Erian refers to a study on globalization by James Manyika (McKinsey Global Institute).

Picture Credits

P. 40: Print Collection/Getty Images; p. 43: Hulton Archive/Getty Images; p. 66: Ullstein Bild; p. 133: private collection of Alexander v. Yxkull; p. 145: private collection of Peter Haas; p. 148: Scherl/Süddeutsche Zeitung Photo; p. 179: with the kind permission of Schöning Publishing Company, Lübeck, p. 197: Archiwum Państwowe w Łodzi (Lodz State Archive), Ghetto Administration, No. 31179, Bl. 453; p. 198: dpa/Ullstein Bild; p. 201: Ullstein Bild; p. 258: dpa-Bildarchiv/Picture Alliance; p. 295: Philipp Holzmann Werkfoto; p. 319: AFP/Getty Images; p. 325: Michael Westdickenberg; p. 331: Reto Zimpel; p. 357: NYSE; p. 369: Incheon Bridge project, South Korea, completed in October 2009 on time and budget by AMEC plc, project manager and shareholder in Incheon Bridge Company (IBC), Photo courtesy of AMEC/IBC; p. 372: Franck Guiziou/Getty Images; end pages: Bernd Ducke

All other images are from the holdings of the Allianz Center for Corporate History.

We made every effort to honor all copyrights of the photographs, graphics, and text documents used in this volume. If you should become aware of a violation of copyright, please contact us with the relevant information.

List of Archives

Archive of Dr. Jürgen-Detlev Freiherr von Üxküll
Mining Archive of Freiberg
Main Archive of the State of Brandenburg, Potsdam (BLHA)
German Federal Archives in Berlin (BArch)
German Federal Archives in Koblenz (BArch)
Centr Chranenijsa Istoriko-Dokumental'nych Kollekcii (Center for Historical Document Collections – "Special Archive, Moscow") (SM)
Allianz Center for Corporate History, Munich (FHA)
Prussian Secret State Archives, Berlin (GStA PK)
Association of the German Insurance Business Archive, Berlin (GDV)
Historical Archive of Deutsche Bank, Frankfurt a. M. (HADB)
Historical Archive of Munich Reinsurance Company, Munich
Berlin State Archive (LAB)
Political Archive of the German Federal Foreign Office (AA)
U. S. National Archives, Washington (NA)

Aachener und Münchener Versicherungs-
  AG 42, 195, 305
accident insurance 14–17, 21–23, 25 f., 39,
  54, 60 f., 68 f., 75, 90, 96, 116, 169, 226,
  265, 276, 284, 304, 312, 336, 350, 365
Act for the Order of National
  Employment 164
Adenauer, Konrad 205, 207, 246
Adolf Hitler Donation of the German
  Business Community 158, 171
Adolf, Hans 133
Adolff, Peter 11, 224, 275 f.
ADVV (Allgemeiner Deutscher
  Versicherungs-Verein) 14–16, 20, 23,
  31–39, 65, 68, 114
Africa 62 f., 137, 139 f., 176, 252, 254, 298,
  336 f., 346, 348, 364, 366
agent 9, 48, 53–56, 58, 61, 67, 75, 80, 87, 92,
  95 f., 98, 106, 111, 116 f., 123, 126, 128 f.,
  133, 137, 143 f., 155–157, 159, 169 f., 176,
  194, 200, 217, 219 f., 223, 226, 230,
  237–244, 253, 274, 283, 310, 331, 333 f.,
  342, 364, 367, 374
agents' clubs 156, 238
Allianz Arena 362, 373
Allianz Center for Corporate History 10,
  330, 332
Allianz Center for Technology
  (AZT) 269–271, 285 f., 345
Allianz Children's Foundation 330
Allianz eagle 24, 126 f., 222, 252, 282–284,
  301, 324, 359 f.

Allianz Environmental Foundation 288,
  324, 329
Allianz Foundation for North America
  330, 332
Allianz Foundation Forum 329
Allianz Global Corporate and Specialty
  (AGCS) 305, 370 f.
Allianz Global Investors (AGI) 355, 357
Allianz Holdings Ltd., Amsterdam 310
Allianz Journal 224, 324, 333, 360
Allianz Leben (Allianz Life) 83, 91, 93 f.,
  108, 114 f., 117, 122, 126, 130, 134, 137,
  139 f., 149 f., 156, 161 f., 169, 177, 184 f.,
  187, 191–193, 196–198, 202 f., 218, 227,
  229 f., 232, 237, 239 f., 244–246,
  260–262, 281, 300, 303 f., 308, 320,
  326, 338, 346, 350, 353, 363
Allianz Pension Fund (AVK) 111, 178, 210,
  212–214, 234, 236, 238
Allianz Zeitung 73, 86, 92, 94 f., 97, 110,
  112, 123 f., 126 f., 131, 139, 163, 168, 195,
  218 f., 222, 239 f., 242, 262, 272, 274,
  287, 294, 334
Alsberg, Aenne 143
Alzheimer, Alois 190 f., 235, 248
America 35, 44–46, 60, 62 f., 67, 109–112,
  122, 127, 130, 136 f., 148 f., 198–200, 202,
  227 f., 249, 254, 287, 289, 291 f., 296,
  298, 300–304, 306, 308, 310 f., 313–315,
  330, 332, 336–338, 345 f., 349, 351, 357
AMOS 372 f.
Andrée, Otto 41, 55

Anglo-Elementar Versicherungs-AG 52, 298
animal insurance 226, 310
Arab International Insurance Company 294
Arendts, Wilhelm 154, 164, 178, 193, 200
Argentina 67, 292
Arnhold, Hans 123
Arps, Ludwig 15, 22, 67
Aryanization 76
Asia Pacific 327 f., 336, 345–349, 355, 365
ASS 94, 108, 116–118, 162, 183, 240, 243, 277
Assecuranz-Companie Mercur 230
association agreement 76–78, 88,189 f., 339
Assurances Générales de France (AGF) 313, 335–337, 339, 345, 349, 354, 370 f.
Australia 62, 137, 184, 296, 298, 310 f., 313 f., 346, 350
Austria 51 f., 59, 62, 64, 85, 87, 137–139, 179, 182, 187, 189, 252, 289, 298, 311 f., 315, 327, 371, 374
automobile insurance 41, 68 f., 83, 122, 125, 162, 191, 215–217, 242, 249, 257, 264–270, 276, 290 f., 296, 304, 310 f., 335, 340, 343, 345
aviation insurance 249, 282, 294, 297, 310, 363 f.
Baer, Willi 176
baggage insurance 226
Bajaj Allianz 351, 353
Bajaj, Rahul 351
Bäte, Oliver 375
Bäumer, Arno Paul 260–263, 275, 279, 302
Beck, Ulrich 288
Becker, Philipp 117–119
Becker, Willy 173
Beckord, Michael 11, 342 f.
Beier, Max 195 f.
Belgium 51, 62, 73, 192, 252, 254, 289, 310, 315
Benner, Ernst 281–284
Berlinische Feuer 23, 52, 158
Berlinische Hagel 23
Berlinische Leben 23, 122, 189, 230
Bernhardt, Victor 20
bicycle theft insurance 40 f.
Bierich, Marcus 306
Big Advertiser Club 238
Big Life Club 144, 238
Bimeh Pars 254, 294

block policy 225–227, 241
Boetius, Jan 306, 319
Bohl, Franz 206
Bore 140, 252 f.
Bossenmaier, Helmut 260 f., 263, 266, 274
Bothe, Heinrich 47 f., 50
Branca, Alexander von 211 f.
Braun, Heinz 285, 287, 295, 300
Brazil 22, 298, 313 f., 374
Breipohl, Diethart 306, 354
Bremen-Hannoversche Lebensversicherung 93
Bremkamp, Detlev 310, 315, 327, 344 f., 347
Bremkamp, Heinz 289 f.
Brinkmann, Gerhard 218, 282, 284
Bruck, Martin 176
Brugger, Werner 266 f.
Bulgaria 66
Bünger, Gottfried 177
Burg, Detlev von der 255, 290, 299 f., 308, 315, 327
burglary and theft insurance 23, 39–42, 52, 58, 60–62, 96, 135, 181, 191, 265
Busekow, Wilhelm 117
Business Group Private Insurance 167, 180, 184
Butzengeiger, Karl 235
California 43–45, 47, 300, 302, 355
Canada 137, 296, 308, 310 f., 313–315, 337
Castell-Castell, Prosper Graf zu 275
Channel Tunnel 319 f.
Chile 67, 137, 146, 289, 292, 298, 314
China 62, 137, 141, 347, 350–352
China International Trust and Investment Corporation 351
codetermination 85, 208, 234 f., 237, 368
collection of premiums 239 f.
collective wage agreement 85, 109, 113, 232
collision insurance 68
cologne model 320
Colombia 313, 374
cominvest 357
commercial credit insurance 88
Commercial Union 291 f., 297
Commerz- und Diskontobank 18
Compagnie de Navigation Mixte (CNM) 316
company health insurance 112, 122, 234
company pension insurance 276

comprehensive automobile insurance 335, 345

Concentra 278, 280

concentration camp 75, 176, 179, 185, 195 f., 330

Constellation Insurance Company 253

construction insurance 249, 286, 292, 297

Cornhill 289, 309–316, 327 f., 337, 346 f., 371

corporate design 217, 224, 281 f., 284, 301, 358 f.

correspondent company 291

Cosmos Versicherungs-AG 305

credit insurance 88, 119, 349, 354, 370

Creditanstalt 187

Cyprus 137

Czechoslovakia 73, 85, 105

DAF (Deutsche Arbeitsfront) 150, 153, 157, 163, 165, 168, 196

Daluege, Kurt 180

Danat Bank 74

Daniel-Hauser, Renate 343

Danner, Max 269 f.

Dazhong 350 f.

Deckers & Meckelbert 254

Decree for the Restoration of the Appearance of the Streets 180

demographic shift 9, 277, 365

Denazification 198–200, 246

denazification court 198, 200

Denmark 62, 73, 311

deportation 146, 183, 185 f., 252

Deutsche Ausrüstungswerke GmbH (DAW) 195

Deutsche Bank 17 f., 26 f., 151, 248, 281 f., 330, 356, 358, 362

Deutsche Investitionsbank 122

Deutsche Krankenversicherung (DKV) 338

Deutsche Lebensversicherungsbank Arminia AG 93 f.

Deutsche Transport Versicherungs-gesellschaft 18

Deutsche Versicherungs-AG 324, 326, 335, 341 f.

Deutsche Versicherungsbank 92

Deutscher Investment Trust (dit) 278, 280, 356

Diekmann, Michael 345, 347–349, 365–367, 369, 375

Dierring, Carl Ludwig 139

disability 365

Dollberg, Heinz 11, 346 f., 349 f.

Dollinger, Werner 270

Dorschel, Hansjörg 11, 218, 222–224, 281–284

dowry insurance 140, 240

Dresdner Bank 17 f., 27, 132, 159, 248, 280 f., 354, 356 f., 363, 365

Drumm, Ernst 48, 86, 90

Dumcke, Paul 81, 89, 92, 117 f., 121

Dümmler, Hans Wilhelm 206, 208, 210

Eagle Star 280, 306 f., 309 f., 313

Eckert, Max 182

education insurance 140, 240

Eggerss, Walter 150 f., 154

Egypt 62, 137

Eichbaum, Maximilian 107, 172, 174–176

Eichberger, Barbara 11, 282, 284, 359 f.

El-Erian, Mohamed 375

ELIAS 272

Elvia 327 f., 335

engineering insurance 285, 287, 294, 297 f.

England 50, 62, 64, 71, 217, 253, 255, 298

Enß, Franz 41

erection insurance 250, 286 f., 292

Erste Oesterreichische Versicherungs-Gesellschaft gegen Einbruch 39

Estonia 60, 132, 135 f.

Euler 370

Europahaus 130, 240

Eversmann, Rudolf 234 f., 275

expropriation 180, 183–185

Faber, Joachim 354

Feder, Gottfried 148, 155

Feldman, Gerald D. 10, 152, 182 f., 330–332

Feldmann, Jürgen 285

Fickel, Horst 11, 291 f.

fidelity bond insurance 39, 41, 51, 61, 88

Fidelity Union Life Insurance Company (FULICO) 301–303

Fides 39, 41

Finck, August von 148, 151, 154, 198, 246 f.

Finck, Wilhelm von 9, 13 f., 16, 25–27, 53, 80, 246

Finland 60

fire insurance 21 f., 24, 26, 30, 42–48, 50 f., 57 f., 60, 62 f., 72, 74, 78, 88, 90, 96,

116, 135, 150 f., 181, 191, 194, 215, 221, 226, 265, 312
Fireman's Fund Insurance Company (FFIC) 44 f., 128, 304 f., 324, 326–328, 360, 371
First Life 349, 351
flexible working hours 234
flooding of the Oder river 343
forced conformity 149, 155
forced labor 173, 194 f.
Foundation "Remembrance, Responsibility, Future" 332
France 22, 39, 62, 64, 67, 73, 128, 137, 140, 158, 192, 252, 254 f., 289, 310 f., 313–317, 335, 337, 356, 360, 370, 374
François-Poncet, André 158
Frankfurter Allgemeine Versicherungs-AG (Favag) 22 f., 42, 50, 80 f., 89, 92, 104, 117–122, 128, 133, 138, 152, 172 f., 189
Frankfurter Versicherungs-AG 89, 120 f., 138, 164, 172 f., 176 f., 189, 196, 198–200, 213, 217, 225 f., 229 f., 237, 249, 275, 283, 369
Fraternal League of German Police Officials 169
Fräulein Block Policy 226 f., 241
Freia 93 f.
Freudenburg, Erika 174
Freudenburg, James 172–175
Freundeskreis Reichsführer-SS 153
Friedländer, Ilse 176
Friedrich Krupp GmbH 279
Friedrich Wilhelm Lebens-Versicherungs-AG 92 f.
Frigessi di Rattalma, Adolfo 313
Frigessi di Rattalma, Arnoldo 313
Frisia 248
Fukushima 287
fund-linked life insurance 279 f., 310
furniture fire insurance 58
Futtig, Hans 168 f.
Galli-Zugaro, Emilio 11, 329
Gavazzi, Roberto 327
Gehrke, Paul 172
Generali 59, 136, 163, 187, 252, 311 f., 335
Georgii, Max 114
Gerlach, Walther 249
German Law for Lending 160
Gestapo 134, 174, 184
ghetto 146, 185, 194, 197

glass insurance 23, 102, 130, 181
Globus Versicherungs-AG 48, 88, 230
Goebbels, Joseph 154, 179 f.
Goetz, Carl 248
Göring, Hermann 148, 150–152, 170, 179–181, 188 f., 194
Gothaer (insurance company) 30, 156
Götte, Klaus 279, 300, 302 f.
Goudefroy, Hans 141, 145, 154, 181, 190 f., 199 f., 205, 207–209, 212, 219, 225, 227, 229, 233, 236, 239, 246, 248, 250, 252–254, 259, 261
Great Britain 66, 128, 137, 296, 306, 309 f., 315, 320, 337
Greece 62, 137, 192, 315, 337, 356
Gross, Bill 355
group insurance policies 122, 162, 280
Grumbt, Ernst 71 f.
Grünebaum, Hans 176 f.
Guehery, Rudolf de 176
Gutmann, Herbert 132
Haas, Leopold 143
Haase, Alfred 200, 206, 208 f., 225, 229 f., 239, 259–262, 264, 289
Haasen, Uwe 300, 303, 308
hail insurance 78, 89, 230, 267 f., 312
Hamburg-Mannheimer Versicherungs-AG 93, 122, 230
Hammacher, Friedrich 17 f.
Hammonia 189
Hansmeyer, Herbert 308
Hartung, Arnold 218
Hauff, Volker 269 f.
health insurance 31, 75, 91, 112, 122, 234, 302 f., 310 f., 334–336, 338, 371
Heiland, Gerhard 176
Helldorf, Wolf von 154
Helms, Walter 135
Helvetia 45
Hensel, Rudolf 9, 66, 93, 96, 110 f., 283
Hermes Kreditversicherungs(bank)-AG 88, 338, 370
Herrhausen, Alfred 362
Herzfelder, Erich 88
Herzog, Martin 154, 252, 290–292, 294
Heß, Hans 79–83, 88 f., 93, 96–98, 101, 106 f., 109–112, 120, 133, 143–145, 154, 157, 173, 175, 177, 190, 198–200, 206–209, 235 f., 238, 242, 253, 259

Heydrich, Reinhard 180
Heymann, Franz 178
Hilgard, Eduard 79, 81–83, 90, 93, 101, 120,
    131–134, 153 f., 157–160, 164 f., 171, 179–
    182, 187, 189 f., 192, 198, 200, 206, 252
Himmler, Heinrich 153
Hindenburg, Paul von 76, 147, 153
Hitler, Adolf 76, 100, 134, 147–149, 151, 155,
    157–159, 164, 167 f., 171, 178, 188, 198, 330
holding company 260, 294, 298, 300,
    304–308, 313, 315 f., 318, 324, 326, 328,
    337, 340, 366
Honsel, Bernd 11, 306
Hooffacker, Alfons 236 f.
Hopefully Covered by Allianz (ad
    campaign) 222, 224, 242, 284
household contents insurance 223, 226,
    343 f.
HTO (Haupttreuhandstelle Ost) 193 f.
Hugenberg, Alfred 133, 147
Hungária Biztosító 323, 335, 340, 343
Hungary 62, 85, 137, 252, 323, 340, 343 f.,
    356
hunting liability insurance 169 f.
hurricane 304, 364
hyperinflation 78, 98–103, 111, 136
IBM 108, 228 f., 272 f.
Iduna-Germania 194
Imperial Automobile Club (KAC) 69, 83
India 62 f., 124, 137, 140 f., 351, 353
inflation 10, 17, 47, 68, 74, 78, 81, 84–88, 93,
    98–103, 105, 110 f., 114, 116, 136, 140,
    188, 303
initial public offering 26 f., 351, 358 f.
Institute of London Underwriters 297
insurance shields 24
International Executive Committee 327 f.
Interunfall 69, 312
Iraq 140 f.
Irneri, Ugo 290
Isar-Lebensversicherung 182
Italy 11, 23, 51, 105, 128, 137, 140, 221, 252,
    254, 289 f., 311 f., 314 f., 356, 368, 373
Jacobi, Ernst 271
Jannott, Horst K. 338
Japan 105, 132, 137, 308, 310, 319, 337,
    345–349
javelin thrower 108–110, 226, 261
Jewish Atonement Tax 180, 184

Johansson, Arvid 21
Jöhl, Josef 156
Kappes, Walter 218, 222, 281
Karlsruher Leben 121 f., 189
Kettner, Hugo 177
Keynes, John Maynard 71
Kisch, Wilhelm 51
Kißkalt, Wilhelm 59, 78 f., 88, 90, 114, 121,
    154, 189 f.
Klang, Dr. James 59
Kleinschmidt, Alwin 30
Knatterton, Nick 218
Knote, Gustav 53
Knote, Manfred 53
Koç-Allianz Sigorta A.S. 361
Koch, Claus 360
Kölnische Rückversicherungs-Gesell-
    schaft 13 f.
Kölnische Unfall 50, 55
König, Georg 144, 154, 168 f., 173
korean war 215
"Kraft" Versicherungs-AG 69, 83
Krupp, Gustav 171
La Cité 192
La Comercial-Libertad 292
La Minerve 192
La Pace Assicurazioni e Riassicurazioni
    S.p.A. Mailand 140, 252–254, 289 f.,
    315, 361
La Préservatrice 192
La Riassicuratrice 312
Lachmann, Aenne 143, 146
Lachmann, Martin 143–147, 331
Ladner, Otto 224, 227, 231, 271
Landschaftliche Brandkasse Hannover 24
Landwehr, Rolf 276, 300 f., 303
Lange, Hans 149, 153
Latvia 60, 135 f., 140
Lauinger, Artur 117 f.
Law for the Seizure of Assets of Enemies of
    the People and the State 184
Lebanon 254
legal expenses insurance 310, 315
Lehman Brothers 357, 374
Lerchenfeld (count) 138
Levison, Jacob Bertha 44
Lewes, Wilhelm 178
Ley, Robert 153, 157, 165, 168
liability insurance 14–16, 30, 41, 45, 47,

52–55, 60 f., 68, 79–80, 83, 96, 116, 129, 169, 172, 191, 210, 217, 226, 249, 262, 284–286, 290, 292, 294, 297, 300–302, 304, 312, 336

Liebermann, Martha 133 f.

Liesen, Klaus 273, 340

life insurance 21, 29, 41, 50, 55, 61, 63, 67, 75, 83, 90–94, 102–104, 108, 111, 114–119, 121 f., 126, 136 f., 140, 156, 160–162, 169, 182–186, 191, 193 f., 202 f., 213, 215, 217, 227, 230 f., 239 f., 242 f., 246, 248, 262 f., 265, 274, 276–281, 296, 301–303, 310–312, 314, 317, 320, 330 f., 334, 336–338, 343, 346–354, 371

Linhof, Gregor 344

Lithuania 60, 136, 140

Lithuanian Lloyd 136

Lloyd 1885 373

Lloyd Adriatico 290, 335, 370

Łódź 146, 194, 197

Logo 24, 69, 94, 125–127, 240, 252, 281–284, 324, 358, 360–362

Lolli, Ettore 312

Louis Dreyfus & Co. 60

Lueg, Heinrich 17

Luftpool 249, 294, 364

Lusitania 66 f.

Lux, Paul 141, 164, 173, 178, 190 f., 198

Luxembourg 51, 62, 140, 192, 254

Macher, Paul 176

machine insurance 50 f., 53, 56, 162, 191, 210, 249, 286 f.

Maffei, Hugo Ritter von 16, 19

Magdeburger Feuer Versicherungs-gesellschaft 24, 50, 54, 90, 128

Maiholzer, Clemens 82 f., 177, 196, 199

Malaysia 349

Mann, Thomas 64, 67, 133

Manufacturers' Mutual Insurance Company (MMI) 350

Marchant, Edward G. 297 f.

Matthes, Gottfried 160

Mauel, Marcus 25, 41

Mazumdar, Dhirendra Rath 140

Merck, Finck & Co. 13 f., 16 f., 246, 248

Merkel, Hedwig 176

Mexico 62, 137, 140, 146, 291 f., 330

Meyer, Ernst 230, 259 f., 262, 270 f., 290

microinsurance 364, 372

Middle East 298, 337

Mietzel, Johanna 179

Mirow, Jürgen 237

Möbius, Karl 108, 110

Molt, Carl 15 f., 31 f., 37 f.

Moltke, Freya von 133

Moltke, Helmuth James von 133–135

Moments (ad campaign) 362, 369

mortgage insurance 88, 119, 161

Mountain, Sir Denis 306

Mühlbauer, Johannes 208

Müller-Lutz, Heinz-Leo 197, 220, 224–231, 266, 271, 273–275

Müller, Gerd 154, 192, 198–200, 209, 245, 259 f., 278 f.

Müller, Wolfgang 300, 315

Munich Hail 267 f.

Munich Re 13–16, 18, 20–25, 27 f., 32, 39, 41 f., 45–53, 56–62, 67, 69, 74, 76–78, 80, 83, 88, 90, 92–94, 114, 121, 137, 141, 149, 151, 164, 175, 187, 189–193, 195, 230, 235, 246- 248, 251–255, 282, 289, 291, 338 f., 345

Nagel, Fanny 178

Nahmer, Paul von der 18, 26–29, 32, 41, 48 f., 51–53, 60, 62, 64, 73 f., 76, 78, 80 f., 85, 125, 132

Nanavati (chief inspector) 139 f.

National Insurance Company 349

National Socialist Lawyers' League 170

National Socialist Model Corporation 167

nationalization 72, 159, 188, 207 f., 350

Nationalsozialistische Volkswohlfahrt (NSV) 171

Navakij 349

Nazi Party (NSDAP) 76, 147–151, 153 f., 164, 167 f., 170 f., 177–179, 189, 199 f., 246

Netherlands 51, 62, 67, 71, 137, 192, 252, 254, 311, 315, 337, 360

Neuhäusler, Johannes 211

Neumüller, Ludwig 154

New York Stock Exchange 119, 357 f.

Nicholas-Applegate 354

Nißl, Karl 211

Norddeutsche Feuer(versicherungs-Gesellschaft) 46 f., 50

Nordstern 18, 74

North American Life and Casualty 301
North British and Mercantile 33
Norway 310
NSBO 149 f., 153, 165, 168
nuclear energy 249 f., 285 f., 324
nuclear insurance 250, 285–287
Nuremberg Laws 177
Nuremberg trials 200
Nyitrai, Sigmund 58 f.
O Trabalho 254
obligation to buckle up 270
Oechelhäuser, Otto 17
Old Savers Law 243
open-plan offices 271, 302
ordinary life insurance 169, 183, 240, 243
Otten, Fritz 242
Pacelli, Eugenio 133
Palestine 140
Parthier, Hans 203
Pastor, Eilert 126
Patria 193
peace treaty 71, 73
Pempeit, Willy 237 f.
Pemsel, Hermann 16, 53, 59
People's Accident Insurance 226
People's Insurance 116
Persia (Iran) 139 f., 252, 254, 298
Peru 313
Pesenti, Carlo 313
Petplan 310
Phoenix 24, 52 f., 59, 61, 89, 106, 175, 182, 187
PIMCO 354 f., 357
Pina, Luca 374
Pohl, Bruno 17, 25, 60
Pohl, Ernst 249 f.
Poland 67, 73, 85, 140, 146, 187, 193, 195, 337, 340
Pomerania 60, 160
Ponto, Jürgen 281, 363
pool of transportation insurers 301
Portugal 254, 337
Preußische Leben 121
Preußische National-Versicherungs-Gesellschaft 30, 50
Pritzbuer, Anna von 122
propaganda 126, 157, 163, 180, 270
protectrice accidents 312
Providentia 51, 53, 59, 89, 106, 189

Prudential 114, 137, 193, 302
public relations work 94, 123, 126, 132, 262, 328–330, 332
Quattroruote (4R) 290
quick-service claims stations 267 f.
Raab, Frank 300 f.
Rasche, Ernst 190
Rathenau, Walther 92
Rationalization Commission 242
RCM 356
Reich Association for Private Insurance 132, 134, 157, 171
Reich Aviation Ministry 179 f.
Reich Citizenship Law, 11th Decree of the 178, 185
Reich Citizenship Law, 13th Decree of the 185
Reich collective wage agreement 85, 109, 113
Reich Flight Tax 184
Reich Group for Insurance 154, 158–160, 179 f., 182, 200, 252
Reich League of Jews in Germany 174, 185
Reich Liability Law 14
Reich, Rudolf 30
Reichsbund "Deutsche Jägerschaft" 170
Reiner Film 223
Reinhardt, Max 133
Reischert, Ernst 54–56
Reuter, Robert 140
Rhein & Mosel 45
Ribbe, Friedrich Wilhelm 194
Riebesell, Paul 182
Rittberg, Joseph 176
Riunione Adriatica di Sicurtà S.p.A. (RAS) 59, 128, 136, 193, 195, 289, 309, 311–316, 320, 327–329, 335, 337, 354, 356, 367, 370, 373 f.
Roehreke, Imai-Alexandra 329
Romania 62, 192, 340
Röse, Robert 172 f.
Rosipal Villa 210 f.
Rosskotten, Heinrich 130, 186
Roßmann, Anton 177
Rostock, Walter 282 f., 294, 300, 346
Royale Belge 280
Ruperti, Ernst-Justus 137, 140
Russia 60, 62, 64, 67, 71, 128, 132, 135, 340
SA 149–151, 154, 156, 171